Framing post-Cold War conflicts

MANCHESTER
1824

Manchester University Press

Framing post-Cold War conflicts

The media and international intervention

Philip Hammond

Manchester University Press

Manchester and New York

distributed exclusively in the USA by Palgrave

Published by Manchester University Press
Oxford Road, Manchester M13 9NR, UK
and Room 400, 175 Fifth Avenue, New York, NY 10010, USA
www.manchesteruniversitypress.co.uk

Distributed in the United States exclusively by
Palgrave Macmillan, 175 Fifth Avenue,
New York, NY 10010, USA

Distributed in Canada exclusively by
UBC Press, University of British Columbia, 2029 West Mall,
Vancouver, BC, Canada V6T 1Z2

British Library Cataloguing-in-Publication Data is available

Library of Congress Cataloging-in-Publication Data is available

ISBN 978 0 7190 8669 4 paperback

First published by Manchester University Press in hardback 2007

This paperback edition first published 2011

Printed by Lightning Source

For Nena, with love

Contents

Tables, figures and boxes

Tables

Figures

Boxes

Acknowledgements

The research for this book was supported by the Arts and Humanities Research Council research leave scheme and by a matching period of leave from London South Bank University. My thanks to the AHRC and to all my colleagues at LSBU, particularly Professor Andrew Dewdney, Professor Jeffrey Weeks, Dr Jenny Owen and Dr Terry Daniels, for their support. I am also very grateful to Professor Howard Davis and Professor Richard Keeble for acting as my referees.

Thanks to George Kenney and David Peterson for helping me with information about media use of the term 'ethnic cleansing' (Chapter 3) and to Nik Gowing for permission to quote from his 1998 paper on 'New Challenges and Problems for Information Management in Complex Emergencies' (Chapter 4). Thanks also to those friends and colleagues who commented on parts of the manuscript during its preparation, particularly Barrie Collins, Tim Fenton and Edward Herman. Responsibility for any errors or omissions which remain is of course mine.

I would like to thank my students at LSBU, especially those who took my 'War and the Media' option and/or wrote their dissertations on this topic, for their insights and enthusiasm.

Finally, special thanks to my family for putting up with me while I was writing this book.

CHAPTER 1

Introduction: post-Cold War conflicts and the media

The fall of the Berlin Wall brought to an end a well established way of looking at the world. Throughout the Cold War era, Western governments were generally clear about who their enemies were and whom they could count on as allies. For the 'free world', united under American leadership against the 'evil empire' in the East, anti-communism provided a stable framework for making sense of international conflict and cooperation. The first major post-Cold War conflict, the 1991 Gulf war, indicated how much had already changed. Saddam Hussein had enjoyed Western support in Iraq's war against Iran in the 1980s, but was abruptly cast as the 'new Hitler' after his invasion of Kuwait in August 1990. Neither the erstwhile Soviet enemy nor Arab states raised any serious objections to a United Nations Security Council resolution authorising massive US-led military action in the Gulf; but whereas American leadership of the Cold War alliance was largely taken for granted, the temporary coalition of 1991 was assembled only through months of diplomacy, as the US persuaded other countries to participate in, or to fund, the war. Long-standing relationships between former friends and enemies were now open to question, the international order suddenly more fluid and uncertain.

The 1990s and early 2000s were characterised by a high level of activism on the part of the major Western powers. More than half of peacekeeping operations mounted by the United Nations (UN) since 1948 were set up in the decade after 1989, for example; at its peak in 1994, the number of troops deployed on such missions reached 72,000 (IISS 1999: 291). The Cold War Nato military alliance first saw action only after the fall of communism, bombing the Bosnian Serbs in 1994 and 1995 and again bombing Yugoslavia in 1999. Britain and France undertook unilateral military missions in former African colonies, and for the first time since 1945 Germany and Japan sent troops overseas on active duty. The rationale and justification for this activism, however, were necessarily different from the past.

This book is about how the media have interpreted conflict and international intervention in the years after the Cold War. By comparing press coverage of a number of different wars and crises, it seeks to establish which have been the dominant themes in explaining the post-Cold War international order and to discover how far the patterns established prior to the 11 September 2001 terrorist attacks have subsequently changed. Throughout, the key concern is with the legitimacy of Western intervention: the aim is to investigate the extent to which Western military action is represented in news reporting as justifiable and necessary. For journalists, charged with writing the first draft of history without benefit of hindsight, the work of interpretation and analysis must be direct and instantaneous. Yet reporters do not work in a vacuum: their writing will be influenced by the stock of ideas circulating in the culture in which they are working, particularly those which are taken up and promulgated by powerful sources. Below we first outline a number of key debates which have been influential in shaping how the post-Cold War world has been understood, before going on to examine the role played by the news media.

Explaining post-Cold War conflicts and interventions

Although the threat of nuclear war has receded, the post-Cold War world has not been peaceful. According to the Stockholm International Peace Research Institute (SIPRI), there were 57 different major armed conflicts in 45 different locations around the globe between 1990 and 2001. In any one year, there were on average around 27 ongoing major armed conflicts (SIPRI 2000: 17; SIPRI 2001: 66).[1] Both the dynamics of these conflicts and the Western response to them seemed to call for new explanations, but such explanations have been controversial, not least because how conflicts are understood would seem to have a bearing on how governments might react to them. As we shall see, much discussion of media coverage of recent crises has centred on whether the 'wrong' interpretation has sometimes inhibited an effective response.

Culture and anarchy

One of the most common ideas about post-Cold War conflicts is that the collapse of communism unleashed pent-up tensions. As the 1992 *SIPRI Yearbook* put it:

> The end of the Cold War ... removed various restraints exercised over parties to ethnic conflicts during the Cold War.... The conflict in Yugoslavia followed the end of the Communist regimes in Eastern and Central Europe. It brought to light old and unresolved animosities between, in particular, Serbs and Croats. The Communist regime had kept these animosities under control through repression. (SIPRI 1992: 420)

In this scenario, 'old animosities' based on ethnic or national identity had been simmering away under the surface only to burst forth once the restraint of communist repression was removed. Two influential variations of this idea were developed by Samuel Huntington and Robert Kaplan.

Huntington argued that the post-Cold War world was riven by a 'clash of civilisations': the motor of conflict was not political ideology but deep-seated ethnic antagonism. Hence, for example, one of the civilisational 'fault lines' which, he argued, divided the world ran 'almost exactly along the line now separating Croatia and Slovenia from the rest of Yugoslavia' (Huntington 1993: 30). Huntington's argument was clearly an attempt to recast the Cold War division: he suggested that 'the Velvet Curtain of culture has replaced the Iron Curtain of ideology as the most significant dividing line in Europe'. Those on the wrong side, according to Huntington (1993: 30–1), are 'Orthodox and Muslim' peoples, who are 'much less likely to develop stable democratic political systems'. As Diana Johnstone (2000: 155) notes, 'an oddity of these "cultural divide" projections is that they find the abyss between Eastern and Western Christianity far deeper and more unbridgeable than the difference between Christianity and Islam'. In trying to find a replacement for the Soviet threat, Huntington lumped Muslims together with Serbs and Russians, since Islamic fundamentalism was already an established propaganda enemy of the West. Such quirks began to look even more odd when, in Bosnia and Kosovo, the dividing line appeared to be between Orthodox Christianity and Islam, and Nato's first ever military engagements were justified as being in defence of Muslims.

The second strand of explanation encountered no such problem, since in this perspective ethnicity itself was the source of conflict. Kaplan (1994) drew on Huntington's 'clash of civilisations' thesis but developed it to describe a collapse of civilisation in 'places where the Western Enlightenment has not penetrated', places constantly threatened by 'cultural and racial war', places populated by 'reprimitivized man', including the Balkans and much of Africa. Where Huntington's argument emphasised competing civilisations in attempting to explain the break-up of states such as Yugoslavia, Kaplan's focused on the breakdown of order in 'failed' states such as Somalia.

The implications of these approaches can diverge significantly when applied to particular circumstances. Huntington's thesis suggests that local, Westernised 'goodies' may be found and that the old East–West boundary can be redrawn, for example between Croatia and Serbia. Illustrating how this perspective could function as a reworking of the Cold War divide, Croatian President Franjo Tudjman argued that 'The struggle here is the same that has been going on in Eastern Europe for the past three years: democracy against communism', and then in the same breath also suggested that Serbs and Croats were 'not just different peoples but different civilisations' (European, 18 August 1991). Local leaders thus sought to use the idea of a cultural divide to their advantage, sometimes exaggerating or inventing linguistic and other cultural differences (Rieff 1995: 67–9). Critics have identified similar ideas in media coverage. Peter Brock (1993–94: 162–3), for example, notes how, in US reporting of Yugoslavia, terms such as 'Eastern', 'Byzantine' and 'Orthodox' were often used pejoratively, to contrast Serbs with 'Westernised' Croats.

Kaplan's approach is less discriminating, tending to see entire regions as outside the civilisational fold. In this view, the resurgence of old antagonisms which had been held in check by the Cold War leads to a disintegration of order and a reversion to a more primitive condition. Military historian John Keegan (1993: xi), for example, argued that:

> The horrors of the war in Yugoslavia, as incomprehensible as they are revolting to the civilised mind, defy explanation in conventional military terms. The pattern of local hatreds they reveal are unfamiliar to anyone but the professional anthropologists who take the warfare of tribal and marginal peoples as their subject of study.... Most intelligent newspaper readers ... will be struck by the parallels to be drawn with the behaviour of pre-state peoples.

Here, civilisation excludes everyone in the Balkans, since all are party to pre-modern, 'tribal' conflicts: rather than looking for local 'goodies and baddies', all sides are tarred with the brush of tribalism, in contrast to the modernity of the West. This approach also informed media reporting. During the Kosovo war, for example, one journalist recalled visiting Yugoslavia in the 1970s, when he had 'felt there was something intractably wild and backward about the people in these parts'. Of the present, he said:

> Here in the Balkans, although there is a veneer of civilised behaviour, the appearance of prosperity and the suggestion of a future, there is truly only history. Nothing else matters. Just history, hatred and ruin. (*Sunday Telegraph*, 4 April 1999)

The invocation of 'history', in this perspective, is not really about seeking historical explanations. Instead, it works as a coded suggestion that the region is beyond the pale of modernity and civilisation.

It is not difficult to see the appeal of these frameworks. Both offer new ways to make sense of the world, which involve a comforting sense of Western superiority. Although it has been subjected to much criticism, Huntington's view in particular has continued to be influential, attracting renewed interest after 9/11, when the concept of a 'clash of civilisations' seemed to describe the confrontation between the West and Islam. At least as important, however, has been the critique of such 'ethnic' explanations, and the elaboration of alternative accounts which view conflicts in terms of political violence and genocide.

Politics and morality

A major objection to explanatory frameworks which rest on the idea of 'ethnicity' is that the concept tends to be used in an essentialist way. In principle, 'ethnicity' is quite different from the notion of natural difference entailed in the concept of 'race'. As a matter of culture rather than biology, 'ethnicity' implies that identity and difference are socially constituted and susceptible to change. In use, however, the concepts of 'race' and 'ethnicity' are often confused or used interchangeably, in a way that implicitly understands 'ethnic' differences as fixed and innate. As Michael Ignatieff (1998: 56) notes, 'Ethnicity is sometimes described as if it were skin, a fate that cannot be changed'. Instead, he emphasises the 'plasticity' of identity. As against what he characterises as Huntington's notion of an 'eruption of ancient historical rivalries and antagonisms', Ignatieff (1998: 58) argues that, in the case of the former Yugoslavia, professed differences of religion and culture were inauthentic and shallow, even fraudulent. The conflict may have been 'about' ethnic identity but, rather than treating ethnicity as a given which causes conflict, Ignatieff suggests that an exclusivist politics of identity was deliberately encouraged and manipulated by local political leaders and the media.

This is a telling critique of 'ethnic' explanations. As noted above, adopting the framework of 'ethnic conflict' is really a refusal of explanation: the tendency is to down-play or ignore historical and political factors, except insofar as these are located in the distant past, and to suggest instead that conflict is somehow inevitable and incomprehensible. However, the critique is not an innocent one: it is tied to an argument about the necessity for the West to adopt a particular policy – that of 'ethical' intervention. Discussing Kaplan's ideas, Ignatieff (1998: 98) complains that portraying the world as anarchic discourages the West from intervening: 'If we could see a pattern in the chaos, or a chance of bringing some order here or there, the rationale for intervention and long-term ethical engagement would become plausible again'. Similarly, Mary Kaldor (1999: 147) rejects the 'essentialist assumptions about culture' shared by Huntington and Kaplan, but this is more than simply an analytical point. Her objection to their arguments is that they 'cannot envisage alternative forms of authority at a global level': Huntington remains wedded to what she sees as an outdated model of state-centric governance, while Kaplan's analysis implies helplessness before the rising tide of chaos. In contrast, Kaldor (1999: 124–5) advocates a system of 'cosmopolitan law-enforcement', whereby the international community would intervene to uphold 'international humanitarian and human rights law'.

The discussion of how to explain conflict is also a debate about how the West should respond. In David Keen's words: 'In so far as the causes of wars ... remain poorly understood, it may be relatively easy for some analysts ... to insist that a proper response is an isolationist one' (Keen 1999: 82). US Secretary of State Warren Christopher, for example, seemed close to Huntington's views when he argued in February 1993 that:

> The death of President Tito and the end of communist domination of the former Yugoslavia raised the lid on the cauldron of ancient hatreds. This is a land where at least three religions and a half-dozen ethnic groups have vied across the centuries. (Quoted in Allen and Seaton 1999: 1)

Kaplan's ideas are thought to have influenced US policy directly: his 1993 book, *Balkan Ghosts*, is 'credited with dissuading the Clinton administration from its initial interventionist line in Bosnia' (Allen 1999: 27). It seems logical that a view of post-Cold War conflicts as intractable 'ethnic wars' could act as an argument for non-involvement, or as an excuse when attempted interventions fail. Yet not all analysts make a connection between 'ethnic' explanations and Western isolationism. David Callahan (1997: 17), for example, argues that an upsurge of ethnic conflict since the end of the Cold War is a reason for greater activism, and suggests that 'Responding to ethnic conflict must be part of a broader strategy for reinvigorating US internationalism'. And despite having taken the view that conflict in Yugoslavia was caused by incomprehensible tribalism, Keegan nevertheless declared that Nato action in Kosovo was 'a victory for that New World Order which, proclaimed by George Bush in the aftermath of the Gulf war, has been so derided since' (quoted in Chomsky 1999: 120).

Furthermore, the argument that there is a connection between an inadequate explanation and a particular policy orientation on the part of Western governments could be turned around: the preference for intervention and 'ethical engagement' might be linked to a tendency to explain conflicts in equally simplistic, good-versus-evil terms. Kaldor (1999: 117–18), for instance, contends that 'Those who argued that [Bosnia] was a civil war were against intervention', asserting instead that 'This was a war of ethnic cleansing and genocide'. In this view of the Bosnian war, in which an analogy is drawn with the Nazi Holocaust, it is possible to identify clear villains and victims for whom the Western powers can intervene, to punish or protect. To explain a conflict as the product of 'ethnic hatred' implicitly treats all sides as equally guilty, but the concern of many commentators has been to suggest that one side is more to blame, or even exclusively to blame. This perspective also involves a selective and distorted understanding. While Serbian President Slobodan Milosevic was routinely condemned as an ultra-nationalist, for example, comparatively little attention was given to the political doctrines of Croatia's President Tudjman or Bosnian leader Alija Izetbegovic, both of whom had espoused an exclusivist nationalism prior to the conflict.

Ultimately, there may be less of a distinction than is usually assumed between a view of post-Cold War conflicts as a 'clash of civilisations' or an expression of 'anarchy' and an approach which instead divides the world between human rights abusers and victims. As Ignatieff (2000: 213) observes:

> While the language of the nation is particularistic – dividing human beings into us and them – human rights is universal. In theory, it will not lend itself to dividing human beings into higher and lower, superior and inferior, civilized and barbarian. Yet something very like a distinction between superior and inferior has been at work in the demonization of human rights violators.

While some analysts explain the superiority of the West in the vocabulary of 'ethnicity' and 'civilisation', the alternative framework of *moral* superiority produces similar results.

Ethical intervention and its critics

President George Bush Snr's proclamation of a 'New World Order' at the time of the 1991 Gulf war soon began to look over-optimistic. Yet the assumption persisted that the West was now in a stronger position to bring order to a chaotic world. The ending of the Cold War was said to have given the UN Security Council a new lease of life, since it was no longer hamstrung by the Soviet veto. As Mark Curtis (1998: 174–6) has shown, the idea that UN efficacy was blocked by the Soviet veto was a myth. Nevertheless, the fact that Western strategy was not now constrained by the need to counter the Soviet threat appeared to allow the possibility of a more principled foreign policy: no longer would it be necessary to support unsavoury regimes or to overlook human rights abuses because of the demands of Cold War *realpolitik*. Following the Gulf war, in April 1991 the US and its allies intervened again in Iraq to set up 'safe havens' for Kurds and other minorities. This was the first of a series of humanitarian interventions which – as Western military forces were sent to deliver food to the starving in Somalia, to protect aid and keep the peace in Bosnia, and to 'restore democracy' in Haiti – seemed to confirm the idea that foreign policy was increasingly driven by ethical and humanitarian concerns.

While mainstream assessments of the end of the Cold War have tended to see it as the start of a new era, however, radical critics have instead emphasised continuity, and have suggested that both the Cold War and the period since have basically been 'business as usual' for the major Western powers. John Pilger, for example, describes the post-Cold War era as a 'New Cold War', and writes of 'the unchanging nature of the 500-year Western imperial crusade' (1999: 38, 21). Pilger has also described the post-9/11 period as the 'Colder War', arguing that 'The parallels are striking' between the Cold War and the war on terrorism (*Daily Mirror*, 29 January 2002). Similarly, Noam Chomsky (1990) has argued that, for the US, the Cold War was 'largely a war against the third world, and a mechanism for retaining a degree of influence over its industrial rivals and, crucially, a mode of domestic social organisation. And nothing has changed in that respect. So the Cold War hasn't ended.' The suggestion of continuity is a useful corrective to official proclamations of a brave New World Order, but much radical criticism is open to the objection that it understates what has changed since 1989.

Of course, Great Power interference in weaker states, sometimes rhetorically justified in 'ethical' terms, is hardly a new phenomenon. Yet the 'ethical' interventions of the 1990s did represent something different from the Cold War era. Under the post-1945 UN system, the governing principle in international affairs, at least formally, was one of sovereign equality. The principle of non-interference in the affairs of sovereign states meant that external intervention was widely understood as illegitimate, and when Western powers, chiefly the US, did intervene they tended to do so indirectly, through covert action or via proxy forces (Keeble 1997: 15–18). As David Chandler (2002) argues, a significant change since 1989 has been the erosion of the principles of sovereign equality and non-interference. From the 1991 Kurdish crisis onwards, the argument has been that sovereignty must not be a barrier to effective intervention to uphold human rights or humanitarian principles. As Javier Perez de Cuellar put it in 1991, when UN Secretary-General:

> We are clearly witnessing what is probably an irresistible shift in public attitudes toward the belief that the defense of the oppressed in the name of morality should prevail over frontiers and legal documents. (Quoted in Rieff 1999: 1)

Over the course of the 1990s, a growing consensus held that, in the words of the sometime French government minister and founder of Médecins Sans

Frontières Bernard Kouchner, 'a new morality can be codified in the "right to intervention" against abuses of national sovereignty' (*Los Angeles Times*, 18 October 1999).

In some respects, the most vociferous critics of actual policies have been the supporters of the ideal of ethical intervention. One frequent criticism is that concern to maintain domestic political support makes Western governments timid about sending their troops into action (Ignatieff 2000: 213–15; Shawcross 2000: 374). A second, related criticism is that this half-hearted commitment, coupled with what advocates of intervention view as an outmoded realist concern with stability and state sovereignty on the part of Western political leaders, has led to an over-emphasis on traditional ideas of neutrality. Rather than intervening to punish abusers and protect victims, humanitarian action has been ineffective, it is argued, because Western forces have been deployed as neutral peacekeepers or aid-givers. According to Kaldor (1999: 118), for instance, a position of neutrality is morally indefensible: 'The failure to protect the victims is a kind of tacit intervention on the side of those who are inflicting humanitarian or human rights abuses'. Similarly, Alex de Waal (1997: 189) argues that: 'international military intervention in Somalia and Bosnia was primarily aimed at protecting aid givers, rather than the populace in the area'. His main target of criticism is the international community's failure to intervene to prevent or halt genocide in Rwanda in 1994. The mistake of the 'humanitarian international', he argues, was 'to introduce and elevate the principle of neutrality' (1997: 192), by calling for a ceasefire and humanitarian access instead of forceful intervention.

Where proponents of ethical intervention tend to see self-interest as limiting the West's willingness to intervene consistently, radical critics have dismissed the claim that humanitarianism and human rights have become central to Western foreign policy as an ideological cover for the pursuit of hidden interests. Uwe-Jens Heuer and Gregor Schirmer (1998), for example, denounce 'human rights imperialism' on the grounds that, in many cases, 'the altruism of the intervening parties was a mere secondary phenomenon to crude self-interested efforts toward the expansion of political and military power, spheres of economic influence, and the like'. Yet it has not been easy for critics to make a convincing case about how interventions in, say, Somalia or Kosovo have furthered the 'crude self-interest' of Western powers. Furthermore, the radical critique is not always as sweeping as it first appears. One line of argument, for example, contrasts the claims made for cases of 'ethical' intervention with comparable cases where the West has not intervened or has actively supported or colluded in abuses (Chomsky 1999, 2000a, 2000b). Yet, while it is not intended as such, this could be taken as an argument for more intervention. Having held up the example of East Timor as one of the places where self-interest prevented Western states from making good on their proclaimed commitment to human rights, radical critics were somewhat wrong-footed when the West did intervene to establish a UN protectorate there in 1999. The underlying assumption of most criticism is that a real commitment to upholding human rights would be desirable, so the possibility of genuinely 'ethical' interventionism is kept open. Despite sharply criticising the role of the West in escalating conflict in former Yugoslavia, for example, Pilger (1993) argued that further intervention was necessary in the form of tightening sanctions against Serbia, extending sanctions to Croatia, arming the Bosnian Muslims, making better use of UN troops, and drawing up a new peace treaty.

Chandler's critique of the erosion of sovereign equality, in contrast, implies that there can be nothing progressive about ethical interventionism, since there is a contradiction between the promotion of human rights, and support for democracy and self-determination. From the perspective of the international community's 'right to intervene', the sovereignty of weaker states becomes conditional on their compliance with 'human rights norms': if a state is judged to be violating these norms the 'international community' has a responsibility to intervene. 'Conditional' sovereignty, of course, is by definition not sovereignty, since it is dependent on the approval of a higher authority. Similarly, human 'rights' are not really rights as traditionally understood. As Chandler (2002: 109) notes, for democratic rights theorists, 'If a right could not be protected, or exercised, by its bearers then it could no longer be a right, an expression of self-government'. Human rights, in contrast, depend not on autonomous self-governing subjects, but on external enforcement in support of victims who cannot exercise those 'rights' on their own behalf. Like 'conditional sovereignty', human rights are in the gift of the powerful. A view of (non-Western) sovereignty as a 'tyrant's charter' and of (non-Western) people as helpless victims implies an outlook which is just as elitist as that which sees the non-Western world as uncivilised and barbaric.

War on terrorism and the problem of legitimacy

Advocacy of 'ethical' interventionism in the 1990s rested on the assumption that 'might', in the form of military action by the most powerful states, broadly coincided with 'right', in that force was used to uphold humanitarian and human rights principles (Chandler 2004). In the war on terrorism, however, this assumption has looked increasingly questionable. Even supporters of American power acknowledge that it is 'suffering a crisis of international legitimacy' (Kagan 2004: 108). Almost immediately after taking office in 2000, George W. Bush's administration was accused of adopting an unacceptably unilateralist foreign policy stance, failing to respect international agreements on climate change and nuclear missiles, for instance. A particularly pertinent example is America's insistence on exemption from the jurisdiction of the International Criminal Court (ICC) established on 1 July 2002. America's refusal to acknowledge any higher authority than its own national sovereignty threatened to expose the notion of an international community based on norms and values as a fiction. The problem came to a head in the run-up to the 2003 invasion of Iraq, when the US declared its intention to act regardless of whether it gained UN approval.

At first glance, the contrast between the liberal consensus in favour of humanitarian intervention and the division and controversy surrounding the invasion of Iraq could not be greater. Yet aspects of 'war on terror' interventions which have attracted criticism were pioneered in the 'ethical' 1990s. Richard Falk contrasts the 'golden age' of humanitarian intervention with the post-9/11 era, complaining that:

> the Bush Administration has been doing its best to wreck world order as it had been evolving, and ... part of the wreckage is the abandonment of legal restraints on the use of international force, the heart and soul of the UN Charter.[2]

Yet the advocates of 'human rights intervention' themselves undermined the UN system by putting the moral duty to intervene above the principle of sovereign equality. Voicing the complaint of ethical interventionists throughout Falk's 'golden age', Ignatieff argues that upholding sovereign equality means 'defending tyranny and terror' (*New York Times*, 7 September 2003). This is what led many, including Falk himself, to approve the Kosovo bombing in 1999 as illegal but moral (see Chapter 5). Similarly, there were many objections to the Bush administration's willingness to use pre-emptive force, yet this idea had been advocated as part of the West's 'right to intervene' for humanitarian or human rights reasons. Kouchner, for example, argued after the Kosovo conflict that it was 'necessary to take the further step of using the right to intervention as a preventive measure to stop wars before they start and to stop murderers before they kill' (*Los Angeles Times*, 18 October 1999).

Many liberal supporters of humanitarianism and human rights, however, disliked the Bush administration, and sought to distinguish between the war on terrorism and the sort of 'moral' intervention they favour. Geoffrey Robertson, for example, whose 1999 book *Crimes Against Humanity* forcefully made the case for international intervention against human rights abuses, criticised US treatment of detainees from Afghanistan (*Independent*, 15 January 2002) and argued that the West was wrong to go to war with Iraq (*Observer*, 8 September 2002). Even Robin Cook, a key architect of Labour's 'ethical foreign policy' and Britain's hawkish Foreign Secretary during the Kosovo conflict, emerged as the 'standard-bearer of the Labour "doves"' over Iraq (*Mail*, 16 August 2002). Despite their attacks on Anglo-American policy, these critics were not against intervention as such. Cook's resignation from government in March 2003, for example, was prompted by the decision of the British and American governments to abandon their pursuit of a second UN resolution authorising force against Iraq, implying that he would have supported military action with such a mandate. Similarly, Robertson advocated using the framework of international human rights law in the war on terrorism and advised that, instead of using self-defence as justification for attacking Afghanistan, 'A more modern and more permissive legal justification for an armed response is provided by the emerging human rights rule that requires international action to prevent and to punish "crimes against humanity"' (*Independent*, 26 September 2001). Self-defence in Afghanistan or imperial ambition in Iraq seemed old-fashioned and illegitimate justifications for war, out of step with the liberal humanitarian consensus.

The question of how conflicts and threats, and the global responses to them, are understood and explained is of some importance, given that the legal and political framework of international relations often seems uncertain in the post-Cold War era. This uncertainty is particularly marked in the case of humanitarian or human rights intervention, where establishing the nature of conflicts and the legitimacy of international responses becomes a crucial but fluid process, in which, as the International Commission on Intervention and State Sovereignty (ICISS) observed, 'media coverage … is a new element in determining military as well as political strategies' (ICISS 2001: 64). The Independent International Commission on Kosovo (IICK) described its proposals for guiding future intervention as 'situated in a gray zone of ambiguity between an extension of international law and a proposal for an international moral consensus', and concluded that 'this gray zone goes beyond strict ideas of *legality* to incorporate more flexible views of *legitimacy*' (IICK 2000: 164). Similarly, the ICISS (2001: 11, 63–4) suggested that a key objective of international actors must be 'to establish the legitimacy of military intervention when necessary', and highlighted the role of the news media in this process. Following the 11 September 2001 attacks, these issues have become more urgent, but the picture remains unclear. Some critics have continued to pursue themes which became prominent in discussion of post-1989 conflicts, such as imperialism, or the 'clash of civilisations' between the West and Islam (Ali 2002; Mahajan 2002). Yet it is evident that other themes, of international terrorism and weapons proliferation, have assumed new prominence, while humanitarian and human rights issues have arguably been neglected (Weiss et al. 2004) or compromised (Rieff 2002). It is also clear from the public debate surrounding the conflict with Iraq in 2003 that the legitimacy of intervention remains a crucial and controversial issue.

The role of the media

The role of the media in war and conflict has long been a topic of interest for academic researchers and others, with the most prominent issue being propaganda. However, propaganda has not been the main focus in studies of post-Cold War conflicts and interventions – at least as regards the Western media[3] – with the exception of the 1991 and 2003 Iraq wars and the partial exception of the Kosovo conflict. This is partly because, in many cases, the Western military has either not intervened directly or has been engaged in non-warlike operations, and partly because intervention has usually been perceived as desirable. Few studies of the post-1989 period have dealt directly with media content or examined themes and patterns of reporting across different conflicts. Where a comparative approach has been taken, attention has largely centred on other issues, such as: the place of recent conflicts in the history of war correspondence (Carruthers 2000; McLaughlin 2002); the relationships between the media and non-governmental organisations (NGOs) in humanitarian emergencies (Giradet 1995; Rotberg and Weiss 1996); or the effects of

coverage on government decision-making (Mermin 1999; Robinson
Nevertheless, many of the issues examined above concerning how con-
_____ınd interventions should be understood have also been raised in debates
about the media.

The CNN effect

The idea developed in the early 1990s that Western foreign policy was being
influenced by media coverage of international events: the so-called 'CNN
effect'. Former US Defense Secretary James Schlesinger, for instance, wrote in
1992 that 'policies seem increasingly subject, especially in democracies, to the
images flickering across the television screen', pointing to the Kurdish refugee
crisis and Somalia as examples (quoted in Livingston 1997: 1). The attraction
of the idea, subsequently elaborated and explored in a number of studies
(Gowing 1994, 1996; Neuman 1996; Hudson and Stanier 1997; Strobel 1997),
had much to do with the fact that Western foreign policy seemed difficult to
explain in terms of conventional geo-strategic interests. Since decisions often
appeared arbitrary, the notion of powerful but fickle media seemed to offer a
plausible explanation for the selective attention paid to some crises rather than
others. For policy-makers, the thought that the media were driving foreign
policy was a disturbing one, as it implied a loss of elite control. For others,
however, it seemed much more positive: the media were able, it was argued, to
facilitate and promote humanitarian action (Giradet 1995; Minear et al. 1996;
Rotberg and Weiss 1996; Shaw 1996).

Academic research into the CNN effect has generally warned against over-
estimating the power and influence of the media: studies have shown that in
Somalia and other cases news coverage followed interest on the part of political
leaders rather than leading it (Livingston and Eachus 1995; Livingston 1997;
Mermin 1999). The most sustained and systematic study is Piers Robinson's *The
CNN Effect* (2002), which suggests that there may be some media influence but
only under specific circumstances: where policy is uncertain and where coverage is both supportive of Western policy and sympathetic to the victims of
war. The present study is not concerned with the relationship between media
reporting and foreign policy, except at the level of ideas. There is no attempt to
assess the extent of media influence on particular decisions: rather, our interest
is in the extent to which the ways that journalists explain conflicts and interventions follow the official script, and how far they help to write it. We have
already seen an example of this in the portrayal of Saddam as the 'new Hitler',
mentioned at the beginning of this chapter. As William Dorman and Steven
Livingston (1994: 70) show, the comparison to Hitler actually originated with
journalists, who used it before Saddam had invaded Kuwait, in reference to
his bellicose attitude toward Israel. Just before the invasion, politicians began
drawing the same analogy, and afterwards, once President Bush had made the
comparison, it pervaded media reports as greater numbers of journalists took
up and elaborated the idea.

Robinson's work is of particular interest because, unlike many other commentators on the CNN effect, he methodically examines the content of news reports, attempting to measure how far coverage adopts either 'empathy' or 'distance' framing in relation to victims, and the extent to which it presents Western policy as likely to succeed. This again raises the issue of the relationship between explanations of crisis and prescriptions for action: only the 'right' sort of reporting has the potential to encourage intervention. Furthermore, the idea of the CNN effect took a dramatic twist early on, when it seemed that graphic media reports of US casualties in October 1993 led to America's subsequent withdrawal from Somalia. This led many to conclude that adverse coverage of intervention could also have what Livingston (1997: 2) calls an 'impediment effect'. Following the decision to pull out of Somalia, the Clinton administration issued a presidential directive setting limits and conditions on any future military deployments, apparently demonstrating the way that fear of losing political support can make leaders reluctant to intervene. The widely publicised failure in Somalia is held to have played a large part in America's decision not to intervene in Rwanda the following year (Livingston and Eachus 2000). The Joint Evaluation of Emergency Assistance to Rwanda (JEEAR), an international study commissioned by the UN, also concluded that 'inadequate and inaccurate reporting by international media' had 'contributed to international indifference and inaction' (JEEAR 1996: study II, section 4.3). For those – including journalists – who wished to promote intervention, these developments accentuated the importance of explaining crises in such a way as to counter elite reluctance to pursue ethical policies.

Explanation and advocacy

Whether or not media coverage actually did pressure governments to adopt policies of 'humanitarian intervention' in the 1990s, it is certainly the case that many journalists began to understand their role in these terms. In Britain, the best-known proponent of this approach is the former BBC correspondent Martin Bell, who coined the phrase 'the journalism of attachment' to describe a style of journalism which 'cares as well as knows', and which 'will not stand neutrally between good and evil, right and wrong, the victim and the oppressor'. Bell rejected the 'dispassionate practices of the past', confessing that he was 'no longer sure what "objective" means' (Bell 1998: 16–18). In the US, a similar argument, in favour of 'advocacy journalism', is perhaps most prominently associated with CNN reporter Christiane Amanpour, who famously scolded President Clinton on live television in May 1994 for failing to articulate a tough policy on Bosnia (Ricchiardi 1996). Notwithstanding Bell's comments, the journalism of attachment does still entail some commitment to 'objectivity' in the sense of truthful, factually accurate reporting: what is rejected is moral neutrality. So, for example, Amanpour maintains that: 'In certain situations, the classic definition of objectivity can mean neutrality, and neutrality can mean you are an accomplice to all sorts of evil' (quoted in Ricchiardi 1996). This moral objection to 'neutral' journalism means that reporters feel compelled to take sides in the conflicts they cover. As Amanpour explains:

> Once you treat all sides the same in a case such as Bosnia, you are drawing a moral equivalence between victim and aggressor. And from here it is a short step to being neutral. And from there it's an even shorter step to becoming an accessory to all manners of evil. (Quoted in Hume 1997: 6)

This line of reasoning is reminiscent of Kaldor's argument that non-intervention is immoral. Journalists have argued that the neutrality of peacekeeping and traditional humanitarianism results at best in helplessness. BBC correspondent Fergal Keane (1995: 124, 186), for example, argues that UN troops in Rwanda 'had a mandate that turned them into little more than spectators to the slaughter', and suggests that the refugee camps which developed on Rwanda's borders in the wake of the mass killings of 1994 were a '"humanitarian haven" for the killers'. Similarly, Bell (1996: 135, 190) sympathises with UN troops in Bosnia, forced into the role of 'bystanders', and sardonically describes humanitarian aid as ensuring that victims 'should not be starving when they were shot'.

From this perspective, failing to report conflicts in the 'right' way is understood as complicity with 'evil'. Advocacy journalists have been highly critical of their fellow reporters for following the allegedly neutral agenda of Western governments. Ed Vulliamy (1999), who reported from Yugoslavia for the *Guardian*, contends that the 'neutrality' of the 'international community' has been 'nowhere more evident than in the media'. Similarly, the BBC's Allan Little (2001) describes how in the early 1990s he was 'bewildered' by what seemed to be the general consensus about Bosnia:

> That the Balkan tribes had been killing each other for centuries and that there was nothing that could be done. It was nobody's fault. It was just, somehow, the nature of the region. It was a lie that Western governments at that time liked. It got the Western world off the hook. When I and others argued that you could not blame all sides equally, the moral implications were that the world should – as it later did – take sides. We were denounced – derided even – by government ministers as laptop bombardiers.

Reporters have described a similar consensus about Rwanda. According to Keane (1995: 6–8):

> The mass of early reporting of the Rwandan killings conveyed the sense that the genocide was the result of some innate inter-ethnic loathing that had erupted into irrational violence.... several of the world's leading newspapers ... bought the line, in the initial stages, that the killings were a straightforward 'tribal war'.

Advocacy journalists, in contrast, sought to identify clear human rights villains and victims, to explain conflicts in unambiguous moral terms and to encourage Western military intervention by bringing public pressure to bear through media reports.

Assessing the extent to which news coverage has indeed adopted an 'ethnic' or 'tribal' framework will be an important issue for this study. As we saw earlier, there is evidence of journalists portraying the break-up of Yugoslavia in terms of ancient 'ethnic' divisions. However, the issue is not clear-cut. Melissa Wall's comparative study of coverage of Bosnia and Rwanda in US news magazines, for example, found that, although in both cases the people of the region concerned were depicted as 'inferior to the more "advanced" civilizations of the West' (Wall 1997: 422), Rwanda was reported in terms of incomprehensible 'tribal' violence, while the conflict in Bosnia was explained in terms of logical, political and historical motivations. A similar study of US press coverage by Garth Myers et al. found that events in Bosnia were reported in terms of military strategy and tactics much more than those in Rwanda, and that, although both crises were understood in terms of 'ethnicity', in the case of Rwanda violence was also described as 'tribal', while that in Bosnia almost never was (Myers et al. 1996: 33). Both studies suggest that Rwanda was depicted as more 'distant' and different. Yet the terms in which these two studies explain the less distant representation of Bosnia – a greater emphasis on military strategy, political decisions and history – are the same as those which have led other critics to conclude that the reporting of Bosnia was also 'distancing'. Alison Preston (1996: 112, 115), for example, notes the existence of 'two co-existent narrative templates ... in the coverage, based around the motifs of either distance or proximity'. The first was associated with 'an emphasis on the complicated or difficult', for example in coverage of political and diplomatic developments; the second accentuated stories of personal suffering. She concludes that 'the motif of "complication" dominated discourse about Bosnia'. It would appear that a style of reporting which seems 'distancing' in one instance may look quite different when compared with coverage of another conflict.

Referring to the journalism of attachment, Preston (1996: 113) notes that 'The wish to highlight emotional proximity is intrinsically bound to a wish to proselytise'. Some reporters 'deliberately emphasised the emotional in their reports in order to signal the extent of their commitment, and their belief that detachment, or distance, should not be inserted'. Critics have charged, however, that, in the process of encouraging empathy, advocacy journalists have been guilty of over-simplification. With regard to Bosnia, for example, *Washington Post* journalist Mary Battiata said that: 'There was only one story – a war of aggression against a largely defenseless, multi-ethnic population. It was very simple.' Similarly, for Amanpour: 'sometimes in life, there are clear examples of black and white ... I think during the three-and-a-half-year war in Bosnia, there was a clear aggressor and clear victim' (quoted in Ricchiardi 1996). Commitment to a 'simple', 'black and white' view of a conflict may produce just as distorted a picture as the mystified notion of 'ethnic' or 'tribal' warfare.

Controversy and critique after 9/11

The vocabulary of 'good versus evil' which appealed to liberal advocates of ethical intervention in the 1990s began to seem crude and dangerous in the context of the war on terrorism. George W. Bush's declaration of war on 'evildoers', his insistence that 'either you are with us, or you are with the terrorists', and his description of Iraq, Iran, North Korea and other states as an 'axis of evil' struck many commentators as simplistic and ill-informed.[4] The huge numbers of people who marched in London and other cities in protest against the proposed invasion of Iraq indicated that political leaders were having difficulty in making a convincing case for war. Yet, ironically, it was at the moment when scepticism about official claims seemed to be at its greatest that most attention was paid to the media's role in perpetuating falsehoods and distortions.

Media coverage of 'ethical' intervention, insofar as it was discussed as propaganda at all, could be understood as 'good' propaganda (Taylor 2003: 324), or as helpful advocacy on behalf of the oppressed (Shaw 1996: 123). Since 9/11, however, particularly in relation to Iraq, discussion has returned to the traditional critical focus on the media's propagandistic role in building support for war. The main issue was the misleading claims about Iraq's possession of 'weapons of mass destruction' (WMD), the ostensible reason for the invasion (Rampton and Stauber 2003; Solomon and Erlich 2003; Miller 2004). Yet some analysts have detected a more critical tone in media reporting. Comparing coverage with that of the 1991 Gulf war, Howard Tumber and Jerry Palmer (2004: 94) argue that in 2003 the reporting of the build-up to war was more 'sensitive to different currents of opinion' and demonstrated greater 'critical distance' on the part of journalists. Drawing a similar comparison, Stephen Reese (2004: 259) also suggests that in 2003 the media were 'less apt to follow government policy'. Certainly in the aftermath of the war, the media played a prominent role in circulating criticism. The claim by BBC reporter Andrew Gilligan that the government had manipulated and falsified intelligence about WMD led to a high-profile public enquiry, and pictures of US troops abusing prisoners in Abu Ghraib prison in Iraq were publicised by all mainstream news organisations.

This last example suggests that the 'ethical' discourse which was so important in establishing the moral legitimacy of Western military intervention in the 1990s may itself have become a source of controversy since 9/11. Following criticism of the treatment of detainees in Guantanamo Bay and in Iraq, for example, Amnesty International Secretary-General Irene Khan suggested that Western governments may be 'losing their moral compass, sacrificing the global values of human rights in a blind pursuit of security' (Amnesty International 2004). As Ignatieff has put it: 'Since the end of the cold war, human rights has become the dominant moral vocabulary in foreign affairs. The question after September 11 is whether the era of human rights has come and gone.' The war on terrorism, he suggested, 'may permanently demote human rights in the hierarchy of America's foreign policy priorities' (*New York Times*, 5 February 2002).

Understandings of the media's role in post-Cold War conflicts and interventions range from the view that news reporting has the power to shape foreign policy, through to the argument that it serves as a conduit for official misinformation and spin. In terms of media content, some contradictory claims have been made. Some critics have suggested there may be new ideological themes emerging in news coverage which are conducive to Western intervention, while others, including some journalists, have suggested that a key problem has been a tendency to frame conflicts so as to hamper effective intervention, or even to act as an alibi for non-intervention. From either perspective, the ways in which conflicts and interventions are explained are seen to have important consequences.

About this book

This study looks at UK press coverage of six conflicts and the international response to them: two instances of 'humanitarian military intervention' (Somalia and Kosovo); two cases in which the international community was criticised for not intervening (Bosnia and Rwanda); and two post-9/11 interventions (Afghanistan and Iraq). These have been chosen because of their political importance, the large amount of media coverage they received, and in order to maximise the comparison of similarities and differences across conflicts. Since in some instances news coverage of one crisis informed and influenced the reporting of others, the case studies are presented chronologically.

While each of the conflicts throws up different issues to be explored in different chapters, the key overall questions posed in this book are as follows:

- *How have post-Cold War conflicts been framed?*
  How have conflicts been explained? Are there common patterns in news framing across different conflicts? Who, in terms of the main sources cited, are the originators of news frames?
- *How are international responses to conflicts framed?*
  Have international interventions been seen as legitimate? To what extent do claims of legitimacy derive from claims about upholding humanitarianism and human rights? Are there alternative sources of legitimacy?
- *Has news framing of conflict changed since 11 September 2001?*
  Have 'ethical' themes been overshadowed by other concerns? Does reporting of human rights issues support or undermine the legitimacy of international intervention?

The remainder of this Introduction explains the approach taken in seeking to address these questions in the chapters which follow.

News frames

'Frames' are the underlying, sometimes only implicit, ideas through which an account of the world is organised. As Robert Entman puts it in his well known explanation of the approach, frames 'diagnose, evaluate, and prescribe':

> To frame is to *select some aspects of a perceived reality and make them more salient in a communicating text, in such a way as to promote a particular problem definition,*

causal interpretation, moral evaluation, and/or treatment recommendation. (Entman 1993: 52, original emphasis)

Similarly, Shanto Iyengar and Adam Simon note that a key issue in news framing is the attribution of responsibility:

Attributions of responsibility are generally divided into causal and treatment dimensions. Causal responsibility focuses on the origin of the issue or problem, while treatment responsibility focuses on who or what has the power either to alleviate or to forestall alleviation of the issue. (Iyengar and Simon 1994: 171)

For our purposes, the issue is how the causes of conflicts and crises are understood, and what the appropriate international response is thought to be.

Identifying frames involves close textual analysis – Entman (1993: 52) suggests that frames are 'manifested by the presence or absence of certain keywords, stock phrases, stereotypical images, sources of information, and sentences that provide thematically reinforcing clusters of facts or judgements' – but it also entails a quantitative assessment of the extent and persistence of a given frame. The qualitative aspect of framing analysis offers greater subtlety than traditional content analysis, although sometimes this advantage can be lost. Commonly, the stages of framing analysis are, firstly, identifying frames through qualitative study of a relatively small sample of texts, and then quantifying the occurrence of keywords associated with these frames across a larger sample. While this can often produce illuminating results, there is also the danger that, at the quantitative stage, a simple count of keywords can lack nuance. As Entman (1993: 57) notes, one of the potential advantages of the framing approach is that it 'avoid[s] treating all negative or positive terms or utterances as equally salient and influential'. The problem is compounded when keywords or categories are predicted in advance rather than derived from qualitative analysis. In the present study, every article was examined qualitatively before proceeding to the quantitative stage of analysis. While this approach is more time-consuming and laborious, it does afford greater validity.

A further problem with the keywords approach is that it segments texts into countable components instead of treating them as coherent wholes. Checking the incidence of key terms can be a useful procedure, and is sometimes used in the present study to give a quick indication of framing devices. However, a more accurate picture seems more likely to come from examining articles in their entirety as far as possible. Particularly in the case of news reports of crises and conflicts, which deal with often controversial, new and fast-moving events, we would expect there to be competing narratives and explanations rather than only one settled perspective. Examining the interaction of different frames within and across texts can reveal much about why some diagnoses and prescriptions become favoured over others. According to Entman (1993: 55), competing frames reflect 'the play of power and boundaries of discourse over an issue':

Framing … plays a major role in the exertion of political power, and the frame in a news text is really the imprint of power – it registers the identity of actors or interests that competed to dominate the text.

The case studies in this book investigate the relationship between framing and power through comparing dominant frames with official perspectives, such as those offered by political leaders, and through examining the sources used by news reports. Particular ways of understanding a problem do not, after all, emerge from nowhere: they are likely to be influenced by a range of factors, including who has access to the media. Each of the case studies assesses the extent to which critique, dissent and non-mainstream views are represented.

In order to appreciate the significance of how a particular event was framed, it is important to consider the range of other possible interpretations: both those which were available at the time and those which have become established since. As Entman (1993: 54) comments, 'the omissions of potential problem definitions, explanations, evaluations, and recommendations may be as critical as the inclusions'. In their study of the public debate leading up to the 1991 Gulf war, for example, Dorman and Livingston (1994: 65, 67) observe that, while 'information regarding the historical root causes of the crisis' received only 'selective attention', news reports were 'rich with references to an alternative historical context: Adolf Hitler and Nazi Germany'. They see this failure of explanation as limiting the policy debate about the crisis, resulting in the 'elimination of complicating alternative interpretations and policy implications' (1994: 73). We might also note that the repeated use of the comparison with Hitler is likely to have been particularly important since, as Entman (1993: 53) notes, 'Texts can make bits of information more salient by placement or repetition, or by associating them with culturally familiar symbols'. The range of possible responses considered in relation to a conflict seems likely to be related in some way to which explanations of the problem are foregrounded and which are marginalised, although, as we have seen with regard to 'ethnic' explanations and non-interventionist policies, no straightforward relationship should be assumed.

Samples and sources

In each case study, four daily newspapers are examined: the *Guardian, Independent, Times* and *Mail*.[5] News articles were acquired electronically from the LexisNexis online database.[6] The main objective was not to compare different newspapers, although similarities and contrasts are noted where relevant. Rather, the reason for examining four newspapers was to establish how far the themes identified informed newspaper coverage as a whole. For each case, the core sample of coverage consists of two four-week periods spanning the beginning and end of each conflict/intervention. However, since the conflicts considered here were of varying length, in many cases this procedure would not have represented a full enough sample: while two such four-week periods encompass the whole of the 2003 Iraq war, for example, they would cover only a small part of the Bosnian war. The picture is further complicated by the fact that some conflicts do not have clear beginning and end points: in Bosnia, for example, different sides have different views about when the war began; and in

Rwanda and other cases highly significant events continued to take place after the main crisis had 'ended'. The same is also true of international interventions: in all the cases examined here, there was significant international intervention of one sort or another before the crisis periods began, and troops, NGOs and other organisations maintained a presence after the main intervention had ended. For these reasons, the core samples are supplemented with additional periods of coverage where appropriate. Particular sampling decisions are explained further in the case study chapters.

CHAPTER 2

Somalia, 1992–94

There were a number of overlapping UN and US interventions in Somalia in the early 1990s. The United Nations Mission to Somalia (UNOSOM) began in April 1992 and was succeeded by UNOSOM II, which operated from March 1993 until March 1995. A US airlift of food aid, Operation Provide Relief, was launched in August 1992, and Operation Restore Hope, a UN-authorised military intervention by the US-led Unified Task Force (UNITAF), operated from December 1992. Operation Restore Hope ended in May 1993 but a US force remained (Operation Continue Hope) to support UNOSOM II. During 1993 the US military became involved in a manhunt for the Somali 'warlord' General Mohammed Farah Aidid, culminating in an abortive raid which resulted in the deaths of 18 US troops in October 1993. US forces pulled out in March 1994 and all other UN troops had left by March 1995. Operation Restore Hope, the largest operation, deployed over 30,000 US and allied forces, with the declared objective of protecting the delivery of humanitarian aid against looting, and was the first major instance of post-Cold War humanitarian military intervention, following the precedent set by the establishment of 'safe havens' for Iraqi Kurds and other minorities at the end of the 1991 Gulf war. It forms the core of this case study, although we shall also look at earlier and later coverage for purposes of comparison.

Context

Divided under British, French and Italian rule during the nineteenth century, Somalia became independent in 1960, uniting the former British and Italian colonial territories. Yet many Somalis remained outside the country's borders – in Kenya, Djibouti (ruled directly by France until 1977) and the Ogaden region of Ethiopia. The objective of unifying all Somalis in a single state remained a source of conflict with the country's neighbours, particularly Ethiopia, and these tensions were exploited by the superpowers. In 1969 the military seized power under the command of General Mohamed Siad Barre, who declared Somalia a socialist republic and provided military facilities for the Soviet Union, principally at the port of Berbera. Ethiopia meanwhile enjoyed US patronage, but in the 1970s the superpowers swapped sides. In 1977, the US identified Somalia as one of a number of states in which the Soviets looked vulnerable, while the Americans' own ability to hold on to Ethiopia seemed highly questionable following the country's 1974 revolution. With Ethiopia in turmoil, Barre supported ethnic Somali rebels in the Ogaden and mounted a full invasion in 1978. The USSR switched its support from Somalia to Ethiopia, sending in Cuban forces to help defeat the Somalis. Barre henceforth had US support, and, in return for US aid and arms, gave the US access to the air and naval facilities at Berbera, which became a base for America's Rapid Deployment Force during the Cold War (Lewis and Mayall 1996).

Western aid had a devastating effect on Somalia in the 1980s, as the country became a dumping ground for excess food produced by US farmers, bought up by the American government and shipped to the Third World. The refugees from the war with Ethiopia – whose numbers were exaggerated by the Barre government – attracted so much foreign aid that it soon accounted for two-thirds of the Somali economy (Maren 1997). The dependency thereby created on foreign food imports undermined the domestic economy, and encouraged political corruption and intensified traditional clan divisions in Somalia, as Barre used aid to favour his allies and weaken his enemies. The Reagan and Bush administrations supported Barre's dictatorship throughout the 1980s, but after the end of the Cold War the US no longer needed to counter Soviet influence in the region and Barre became expendable. Following protests by human rights activists in 1990 over the Somali government's suppression of opposition, the US withdrew its troops and aid. In January 1991 the government collapsed and the opposition United Somali Congress (USC) took power, declaring businessman Ali Mahdi Mohammed interim president.

In May 1991 another opposition organisation, the Somali National Movement (SNM), declared the independence of the Republic of Somaliland, the former British protectorate, while continued fighting between the USC and Barre's forces in autumn 1991 ruined Somalia's agricultural region, leading to famine. During the winter, fighting between supporters of Ali Mahdi and a breakaway faction of the USC, the Somali National Alliance (SNA), led by General Aidid, laid waste to the capital, Mogadishu. At the point at which the UN and US intervened in 1992, Somalia was sharply divided and lacked any clear central authority. Yet this situation was largely the product of previous Western intervention in the country. It was, after all, with US support that Barre had manipulated and sharpened clan divisions; they were US arms that Barre had used to suppress opposition; and it was US food aid which had weakened the economy. Having become a society dependent on foreign sponsorship during the Cold War, it seems unsurprising that the country should collapse when that prop was withdrawn. One question for this study is how far press reporting referred to this historical background in explaining the crisis in Somalia. In a review of European news coverage, Rune Ottosen (1999: 181–2) suggests that there was generally a lack of historical perspective and a failure to link present violence to previous Great Power interference.

Discussion of the US/UN intervention in Somalia has been dominated by the controversial manner in which it ended: with a seemingly hasty withdrawal following the death of US troops in clashes with Aidid's militia in 1993. Many accounts focus on how what began as a limited, ostensibly humanitarian mission turned into a 'quagmire', as US forces became bogged down in a hunt for Aidid. Some assessments have followed the suggestion made by the US government at the time that the UN was to blame for this failure. The argument is that, after the UN assumed control in May 1993, unclear and over-ambitious objectives led to disaster, turning the humanitarian mission into a misconceived attempt at 'nation building' and 'peace enforcement' (Allard 1995; Crocker 1995). Subsequent assessments have challenged this view, however, and made it clear that this claim was simply an attempt by the US to shift the blame for its own ignominious defeat to the UN. As Walter Clarke and Jeffrey Herbst (1996) point out, for instance, despite formally handing over to the UN, all the main Security Council resolutions were written by US officials and the US retained operational control, with Jonathan Howe, a retired American admiral and former deputy national security advisor, in charge of UNOSOM II.

In terms of the analysis of media coverage, much discussion has also been rather narrowly focused, concentrating on the issue of the 'CNN effect'. As noted in Chapter 1, a number of studies have demonstrated that the relationship between media reporting and the US government's policy on Somalia was more or less the opposite of that supposed by the CNN effect thesis, in that news coverage largely followed elite attention to Somalia rather than preceding and causing it (Livingston 1997; Mermin 1999; Robinson 2002). There is more evidence for the less significant claim that media coverage led to the US leaving Somalia, as dramatic pictures of the killing of American troops provoked calls for withdrawal, but even here it seems to have been more a case of speeding up the decision rather than causing it. News reports at the time noted that President Clinton was 'already under intense pressure to pull American troops out' (*Independent*, 5 October 1993) and had 'already begun to make clear that he intended to withdraw' (*Times*, 4 October 1993). The fact that much subsequent commentary has been preoccupied with these essentially misleading ideas about media influence and the causes of the mission's failure indicates a certain narrowness of debate.

There are, nevertheless, some more substantial and significant issues raised by the intervention in Somalia. The first concerns the reasons for the intervention. As a number of critics have pointed out, while the ostensible rationale was to ensure that emergency food aid reached famine victims, the famine was actually waning by the time of Operation Restore Hope: the famine peaked in August 1992 but it was not until November that the US decided to send in the marines, by which time the worst was over (Maren 1997: 204). This raises questions about how far media coverage took the official reasons for intervention at face value, and how far reporters looked for alternative explanations (Ottosen 1999: 186–91). It has been suggested that media coverage of famine was misleading, focusing on the worst cases of individual suffering and ignoring the broader picture. Michael Maren (1997: 211) notes that the impact of the famine was localised but 'there was very little reporting that let people know that most of Somalia was fine'. Instead, anecdotal evidence suggests that journalists sought out the most sensational and emotive images (Carruthers 2000: 240). This accusation was made at the time, rather than only retrospectively: at the beginning of Operation Restore Hope, Rakiya Omaar and Alex de Waal accused the media of producing 'disaster pornography'.[1] Omaar was sacked from the human rights NGO Africa Watch for her outspoken criticism of the US military intervention in Somalia, and her colleague, de Waal, resigned. Together they formed a new organisation, African Rights, which continued to comment critically on the mission. In a May 1993 report, African Rights also observed that 'the intervention was designed to address a problem that had already been largely solved', and disputed the UN claim that before the launch of Operation Restore Hope 80 per cent of food aid was being looted by armed gangs. The proportion of aid being lost through looting prior to the intervention had been exaggerated and was not exceptional, it was noted, and the massive amount of aid which flowed into the country after the arrival of US/UN forces was not well targeted and had damaged Somalia's prospects for economic recovery (African Rights 1993a). The question for this study is how the media explained the reasons for the intervention.

A second issue, also raised at the time by African Rights in a July 1993 report, is the conduct of the military deployed in Operation Restore Hope. There were numerous instances of ill-treatment of Somalis by UN troops, including rape, sexual abuse, detention without trial, torture and the indiscriminate killing of civilians. Although in many cases these abuses were carried out by individuals or small groups of soldiers, it was under the direction of official orders that UN troops attacked a hospital and opened fire on civilian demonstrations (African Rights 1993b; de Waal 1997, 1998). Estimates of Somali casualties vary, but seem certainly to have been in the thousands: at the upper end, Chomsky (1999: 69) cites an estimate produced by the US Central Intelligence Agency (CIA) of 7,000–10,000 killed. How a 'humanitarian mission' could have resulted in the abuse and killing of those it was purportedly designed to help has attracted less comment than might be expected, but some critics have sought to address it. Part of the explanation seems to lie in the American military doctrine of using 'overwhelming force' against any threat to US personnel (de Waal 1998: 142; Chomsky 1999: 69), although many of the abuses were committed by non-American troops. Perhaps more importantly, the misconduct of the international military at all levels flowed from an attitude of what de Waal (1997: 188) calls 'humanitarian impunity', whereby almost anything can appear justified if it is done for 'good' ends. As Maren (1997: 217–18) comments: 'the people running a humanitarian mission became so dedicated to their cause that they started to see strafing, bombing and killing as humanitarian acts'. In its own retrospective assessment of the mission to Somalia, the UN suggested that media coverage had been skewed toward dramatic stories involving the military, while the progress made by the aid operation was neglected,[2] and studies of media coverage have also indicated a disproportionate emphasis on the military rather than on the humanitarian aspects of the mission (Ottosen 1999: 182; Bantimaroudis and Ban 2001: 182–3). The more significant question, however, is how far the media reported the sometimes brutal and violent conduct of the UN military.

A third, related issue raised by Operation Restore Hope is the changing perception of Third World sovereignty and the doctrine of humanitarian intervention. Maren (1997: 218) argues that the violent conclusion of the international mission was the logical extension of humanitarianism, as the 'desire to help ... [became] the desire to control'. In a national television address on 4 December 1992, at the launch of Operation Restore Hope, President Bush promised the Somali people: 'We do not plan to dictate political outcomes. We respect your sovereignty and independence.'[3] Yet Somalia was particularly open to a revision of the principles of sovereign equality and non-interference in the internal affairs of states, in that it lacked an established government. As Ioan Lewis and James Mayall argue, the UN's operations in Somalia 'broke new ground in two ways', both of which concern the way that intervention was justified. Firstly, the crisis which was said to justify international involvement was, according to Lewis and Mayall, 'unambiguously internal': Somalia was not threatening another state but was nevertheless perceived as a 'threat to international peace and security'. Secondly, although the UN Security Council referred to 'urgent calls from Somalia' for intervention, there was little pretence that outside involvement was at the request of the Somali authorities. With no effective central authority in Somalia, intervention was seen as justified by the country's lack of statehood: 'statelessness was acknowledged to be a threat to ... international society' (Lewis and Mayall 1996: 94). How far did these novel justifications of outside involvement attract critical analysis and commentary in news coverage?

In the literature, censure of the mission's shortcomings is often tempered by a reluctance to interpret failure in Somalia as an argument against intervention elsewhere. African Rights devoted a substantial part of its May 1993 report to the questions surrounding 'humanitarian intervention', but ultimately fudged the issue. While sensitive to its problems and dangers, the authors could find no argument against it in principle, and suggested instead that 'No reasonable person could object to the idea that when a human rights or humanitarian emergency reaches a state of mass death, sovereignty should not be an obstacle to international intervention' (African Rights 1993a: 57). They also argued that, in some respects, the intervention did not go far enough: 'a major opportunity for a programme of disarmament ... was missed', they suggested, because the US showed insufficient commitment to 'nation building' (1993a: ii, 27). In part, this agreement on the desirability of extensive Western involvement in reshaping Somali society, even among some of the mission's harshest critics, flowed from shared assumptions about the potential for positive and 'ethical' foreign policy actions. Agreement was reinforced by the linking of Somalia with cases of non-intervention. Operation Restore Hope came to be understood by many as having been an alternative to intervention in Bosnia: a target picked out by US planners as a relatively easy option compared with the greater potential dangers of taking military action in the Balkans (Maren 1997: 219–20). This was somewhat ironic, since Somalia was initially perceived as having been ignored because of a Eurocentric preoccupation with what UN Secretary-General Boutros Boutros-Ghali described as the 'rich man's war' in former Yugoslavia (Maren 1997: 207–8). Once Operation Restore Hope was underway, commentators who wished to see greater Western commitment in Bosnia must have thought twice about damning US intervention in Somalia. After the US withdrawal, the West's widely condemned failure to intervene in Rwanda also coloured views of the action in Somalia: some commentators reassessed it as having been a success (Crocker 1995; Clarke and Herbst 1996); others balanced criticism of its failures against regret that the US had not done more in Rwanda (de Waal 1997). It seems likely that this consensus around the desirability of ethical interventionism would have set limits on the critical perspectives available in news reporting.

Questions

The main questions addressed in this chapter are:

- How were the famine and civil conflict in Somalia explained? How far did media reporting put Somalia's problems into their historical context?
- What solutions were proposed? How was intervention explained and evaluated? Was the international intervention viewed as legitimate? To what extent was the misconduct of the international military reported at the time?
- How far did reporting offer critical alternatives to the official narrative, and what were the limits to critical debate?

In line with the overall research design of the book, two four-week periods of coverage, spanning the beginning and end of Operation Restore Hope, form the core of the data sample for this case study. However, since the end of the operation attracted little press attention, the later withdrawal of US forces in March 1994 was also examined. In addition, for purposes of comparison, two further four-week periods of coverage were selected, coinciding with the months which saw the beginning of major US involvement (the August 1992 airlift) and the events which precipitated US withdrawal (the October 1993 clashes with General Aidid's forces). The numbers of articles with relevant coverage are shown in Table 2.1.[4]

Explanations

Articles were classified according to whether they were mainly about the causes of crisis or whether they mentioned causes only in passing. In the case of Somalia, 'causes' could refer to one of two things (and occasionally both): the causes of famine or of conflict. Overall, 22.1 per cent of coverage attempted

Table 2.1 Numbers of articles about Somalia

	Start of Operation Provide Relief (1–31 August 1992)	Start of Operation Restore Hope (27 November–25 December 1992)	End of Operation Restore Hope (13 April–11 May 1993)	US battle with General Aidid (1–31 October 1993)	Withdrawal of US forces (4 March–1 April 1994)	Totals
Guardian	24	44	4	30	9	111
Independent	36	43	3	43	7	132
Times	26	52	4	27	5	114
Mail	8	11	0	7	1	27
Totals	94	150	11	107	22	384

some explanation of the famine or the conflict in Somalia (85 out of 384 articles). However, only 14 articles (3.6 per cent of the coverage) were mainly focused on explanations and causes, the remainder mentioning causes only in passing. The *Guardian* offered the greatest amount of explanatory material, with 10 articles mainly focused on causes, as against two each in the *Times* and *Independent*, and none in the *Mail*. The *Guardian* also carried the most articles mentioning causes in passing.[5] The majority of explanatory articles were published during the earlier periods examined in this study: August and November/December 1992. All the articles which were mainly concerned with the causes of the crisis appeared during these periods (six in August and eight in November/December), as did 57 of the 71 articles which included a brief mention of causes (24 in August, 33 in November/December). The period with the fewest explanatory articles was October 1993, when the conflict with Aidid's forces was at its height, with only nine articles addressing causes (8.4 per cent of the total for this period), despite the relatively large quantity of coverage.[6]

Major explanatory articles

Looking firstly at those articles in which causes were a major focus, discussion of the crisis in terms of past superpower intervention was a theme in both the August and November/December 1992 periods. Yet this theme appeared almost exclusively in the *Guardian*, and overall the accent tended to be on internal factors, particularly Somalia's culture and social structure. In August 1992, two articles by Mark Huband, the *Guardian*'s Africa correspondent, described Somalia as 'perhaps the world's most vivid example of the devastation bequeathed to developing countries by the end of the cold war and the end of superpower interest in the Third World' (7 August). The country's 'internal problems must be seen as having been exacerbated by [its] relationship to the superpowers', he suggested, and argued that 'the seeds of Africa's current destruction were sown by Western powers eager to do business with dictators' (31 August). Huband drew attention to the role of both the Soviets and the Americans in propping up Barre's dictatorship and supplying him with the arms and aid which allowed him to exploit and encourage clan rivalries (7 August). Similarly, in the *Times* (7 August), Africa correspondent Sam Kiley noted that 'the seeds of the disaster were sown during the dictatorship of Mohamed Siad Barre' and recalled that 'first the former Soviet Union and later the United States boosted Mr Siad Barre's regime with weapons'. However, Kiley also wrote that the followers of the different Somali factions were people 'who recognise no loyalty beyond their families and to whom concepts of democracy and consensus are alien', implying that the explanation for the conflict also lay in the nature of Somali society. Kiley emphasised the importance of clan and sub-clan groupings, rather than political divisions, and argued that the term 'warlord' was misleading, insofar as it suggested that Somali leaders were 'major figures' with substantial support. Rather, he maintained, they were 'the heads of disorganised armed gangs'. The conflict was thereby framed less as a contest for political power than as a quasi-criminal competition for resources, in which 'only the armed may eat'.

In the *Guardian*, while Huband's articles clearly suggested that the roots of famine and conflict were ultimately to be found in previous foreign involvement in Somalia, other writers highlighted more immediate causes. Rakiya Omaar suggested that 'The famine is largely man-made, the result of nearly three years of fighting between the former government and armed movements, and between various warring factions' (14 August), and a Reuters story described Somalia as caught in a 'tragic cycle' of 'abuse and violence', citing an Amnesty International report to the effect that 'Civil war, insecurity and anarchic violence in much of the country combine with the drought and famine sweeping through the Horn of Africa to threaten much of the surviving Somali population with further massive loss of life' (4 August). In these last two articles, the country's problems were explained more in terms of internal causes, but these were understood as contingent and recent rather than endemic to Somali society. The idea of internal collapse was taken further in a commentary by Martin Woollacott (1 August), which described Somalia as having committed 'the state equivalent of suicide'. Arguing that 'Somalia now has no government whatever', Woollacott said that it 'was never genuinely unified', and was now the 'prime example' of a type of society that had 'become so divided and so regressed that a state structure simply cannot be maintained, or if it is, only as a facade concealing chaos'. In August, then, criticism of past interference by the superpowers was a relatively prominent theme, featuring in two out of five of the *Guardian's* explanatory articles during this period and also appearing in Kiley's 7 August report in the *Times*. At the same time, however, other explanations were also developed, emphasising the internal causes of Somalia's collapse.

In the November/December 1992 coverage, the theme of internal collapse tended to dominate. One clear but unusual example was a 12 December *Guardian* article by Mary Gooderham, which put the blame for the country's crisis on *qat*, the mildly narcotic leaf chewed by many Somalis. The negative effects of the drug, she suggested, had 'become all too obvious': it had 'crippled the economy and enervated a generation', exacerbating 'the present culture of guns and violence'. More commonly, the *Guardian's* coverage continued to discuss the effects of previous superpower intervention, while introducing other ideas about the internal causes of conflict, particularly inter-clan rivalry. Shortly before the start of Operation Restore Hope, for example, in an article from 28 November entitled 'Rambo's Boot Has No Place on Somalia's Door', Woollacott emphasised the legacy of past US involvement. Quoting a former US ambassador, he said that when America withdrew in 1991 'it was as if ... the United States "turned out the light, closed the door, and forgot about Somalia"'. The US, Woollacott argued, bore a 'special responsibility' for the country's plight, having underpinned the 'repressive apparatus' of the Barre regime:

> Somali society regressed badly under Barre, and the United States assisted in the process. First it sustained him, while making no serious attempt to persuade him into reform, and then, abruptly, it undercut him as the contest with the Soviets dwindled away and Berbera's value seemed dubious.

After the Barre regime's collapse, Woollacott concluded, a new type of violence had emerged, 'still clan-based, but with vicious differences', involving a new set of leaders, more sophisticated weapons, the decline of traditional institutions and the rise of trade in drugs. Here, conflict in Somalia is presented as the outcome of past policies pursued by Barre with US support, but the importance of more recent factors leading to new types of 'clan-based' violence is also emphasised. Similarly, writing in the *Guardian* on 24 December, former Africa correspondent Andrew Buckoke derided the hypocrisy of Bush's declaration that 'we will not tolerate armed gangs ripping off their own people', observing that the US had 'supported the biggest warlord and armed gang, ex-President Siad Barre and his army, for a decade, and thus sowed the seeds of the mayhem'. Describing America as 'claiming credit for an attempt to sort out the mess it helped create', Buckoke argued that when the US withdrew its support at the end of the Cold War 'Somalis' remarkable capacity for vengeance was unleashed'. From this perspective, the causes of conflict lay partly in past US involvement and partly in what Buckoke called 'the Somali clans' tendency to internecine savagery'.

Woollacott's idea that clan conflict now had a new social basis was supported by Somali professor of African history Said Samatar, from Rutgers University (*Guardian*, 3 December). Samatar suggested that: 'The Somali disaster is directly traceable to a tragic mismatch between moral authority possessed by the elders and senior notables of the clans, and physical coercive authority usurped by self-made warlords'. Samatar sought to dispel the 'dangerous misconception' that 'Somalia as a country has gone completely to hell and is under the sway of random violence and mass starvation'. In fact, he argued, the crisis was confined to 'a limited portion' of the country, while the rest was 'relatively peaceful and well governed by an alliance of traditional elders and local leaders that has re-emerged in the wake of the collapse of the central authority'. Only General Aidid, he suggested, was 'worthy of the name' of warlord, and even he attracted only opportunistic support. Here, the traditional, clan-based structures of Somali society are seen as a source of stability and peace, while violence is caused by the recent emergence of new military leaders. As these last few examples indicate, the Somali clan system was viewed somewhat ambivalently. On one hand, traditional clan structures were seen as distinct from the current violence; on the other hand, that violence was also understood as being 'clan-based'.

In a 5 December 1992 article, Mark Huband noted that 'violence, hunger, desperation and humiliation in the eyes of the world are the basic instincts governing everyday life in Somalia', but he challenged explanations which 'result in the conclusion that the prevailing anarchy suddenly emerged as a sign of these instincts being allowed to take an entire country in their grip'. Instead, Huband drew attention to how Barre had 'exploited clan rivalries … as a way of dividing his enemies'. While suggesting that the traditional authority of clan elders had been undermined by the emergence of new military leaders and ill-disciplined gangs of 'drugged gunmen', Huband also argued that 'The clan structure upon which Somali society is based lies at the heart of the political crisis which has prolonged the starvation from which at least 500,000 people have died'. The crisis, he suggested, had exposed 'the emptiness of Somalia's proud boast that it is the only country in Africa with a single tribe'. The conflict was an expression not of political ideologies, which were shallow and had been adopted in order to encourage foreign support, but of 'clan-based xenophobia and distrust'.

The idea that the roots of conflict were to be found in the clan system was prominent in the remaining articles which took causes as their main theme, in the *Times* and *Independent*, this time without the ambiguity and complexity present in some of the *Guardian*'s coverage. The *Independent*'s Africa editor, Richard Dowden, argued in a 21 December 1992 article that the roots of the conflict lay deep in Somali culture. As Barre's supporters fought the USC in early 1991, they 'pursued a scorched earth policy whose effect was genocide'. 'Genocide' was understood here not as a deliberate policy but as an effect of fighting which had been vengeful because of the character of Somali culture: 'Revenge, blood or blood money is central to Somali culture and there are some horrendous scores to settle'. Accordingly, Dowden argued that 'the substance of the problem' in Somalia remained 'as deranged and nihilistic as ever'. In another article, on 24 December, about the *Independent*'s local bodyguards, Dowden pursued similar themes, interviewing his Somali employees about their clan loyalties and desire for revenge against rival clans. Dowden invoked a 'nomad saying' to explain these divisions:

> My brother and I against my half-brother, my brothers and I against my father, my father's household against my uncle's household, our two households against the rest of the kin, the kin against the clan, my clan against other clans and my nation and I against the world.

He concluded that conflict resulted from 'madness' and described it as 'suigenocide' – presumably a combination of suicide and genocide – 'based on blood revenge'. In the *Times*, Sam Kiley cited a version of the same adage, on 2 December:

> The Somalis have an old explanation (which is also much heard among the Bedouin in the Middle East): 'My country against the others, my clan against my country, my sub-clan against my clan, my family against my clan, my brothers against my family; me against my brothers'.

Somali society had been criminalised by the civil war, Kiley argued, contending that 'most of the religious and social structures, including familial relationships, have collapsed'. However, while this implied that the crisis in Somalia was of recent origin and had specific causes, he also offered another explanation, which located the fundamental roots of conflict in the fact that Somalis are 'predominantly nomadic pasturalists living on the edge of starvation for much of their lives'. This fact meant that they 'inevitably regard their relationship with the world as a battle for existence' and that they 'attach no great sentimentality to family or clan bonds but see their social system as a means of survival'. As in his 7 August article discussed above, Kiley again said that 'to characterise the main players on the Somali stage today as "warlords" is to do them unjust credit', once more framing the conflict in criminal terms: 'They are now simply godfathers presiding over families running extortion and protection rackets, using teenage gunmen high on khat, a narcotic plant, or looted Valium, morphine, slimming pills, pharmaceutical cocaine, and lately, heroin'. Kiley explicitly repudiated any political explanation of the conflict, arguing that no Somali leader had 'a coherent aim or set of policies other than the pursuit of power and of profit'.

The small number of articles mainly concerned with explanations are divided between those which understand the crisis as largely resulting from past foreign interference, and those which present it mostly in terms of the internal collapse of Somali society. In order to get a sense of how common these different explanations were in the rest of the coverage, we need to look at the greater number of articles which offered only brief explanations. First, however, we can gain a quick indication of the types of explanation which were favoured by looking at the shorthand descriptions of Somalia and its society or culture presented in Box 2.1. These snapshot descriptions, taken from all articles in all periods, tend to emphasise themes of collapse, chaos, criminality and division: the implied understanding of the problem is as something self-inflicted. Perhaps surprisingly, starvation features in relatively few descriptions: the more important issue is disorder.

Brief explanations

Turning now to the greater number of articles which mentioned causes in passing, although these offered only brief explanations this in a sense makes them more significant: their more regular summing up of the situation provides a stronger indication of what the most common ideas were about the reasons for Somalia's crisis. The scope of the explanations offered varied greatly. At one end of the scale, explanation was limited by a focus on immediate causes or on only some aspects of the crisis. A report in the *Independent* on 14 December 1992 by Dowden described a particular 'inter-clan battle' over disputed territory around Mogadishu and noted that, elsewhere, 'gunmen and bandits ... are looting and killing', leading to starvation. Similarly, in a 15 October 1993 article in the *Guardian*, Julie Flint reported on the breakaway Republic of Somaliland, against which Barre had waged 'a genocidal war'. In these articles, only particular events or areas were discussed, without any attempt at broader explanation.[7]

In other articles, explanation was limited by a focus on only the most immediate causes of crisis. Dowden said, for example, that 'thousands more will die if the warlords and armed gangs continue to steal the food and prevent distribution' (*Independent*, 27 November 1992). This purported to explain the immediate cause of starvation, but not why the famine had occurred in the first place. Similarly, at the beginning of Operation Restore Hope, a 5 December 1992 editorial in the *Mail* commented on the emergence of 'A new enemy for the marines': they would be 'taking on an undisciplined rabble of gun-happy warlords in Somalia'. Who this 'rabble' were or why they were fighting was left unexamined. The *Mail* continued: 'The real enemy, though, is ... mass

Box 2.1 Descriptions of Somalia

Chaotic
- corrupt and chaotic
- far advanced toward chaos
- imploded
- thoroughly smashed up
- shattered nation
- shattered country
- 'like a giant mirror that has been shattered into a million pieces' (aid worker)
- a country that has ... dissolved into murderous anarchy
- tragic disintegration
- torn to pieces by civil strife
- where drought is compounded by anarchy
- collapsed into anarchy
- anarchy ... stalks
- strife-torn African state
- strife-torn country
- benighted country
- [Mogadishu] has earned the reputation of 'the craziest place in a madhouse'
- no longer exists as a country
- ceased to exist as a functioning country
- the entire territory is simply without a government
- without a government
- collapsed into ... squalor, chaos and misery
- blighted country with no government, bedevilled by banditry and ravaged by cholera[a]
- a country with no government, bedevilled by banditry and ravaged by cholera[a]

Apocalyptic
- hellish
- parts ... resemble a post-nuclear wasteland
- 'hell on earth' (French minister Bernard Kouchner)
- It is hell on earth
- nightmarish

Lawless
- turmoil and lawlessness
- a land now ruled by marauding gangs of gunmen, often high on drugs
- bandit-ridden interior
- 'a place where automatic rifles are a dime a dozen and there's no law' (US official)
- lawless and famine-stricken country
- prey to looters and bandits
- criminalis[ed]

Divided and war-torn
- divided and desperate society
- divided ... into a patchwork of clan fiefdoms
- a nation now riven by inter-clan hatreds
- a country in the thrall of rival warlords
- a society where terrorism and despair are intertwined among the same people
- this snakepit
- culture of nationalistic xenophobia, clan solidarity and blood revenge
- steeped in retaliation and blood revenge
- Revenge, blood or blood money is central
- a human-rights disaster area where thousands are killed, raped and mutilated in factional fighting and countless others face drought and famine (Amnesty International)

Starving
- starving Somalia
- famine-stricken country
- famine-stricken nation
- caught in a vicious circle of war and famine
- starving interior
- war and famine-ravaged interior

- vast, harsh hinterlands
- stage of the world's greatest human disaster
- the 'worst humanitarian crisis in the world'
- the worst humanitarian crisis in the world (UN officials)
- 'a nation in which over 300,000 people have lost their lives, many of them children' (Clinton)
- the East African state affected by drought and civil war

Once-proud
- once the proudest nation of the Horn of Africa
- unique in Africa ... on the surface appears to be the only country with a natural claim to nationhood ... alone in having just one tribe speaking one language ... and following one religion
- proud Somalis were famed for their graciousness and hospitality and their yearning for education

Counter-descriptions
- [most] of the country is relatively peaceful and well governed
- reasonable security and functioning markets in the northern half of the country
- not a nation of warlords, looters and starving people ... also a nation with civic leaders
- elders, professionals, entrepreneurs, experienced relief workers and volunteers who take daily risks to end the bloodshed and the suffering

Three descriptions did not fit any of the categories here: 'a much softer option than Bosnia'; 'this oral society'; and 'To the newcomer ... alarming and layered with illusion and contradiction'.

Descriptions are in quotation marks where they appeared that way in the original; attributions are given where the article attributed a phrase.

[a] *Guardian* and *Independent*, 26 March 1994, respectively. The common source was a Reuters report.

starvation.... The urgent priority is to help those desperate people by taming the gunmen who have prevented the food and medical supplies from getting through.' Again, this was a limited explanation in that it identified the immediate problem (gunmen preventing aid distribution) but ignored the question of wider causes (why the aid was needed and why the gunmen were fighting). Sometimes, these immediate causes were presented as if they were sufficient explanation in themselves, as when a *Times* editorial from 28 March 1994 commented that: 'Unlike the Ethiopian famine of 1984, the Somalian famine was entirely man-made: Operation Restore Hope sought to end the looting of food aid and protection rackets, the main causes of starvation.' Overall, 11 articles (15.5 per cent of the 71 in which explanations were mentioned in passing) focused on the immediate causes of the problem, which was invariably understood as the disruption of aid delivery and distribution. In most instances, this disruption was explained in terms of criminality: 'looting gunmen', 'armed gangs', 'hoodlums', 'banditry', 'hijacking' and 'protection rackets'.[8]

More often, however, somewhat wider causes were examined as reporters sought to explain how the immediate problem had come about. Sometimes the crisis was seen as the result of a breakdown of order and government, as when James Bone and David Watts reported that 'About 300,000 people have died in Somalia since the collapse of law and order after the overthrow of President Mohamed Siad Barre in 1991' (*Times*, 28 November 1992). Eleven articles mentioning causes in passing simply 'explained' the crisis in terms of a breakdown of society and order: the *Times* identified the problem as a 'collapse of law and order' (28 November 1992), for example; the *Guardian* reported that Mogadishu had 'collapsed into anarchy' (10 December 1992); the *Mail* said that 'The country has descended into anarchy since rebels drove out dictator Mohamed Siad Barre ... then turned on one another' (18 August 1992); and the *Independent* said that 'Somalia plunged into anarchy' and 'collapsed into anarchy' after rebels 'fell on each other' (11 and 17 August 1992). In the absence of any wider context, this collapse appeared irrational, so that the notion of a 'descent into anarchy' was in itself also a limited explanation.

In addressing the causes of famine, the most common approach was to see it as the result of civil war.[9] In a 27 November 1992 editorial, for instance, the *Guardian* distinguished its (erroneous) diagnosis of the immediate problem – 'At present 80 per cent of humanitarian supplies are intercepted and stolen by rival warlords' – from the broader context: 'Thousands are dying from starvation as the civil war has intensified and the country [has] fragmented between the various warlords.' This was true as far as it went, but it begged the question of how the war should be explained, and here accounts diverged. Occasionally, the conflict was understood as political, as when Dowden discussed the fighting in terms of divisions within the USC (*Independent*, 7 December 1992). Similarly, in a 7 August 1992 *Guardian* report Huband explained the famine as resulting from a 'political and military conflict' between different 'faction leaders'; and in a 12 December article he explained that it had been the split in the USC which had 'led to civil war and famine'. Huband also noted that the USC was still fighting supporters of Barre, 'America's firm ally who was ousted by congress rebels in January 1991'. These political and historical explanations were rare, however. Overall, of the 71 articles which made brief reference to causes and explanations, only seven framed the conflict in political terms. Eight articles contained references to the legacy of past external intervention in Somalia, and in all but one instance this was combined with discussion of internal causes of conflict. Five of these eight articles appeared in August 1992 and three in December 1992. As we have seen, these were also the periods when all 14 of the articles which focused mainly on causes appeared, so that after December 1992 the historical context of prior foreign involvement in Somalia disappeared entirely from the sampled coverage. This inevitably impoverished understanding of the crisis, given the significant role played in previous years by the main intervening power, the US, which had withdrawn its military and its aid only the year before it sent its troops back in.

The most common explanation was that the war was based not on politics but on clan divisions. This featured in 40 per cent of all explanations: seven of the 14 articles in which causes formed the main topic and 27 of the 71 articles offering brief discussion of causes. One typical example was a Reuters report which said that people were 'dying of hunger … after months of savage fighting between clans'. In this account, after the overthrow of Barre, Somalia had 'plunged into anarchy as rival clans turned on each other'; and the division between rival USC factions was understood as a personal 'feud between the two men [Aidid and Ali Mahdi]' (*Independent*, 13 August 1992). As this example suggests, the 'clan warfare' frame could readily be combined with other ideas about criminality, anarchy and breakdown as Somalis began 'turning on each other'. In the *Guardian*, Huband noted that 'Clans responsible for the division and cohesion of Somali society are turning in on themselves' (4 October 1993). In the *Times*, Kiley described a 'genocidal civil war' between clans (13 August 1992), and in a 5 May 1993 article[10] he noted that after 'Clan warfare destroyed much of the country's crops', the 'careful manipulation of relief efforts by looting gangs run by warlords meant that most of the food brought in to save the starving was stolen'.

This last article was entitled 'Can Somalia Ever Be Saved?', and indeed an understanding of the conflict as resulting from clan divisions could be taken to imply that conflict was endemic to Somalia. Sometimes this led journalists to draw the conclusion that the country was simply incapable of self-governance. Near the start of Operation Restore Hope, discussing the 'new age of colonialism', Kiley said he had felt 'an initial thrill in seeing teenage gunmen, whose looting and atrocities have impeded relief efforts since the country collapsed into anarchy, put in their place' (*Times*, 15 December 1992). Yet the root of the problem, he suggested, was more intractable: 'the continent is crumbling under tribal pressures caused by boundaries drawn with a disregard for ethnicity by the outgoing colonial powers'. In this view, reminiscent of the ideas later developed by Huntington and Kaplan (see Chapter 1), the conflicts caused by underlying 'tribal' or 'ethnic' divisions are seen as more powerful factors than recent political settlements. This did not mean, however, that Kiley thought intervention would not work. Rather, he argued that there should be more of it: 'The international community may yet have to admit that Somalia is not unique, that other countries, too, are incapable of governing themselves, or are putting citizens at risk, and that UN troops should be sent in'. A similar view was taken by *Guardian* columnist Edward Pearce, who argued that 'great parts of the recently independent world do not work':

> The pattern, of which Somalia is the extreme example, is for ordinary authority to shift from legality to despotism of the most stupid and destructive kind, then to tribal factionalism which in turn becomes simple criminal gangsterism in the hands of the very young and very armed.

Again, this view of Somalia and other nations as being unable to rule themselves led to a forceful advocacy of intervention. Arguing that 'You can only put to rights a country as thoroughly smashed up as Somalia by ruling it', Pearce advised that 'The gangs who are symptom and cause' of the crisis in Somalia 'must be put down, which is to say enough of their members must be killed' (*Guardian*, 9 December 1992).

Prescriptions

These last two articles raise the question of what solutions journalists proposed for the problems of Somalia. This section examines these prescriptions in more detail by looking at the explicit editorial stance of each paper.

August 1992: calls for action

The *Times* was the most forceful advocate of action in August 1992. In a 6 August editorial entitled 'Force for Humanity', the paper noted that the West had 'inexcusably tolerated' Barre's 'cruel, corrupt and tribally divisive' regime and said that for months after the UN withdrew its personnel in 1991 it had 'stuck by the rules under which it provides emergency relief only at the invitation of a country's government when Somalia had no recognised government'. The *Times* welcomed the fact that now 'The case for determined humanitarian intervention has at last been formally acknowledged by the Security Council'. It is noteworthy that factors which might be adduced as arguments against intervention – the US record of support for Barre and the principle of non-interference in sovereign states – are here presented as reasons to intervene. Neither was the paper deterred from advocating action by its understanding of the conflict as 'armed anarchy' among 'tribal gangs': it argued that 'Well-armed UN troops, backed if necessary by air power, are needed to establish authority over the gangs which pass in Somalia for armies and which control no more than a few square miles each'. Its editorial on 20 August 1992 again pre-empted possible objections to intervention, noting the argument that the 'big powers' had 'created the catastrophe' but contending that 'African countries have railed at the West for turning a blind eye for so long'. It also acknowledged that 'independence is extolled as the basic right of any nation' and said that 'entrusting a country to outsiders is a last resort'. However, the extent of the crisis was said to justify extreme measures: 'such is the horror of Somalia today that only UN trusteeship in all but name can save the country from self-inflicted genocide'. Arguing that Somalia had 'ceased to exist as a functioning country', the *Times* dwelt on the breakdown of Somali society: 'No independent nation in modern times has collapsed into such squalor, chaos and misery as Somalia.... The country has no water, electricity, law or government. Even tribal loyalties have broken down'. This collapse, according to the *Times*, meant that the US airlift of food was 'just a beginning': 'If chaos is to subside, somebody must assume virtually all functions of government: the repair of the ruined infrastructure, the running of hospitals, the re-establishment of agriculture, the opening of schools and markets'. In effect, the paper was calling for the re-colonisation of Somalia, proposing 'what amounts to an old-fashioned protectorate' and claiming that 'There is strong world support for such intervention'.

Other papers were more cautious, but did call for action of some sort. In an 18 August editorial about the crises in both Somalia and Bosnia, the *Mail* asked 'What can we do to help?' While it recommended 'Safe corridors for aid in Bosnia', the paper offered no specific prescription for Somalia and implied that action would necessarily be limited: 'If we can't stop the killing, at least we must provide the anaesthetic'. Taking a similar line, the *Independent* also linked the crisis with the Bosnian war, seeing both as part of the same pattern: 'The end of the Cold War has released long pent-up ethnic hatreds across Eastern Europe, just as the overthrow of Siad Barre unlocked similar inter-clan tensions in Somalia' (8 August). The difference, however, was that while the Bosnian conflict was 'widely seen as a crazy aberration from European norms', in Africa 'internecine wars have, sadly, become all too familiar'. In the case of Bosnia, the paper hoped 'it will be possible to settle differences without resorting to arms', implying that no such hope was plausible for Africa. Warning of 'compassion fatigue', the *Independent* said that 'The war in Somalia induces a sense of hopelessness: if these people hate each other so much that they will not let food through to the starving, how can they be helped?' While the prospects for solving the problem seemed remote, the paper nevertheless welcomed the fact that Somalia was 'at last ... creeping up the international agenda' and said that the UN had a 'great duty' to deal with the crisis.

The *Independent* also reported calls for action by Amnesty International (5 August) and Oxfam (8 August), and a 31 August report from Mogadishu by James Roberts concluded that: 'A world that believes in any kind of decency cannot stand by while this happens'. In addition, the paper ran a comment piece by Alex de Waal on 14 August, the day the US food airlift began, which accused the UN of 'Fiddling while Somalia starves' and advocated greater UN accountability: 'A cataclysm on this scale requires at least several charges of criminal negligence against senior officials'. In the *Guardian*, there were no editorials about Somalia during August, although the paper did launch its own famine appeal (6 August). The *Guardian* also published comment pieces calling for action: Rakiya Omaar advocated a 'massive' relief operation with 'armed escorts' (14 August), and columnist Martin Woollacott said that 'we may now have to try to devise measures to deal with the state equivalent of suicide' (1 August), although he did not specify what these might be.

November–December 1992: 'A Benign Imperium'

'A Benign Imperium' was the title of the *Independent*'s editorial of 1 December 1992. Criticising the UN for having 'taken the rather supine view that its representatives do not have the authority to use force', the paper suggested that 'Things may be about to change for the better' with the arrival of US troops. It warned that a 'short, sharp intervention' would not solve the country's problems: intervention would have to be 'prolonged' and 'on a scale grand enough to signal that a fundamental change in international attitudes and law has occurred'. The perceived danger that the US might leave too soon was also raised in two further editorials, on 10 and 23 December. In all three articles, the *Independent* sought to draw out the implications of the long-term intervention it hoped would happen. In its 10 December leader, the paper predicted that action in Somalia would 'have a profound effect on how – and even whether – American power is deployed in the post-Communist world' and suggested that it showed 'the American character at its best – generous, brave and imaginative'. These qualities had been 'too often frustrated or contaminated by power politics' during the Cold War, but 'Now they can be liberated'. Similarly, on 23 December the paper said that since the end of the Cold War the US and UN had both been 'moving towards a new role: that of guarding innocent civilians from the grossest abuses of criminal governments or warlords'. This new role was 'no less noble' than the Cold War aim of 'guaranteeing the security of the free world'. As the *Independent* accurately observed, the mission established 'an important precedent', in that Western troops were 'being used to intervene under UN auspices in the affairs of a notionally sovereign state for essentially humanitarian reasons' (23 December).

This view of Somalia as a 'notionally sovereign state' was the basis of the *Independent*'s argument that a 'fundamental change' had occurred. In its 1 December leader, the paper noted 'suggestions from some members of the outgoing Bush administration' that, by using the military to impose a solution, 'the United States would thus have accepted the need to create an indefinite UN protectorate in Somalia, whatever the objections of the warlords and those nominally in charge of parts of the country'. Arguing that 'Such an initiative would be a welcome recognition of reality', the paper observed that 'The concept of absolute national sovereignty has already been severely eroded in recent years'. The *Independent* welcomed 'the idea of imposing formal and continuing UN mandates on once-sovereign states' and characterised the situation in Somalia as a 'total breakdown of internal authority'. The 'benign imperium' which it wished to see established was thus based on the argument that 'Outside intervention is ... justified' when 'national law and order break down and the state has effectively ceased to exist'.

While the *Independent* endorsed the position taken by the *Times* in August, the *Guardian* remained rather more cautious, describing Operation Restore Hope as 'a complex mission' (3 December) which deserved 'a qualified welcome' (27 November). In its two editorials about Somalia during this period, the *Guardian* recalled the history of interference in the country, reminding its readers that the US had 'propped up the notorious Mohamed Siad Barre for many years' (27 November). Where the *Independent* (10 December) argued that 'There is no need to look for motives much beyond pressure from the American people, who could not face tucking into Christmas dinners while watching Somali children starving to death on television', the *Guardian* raised some suspicions about US motivations. Noting that the proposed military action represented a 'dramatic reversal in American policy', the *Guardian* said that 'the reasons for this change of heart can only be guessed', suggesting both Bush's desire to end his presidency 'on a strong humanitarian note' and US concerns about 'the radical Islamic element which has begun to surface in Somalia' as possible underlying motives (27 November). By 3 December the *Guardian* was willing to concede that 'The horror of Somalia seems to have touched a genuine nerve of compassion' in the Bush administration, but it continued to highlight possible problems. The paper worried that if the operation was run from Washington it would not be genuinely internationalist and warned against 'a Rambo approach in which the intervening troops simply attempt to blow away the Somali gunmen' (3 December). Instead, the *Guardian* argued that 'Military intervention can only be part of any solution': rather than a 'quick in-and-out operation', the US mission should be 'meshed with a wider UN presence, a continuing infrastructure on the ground and the start of a political process among Somalis themselves' (3 December). The paper said that 'international neglect' had created huge problems and wondered: 'are we witnessing the beginnings of a UN mandate in Somalia?' (27 November). The *Guardian* stopped short of endorsing UN trusteeship but, despite its reservations, it broadly supported the proposed intervention. Ensuring the delivery of aid would be 'An enormous humanitarian advance' (27 November); action was 'direly needed'; it had taken the international community 'far too long' to act and 'More forceful measures may have to be used, as selectively as possible' (3 December).

Perhaps the *Guardian* was among those the *Mail* had in mind when it wrote in a 5 December editorial that: 'Ironically, the liberal souls who 20 and more years ago were demanding that the white man should leave Africa are now equally keen that he should return'. Arguing that the US was 'acting as a world policeman with general approval', the *Mail* raised some of the same potential problems as other papers, warning, like the *Guardian*, that the task was 'complex', that it would 'not be accomplished by military means alone' and that it was not susceptible to a 'quick fix'. The extent of press criticism of the intervention is explored below, but it might be noted here that the warning against 'quick' solutions and the suggestion that more was needed beyond the use of military force were not arguments against intervention: rather, they were arguments for more extensive and long-term involvement.

The *Times* maintained its vigorous advocacy of intervention. Under the headline 'Shoot to Feed' (a phrase borrowed from a US official), its 1 December editorial argued that 'If only force will save Somali lives, force should be used'. Acknowledging that the peace-enforcement mission represented 'a radical departure in international law', the *Times* argued that the extremity of the crisis made such a change necessary: 'for humanity's sake, governments must set aside their fears of setting precedents for external intervention. So desperate is Somalia's plight'. As in August, the *Times* supported the idea of 'putting Somalia under temporary trusteeship'. On 9 December the paper argued that other countries should support the mission in order to avert the danger of any 'lack of American staying power'. Describing the US as a 'Gentle Giant', the *Times* drew out the 'broader purpose' of the mission: to 'show that force can be used, under the UN umbrella, to help non-white, Muslim people, and not just where vital American interests are at stake'. Somalia, in other words, would be the proving-ground of a new post-1989 order, 'an important test of international determination to use the opportunities created by the end of the Cold War'.

Overall, the different explanations for the crisis explored earlier were coupled with strikingly similar prescriptions for action. In each case, the logical conclusion of the way that Somalia's problems were understood appeared to be intervention. Where only the immediate problem of looting of food aid was considered, this fitted with the US government's own diagnosis of the problem, as articulated in Bush's television address of 4 December 1992, and the proposed solution was the imposition of order. Where this immediate problem was set in the context of the civil war, again armed intervention was taken to be the answer, either as part of a package of measures which would include diplomatic brokering of a political settlement, or more often as the only hope for a nation which was understood to be caught in a 'tragic cycle' of abuse, divided by deep-rooted clan hatreds, or simply incapable of self-rule. The characterisation of Somalia as prey to chaos and anarchy – whether this was understood in terms of criminality, clan divisions or an incapacity for governance – was particularly important, since it was the breakdown of the state which was held to justify exceptional interventionist measures. The view of Somalia, and Africa generally, as prone to 'internecine wars', particularly because of 'long pent-up ethnic hatreds' unleashed after the end of the Cold War, did give rise to a scepticism about the efficacy of intervention in the *Independent*'s editorial of 8 August 1992. Yet the paper had changed its position by the start of Operation Restore Hope. Reflecting on his experiences of reporting from Somalia, Richard Dowden (1995a: 95) describes himself as having been a 'prophet of doom', claiming: 'I don't think that I wrote a single story which did not mention the possibility of disaster'. In his reporting, and in his retrospective assessment of it, Dowden understood his emphasis on the intractable nature of the conflict, rooted in the cultural and social peculiarities of Somali society and culture, as implying that the mission would not work: the intervention foundered 'not just on ignorance, but ignorance of ignorance', since US commanders 'had no idea that Somalis thought and acted differently to Americans' (1995a: 97). Yet an understanding of the conflict as endemic to Somalia could just as easily be interpreted as an argument for trusteeship, as in the *Independent*'s editorials and in the commentaries by Kiley and Pearce discussed earlier.

The more incapable Somalis were thought to be, or the more deep-rooted in Somali culture the conflict was understood to be, the more far-reaching was the proposed intervention. Hence, as we have seen, the *Times* and later the *Independent* were the most enthusiastic advocates of intervention, emphasising the 'chaos' and 'anarchy' in Somalia, and urging a complete takeover of the country under some form of trusteeship. The characterisation in the *Times* of the crisis as 'feudal violence' (22 December 1992), for example, supported the paper's view that Somalia's effective loss of modern statehood justified far-reaching international intervention. For the editorialists of both papers, the crisis was clearly understood as a defining moment in changing the post-Cold War international order and abandoning the principles of sovereign equality and non-interference. It is notable that these two papers continued to carry explicitly pro-intervention editorials during the later periods examined in this study: the *Independent* making 'The case for intervention' in a 15 October 1993 editorial, for example; and the *Times* still pushing the issue of trusteeship as late as 28 March 1994.

The *Mail* was less interested in Somalia, but offered mild support for intervention. The *Guardian* was the most cautious, paying greatest attention to potential problems and pitfalls, although broadly agreeing that international action was necessary. As we saw earlier, the *Guardian* was much more likely than other papers to recall the history of foreign involvement in Somalia, although this in itself did not result in any questioning of the need for intervention. Rather, America's past role tended to be taken as placing a 'special responsibility' on the US to act in the present. In a 31 August 1992 article, for example, Huband noted that aid had been used as 'weapon' in the Cold War, a way of recruiting and rewarding African allies, but argued that now such countries 'will require more and more support from the West'. Acknowledging their own destructive role in the past was a necessary precursor to the Western powers ensuring 'the provision of the real amount of assistance needed' in the future. The *Guardian*'s apparently keener awareness of the West's destructive history in Somalia may have contributed to its more cautious stance, by heightening suspicion of US motives, but perhaps a more important factor was that – judging from the periods of coverage sampled in this study – the paper offered the greatest amount of explanatory material and was more inclined to question the view of Somalia as entirely collapsed into anarchy and chaos. The three 'counter-descriptions' in Box 2.1 which refused this explanation, for example, all appeared in the *Guardian*, one of them in an editorial column.

Criticism

Notwithstanding newspapers' overall support for international action in Somalia, they also presented much criticism of it. Of the 384 articles in our sample, 116 featured some form of criticism, representing 30.2 per cent of the total coverage. The military operation was the focus of criticism in 69 of these 116 articles (59.5 per cent), far more than the other two topics they covered: the media and the public relations tactics of the US and UN (19 articles, or 16.4 per cent); and the aid operation (13 articles, or 11.2 per cent).[11] However, this criticism was limited in various ways.

The military

Many criticisms of the military operation were superficial and in fact implied underlying approval, in that they highlighted only tactical problems or suggested that the intervention did not go far enough. Nine articles, for example, made the point that while military intervention was useful, it could be only a partial solution to Somalia's problems. The *Guardian*'s 27 November 1992 editorial argued that 'the American offer [of troops] will only be effective in the short-term.... Military intervention can only be part of any solution'; and the *Mail*'s 5 December leader said that 'the task is complex. It will not be accomplished by military means alone.' Similarly, the *Times* reported the view of a German aid worker in Somalia that 'it was vital that the military option be exercised in tandem with development' (3 December). Other frequent criticisms were that the forces would not stay long enough, that they were initially too slow in reaching other parts of the country, that they had failed to disarm the Somali factions, or that they were too fixated on capturing Aidid. These were not criticisms of military intervention as such, but disagreements about the way it should be conducted.

A more far-reaching criticism did receive a relatively high degree of attention, though: that military action could overshadow the humanitarian effort or make it more difficult. Reporting the first killings of Somalis by US troops in December 1992, for example, Dowden commented: 'it is clear that Operation Restore Hope is now driven by purely military considerations'. Noting the 'intense pressure from aid agencies' for the military to move more quickly into other parts of Somalia, his report also suggested the aid operation was being driven by military planners, who were concerned above all for the safety of their own troops (*Independent*, 14 December 1992). At the beginning of the intervention the *Guardian* reported the comment of an aid agency director that it was planned in accordance with an 'invasion mentality which will accelerate the problem of moving food' (3 December 1992); and towards the end, after the deaths of US troops, Woollacott noted that 'UN officials have privately objected for some time to the sidelining of the humanitarian relief effort in favour of the military campaign' (*Guardian*, 11 October 1993). This was a more forceful criticism, in that it suggested the military might be impeding effective humanitarian relief instead of facilitating it, although the desirability of intervention *per se* was not questioned. Even Rakiya Omaar, who commented that 'any sudden arrival [of troops] will only provoke an escalation of violence and will force any responsible relief organisation to withdraw', prefaced her criticism by saying she was 'not opposed to the use of force as such' (*Times*, 5 December 1992).

Overall, 18 articles objected to the use of military force on the grounds that it interfered with the aid operation. The examples above are typical, in that the main source of the criticism was aid agencies: this was the case in two-thirds of the articles making this point. If aid organisations were a significant source of criticism, however, they were also an ambivalent and inconsistent one. Firstly, before the start of Operation Restore Hope, aid agencies played an important role in calling for armed intervention. Interviewed in August 1992, the director of Save the Children, Nicholas Hinton, characterised the mood in Somalia as 'psychotic' and called for 'armed intervention' (*Times*, 14 August 1992); and in December the charity's president, Princess Anne, said aid agencies were beginning to accept that military intervention was 'almost the only answer' (*Times*, 7 December 1992). In the US, aid organisations lobbied both the UN and the Bush administration for security protection, the US Agency for International Development calling for military action even without UN approval (Robinson 2002: 48–9). Secondly, as the potentially controversial deployment of troops got underway, many aid agencies were reported to be welcoming them. Perhaps because of its strong support for armed intervention, the *Times* devoted particular attention to this theme and ran a series of 13 articles between 2 and 19 December 1992 featuring the opinions of relief workers. At the beginning of this period, reports acknowledged the concerns of some agencies but then always countered them. 'Some relief agency officials maintain that troops are not necessary', noted Kiley on 2 December, for example. 'But', he continued, 'more experienced workers in the field believe that if the world is serious about doing something for Somalia, then troops will be needed to protect food convoys that are being constantly looted'. The title of the article – 'Gunmen Fire at Children on a Road of Terror' – also implied that these 'more experienced' fieldworkers knew better than the officials. In some of these reports aid workers called not just for protection but for the use of force to sort out the Somalis. One British aid worker said it was 'essential that the US come in and give them a short, sharp, shock' (3 December), while another seemed ready to compile a hit-list of locals: 'We in aid are supposed to be liberals, but after a few months here I could give the Yanks a list of lads that should be put out of business, permanently' (9 December). As Maren (1997: 219) suggests, charities were somewhat naive in calling for military intervention: 'they wanted it on their own terms … [and] were dismayed to find that the soldiers were acting like soldiers'. Their belated criticisms were undercut by their earlier enthusiasm for the military intervention.

Eleven articles – around 3 per cent of our total sample – dealt with the mistreatment or killing of Somalis by UN troops: five each in the *Guardian* and *Independent*, one the *Times* and none in the *Mail*. Seven of these appeared in October 1993, when violence between the US/UN troops and Aidid's militia was at its height; and three in March/April 1994 – two of them about a UN report on the mission, and one about the trial of a Canadian peacekeeper found guilty of torture and manslaughter. The remaining article, in the *Guardian* on 11 May 1993, reporting the killing of Somalis by Belgian troops, was very brief, consisting of only one sentence. It seems fair to conclude that this was not a prominent theme in the coverage. To offset any distortion which might have occurred as a result of the sampling periods chosen, an additional search was conducted to gauge the extent of coverage given to the July 1993 African Rights report, which detailed abuses and killings by UN troops.[12] The *Guardian* ran three articles mentioning the African Rights report (on 30 July, 31 July and 9 August 1993) and carried a comment piece by Rakiya Omaar on 15 June 1993, while the *Independent* published one report on 30 July and a profile of Omaar on 14 July 1993. Other newspapers ignored the story.

Even more marginal was criticism of the fact that the military intervention undermined Somali sovereignty. This barely registered in the coverage, featuring in just two articles that offered criticism of the military operation. In the *Independent*, Dowden reported the reaction of the USC to the imminent arrival of US troops: the USC warned of a 'new colonisation' and promised to 'defend the interest of the Somali people' (7 December 1992). In the *Times*, columnist Simon Jenkins made some stinging criticisms of 'this caring imperialism', challenging the strident interventionism of the US press (5 December). Although Jenkins offered a powerful critique, his was a lonely voice.

The aid operation

Not surprisingly, given the limited criticism of the military, much critical commentary on the aid operation was also mild, the most common complaint being that the Western response was too slow or poorly coordinated. Eight articles made this point, seven of them in August 1992. The criticism here was generally limited, in that it focused on issues of timing and logistics, highlighting problems with the UN's past performance or pointing to the limitations of the US airlift of supplies in the absence of an effective distribution system. De Waal criticised UN famine relief programmes as 'slow, wasteful, poorly planned and executed', for instance, concluding that they 'do as much damage as good' (*Independent*, 14 August); and the *Times* reported Save the Children's Nicholas Hinton condemning the UN operation in Somalia as 'shameful', 'piecemeal' and 'haphazard' (31 August). On the US airlift of food, James Roberts argued in the *Independent* that it would arrive 'too late' (24 August) and that aid organisations were incapable of distributing it without help (26 August). In effect, these articles airing disagreements over the practicalities of the aid operation were part of the chorus calling for greater intervention. In an article criticising 'a year and a half of inaction' by the UN, Omaar called for Somalia to be 'flooded' with food, accompanied by 'armed escorts' (*Guardian*, 14 August). Perhaps Operation Restore Hope was not quite what she had it mind, but it did seem to meet her earlier description of what was needed.

A more hard-hitting point was made by articles noting that the extent of both the famine and the looting had been exaggerated at the start of Operation Restore Hope, although these were few in number. As the troops went ashore, Robert Block reported in the *Independent* that 'The Bush administration exaggerated the magnitude of the problems in Somalia'. Citing the Red

Cross, Oxfam and Save the Children, Block questioned the claim that 80 per cent of food was being looted and suggested the true figure was nearer 20–30 per cent. Block also quoted Omaar and de Waal's criticisms of 'disaster pornography' and argued that the intervention had been driven by 'pressure from the press and television images' (10 December 1992). In the *Guardian* (9 December), Huband made similar points, quoting a UN official who challenged the 'bullshit about 80 per cent of food being looted' and described the US operation as 'very well stage-managed'. The *Guardian* also featured articles by guest writers making similar points. On 5 December Omaar and de Waal argued that the 'United States military intervention in Somalia has followed from a gross misrepresentation of the situation in the country, and is a complete failure to pay the most elementary respect to Somalis'. They disputed four 'major errors' which had been made about the situation: 'that Somalia has descended into complete anarchy and chaos'; 'that two million people are at risk of death by starvation'; that 'most of the food [is being] looted'; and that 'diplomatic options have … been exhausted'. On 3 December Said Samatar questioned the 'dangerous misconception' that the whole country was in crisis, and on 24 December Andrew Buckoke challenged 'the received wisdom of the media', particularly claims that there were 'two million starving' and that '50 per cent of the population was displaced'. Buckoke conceded that UN troops could help in 'a few blackspots', but argued that 'as far as the rest of the country is concerned the Somalis should be allowed to take responsibility for themselves'. This story then disappeared from the coverage, aside from a report in the *Guardian* on 29 April 1993 which noted that 'the famine was over before the marines landed'. It is perhaps worth asking why the story did not receive more attention. One reason is probably that few potential sources questioned the official line: only writers with specialist knowledge, such as Buckoke and Omaar, or aid officials who were unhappy with the US military presence were voicing these doubts about the rationale for military action. Secondly, the picture was skewed because reporters on the ground tended to go where the action was: Mogadishu and the worst-affected provincial areas. Thirdly, given the general enthusiasm for the intervention as 'an important test of international determination' (in the words of the 9 December 1992 *Times* editorial cited earlier), there was probably little inclination among editors and commentators to emphasise unpopular views. As Dowden (1995a: 95) later recalled, 'questions were not easy to raise against the background of self-congratulation'.

The media

A related point was made in the 19 articles which criticised the sensationalistic, insensitive or inaccurate reporting of the famine. Huband described reporters' callous and ruthless pursuit of the 'best photographs' of starvation, recounting how one American journalist 'was seen openly consuming a diet drink in front of famine victims' (*Guardian*, 16 December 1992). In the *Mail*,

Conor Cruise O'Brien argued that the UN had been 'tainted by those forms of manipulation that go under the generic name of "public relations"', so that the 'image of the giver [had] become more important than the effectiveness of the giving' (2 December). In the *Times* (12 December), academic Ioan Lewis also criticised 'the rather poorly informed media coverage'. Perhaps it is not surprising that newspapers gave little space to reflecting on whether reporting had been adequate, given that, as we have seen, their own coverage rarely questioned official claims about the famine and violence in the country. The less critical and questioning the coverage of events, the less self-criticism there is likely to be.

An illustration of this is the tendency to focus on the suffering of children. A *Times* feature by media analyst Patricia Holland examined how images of children in reports of war and disaster offer 'a forbidden pleasure that almost becomes a pornography of suffering' (25 August 1992). Discussing Somalia and other examples, she argued that such photographs:

> arouse unfocused emotions that are pleasurable because they lead nowhere. It is easier to pity the children because they allow us to overlook the ambivalences and muddles of social conflict in which one side is never entirely in the right.

In later reporting, the focus on children was occasionally commented upon: Martin Walker noted that Bush's national television address 'refer[red] repeatedly to Somalia's starving children' (*Guardian*, 5 December 1992); and Edward Pilkington argued that the 'shocking, and arguably manipulative, television image that brought US troops to Somalia in the first place' was of 'a starving child crawling across barren earth in a fruitless search for food' (*Guardian*, 11 October 1993).

As against these three articles commenting critically on the use of such images, in our sample there were 33 articles which emphasised the plight of Somali children. Two-thirds of these appeared in August 1992, heightening the call for intervention: in fact nearly 25 per cent of all coverage in that month specifically drew attention to children's suffering. As discussed earlier, we may doubt whether it was emotive media images which caused the intervention, but political leaders certainly drew on public sympathy for children in seeking to justify military action. At the start of Operation Restore Hope, Bush said that 'The people of Somalia, especially the children of Somalia, need our help.... When we see Somalia's children starving, all of America hurts.'[13] As the mission ran into crisis in October 1993, President Clinton responded to the deaths of US servicemen by reminding people that the troops had been 'working to ensure that anarchy and starvation do not return to a nation in which over 300,000 people have lost their lives, many of them children' (*Times*, 5 October 1993). By this stage, however, an emphasis on children was relatively unusual. When Dowden likened Aidid's supporters to 'wild children who lash out at the teacher and catch him in the crotch: 18 Americans died and 75 were wounded', it seemed a somewhat inappropriate comparison. After August 1992, other terms for Somalis, such as 'guerrilla', 'militia' and 'warlord', gained in prominence. A rough indication of this is provided in Figure 2.1, which

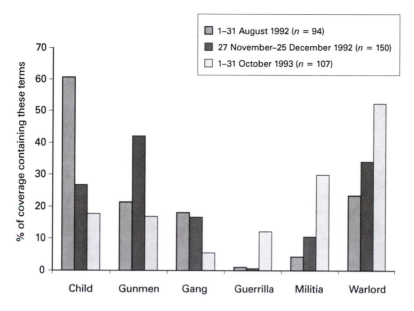

Figure 2.1 Terms used for Somalis.

shows the percentage of articles mentioning a number of key terms in the August 1992, November/December 1992 and October 1993 periods.[14] It is also worth noting that the terms used more in October 1993 to describe Somalis engaged in violent activity – particularly 'guerrilla' and 'militia' – imply greater discipline and organisation than terms such as 'gunmen' and 'gang', which were favoured in earlier periods.

As we saw, articles critically discussing the mistreatment of Somalis by UN troops were rare. Not surprisingly, there were also very few articles criticising the lack of media coverage of Somali casualties. In the *Independent*, O'Brien wrote that 'there is no doubt that Somali casualties (including women and children) considerably outnumber American casualties'. He noted that the extent of Somali casualties remained unknown, however, since 'the international media are not particularly investigative in the matter of Somali body counts' (1 October 1993). In the same newspaper, Peter Pringle contrasted the Americans' 'national outpouring of grief' over their own losses with their ignorance of what 'their soldiers had done to the other side', since they had not been shown 'the pictures of the 200 Somalis that the international Red Cross estimated had died in the battle [with Aidid] and the hundreds of wounded piled into hospitals short of drugs and plasma' (13 October). These criticisms were equally applicable to the British media.

The event which prompted the greatest number of articles critically evaluating the role of the media was the landing of US troops at the start of Operation Restore Hope. Fifteen articles in December 1992 commented on the publicity surrounding the arrival of the marines, who came ashore as if they were mounting an assault on a military objective only to be met by scores of Western journalists.[15] The sardonic tone of Dowden's reports was typical of many. Describing the operation as a 'dangerous farce', he captured the absurdity of the situation:

> Caught in the glare of television lights and flashing cameras, the Seals first of all threatened to shoot the journalists if they didn't go away, then fled into the bushes behind the sand dunes to do whatever special forces are supposed to do when they land secretly in enemy territory.... Such are the perils of a pre-announced seizure of an airport, which has been in the hands of United Nations troops for four months, as if it were heavily defended enemy territory. (*Independent*, 10 December 1992)

Dowden's main target of criticism was the public relations strategy of the Pentagon, which had invited the media to witness the landings in the first place. After the first landing, Dowden reported, some journalists 'suggested the second phase was planned to take place after a commercial break' (*Independent*, 9 December). It was more the US government's attempt to generate dramatic pictures which was seen as problematic here, rather than the media themselves. However, this was not always the case. While Dowden reported being questioned at gunpoint by confused and angry marines, in the *Mail* readers were invited to sympathise with the soldiers, who 'had to escape news gatherers armed with notebooks, cameras and silly questions'. Whereas reporters behaved as if they were 'having a day out in Disneyland', commented Jane Kelly, the marines tried to 'keep their minds on the job in hand' while 'desperately trying to evade the constant barrage of questions shouted by reporters' (*Mail*, 10 December 1992). In this telling, it was the journalists who were a threat to the military. Indeed, Kelly also reported that, according to a Pentagon official, 'many relatives of the troops were angry that their loved ones had been put at risk'.

The emphasis and the extent of criticism varied. Overall, commentary on media coverage of the troops' arrival was linked to a broader questioning of the motives behind the US intervention in seven articles. The most extensive criticism was in the *Times*: O'Brien described the intervention as 'a cynical pseudo-humanitarian publicity exercise' (15 December 1992), for example; and Ben Macintyre characterised it as 'a piece of charity showbusiness' which was also designed 'to restore hope in America and the Republican Party' (10 December). This is not to say that such reports criticised the intervention as such: rather, it was the emphasis on generating good publicity which was questioned. Macintyre, for instance, argued that the 'prime-time invasion' had 'exposed a creditable, life-saving enterprise to ridicule'. Furthermore, three articles coupled discussion of the staged beach landings with pointed exoneration of US motives. In a 10 December report in the *Independent*, Rupert Cornwell noted that the mission's 'goal of bringing succour to starving Somalia is impeccable ... the operation that really counts, of securing supply lines for an effective relief effort, seems to be moving ahead'; and the same edition's leader column argued that the television spectacle 'should not obscure the seriousness of the enterprise'. In the *Times* (9 December), Martin Fletcher and Sam Kiley also made it clear that the media circus did not diminish the value of the operation: "'This is just great!" said one unidentified Somali. "What a relief.'" It is notable that the August 1992 US airlift occasioned only one report raising similar points to those made in December: Huband argued that 'a rather shady picture of White House motives' was suggested by the Bush administration's 'sudden interest in a famine the world … has known about for months … just as an election in the US is drawing closer' (31 August). In December, while the absurdity of the situation could not be ignored, the effort to generate maximum good publicity led at most to a suggestion that the US action might have mixed motives: it did not shake the consensus in favour of intervention.

Conclusions

The crisis in Somalia tended to be understood as a problem of disorder and division. Terms such as 'chaotic', 'shattered' and 'anarchic' were commonly used to characterise Somali society, although they did not accurately describe the whole country. The causes of conflict were most usually understood as internal to Somali society, with the most prominent idea being that of clan hatred. It was these internal divisions which were generally seen as having led to social breakdown and criminality. These were limited explanations, which for the most part lacked historical background and context: relatively few articles in 1992 addressed the recent history of foreign involvement in Somalia, despite its obvious relevance to the contemporary situation, and this theme was not present at all in the later periods examined.

The way news reports framed the problem chimed with official rhetoric. In an August 1992 report to the UN Security Council, for example, Boutros-Ghali was reported as characterising the situation in terms of 'anarchy and lawlessness', emphasising the 'almost complete absence of central, regional, or local government' (*Independent*, 26 August; *Guardian*, 29 August). In his December

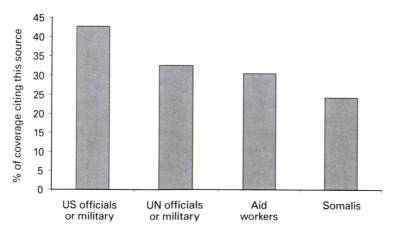

Figure 2.2 Prominence of the different types of source, Somalia coverage.

1992 television address, Bush described the crisis in similar terms: 'There is no government in Somalia. Law and order have broken down. Anarchy prevails … we will not tolerate armed gangs ripping off their own people.'[16] In June 1993 the American head of UNOSOM II, Jonathan Howe, also reinforced the idea that the problem was one of law and order when he announced a $25,000 reward for information leading to Aidid's arrest. We would expect there to be considerable similarity between the way that journalists and influential sources framed the crisis, if only because such sources tend to predominate.

As indicated in Figure 2.2, the most frequently cited sources were US officials and military personnel, featuring in 42.7 per cent of the coverage. It was the perspective of those intervening in Somalia which was best represented. The two next most frequently cited sources, UN personnel and aid workers, sometimes voiced criticisms, particularly with regard to the US military presence, but since both the UN and NGOs were themselves involved in the international intervention it is not surprising that they tended to raise only superficial objections. While criticism was quite extensive, it was limited in its substance. Few articles criticised the conduct of the UN military and any broader questioning of the rationale for intervention was also limited. Instead, the need for international action of some sort tended to be assumed.

This consensus meant that however the crisis was explained, the proposed solution involved outside intervention. Even when the history of Western interference was taken into account, the recommendation was for more benign future intervention. Perhaps the most interesting point to emerge from our examination of the relationship between explanations and prescriptions, though, is that an understanding of conflict as endemic to Somali society, involving 'clan hatreds' or a 'culture of blood revenge', was not in any way an argument against intervention. Indeed, framing the problem in this way tended to lead to calls for longer-term and more wide-ranging intervention, involving a colonial-style relationship. This was because the key to legitimising intervention in Somalia was the argument that the country was not a proper state. Editorial commentators in the two newspapers which emerged as the most forceful advocates of neo-colonial intervention, the *Times* and the *Independent*, understood very well that Operation Restore Hope was a defining moment for the post-Cold War international order. Yet although they were remarkably clear-sighted about the mission's implications, they offered almost no critical discussion of the fact that it overturned the principles of sovereign equality and non-interference. Instead, there was a tendency to talk up the crisis, and to argue that its severity justified a revision of previously established rules. The more critical and informed view of the crisis offered in a minority of articles – that the conflict was affecting only part of the country, that the famine was waning, that past foreign involvement lay at the root of many of Somalia's problems – could perhaps have led to a different conclusion.

CHAPTER 3

Bosnia, 1992–95

Of the crises and conflicts considered in this book, Bosnia has generated the greatest controversy. There is even some disagreement over the date on which the war began: the Bosnian Serbs argue that it started on 1 March 1992, with the shooting of a guest at a Serbian wedding in Sarajevo; others maintain that it began with the recognition by the European Community (EC) of Bosnia-Herzegovina as an independent state, on 6 April 1992.[1] The latter, most common view, will be taken as the starting point in this chapter. Bosnia is also challenging to study because it was a longer conflict than most of the others covered in this book: it did not end until 21 November 1995, when a peace agreement was reached by the main parties at Dayton, Ohio.[2] During the war there were numerous initiatives by the EC, the United States, the UN, Nato and other international actors, including: imposing economic sanctions against Yugoslavia and providing humanitarian aid; deploying UN peacekeepers and establishing 'safe areas'; mediating in ceasefires and hosting peace conferences; brokering an alliance between the Bosnian Muslim and Croatian governments; setting up a war crimes tribunal; and bombing the Bosnian Serbs. While it will not be possible to examine coverage of all of these interventions, the main concern of this study is international involvement in the Bosnian war.

Context

Recognition of Bosnian independence in 1992 followed the secession of the republics of Croatia and Slovenia from the federal Yugoslav state the previous year. While the separation of Slovenia involved little bloodshed, Croatian and Bosnian claims to statehood were violently contested, both by the federal state and by substantial ethnic minorities in both republics. In 1991, 12 per cent of Croatia's population were Serbs, and in Bosnia the population consisted of 44 per cent Muslims,[3] 31 per cent Serbs and 17 per cent Croats. The Yugoslav state deployed the army in an attempt to preserve its territorial integrity. After the independence of the breakaway republics had been internationally recognised, this deployment was defined as an act of inter-state aggression and was judged by the EC to be illegal. The Yugoslav army withdrew, although accusations persisted that it was continuing to help local Serbian forces. Serbian minorities in Croatia and Bosnia resisted incorporation into these newly created states and, unable to remain part of Yugoslavia, declared their own right to secede, claiming independence for the Serbian Krajina in Croatia and for a separate Bosnian Serb Republic. Croatia also laid claim to part of Bosnian territory, Herceg-Bosna, a claim which persisted after the US-brokered 'federation' between Croatia and the Bosnian Muslim government in 1994 and indeed even after the Dayton Agreement.

Susan Woodward (1995: 7–8, 333–4) identifies two competing views of the causes of the Bosnian war, both of which informed the policies of Western governments: the first understood it as an 'ethnic' conflict, arising from long-standing mutual antagonisms which had been given free rein with the end of the Cold War; the second explained the war as the result of Serbia's aggressive territorial ambitions. Although in practice these perspectives may not always have been clearly distinguished, they implied different policy orientations. Understanding the conflict as an ethnic civil war suggested that all sides were at least partly to blame, and that outside intervention ought to be neutral. The overall policy would logically be one of containment, preventing the conflict from spreading, providing humanitarian relief to victims, and encouraging the warring parties to reach agreement on the division of territory. If, on the other hand, the main cause of the war was understood to be Serbian aggression, these sorts of policies might be viewed as tantamount to appeasement. Instead, intervention ought to punish the aggressors and actively defend the victims by military means. Outside mediation of a final territorial settlement ought at best to preserve Bosnian unity against Serbian (and Croatian) ambitions, or at least ensure that a division did not favour the aggressors.

The first view, which Woodward suggests found more favour among European governments, could be seen as underpinning the policies of Britain, France and other states which sent troops to act as UN peacekeepers and sponsored diplomatic initiatives aimed at dividing the country along ethnic lines. The view that the cause of war was Serbian aggression, on the other hand, 'came to be identified most consistently with the US government' (Woodward 1995: 7). The US repeatedly suggested airstrikes and lifting the arms embargo on the Bosnian Muslims as ways to deter or defeat such aggression, options which were resisted for most of the war by the Europeans, concerned that their own troops on the ground would thereby be drawn into the conflict (the US was reluctant to commit its ground forces until after a final settlement had been reached). After many threats, direct military force was eventually used, in the form of Nato airstrikes, sporadically in 1994 and then more intensively in 1995, when the US simultaneously provided support to a ground offensive by the Muslim–Croat Federation.

Although contributors to the debate about how to understand the war often present it in terms of a straight choice between either the 'ethnic war' or the 'Serbian aggression' explanations, these are not the only two options.

For one thing, there are variations on both themes: for example, the view that 'ethnic' conflict was not innate to the culture of the Balkans but a product of recent history, particularly the bitter divisions of the Second World War era; or that multi-ethnic Bosnia was a victim of both Serbian and Croatian nationalist aggression. More importantly, some analysts reject both main views of the conflict. Woodward (1995: 13, 333), for example, is dismissive of both the 'ethnic' and 'Serbian aggression' explanations as simplifications which impeded understanding. Instead, she presents the break-up of Yugoslavia as a process involving complex interactions between internal and external factors, resulting in the rise of destructive nationalist politics on all sides.

For the purposes of our discussion, the most important alternative view is that which sees outside interference as the key cause of war. Analysts such as David Chandler (2000a), Raju Thomas (2003b), Diana Johnstone (2002) and Kate Hudson (2003) attribute decisive importance to international recognition, arguing that, while there were internal economic and political developments which created a tendency to fragmentation, insecurity and the rise of national-ist politics in Yugoslavia in the 1980s and early 1990s, the factor which tipped a volatile situation into outright civil war was Western support for secession. As Woodward (1995: 198) puts it, 'Western intervention … provided the irreversible turning point in [the] escalation toward … war'. European, par-ticularly German and Austrian, backing of Slovenian and Croatian claims to independence in 1991, and then US-led recognition of Bosnia the following year, meant that the leaders of these republics had little incentive to pursue a negotiated settlement with the federal state. Although recognition was pre-sented as a measure to prevent war, in fact it made it more likely, since the status of minorities had not been settled prior to independence. Indeed, it was widely predicted at the time that war was the most likely outcome of precipi-tate recognition. The US is also accused of prolonging the war by encouraging the Bosnian Muslims to reject peace agreements negotiated by the Europeans, for example in Lisbon in 1992 (a proposed settlement which was in fact similar to that adopted in 1995) and in Geneva in 1993 (Woodward 1995: 243–4; Chandler 2000a: 24). This destructive intervention, like the initial support for secessionist claims, was the product of rivalries between the European powers and the US, each attempting to assert its authority in the fluid post-Cold War international order. Similarly, Woodward argues that Western accusations of war crimes were 'a servant of American policy toward the conflict'. By pressing for war crimes prosecutions at points when the Serbs were suing for peace, the US prioritised the defence of supposedly universal moral norms over the resolution of the conflict, even though such a policy 'required a conspiracy of silence about atrocities committed by parties who were not considered aggressors' (Woodward 1995: 323).

In the literature, the 'Serbian aggression' thesis tends to predominate (Cigar 1995; Rieff 1995; Cushman and Mestrovic 1996), including in histories of the conflict written by journalists (Vulliamy 1994; Malcolm 1996; Silber and Little 1996). These accounts explain the war largely in terms of aggressive policies of 'ethnic cleansing' and genocide pursued in order to create a 'Greater Serbia'.

At the same time, reporters who took this view also contended that they were challenging a prevailing consensus which allegedly saw the war in 'ethnic' terms and adopted a neutral policy stance (Vulliamy 1999; Little 2001). Western policy and the majority of media reporting are held to have been mutually reinforcing in this respect. One obvious question for this study is whether this is accurate: did the 'ethnic war' perspective dominate the coverage? We also need to ask whether and to what extent alternatives to either of these main explanations were present in news reporting and commentary. Thomas (2003a: xiii) argues that alternative views were always available but received little attention.

Much of the controversy surrounding the Bosnian war concerns the adequacy of the explanations on offer, as proponents of different perspectives accuse each other of bias, distortion and over-simplification. The 'ethnic war' explanation has been subjected to most criticism, and indeed seems weak, both because of its faulty assumptions about 'ethnicity' (Allen and Seaton 1999; Banks and Wolfe Murray 1999) and because there are many aspects of the war which do not fit. For example, while adherents to this viewpoint see Yugoslavia as an artificial creation which inevitably fell apart as the primordial force of ethno-national identity reasserted itself, the evidence does not seem to support this. Although voters in Bosnia's first free elections split along nationalist lines in 1990, just six months earlier '74 per cent of the population had been in favour of a ban on nationally- or confessionally-based parties', and opinion polls in 1990 and 1991 showed 70–90 per cent majorities against separation from Yugoslavia (Woodward 1995: 228; Chandler 2000a: 24). Furthermore, divisions and allegiances during the war did not always follow neat 'ethnic' lines: in some areas Serbs and Croats allied against Muslims; elsewhere Serbs and Muslims joined forces against Croats; and in the area around Bihac the Muslim leader Fikret Abdic (who had won the greatest share of the vote in the 1990 Bosnian presidential elections but stepped aside in favour of Alija Izetbegovic) struck his own agreements with Bosnian Serbs and Croats, instead coming into conflict with Izetbegovic's Bosnian Muslim forces (Chandler 2000a: 26; Johnstone 2002: 159–60).

Such details do not sit easily with the 'Serbian aggression' thesis either, and this perspective has also been subjected to much criticism. A good case can be made that, like other former communist leaders, Serbian President Slobodan Milosevic opportunistically used nationalism to cohere popular support, but claims that he provoked the war by arousing a uniquely virulent and aggressive nationalist fervour, linked to a plan to create a 'Greater Serbia' at the expense of the other Yugoslav republics, are overstated. Milosevic's 1989 speech on the 600th anniversary of the battle of Kosovo Polje (an historic defeat at the hands of the Ottoman Turks), for example, is often cited as evidence of his responsibility for sparking off the war (Silber and Little 1996: 72; Malcolm 1996: 213) and has been portrayed in media reports in the most lurid terms. Yet the speech itself bears no relation to such descriptions, instead offering precisely the opposite sentiments – for instance that 'Yugoslavia is a multinational community, and it can survive only on condition of full equality of all nations that live in it' (Gil-White 2002; Johnstone 2002: 15–16). The main criticism of the

'Serbian aggression' explanation insofar as it influenced media reporting is that it led to a drastic over-simplification of the war, in that it demonised the Serbs and downplayed atrocities or provocations by the other parties to the conflict (Brock 1993–94, 1995, 2005; Hume 1997, 2000; Parenti 2000). BBC journalist Nik Gowing (1994: 55) argues that 'by and large the media took their cue from the regular declarations by Western ministers. The Serbs were the main guilty party.' This one-dimensional approach meant that violence by other parties to the conflict tended to be played down, so that, for example, the Croat siege of Mostar was 'virtually unreported', despite that city suffering at least as much as Sarajevo (Gowing 1994: 35). It also meant that attacks by Serbian forces tended to be taken out of context. Although Sarajevo was a supposedly demilitarised 'safe area', for example, UN General Francis Briquemont accused Bosnian government forces in the city of provoking attacks by Bosnian Serbs 'on a daily basis' (quoted in Binder 1994–95: 73), a charge echoed by EC mediator David Owen and UN General Phillipe Morillon, who accused Bosnian Muslim forces of trying to draw fire against Sarajevo's Kosevo hospital by using it as a mortar position (Woodward 1995: 236; Bogdanich and Lettmayer 2000). By reporting the responses but not the provocations, it is argued, the media depicted the war as a case of one-sided aggression. Another BBC correspondent, John Simpson (1998: 444–5), subsequently wrote that, in the reporting of Bosnia: 'a climate was created in which it was very hard to understand what was really going on, because everything came to be seen through the filter of the Holocaust'. This framing device, whereby the Serbs were depicted as Nazis committing genocide against innocent Bosnian Muslims, clearly needs to be investigated in this study. Some analysts (for example, Coleman 1993) argue that the comparison of Serbs and Nazis is entirely legitimate, but more often it is understood to have distorted perceptions of the war. In either case, the use of this device would seem to contradict the view that the war was framed largely in terms of mutual 'ethnic hatreds'. It would also contradict the entirely contrary assertion by a few writers that the Western media exhibited a pro-Serb bias (Sadkovich 1998) or that, as Stjepan Mestrovic (1995: 74) suggests, the frame was applied to Croats rather than Serbs, whereby the former were depicted as 'an essentially pro-Nazi genocidal people'.

The perspective which sees outside intervention as the main cause of war has received relatively little direct criticism. This is perhaps partly because the negative impact of early international recognition of Croatian and Bosnian independence is widely acknowledged, but usually in combination with other explanations of the war – as a factor in igniting latent ethnic antagonisms, for instance, or as the trigger for long-planned Serbian expansion. The approach which primarily blames the West for the war is a minority viewpoint and is often simply ignored, but where it has provoked criticism this has mostly come from proponents of the 'Serbian aggression' thesis and has been severe. Where critics such as Johnstone claim to have found evidence of anti-Serb bias, they are accused in turn of having pro-Serb sympathies or being dupes of Serbian propaganda, and of paying insufficient attention to the atrocities committed by Serbian forces in the war. In some cases it may plausibly be argued that criticism of Western involvement is coloured by a certain idealisation of socialist Yugoslavia (for example, Hudson 2003), but this by no means applies to all analysts who blame the war on outside interference. For the most part, what appears to some critics as a 'pro-Serb' perspective may more accurately be characterised as an anti-interventionist one. Of course, it is true that the Serbs produced partisan propaganda glorifying their own cause and denigrating their enemies, some of which was aimed at influencing international opinion. Yet it is equally true that the Slovenes, Croats and Bosnian Muslims did the same, justifying their secession and appealing for Western support on the basis that they were victims of Serbian aggression. There seems no reason for critics to take any of these claims at face value. The core of the disagreement is over whether Serbian violence was qualitatively different and justified a forceful Western response: hence the importance of comparisons with the Nazi Holocaust. The accusations and counter-accusations of bias among both reporters and analysts of the Bosnian war can sometimes become exaggerated, partly because of the emotive issues involved, but mainly because of a fundamental disagreement about the legitimacy of Western intervention in the post-Cold War world.

As we have seen, the debate about explanations and causes is also a debate about prescriptions and solutions. Thus, criticism of 'ethnic' explanations entailed the complaint that adopting this approach disabled or discouraged an effective international response to the war. Conversely, journalists who, in Gowing's (1997: 25–6) words, 'embarked on crusades and became partial', siding with the Bosnian Muslim government and demonising the Serbs, are criticised not simply for distorting events but also for doing so in order to encourage forceful intervention. This study investigates the relationship between the way that the causes of the war were explained in news coverage and the sorts of policy responses proposed. This will also entail asking how far coverage was critical of the actual policies adopted. Although Western policy appeared to be in support of the principles of national sovereignty and self-determination, this was applied in a peculiarly selective fashion. While Slovenia and Croatia achieved statehood, Bosnia remained divided and subject to extensive international regulation, ruled as a UN protectorate and policed by international troops (Chandler 2000b; Knaus and Martin 2003). As in Somalia, Western governments assumed the right to intervene extensively in the internal affairs of the former Yugoslavia, ruling on the legality of rival territorial claims, influencing the outcome of the war, devising new constitutional arrangements, redrawing the maps, and sitting in judgement on the conduct of the war by establishing a special judicial body – the International Criminal Tribunal for the former Yugoslavia (ICTY) – to prosecute alleged war criminals and political leaders. From the literature, it seems likely that these actions will generally have been seen as justified and legitimate.

Questions

The main questions considered in this chapter are:

- How was the war in Bosnia explained? Was there a consensus in favour of 'ethnic' explanations?
- Is there evidence of bias for or against particular parties to the war?
- What solutions were proposed and how was Western involvement evaluated?

Since examining coverage across more than three and a half years would likely skew the comparison with other case studies, as well as being impractical, it has been necessary to choose samples of coverage. Following the book's overall research design, the core sample consists of the two four-week periods spanning the beginning and end of the conflict: the week before the onset of hostilities and the following three weeks (30 March–27 April 1992); and the three weeks preceding and one week following the ending of the war (31 October–28 November 1995).

In order to gain as full a sense of the overall pattern of coverage as possible across the whole duration of the conflict, it was important that additional samples be drawn, from both 1993 and 1994. With any complex and relatively prolonged conflict, however, particularly one as controversial as Bosnia, sampling decisions are liable to raise objections that important events have been deliberately included or omitted in order to produce particular results. To minimise this problem, it was decided not to choose particular 'significant' events or periods, but simply to replicate the dates of the first sample period in both the remaining two years. Although a longer period of time could have been covered by constructing 'artificial weeks' (for example by collecting coverage from alternate days), continuous four-week periods were preferred, as then the development of news stories could be followed across 'natural' samples, comparable to those for the core periods. This procedure gives two further sample periods, of 30 March–27 April 1993 and 1994. The likelihood that, in both years, this period would include some discussion of the anniversary of the start of the war made it preferable to the alternative dates of 31 October–28 November, corresponding to the final sample period.

Given that the war involved phases of relative inactivity, selecting coverage in this fashion potentially raises the opposite problem to that discussed above: that the samples may cover periods when little of significance occurred. A cross-check with the Bosnian Institute's chronology of the war[4] confirmed, however, that these periods saw important local and international developments, including: in 1993, UN Security Council resolutions authorising Nato enforcement of the no-fly zone over Bosnia and designating Srebrenica a 'safe area'; and in 1994, a Nato airstrike against Serbian forces around Gorazde. The total coverage[5] for the periods selected is shown in Table 3.1.

Explanations

The most striking thing about articles explaining the causes of the war is that they were so rare, accounting for less than 8 per cent of the total coverage. Overall, only 14 articles (1.4 per cent of total coverage) took the cause of the

Table 3.1 Numbers of articles about Bosnia

	Start of war (30 March– 27 April 1992)	1993 sample (30 March– 27 April 1993)	1994 sample (30 March– 27 April 1994)	End of war (31 October– 28 November 1995)	Totals
Guardian	32	98	84	59	273
Independent	40	102	95	62	299
Times	32	136	89	51	308
Mail	7	61	37	14	119
Totals	111	397	305	186	999

war as their main theme; a further 65 (6.5 per cent) mentioned causes in passing. The *Guardian* offered the greatest amount of explanatory material, with nine articles taking causes as their main theme and 18 addressing causes in passing. Most articles (nine of the 14 with a major focus on causes; 37 of the 65 mentioning causes briefly) appeared in the first sample period, incorporating the start of the war, with the fewest appearing in 1995.[6] It is possible that more material would have been found if other periods had been chosen, but from our samples it appears that there was very little explicit discussion of the causes of the war. As we shall see, however, an explanation of causes could also be implied through the use of different framing devices.

Ethnic war

In April 1993 each of the four newspapers examined in this study published one article mentioning 'ethnicity' briefly as the cause of the war. The most significant of these were in the *Mail* and the *Independent*, since these were both editorials. Commenting on calls for an international conference on European stability, the *Independent* (9 April) highlighted the difficulty of settling 'what are essentially civil wars based on centuries of ethnic strife and accumulated hatred – especially when hundreds of potential conflicts over borders lurk beneath the surface'. Bosnia was included in this category of 'essentially civil wars' by implication, and was seen as part of a broader pattern which could lead to 'hundreds' of other conflicts. The *Mail*'s 7 April editorial was more explicit in its characterisation of Bosnia. Reflecting on the anniversary of the start of the war, it commented that: 'Proposals to divide the country into cantons only increase the blood-lust of the different warring tribes – for that is what they are – to grab by violence more land'. The article also suggested that Muslims in Srebrenica 'look like being condemned to die from hunger or genocide', but the mention of 'genocide' did not appear to imply that the war was to be understood as one-sided aggression: the *Mail* also characterised it in terms of 'the torture of one side by another' and intimated that all sides were driven by tribal 'blood-lust'.

Also during this period, the *Guardian* published a comment piece by Conservative MP Nicholas Budgen, who described the war as no different 'from any other very unpleasant tribal struggle' (19 April) and the *Times* reported that 'Warren Christopher, the Secretary of State, has subtly changed tune, no longer portraying Bosnia as a moral outrage demanding US action but as a centuries-old tribal feud from which, by implication, America is prudent to keep its distance' (10 April). In the latter case there was no suggestion that the reporter agreed with this portrayal.

These four articles from 1993 mentioned the causes of war only in passing, but 'ethnic conflict' was a major theme in one article from our 1994 sample: a commentary by Geoffrey Wheatcroft, headlined 'Is Tribal Conflict Now the World's Greatest Threat?' (*Mail*, 11 April). Comparing Bosnia, Rwanda and Northern Ireland, Wheatcroft argued that, 'After a century when we all believed in Progress ... we are back to the oldest and most deadly form of conflict of all: between tribes'. In relation to Bosnia specifically, the article suggested that communist repression in Yugoslavia had 'held different people in check, or held them apart', but that now 'the old national – or, yes tribal – enmities have torn the Balkans apart once more'. Here, ethnic animosity is seen as a primordial force, always lurking beneath the surface of modern civilisation.

These five articles, however, were the only ones to mention the argument that the Bosnian war was an 'ethnic conflict'. Looking at the coverage overall, the 'ethnic war' perspective was barely visible, appearing in only one of the articles mainly concerned with causes, and four of those mentioning causes briefly. The theme was entirely absent from the 1992 and 1995 samples. There is, in other words, no evidence found to support Little's (2001) claim of a consensus that this was an intractable 'tribal' war or a matter of 'ancient ethnic hatreds'. The *Times* report cited above suggests that official sources may have favoured different explanations at different times in order to justify different policies,[7] but as regards 'ethnic' explanations this was not reflected in news coverage during any of our sample periods. It appears that the 'ethnic war' perspective was something of a straw man, set up by those who wished to argue for other explanations and for forceful international responses to the crisis.

Serbian aggression

The major theme in articles addressing the causes of the war was Serbian aggression; this theme appeared in six of the articles focused mainly on causes (42.9 per cent of such articles) and 43 of those mentioning causes briefly (66.2 per cent), or 62.0 per cent of the explanatory material overall. This held true right from the start of the war: of the 46 articles in the first sample period that included any mention of causes, 32 (69.6 per cent) explained the war as a result of Serbian aggression. A similar pattern emerged across the other periods examined, with this type of explanation accounting for 41.6 per cent of articles mentioning causes in 1993, 60.0 per cent in 1994 and 100.0 per cent in 1995. These high percentages have to be tempered by the fact that the total amount of explanatory material was very low, but this explanation was certainly more prominent than any other.[8] The 1993 sample included the most variation among explanatory themes, so that although the 'Serbian aggression' explanation was at its lowest as a proportion of the total explanatory material in this period, it was still the theme which attracted the greatest number of articles. If any view can be described as a consensus, this is it.

Looking more closely at these articles, it is evident that the 'Serbian aggression' explanation was favoured from the outset by a variety of influential sources. In 1992, official approval of this explanation was made explicit in reports in all three of the broadsheets examined in this study.[9] The *Guardian* reported, for example: that the US government might sever diplomatic relations with Belgrade 'to emphasise its opposition to what it regards as Serbian aggression against Bosnia' (21 April 1992); that Milosevic had been 'identified by the US, Germany and others ... as the prime culprit' (24 April); and that the US was 'leading the [verbal] attacks on Belgrade' (25 April). The *Independent* said: that Izetbegovic's claim that 'Bosnia is the victim of classic aggression from outside' was 'backed by several foreign governments, including the United States, Germany and Austria' (15 April); that a US State Department spokeswoman, Secretary of State for Public Affairs Margaret Tutwiler, had 'singled out by name President Slobodan Milosevic of Serbia and federal army leaders as the chief culprits behind Bosnia's violence' (16 April); that the EC and US 'agree in holding the Serbs responsible for the fighting' (22 April); and that German Foreign Minister Hans-Dietrich Genscher had 'described Serbia as "the aggressor" in the Bosnian conflict' (24 April). The *Times* reported: that the British Foreign Office had 'said Serb paramilitary units bore the main responsibility for bloodshed and ... deplored the activities of the federal army, which ... had openly sided with terrorists' (17 April); and that the EC's special envoy, Lord Peter Carrington, had said 'that the Serbs and the army were largely to blame for the violence' (22 April). The relative prominence of this explanation in news coverage is therefore not surprising: it reflected a powerful official consensus established quickly at the beginning of the war.

Each paper published an editorial in April 1992 explaining the causes of the war in terms of Serbian aggression, suggesting that they had adopted this perspective as their own. Arguing that 'The root of the problem lies in Belgrade', the *Guardian* described Bosnia as an 'innocent multi-racial [*sic*] victim of Serbian malevolence' (13 April). The *Independent* acknowledged that the Croats 'do not have wholly clean hands', but said the Serbs had 'started the fighting' and suggested that more governments should be 'pressured into recognising that this is now a case of international aggression' by the Yugoslav army (24 April). According to the *Times* (23 April), the 'pattern of Serbian expansionism in Croatia' was now 'being repeated on a potentially far bloodier scale' and the 'Serbian offensive' was 'nothing less than the invasion of an independent country'. Arguing that 'The Serbs are still on the rampage', the *Mail* characterised the war in terms of 'the unbridled ambition of the Serbs to grab what they can by force' (23 April). This explanation accounted for 66.6 per cent of all explanatory material across all sample periods in both the *Guardian* and the *Independent*, 61.9 per cent in the *Times* and 40.0 per cent in the *Mail*.

Newspapers' endorsement of this explanation is also indicated by the way it was sometimes explicitly reproduced in news reports, where it was taken up by journalists themselves rather than only reported as the opinion of sources. The *Independent's* East Europe editor, Tony Barber, argued that 'Conquest is a national crusade for Belgrade' (17 April 1992), for example; a view echoed by Anne McElvoy in the *Times* the following day in an article headlined 'Serb Crusaders Brush Aside Final Warnings' (18 April). The adoption of this officially favoured explanation was most marked in the case of the *Guardian's* East Europe correspondent, Ian Traynor, who also took up the 'crusade' theme in suggesting that 'Serbians view Bosnia as the front line in a new holy war' (16 April).[10] Traynor explained the war as 'an increasingly aggressive Serbian campaign to take control of coveted territory and drive Muslims or Croats out' (6 April) and as a 'land grab campaign to dismember the newly independent state of Bosnia' (16 April). He acknowledged that 'radical Croats' were 'probably' also 'bent on unravelling Bosnia's complex weave of interlocking and intermingled communities' (13 April), but identified Milosevic as 'the main villain of the piece' (25 April). Traynor's own opinion, freely aired in news reports, was that while international recognition of Bosnia may have accelerated the drive toward war, the violence was clearly the result of a premeditated plan. In 1992 he argued that 'For months the Serbs, and to a lesser extent the Croats, were sharpening their knives for the Bosnian carve-up' (25 April), and evidently maintained a similar view throughout the conflict, the only discernible change being to drop the suggestion that Croatia may have shared in the blame. In 1995 he wrote that, before the outbreak of war, 'the Serb leaderships in Belgrade and Bosnia had been plotting annexation campaigns for months' (21 November).

Western interference

The role of Western recognition of Bosnia in causing the war was mentioned in five articles, the same number as explained it as an 'ethnic' conflict, but in this case all but one of the articles appeared in our 1992 sample, suggesting this was an explanation which attracted less attention as the war went on.

Two articles took the cause of the war as their main topic. The first of these was a comment piece by John Zametica in the *Guardian*, in which he argued that 'Conflict in Bosnia-Herzogovina is the price of hasty recognition' (16 April 1992). By treating Yugoslavia's internal administrative divisions as inviolable national frontiers, despite the fact that they did not match the territory occupied by the country's constituent nations, the EC had made conflict over the division of territory inevitable, he suggested. In the *Times* (24 April), George Brock argued that the EC's diplomatic 'blundering' illustrated the continuing importance of 'differences of national interest' between the major powers. Instead of maintaining a common policy, European governments had given in to German pressure for recognition of Slovenian and Croatian independence, and ignored warnings from the chair of the EC peace talks, Lord Carrington, that such a move 'would aggravate the insecurity of Serbian minorities and could be the "spark" which set Bosnia-Herzegovina alight'. Since critical views of Western intervention are sometimes accused of being pro-Serb, it should be pointed out that although at the time of writing the *Guardian* article cited above Zametica was a research associate at the International Institute for Strategic Studies, in September 1993 he became a spokesman for the Bosnian Serbs and was later denounced in the *Mail* as 'the Serbs' Lord Haw-Haw' (12 April 1994). It seems unlikely, however, that both Brock and the main source cited in support of his argument, Lord Carrington, were also motivated by pro-Serb sympathies.

Two articles featured this explanation as a minor theme in our 1992 sample: Steve Doughty argued that the outbreak of war 'bore out the British Government's fears – voiced last year – that premature international recognition of former Yugoslav republics would lead to further violence' (*Mail*, 23 April); and Tim Judah said that international recognition of Bosnia had 'prompted Serbs to declare their own republic and fighting has flared ... ever since' (*Times*, 14 April). After this, however, such views did not reappear in our sampled coverage until a 10 April 1993 *Guardian* commentary by Ian Aitken, who remarked that Germany had 'more or less railroaded the rest of Europe into recognising the new "independent" states by proclaiming unilateral recognition', and had thereby 'made war in Bosnia virtually inevitable'. Notably, the *Independent* was the only paper not to include any critical commentary on Western recognition as the cause of the war. Instead, the *Independent* seemed to take the opposite view. Steve Crawshaw argued that EC recognition of Bosnia was an attempt 'not to repeat the mistake that was made with Croatia', for which recognition had come too late, and suggested the policy was designed to 'prevent more bloodshed' (7 April 1992). In the same edition, a report by Tim Jackson and Sarah Lambert said that 'recognition comes too late to avert a split inside Bosnia', but explained the logic behind the decision in terms of a 'hope ... that Bosnian Serbs will see that further bloodshed will not prevent Bosnia from becoming independent'. This echoed the official rationale for recognition (of Croatia and Slovenia as well as Bosnia): that international support for the independence and integrity of new states would discourage the pursuit of a division of territory by force. Jackson also reported that EC diplomats 'feel they have been outmanoeuvred by the Serbian government' (*Independent*, 22 April). Citing a Portuguese government spokesman, he suggested that 'the Serbs misled the EC into recognising Bosnia', implying that while recognition may have had negative consequences, these could be blamed on the duplicity of the Serbs.

Serb–Croat carve-up

A 10 April 1992 editorial in the *Times* took a similar line, arguing that 'European Community recognition is not the cause of the fighting'. Rather, the

Times suggested, it merely provided the 'pretext for Serbian extremists to try to enforce with bullets what they have constantly failed to secure by ballot: the creation of a Greater Serbia'. Although this seems to view the war in terms of Serbian aggression, in fact this article advanced a somewhat different explanation: that both Serbia and Croatia had 'designs on the territories inhabited by their ethnic kinsmen' and that 'Hardliners round both President Milosevic and President Tudjman are looking for ways to stir up trouble in the hope that they can change frontiers'.

This view of the war as a carve-up of Bosnia by both Serbia and Croatia featured in six further articles. In the *Guardian* (21 April 1992) Maggie O'Kane suggested that both Serbia and Croatia were operating a 'smash and grab' policy in Bosnia; in the *Mail* (24 April) Doughty reported that British Foreign Secretary Douglas Hurd 'blamed Serbia and Croatia for the fighting'; and in the *Independent* (13 April) Steve Crawshaw noted that the Croats were 'fiercely intent on [a] Bosnian carve-up', raising the possibility of violence 'almost as deadly' as that 'being committed daily by the Yugoslav armed forces and the Serbs'.

The remaining articles advancing this explanation all appeared in our 1993 sample period, when there was a flare-up of fighting between Bosnian Croats and Muslims. This prompted some commentators to suggest that the war was not such a straightforward case of Serbian aggression as had previously been thought. In the *Independent* (3 April 1993), Barber described the war as 'several conflicts all at once: Serb against Muslim, Serb against Croat, Croat against Muslim, and, in the special case of Sarajevo, the defenders of a city renowned for its national diversity and tolerance against Serbian tanks and artillery'. Despite the complexity, he argued, 'one constant factor stands out', namely 'the relentless Serbian and Croatian drive to divide Bosnia at the Muslims' expense'. Later the same month, reporting on 'Bosnia's other conflict', Barber suggested that 'The Muslim–Croat fighting demonstrates that the Bosnian war is not a clear-cut case of Serbian aggression against Muslims' (20 April). Barber's suggestion that 'the Serbs and Croats … have agreed to carve up Bosnia at the expense of the Muslims', reiterated here, was also echoed in a *Times* commentary by Woodrow Wyatt (21 April). Observing that 'Because the Serbs are the strongest, we hear mostly of their cruelty [but] Croats and Muslims are also guilty of war crimes', Wyatt concluded that 'Serbia and Croatia intend to carve the place up between them.'

Other explanations

Other explanations for the war were advanced in four articles. In the *Independent* (9 April 1992), Marcus Tanner said the Serbs had caused the war but in this instance did not see this simply in terms of aggressive territorial ambitions. The presence of the federal army in Bosnia, he suggested, was 'a constant encouragement to Serb extremists to try to win their political demands by force', but he appeared to acknowledge that the Bosnian Serbs might have legitimate claims when he explained the war as being 'caused by the opposition to independence from Yugoslavia of the Serbs who form 31 per cent of the community'. Similarly, Barber noted Western condemnation of Serbia as 'a new world pariah', but commented that 'Serbia's tragedy lies in its failure to convince foreign opinion that the Serbs of Croatia and Bosnia-Herzegovina have legitimate fears for their future as minorities in two newly-independent states' (*Independent*, 22 April 1992).

Also conceding the legitimacy of Serb concerns, two further articles located the causes of the war in the Second World War era. *Guardian* columnist Edward Pearce argued that the war grew 'in the soil of the German creation in 1941 of Greater Croatia' (21 April 1993). International policy ignored this history, he suggested, and instead demanded that Serbs 'surrender the third of the population in Bosnia and the fifth in Croatia which are Serbian, to a German-sponsored Bosnia and Croatia when in the lifetime of a middle-aged man, Serbs were ploughed under in those places like bonemeal!' Somewhat similarly, in the *Independent* Cambridge academic C. B. Goodhart reminded readers that 'The Serbs suffered terribly during the last war at the hands of the fascist Croatian Ustasha regime … [and] almost as much from the Muslim SS Legion' (12 April 1994). 'Given this history', Goodhard argued, it was 'unrealistic to expect that the three communities should be able to live peaceably together for the foreseeable future'.

Mixed explanations

Finally, nine articles offered mixed explanations for the war, in most cases combining two of the main explanations identified above. In two cases (both in the *Guardian*, on 25 and 27 April 1992), this was simply a case of reporting the statements of different international actors: the UN blamed 'all three sides', while the US and the EC blamed the Serbs. More significantly, in three articles international recognition of Bosnia was understood as having caused the war, but only insofar as it had 'persuaded the Serbs to start the war' (*Mail*, 15 April 1993),[11] combining the 'Serb aggression' and 'Western interference' explanations. In three further articles, the idea that recognition had 'played a role in sparking the war' was combined with the view that the war was 'a deliberately manufactured conflict fuelled by vicious populist leaders' in both Serbia and Croatia (*Guardian*, 27 April 1993).[12] In addition, a commentary by Roger Boyes in the *Times* (7 April 1993) argued that the war in fact comprised 'several conflicts' and ought to be understood as simultaneously involving 'the proxy war between Serbs and Croats, the war for an ethnically pure Greater Serbia, the war between the hill people and the city-dwellers of Bosnia, and countless small wars waged by local commanders for territorial advantage'. Here the familiar idea of Serbian aggression is combined with some implicit acknowledgement of Croatian belligerence, but also with the idea that conflict was driven by local score-settling and an urban/rural division.

Overall, while there was a variety of explanations available in press coverage of Bosnia, the predominance of the 'Serbian aggression' explanation is striking. On its own, this does not necessarily support the allegation of an anti-Serb bias in news coverage, as it may simply reflect the fact that this explanation tended to be favoured by influential sources. The evidence of journalists endorsing this explanation in editorial columns and news reports does indicate such a bias, however, even if this was sometimes tempered by an acknowledgement of other factors.

Bias

To investigate this issue further, two strategies were employed. First, the descriptions of key political and military leaders were compared, as likely indicators of newspapers' attitudes to the different sides in the war. Second, the use was examined of 'ethnic cleansing' and 'genocide' as framing devices which, as noted above, have been identified by analysts as suggestive of anti-Serb bias. Both the descriptions of leaders and the 'ethnic cleansing' frame implied a particular understanding of the war.

Descriptions of leaders

The descriptive terms used to characterise different political leaders are listed in Box 3.1. While nobody comes off well, criticism of Izetbegovic is very mild by comparison. There were some highly disparaging descriptions of Franjo Tudjman, particularly the comparison with Hitler, although the extent of this should not be exaggerated: the description (in a commentary by Conor Cruise O'Brien) of him as 'go[ing] on ... about the Jews' was prefaced by the observation that 'nobody compares Tudjman to Hitler' (*Independent*, 23 April 1993) – an observation which was largely true. In our samples, there were only two such comparisons and these were of little wider significance. One was a quotation from an advertisement taken out by Serbian-Americans to protest Tudjman's attendance at the opening of Washington's Holocaust museum, and the report of this occasion (published on the same day as O'Brien's piece) noted that 'no invitation had been extended to Serbia's Slobodan Milosevic, perpetrator of today's "ethnic cleansing" in the heart of Europe' (*Independent*, 23 April 1993). The other came from a comment piece by Lord Denis Healey which appeared after the war had finished (*Guardian*, 24 November 1995). There was some suggestion that Tudjman was jointly responsible for the war in Bosnia, but the blame more often fell on Milosevic – frequently presented as a powerful, threatening and dishonest figure who was the cause of the conflict – reinforcing the pattern of explanatory articles discussed above.

The Bosnian Serb leader, Radovan Karadzic, attracted far less attention than Milosevic (in line with the thesis that the war resulted primarily from international aggression by Serbia), although much more than the Bosnian Croat

---

Box 3.1 Descriptions of political leaders, Bosnia coverage

Milosevic
- identified by most as the principal agent of fighting in former Yugoslavia
- named as the prime villain of the piece by Washington and Bonn
- the main villain of the piece
- The man who more than any other was responsible for the break-up of Yugoslavia and the Serb attempt to dominate the Balkans
- The reputed mastermind of 'ethnic cleansing'
- the man who is variously President of Serbia, prime architect of four years of Balkan misery, and reputed connoisseur of Scotch whisky
- the whisky-slugging Serbian strongman
- Serbia's strongman
- Serbian strongman
- a dictator
- aggressive dictator
- [Saddam Hussein and Milosevic are] essentially local dictators riding bloody tigers of ethnic conflict
- a Balkan warlord
- 'an absolute fighter' (Belgrade opposition leader)
- the most powerful man in former Yugoslavia
- a figure seen by many as the most dangerous in Europe
- the boldest political schemer of all in former Yugoslavia
- probably the most skilful practitioner of mendacity in the Balkans
- 'a liar and a conman ... a Machiavellian character for whom truth has no inherent

value' (US ambassador Warren Zimmermann)
- malign figure
- brooding communist banker
- 'a murderous demagogue' (US journalist)
- stubborn, pudgy face[d] ... a man who rules by intimidation and sheer nerve
- the champion of inat[a]

Karadzic
- has the air of a gambler doubling up from a weak hand
- The Serb strongman in Bosnia
- the ruthless warlord of the Bosnian Serbs
- indicted war criminal
- the Bosnian Serb leader who is wanted by a United Nations war crimes tribunal
- [Mladic's] bouffant-haired sidekick
- the poet-psychiatrist

Karadzic with Mladic
- 'indicted war criminals' (US official)
- indicted war criminals
- suspected war criminals
- the two suspected war criminals
- thuggish Balkan chieftains
- warlords
- deadly duo

Tudjman
- A former Communist and general in the Yugoslav Army
- the former partisan general
- a former communist general turned nationalist icon ... the region's strongman [after Dayton]

- the nationalist President of Croatia
- a politician pandering to the hardline nationalists who sponsored his rise to power
- a former communist general, who ... adopted the flag and insignia of the wartime fascists who fought with Hitler against the allies
- 'the spiritual heir of Adolf Hitler' (Serbian-American advertisement in the *Washington Post*)
- goes on in a similar vein [to Hitler] about the Jews
- [together with Milosevic] primarily responsible for the Bosnian tragedy
- a bitter enemy of President Milosevic [but] ... conspired in carving up Bosnia
- equally nasty Balkan warlord
- a lot less formidable ... a lot less shrewd [than Milosevic]
- authoritarian, insensitive and unsympathetic
- the most sinister figure present [at Dayton]
- the supposed ally of the Muslims ... radiated a chilling and ominous disinterest in [their] fate
- portly and avuncular

Izetbegovic
- notorious for going back on agreements
- a difficult negotiator who counted on the obstinacy of the Serbs to win Western sympathy

Descriptions are in quotation marks where they appeared like this in the original, with the attributions given in parenthesis. Formal titles such as 'President of Croatia' and informal titles such as 'rebel Serb commander' were excluded.

[a] 'Inat' was explained in this article as 'an untranslatable word combining defiance, spite, stubbornness and challenge' (*Times*, 27 April 1993). A few days earlier the *Times* had said that 'Serbs use the word inat to describe a national characteristic loosely translated as an eagerness to meet challenges' (21 April).

---

leader, Mate Boban, who is not included in Box 3.1 since he was only ever designated with informal titular phrases, such as 'the Croat Bosnian leader' or 'the Croatian defence leader'. The joint description of Karadzic and Bosnian Serb General Ratko Mladic at the end of the war as 'indicted war criminals' is worthy of comment, since it violated the principle maintained in reporting domestic

---

Box 3.2 Descriptions of Mladic

Violent nationalist
- driving force behind the three-week-old onslaught [on Gorazde]
- the general at the head of the campaign of 'ethnic cleansing'
- the man who pushed through much of the ethnic cleansing
- the chief strategist of this campaign [of ethnic cleansing]
- one of the architects of the Serbian programme of 'ethnic cleansing'
- this most ruthless of ethnic cleansers
- a fearsome reputation for megalomania, brutality and bloodlust
- a psychopath
- 'profoundly violent'
- 'highly intelligent and extremely violent' (former UN official)
- a butcher
- 'the butcher of Bosnia'
- the beast of Bosnia
- Beast of Bosnia
- born into the kind of bloodbath that he has proved so adept at orchestrating
- [one of] the kind of frontiers folk that make the most fanatical breed of nationalists
- prosecuting the Serb cause with the zeal of a Crusader, utterly sure of his faith
- Ruddy, stockily built and exuding an image of power, General Mladic is a believer

- the rabid Serbian nationalist was also a docile and subordinate communist under the old regime

Brutal warrior
- Brutal Serbian general
- hardline military commander
- hardline Serbian commander
- A man who has got used to winning
- warrior king
- Serbia's warrior king
- the warlord
- warmonger
- ruthless war-baby
- describes himself as a 'super-general'
- 'I have an attacking character'
- 'a brilliant officer and a great organiser ... bold and flamboyant' (Belgrade military analyst)
- one of the most talented and ruthless army officers of his generation in the Balkans
- a reputation as a brilliant and brutal strategist

Hero to Serbs
- hugely popular with the general staff in Belgrade
- loved by his men and civilians alike
- the hero of the Bosnian Serbs who has been barred by Mr Clinton from political office
- [Bosnian Serbs] see him as their saviour from the Croat and Muslim threat

Comical
- the little general in the funny peaked cap ... strutting and bragging
- regards himself as 'a bit too short'
- has a Napoleon complex
- calls himself 'the Napoleon of Bosnia'
- Napoleon Mladic
- the general with the manic grin

Other descriptions
- 'public bully, private calculator' (David Owen)
- virtually impervious to the outrage his forces have stirred
- enjoys his power
- His enemies condemn him as an evil figure and a war criminal who has seized land thanks to a policy of firing on defenceless people
- 'a cynic and a sadist' (retired Yugoslav colonel)
- 'out of control'
- the general politician
- Goliath
- stocky, ruddy-faced
- a stocky, florid 51-year-old whose father died fighting with Tito's communist partisans
- short, stocky and ruddy-faced, oozes confidence, charm, and bawdy good humour, happy in the knowledge that he is at the pinnacle of his powers

Descriptions are in quotation marks where they appeared like this in the original, with the attributions given in parenthesis. Formal titles were excluded.

---

trials whereby journalists avoid calling defendants 'criminals' because there is a presumption of innocence. As Mirjana Skoco and William Woodger (2000: 36–7) argue, the phrase is 'the approximate equivalent of "charged murderers"' and its routine use suggests an erosion of the concept of 'innocent until proved guilty' in war crimes cases.

Mladic himself attracted a great many descriptions, including three articles devoted entirely to profiling him (*Guardian*, 14 April 1993 and 18 April 1994; *Times*, 12 April 1994), listed in Box 3.2. These descriptions leave us in no doubt that Mladic was largely to blame for most of the violence, but strikingly few imply a political understanding of this. Even though Mladic was often characterised in terms of his nationalism and responsibility for 'ethnic cleansing', terms such as 'beast', 'rabid', 'butcher', 'bloodlust' and 'warrior king' evoke primitive, even animalistic qualities, while terms such as 'zeal', 'fanatical', 'manic' and 'psychopath' suggest irrationality. The sorts of terms which journalists mostly rejected as explanations for the conflict re-emerge here in describing the military leader of one side. While the war as a whole was rarely explained in terms of primitive 'ethnic hatreds' in our samples of coverage, the military actions of the Serbs were explained in terminology which does evoke this idea. It is also notable that many descriptions are highly personalised: the accent is less on his politics than on his character, psychology, background and even appearance. Such descriptions are best understood as expressions of dislike or even anger on the part of journalists.

Ethnic cleansing and genocide

While several commentators have examined both the term 'ethnic cleansing' and the actions to which it refers, in many respects the discussion is somewhat unsatisfactory.[13] One key problem is that of definition. In common with other analysts, Andrew Bell-Fialkoff (1993: 110) argues that 'ethnic cleansing' covers a continuum, 'from forced population transfers and population exchange ... [to] deportation and genocide'. On this basis, he maintains that 'cleansing has been practiced for nearly 3,000 years', originating with the Assyrians (Bell-Fialkoff 1993: 111; see also Bell-Fialkoff 1999: 10, 281). Similarly, arguing that 'Ethnic cleansing is the dark and ugly side of human nature', Akbar Ahmed suggests that in 'various degrees and in different forms ethnic cleansing is in evidence everywhere', including, in his examples, the Spanish *Reconquista*, the establishment of American Indian reservations and apartheid South Africa (Ahmed 1995: 3, 7–9). In this approach the idea quickly becomes too loose to be specific, seeming to take in virtually all of world history. A more tightly focused discussion is offered by Drazen Petrovic, from Sarajevo University, who identifies the problems which arise when the starting point for defining the term is the range of different 'practices' to which it is applied. Individual acts – from low-level harassment through to atrocities and war crimes – may fall into the category of 'ethnic cleansing', but these various acts can be related together as part of a coherent phenomenon only on the basis of there being a common policy or intent behind them. After examining official usage of the term by a number of international actors, particularly the UN, he defines 'ethnic cleansing' as: 'a well-defined policy of a particular group of persons to systematically eliminate another group from a given territory on the basis of religious, ethnic or national origin', noting that this policy may be pursued 'by all possible means, from discrimination to extermination' (Petrovic 1994: 351). This, however, raises a different issue: how to distinguish 'ethnic cleansing' from genocide, defined as acts 'committed with intent to destroy, in whole or in part, a national, ethnic, racial or religious group as such'.[14] The term 'ethnic cleansing' is often used in such a way as to evoke genocide, but also to maintain a distinction. In December 1992, for example, the UN General Assembly declared 'ethnic cleansing' to be 'a form of genocide' (quoted in Petrovic 1994: 355), but left the relationship between the two unclear. Petrovic himself is led back to the idea of 'ethnic cleansing' as a continuum, and he concludes that lower-level acts 'not aimed at extermination' may be treated as individual crimes against humanity, while more serious 'genocidal acts' come within the definition of genocide (1994: 359). Effectively, this eliminates the need for a separate (legal) category of 'ethnic cleansing': the various actions to which it refers are treated either as individual crimes or as part of a policy of genocide.

The origins of the term also remain obscure. A comparison is often made with Nazi terms such as *Judenrein*, although this seems tendentious, as it suggests an ideological relationship where none has been shown to exist.[15] News articles in our sample took this line when they commented on the meaning of the term, comparing it to 'Hitlerism' (*Guardian*, 15 April 1993) and 'Hitler's Final Solution' (*Independent*, 2 April 1993). Petrovic (1994: 343) speculates that the term 'has its origin in military vocabulary' (to English speakers it perhaps has some similarity to phrases such as 'clean-up operation'). More significantly, he notes that the term first entered Yugoslav political discourse to describe the actions of ethnic-Albanians in the Serbian province of Kosovo in the 1980s, who were said to be establishing 'ethnically clean' territories at the expense of the local Serbs. Ironically, despite the term first having been used in Yugoslavia to describe actions against Serbs, it is often discussed as a specifically Serbian practice or as a kind of semi-official Serbian ideology (Cohen 1999; Hartmann 1999).

As this implies, the discussion of 'ethnic cleansing' and genocide is closely related to the issue of how the war is explained and understood. This is clear from the report produced by the Commission of Experts established by the UN to investigate war crimes in Bosnia. Defining ethnic cleansing as 'rendering an area ethnically homogenous by using force or intimidation to remove from a given area persons from another ethnic or religious group', the Commission argued that although 'All parties involved in the conflict have committed "grave breaches" of the Geneva Conventions and other violations of international humanitarian law', there were 'significant qualitative differences' between the actions of different sides, and that 'no "moral equivalence" argument should be advanced' (UN Commission of Experts 1994: 6, 25). The Commission understood Serbian 'ethnic cleansing' as 'the result of a highly-developed policy', making it 'Unlike the violations committed by the other warring factions'. The Bosnian Muslims were said to have engaged in 'forceful population removal [of Serbs] ... but not as a policy'. The actions of the Croats were viewed somewhat ambiguously, either as evidence of 'similar policies [to those of the Serbs], but on a more restricted scale', or as 'practices' which did not amount to a policy. Hence the Experts noted that:

> while 'Ethnic Cleansing', as a practice, is not new to history, nor ... is it entirely new to the Balkans.... This report ... discusses 'ethnic cleansing' as part of a broader policy, pursued by Serbian forces within [Bosnia], Croatia, and the [Federal Republic of Yugoslavia], to create a 'Greater Serbia'. (UN Commission of Experts 1994: 25)

This official use of the term to reinforce the explanation of the war in terms of Serbian aggression is also apparent in the circumstances surrounding how the phrase 'ethnic cleansing' started to become common in media reports from May 1992 onwards. In April 1992 the Bosnian Muslim Foreign Minister, Haris Silajdzic, visited Washington, where he met with Secretary of State James Baker. In his memoirs Baker recounts how:

> After the meeting, I ... asked Margaret Tutwiler [Assistant Secretary of State] to talk to the Foreign Minister about the importance of using Western mass media to build support in Europe and North America for the Bosnian cause. I also had her talk to her contacts at the four television networks, the *Washington Post* and the *New York Times* to try to get more attention focused on the story. (Baker 1995: 643–4)

Johanna Neuman describes Tutwiler as having 'an extraordinary antenna for the winds of public opinion'. Despite the Bush administration's resistance to military intervention in Bosnia,

> Tutwiler was convinced that the West should at least end the suffering that was being beamed across the miles every night on satellite television. Knowing this too would be resisted by key administration figures, Tutwiler adopted the term *ethnic cleansing* to describe from her podium at the State Department the plight of Bosnian civilians. (Neuman 1996: 236, original emphasis)

Neuman is referring to a 14 May 1992 press briefing at which Tutwiler said: 'We are concerned about reports that Serb forces ... have begun to remove non-Serbs in an ethnic, quote, "cleansing", unquote, operation.'[16] This briefing was written by George Kenney, a State Department official who wished to encourage greater US involvement in the Balkans, and to that end looked for ways to add 'colour' to the daily briefings he wrote, most of which was edited out by senior officials, but some of which found its way through.[17] Kenney obtained this 'colour' from early-morning telephone calls with a contact at the US embassy in Belgrade, and, as he recounts:

> When the term 'ethnic cleansing' came up in one such conversation I knew I had a potentially red-hot bit of prose. I put it in the briefing material, fully expecting it to be excised.... Margaret [Tutwiler] herself ... was somewhat unaware of the images this term could conjure up and did not carefully consider the implications.

The implications and images evoked by the term – that Serbian actions resembled the Nazi extermination of the Jews – may not have been fully intended by Tutwiler, who declined to elaborate on the phrase when asked about it by reporters, but they were intended by Kenney, keen to push the US towards a tougher policy. Furthermore, Tutwiler's use of the term came at just the moment when she, and apparently Baker, were attempting to use the media to generate greater 'support ... for the Bosnian cause'.

The effect on news coverage was immediately visible. In the US media, from a total of only three mentions of 'ethnic cleansing' in April 1992, the phrase was used 29 times in May (27 times after Tutwiler's briefing) and its use continued to rise thereafter, peaking at 717 mentions in August 1992. By the end of the year, the term 'ethnic cleansing' had been used in 2,332 US media reports.[18] The pattern was the same in the newspapers examined in this study. The phrase appeared only once before 14 May 1992, and that was in a letter to the *Independent* (20 April) from a representative of the Croatian Aid Organisation.[19] The phrase appeared in seven articles during the second half of May; thereafter the number of articles using it rose to a peak of 201 in August and reached a total of 560 by the end of the year. In our samples of coverage, the vast majority of articles mentioning 'ethnic cleansing' or genocide applied these terms to the Serbs, as shown in Table 3.2. While (Bosnian) Croat and Bosnian Muslim forces were sometimes said to be engaged in 'ethnic cleansing', their actions were never discussed in terms of genocide. This study found no evidence to support Mestrovic's (1995: 74) assertion that Croats were prejudicially portrayed as 'an essentially pro-Nazi genocidal people', but there is evidence of Serbs being depicted in this fashion, in line with the pronouncements of the UN Commission of Experts and the policy stance of the US.

For those wishing to encourage international military action in Bosnia, the accusation that the Serbs were committing genocide was used to put Western political leaders under moral pressure. In 1993, for example, there were reports of intense disagreement within the US administration as a memorandum from State Department officials was leaked to the press accusing the West of 'capitulation to Serbian aggression and … genocide' (*Guardian*, 24 April 1993).[20] Although the phrase 'ethnic cleansing' evokes the Nazi genocide, however, it also contains an element of ambiguity. Postponing a decision on airstrikes, US President Bill Clinton responded by saying that 'Ethnic cleansing is the kind of inhumanity that the Holocaust took to the nth degree. You have to stand up against it. I think it's wrong.' This is one way in which the ambiguity of the term 'ethnic cleansing' could be politically helpful: Clinton's remarks compare ethnic cleansing and genocide, but do not straightforwardly equate the two – they are the same 'kind of' thing, but it seems to be a question of degree. 'Ethnic cleansing' was thus a useful term in Western policy discourse, since it delineated a clear moral stance while avoiding any commitment to act decisively. Kenney suggests that 'even the higher ups [in the Bush administration] who objected to a greater US involvement in the Yugoslav war took a rather perverse satisfaction in having a new term with which to denigrate those heathen upstarts'. As the West moved towards a tougher military stance, the term 'genocide' could be more freely employed and indeed Serbian leaders

Table 3.2 Numbers of articles mentioning 'ethnic cleansing' and 'genocide', Bosnia coverage

	Ethnic cleansing	Genocide
By Serbs	116	37
By Croats	25	0
By Muslims	8	0
Unspecified	13	4

were indicted for genocide by the ICTY. Secondly, the term's ambiguous relationship to genocide also allowed actions by Croats and Bosnian Muslims to be described as 'ethnic cleansing' but without this necessarily implying that they were the same as actions by Serbs.

In seeking to understand the selective application of these terms to the different parties to the conflict, much turns on whether the actions of the Serbs should be seen in terms of an underlying 'policy' of 'ethnic cleansing', since it is this which would make it directly comparable to genocide. As Banks and Wolfe Murray (1999: 155) note, different writers reach different verdicts on this issue. Ed Vulliamy (1994: 96), for example, maintains what became the most common view, that ethnic cleansing was the central war aim of the Serbs, and 'not a side-effect of the war'. Conversely, Misha Glenny (1996: 187) argues that, at least initially, '"cleansing" is a military tactic which is mistaken for the central war aim because it is executed in such a horrifying fashion'. As the war went on, however, he suggests that this 'tactic' solidified into a policy: 'the idea of including a minority population in the conquered territory becomes less acceptable as the doctrine of "national purity" strengthens'. A somewhat similar approach is taken by Woodward (1995: 242), who argues that 'the association between persons and rights to land became a deliberate policy to clear a territory of all those who were considered not to belong in their national territory and who might be suspected of disloyalty'.

As Bell-Fialkoff (1993: 118) notes, there were large numbers of people who left their homes 'voluntarily' during the break-up of Yugoslavia (for example, even before the beginning of full-scale hostilities, 20,000 Serbs had fled from Croatia) and many more who fled to escape fighting. In many other instances, however, there clearly were deliberate attempts to force people out of particular areas, and to that extent it seems reasonable to argue that this was or became a 'policy'. Woodward's discussion, however, suggests that this policy derived not from any 'doctrine of "national purity"' but from the pragmatic pursuit of political goals. At the beginning of the war it was established that 'international recognition ... required a referendum of residents in a territory on their choice of state'. This led directly to the different sides attempting to 'match' populations to territories under their control, often by the most brutal and violent means. Even where temporary ceasefires had been agreed, local authorities continued to negotiate population transfers, 'to consolidate ethnically pure territories that would vote correctly in a referendum on sovereignty and in future elections' (Woodward 1995: 242). A further consideration was the quality and integrity of territory in any final settlement: all sides attacked cities and towns for their strategic location or the value of their industrial or military assets (Woodward 1995: 269–70).

There were extreme nationalist political and paramilitary groups involved in the war – such as the Croatian Defence League, the Serbian Radical Party, or the mujahideen Islamists invited in by the Bosnian Muslim government (Woodward 1995: 355–6). If Woodward's persuasive account is correct, however, we would have to conclude that the understanding which outside observers tended to favour for the actions of different parties to the war, in terms of their pursuit of coherent political doctrines, ideals or ideologies – whether of committed multiculturalism in the case of the Bosnian Muslims, or of extreme nationalism or fascism in the case of the Serbs and sometimes the Croats – was misleading. The basis of the distinction between parties was not different ideologies but the different position in which each found itself. For Croatia, the goal was to get rid of the disloyal minorities who made a substantial part of its claimed territory ungovernable, and to annex part of Bosnia to enlarge its newly independent state. For Serbian minorities in both Croatia and Bosnia, the goal was to establish viable entities which could either survive separately or, ideally, join the rest of Yugoslavia. Both Serbs and Croats justified such goals on the basis of historic and 'ethnic' claims; but their nationalism derived from these goals, rather than the goals deriving from a 'doctrine' of ethnic purity.

The territorial claims of the Bosnian Muslims, meanwhile, would necessarily be diminished if they were linked to only a part of the population (Woodward 1995: 243). Like the other sides in the war, the Bosnian Muslim government sought to deal militarily with disloyal sections of the population, including Muslims loyal to Abdic. Yet the claim to the entire territory could not be justified on the basis of representing less than half the population. The 'multiculturalism' of the Bosnian Muslims derived not from a uniquely strong attachment to the idea of 'brotherhood and unity' (which had been an official ideology of the entire federal Yugoslav state), but from the fact that, unlike for the other sides in the war, it was more difficult to justify territorial claims in terms of 'ethnicity'. If ethnicity was taken as the sole basis for territorial division, the Serbs would have had a plausible claim to most of Bosnia, since they legally owned and occupied most of the land. In addition, the Bosnian Muslims were more dependent on outside sponsorship, and while the support of Saudi Arabia or Iran could be secured on the basis of a Muslim identity, the backing of Western powers was sought on the basis of an avowed multiculturalism. It might be suggested that the perceived significance of Bosnia for the West's own self-image also contributed greatly to distorting outside views of the conflict. As Lene Hansen (1998: 168–9, 172) argues, in Western political discourse Bosnia became an 'ideal Western self' – a romanticised embodiment of the tolerant values the West supposedly represents – while the Serbs were constructed as the 'Other', exemplifying a nationalistic past to be repudiated.

Looking more closely at the articles in our sample, Box 3.3 shows the different descriptive terms applied to 'ethnic cleansing' for each side. In the case of the Serbs, terms such as 'policy', 'plan', 'aim', 'objective' and 'goal' predominate, which suggest the consistent pursuit of a deliberate policy, as do terms such as 'systematic', 'campaign' and 'strategy'. As Petrovic (1994: 344) demonstrates, these were also the terms used by the UN and Western NGOs to characterise 'ethnic cleansing'. It is a moot point who followed whose usage in this respect: while journalists no doubt picked up the language of official sources, the latter also seem to have been influenced by media reports. In the section of the report from the UN Commission of Experts (1994: 36–41) dealing with 'Assigning Responsibility for "Ethnic Cleansing"', for example, the majority of

---

Box 3.3 Descriptions of ethnic cleansing, Bosnia coverage

By Serbs
- 'unlawful, unacceptable and abhorrent policy of "ethnic cleansing" aimed at territorial aggrandisement' (UN Security Council)
- Serbian policy of 'ethnic cleansing'
- their 'ethnic cleansing' policy
- the Serbian policy of ethnic cleansing – clearing out Moslems from a 'greater Serbia'
- Serb 'ethnic cleansing' policies
- policy of ethnic cleansing and territorial conquest
- the attacking Serbs' policy of so-called ethnic cleansing
- the Serb policy of 'ethnic cleansing'
- part of the military policy
- Serbian programme of 'ethnic cleansing'
- Serbian plans for 'ethnic cleansing'
- the Serbian ethnic cleansing aim
- aim of seizing territory and clearing it of non-Serbs
- Bosnian Serb objective of 'cleansing'
- a ruthless army whose goal was 'ethnic cleansing'
- target list for 'ethnic cleansing'
- the Serbian campaign of ethnic cleansing
- increasingly murderous terror campaign

- the Serb campaign of ethnic cleansing
- the Bosnian Serb campaign of 'ethnic cleansing'
- campaigns of 'ethnic cleansing'
- the strategy of 'ethnic cleansing'
- cold-blooded 'cleansing' strategy carried out by the Serbs and latterly the Croats
- atrocities and ... systematic rape ... as part of 'ethnic cleansing'
- A ... tactic
- tactics of terror, ethnic cleansing, and camps
- hundreds of middle-ranking Serb bureaucrats, skilled in the techniques of 'ethnic cleansing'
- the job of 'ethnic cleansing'
- process of 'ethnic cleansing'
- architects of this vile practice
- systematic murder and dispossession known as ethnic cleansing
- systematic ethnic cleansing was the aim ... not an incidental by-product of the fighting
- another bout of 'ethnic cleansing'
- dreaming of the ethnically pure Greater Serbia
- drive to help build a bigger Serbia through ethnic apartheid

- proceeding with 'ethnic cleansing' to establish their mini-state
- attempts to build an ethnically pure mini-state
- fighting to establish and preserve an ethnically cleansed state
- only 'ethnically pure' cantons made any sense for the Serbs
- idea of exclusive ethnic states
- Hitlerism of a kind
- what ... the Second World War was fought to end
- fascism and ethnic-cleansing
- an easy blitzkrieg
- systematic ... on a scale and in a manner not witnessed in Europe for half a century
- genocidal slaughter
- The Serbs' final solution for Bosnia
- the Serbs' final solution for Muslims
- what the Muslims claim is Serbian genocide aimed at exterminating them and their culture
- ethnic cleansing, Serbian-style
- a quality ... which is fundamentally different
- latest wave of ethnic cleansing
- new wave of Serbian ethnic atrocities
- outbreak of 'ethnic cleansing'
- bouts of Serbian 'ethnic cleansing'
- horrific daily practices

---

the sources cited are news reports, with the *New York Times* being the most often cited source of information.[21]

While similar terminology is sometimes used in news reports of 'ethnic cleansing' by Croats and Muslims, more often their actions are described differently. Here, 'ethnic cleansing' is seen as mutual (it is 'tit-for-tat' cleansing which takes place 'between ... former allies' and involves them attacking 'each other's villages') and reactive (Croats are said to be 'anticipating a Muslim assault', while Muslims are out to 'exact revenge'). Rather than a conscious policy or strategy, terms such as 'insanity', 'frenzy', 'crazy' and 'epidemic' suggest irrationality and illness. All the articles referring to ethnic cleansing by Muslims and most of those concerning Croats were from our 1993 sample, with the remaining articles about Croatian ethnic cleansing appearing at the end of the war in 1995. As Gowing (1994: 55–6) notes, 'the surge in fighting between Croats and Muslims in the Spring of 1993 received virtually no coverage' and was played down by Western governments because of a perceived need

- trying to force their enemies to flee, not to exterminate them

By Croats
- Insanity of tit-for-tat cleansing
- frenzy of tit-for-tat murder
- rampaged through each other's villages
- 'ethnic cleansing' between ... former allies
- Anticipating a Muslim assault ... the Croats have 'ethnically cleansed' the valley
- 'crazy ... very thorough in their ethnic cleansing' (British soldier)
- epidemic ... has erupted
- epidemic of ethnic cleansing
- latest spate of 'ethnic cleansing'
- appallingly brutal wave of ethnic cleansing
- renewed wave of ethnic cleansing as the defeated flee possible revenge
- evening ritual of 'cleansing'
- aped Serb tactics ... to establish their ethnically pure mini-state

- 'exactly the same pattern here as in eastern Bosnia but it's Croats versus Moslems'
- [no] proof of 'orchestrated mass killings'
- 'systematically going through houses shooting people and setting them ablaze' (British soldier)
- ruthless quest for territorial control
- horrific ethnic cleansing and ... constant aggression (Muslim officer)
- [Tudjman] will have carved out and 'ethnically purified' a powerful state
- ethnically cleansed Croatia, bent on final absorption of Croatian Bosnia
- Zagreb-controlled puppet state ... its Serbs have been 'ethnically cleansed' or killed
- 'a disgrace, a criminal act ... not ethnic cleansing: it is ethnic extermination' (UN envoy Diego Arria)
- [like] Croat fascists of the second world war and ... Serb forces (Muslim officer)

- cold-blooded 'cleansing' strategy carried out by the Serbs and latterly the Croats
- goal of building a 'nationally pure' state

By Muslims
- 'ethnically cleansed' by both sides
- Insanity of tit-for-tat cleansing
- frenzy of tit-for-tat murder
- 'ethnic cleansing' between ... former allies
- rampaged through each other's villages
- Moslems exact revenge for Croat attacks
- ruthless quest for territorial control
- 'Their plan is to ethnically cleanse the areas where Croats have been living for centuries' (Croatian spokesman)
- [no] proof of 'orchestrated mass killings'
- an ethnic cleansing operation
- 'cleansing the area ... like the Chetniks (Serb extremists)' (Bosnian Croat)

Descriptions are in quotation marks where they appeared that way in the original; attributions are given where the article attributed a phrase.

to simplify the picture. However, the chance discovery, by British troops, of a Croatian massacre of Muslims in the village of Ahmici in April 1993 meant the story could not be ignored. Even then, however, it appears from our sample that the seriousness of Croatian actions tended to be downplayed relative to those of the Bosnian Serbs.

Occasionally it was argued that the behaviour of all sides was similar, as when O'Brien said that 'ethnic cleansing is not just a Serbian idea [but] a fancy recent label for standard practice in a Balkan civil war' (*Independent*, 23 April 1993). More often, however, it was suggested that 'ethnic cleansing' by Serbs possessed 'a quality ... which is fundamentally different' (*Mail*, 18 April 1993). Hence, for the Serbs, 'systematic ethnic cleansing was the aim ... not an incidental by-product of the fighting' (*Times*, 9 November 1995), but in the case of Croats and Bosnian Muslims there was said to be '[no] proof of "orchestrated mass killings"' (*Guardian*, 21 April 1993). This last article, a report by Traynor on 'ethnic slaughter around Vitez' by Muslims and Croats, found a way to depict 'ethnic cleansing' as an essentially Serbian practice even while it acknowledged that the Serbs were 'not involved this time', by describing the Serbs as the 'architects' of 'ethnic cleansing'. Looking back at the end of the war, Traynor also recalled these events in terms of the Croats having 'aped Serb tactics' (*Guardian*, 21 November 1995). With only a little more subtlety, in the *Independent* (26 April 1993) Marcus Tanner wrote of 'Serb "ethnic cleansing" in northern Bosnia and worsening Croat-on-Muslim violence in nearby Vitez', implying that the latter did not merit the label 'ethnic cleansing'.

'Ethnic cleansing' by Bosnian Muslims was only once said to be part of a strategic 'plan', and the source for this was a spokesman for the Croatian Defence Council (*Independent*, 2 April 1993). 'Ethnic cleansing' by Croats was sometimes explicitly linked to strategic policy goals, as a 'cold-blooded ... strategy' involving an attempt to 'establish [an] ethnically pure mini-state' or to 'ethnically [purify]' their territory, for example, but almost all examples of this were in reports from 1995, when the war was over. The only exception was a *Times* article by Judah (15 April 1993) which reported the complaints of an unnamed 'senior UN official' that a double standard was being applied to Serbs and Croats. Judah noted that the existence of a 'Zagreb-controlled puppet state' in Bosnia was 'regularly ignored' and, even more unusually, wrote that it 'permits no dissent from its Muslim minority and its Serbs have been "ethnically cleansed" or killed'. This was exceptional because Serbs were almost never said to be the victims of 'ethnic cleansing', even when they clearly were. Retrospective accounts of the war in 1995, for example, often mentioned 'Operation Storm', the US-backed Croatian offensive against Serbs in the Krajina region, but there was no consensus on whether this could be described as 'ethnic cleansing'. A commentary by Michael Ignatieff in the *Independent* (22 November 1995) was most forthright, arguing that US 'permission to drive the Serbs from Krajina' amounted to American 'ratification of Croatian ethnic cleansing'. In the *Mail* (23 November), Mark Almond blurred the issue by arguing that 'the return of refugees usually leads to a renewed wave of ethnic cleansing as the defeated flee possible revenge (as happened in the Krajina in August when the Croats turned the tables on the Serbs)'. Here, the violent expulsion of Serbs by the Croatian military is portrayed as a flight, prompted by returning refugees, from the mere possibility of 'revenge'.

In other cases, reporters seemingly went out of their way to avoid describing Croatian actions against Serbs as 'ethnic cleansing'. In the *Times* (24 November 1995), Michael Binyon noted 'the expulsion of Serbs from Krajina', but it was Milosevic whom he described as the 'mastermind of "ethnic cleansing"'; similarly, in the *Guardian* (22 November) Julian Borger acknowledged that Tudjman had 'carved out and "ethnically purified" a powerful state', but it was Milosevic who was said to be the originator of a 'vision of an ethnically-divided Balkans'. Also in the *Guardian* (17 November), David Fairhall said that 'the Croatian army ... drove 150,000 Serbs out of Krajina', but it was only 'the Bosnian Serb militia, who "cleansed" the unsafe havens of Srebrenica and Zepa of 50,000 Muslims'. Even more pointedly, the *Independent*'s Barber wrote that the Serb community in Krajina had been 'ruined by its armed revolt against Zagreb and by Croatia's military revenge last August, which triggered the flight or expulsion of more than 150,000 Serbs' (18 November). While the Bosnian Muslims were said to have suffered 'savage "ethnic cleansing"', the Serbs had apparently brought 'ruin' on themselves by provoking 'revenge'. In a further article, on 22 November 1995, Barber noted that 'Mr Tudjman's armies overran' the 'secessionist Serbs of Croatia', before describing Bosnian Serb leaders as 'indicted war criminals' and claiming there were 'hundreds of middle-ranking Serb bureaucrats, skilled in the techniques of "ethnic cleansing"'.

A double standard was thus applied in describing actions perpetrated by and against Serbs. Given the relative prominence of articles explaining the conflict in terms of Serb aggression, the selective use of the terms 'ethnic cleansing' and 'genocide' may be understood as reinforcing this explanation.

Prescriptions and attitudes to Western policy

Given how newspapers understood the causes of war, it is not surprising that, from the start, the solutions proposed in editorial and comment columns centred on what the West could do to the Serbs. On 24 April 1992 the *Independent* announced it was 'Time for action against Serbia' and advocated 'punitive sanctions' – a line which had already been taken by the *Guardian* (13 April) and the *Mail* (23 April). The *Times* (23 April), describing Serbia as 'The new Pariah', argued that the US and EC 'should withdraw recognition of Yugoslavia' in order to 'hurt Serbia, politically and psychologically', a suggestion also made by columnist Anne McElvoy (22 April). Newspapers were initially cautious about advancing any more forceful measures, however. The *Independent* noted that the UN troops originally deployed to keep the peace in the aftermath of the conflict between Serbia and Croatia were now at risk from fighting in Bosnia, and advised that 'Decisions are required now to ensure their safety and limit their numbers until peace returns' (7 April), while the *Times* argued that 'the scope for peacemaking by outsiders is limited' (10 April).

1993: debating force

Of the four periods examined, Bosnia attracted most editorial attention during 1993, with most discussion centring on the possible use of Western military force. Several developments put this issue on the agenda in April 1993. The UN Security Council authorised Nato enforcement of the no-fly zone over Bosnia (Resolution 816, 31 March) and designated Srebrenica a 'safe area' (Resolution 819, 16 April). The latter move was in response to a Bosnian Serb assault on the town, which also prompted high-profile demands for intervention from former Prime Minister Margaret Thatcher (initially on 13 April) and from US State Department officials who leaked a memo to the press (on 23 April) demanding a US military response to the conflict. The Croat massacre of Muslims in Ahmici and attacks on other villages in central Bosnia, also during April 1993, drew no similar calls for action: invariably the Serbs were the proposed target for the use of force. The *Guardian* did, though, express concern that what it called 'The more confused agony of Vitez' would encourage 'the ... school of thought that nothing should be done' (22 April). Two days later, reflecting on the influence of the media, the paper again worried that increased coverage of Bosnia would not 'necessarily lead to increased commitment', and argued that 'scenes of barbaric Croat violence' would 'serve to convince people that if the Croats are as bad as the Serbs (and perhaps the Muslims as well) then our boys would be better off out of it' (*Guardian*, 24 April). As we shall see, however, this conclusion was rarely drawn.

The *Guardian* and the *Mail* were least impressed, but for different reasons, with proposals to arm the Bosnian Muslims and carry out airstrikes against the Serbs, while the *Times* and the *Independent* were the most bellicose. The *Mail* was the most unenthusiastic about military action, although it generally avoided taking a definitive stand either for or against. The only concrete proposal made in its editorials during the 1993 study period was that bets placed on that year's Grand National horserace, which had been declared void, should be 'transformed into help for the starving children of Bosnia' via a charity fund (5 April). The paper did repeatedly address the issue of using force, however, and devoted five editorials to debating the 'agonising' questions it raised. The question was most directly posed in a 19 April leader entitled 'Should We Wage War Against the Serbs?' Emphasising the risks of 'a Balkan version of Vietnam', the *Mail* concluded that: 'Only after full debate in Parliament and in complete agreement with his Nato allies, would [Prime Minister] John Major be justified in making the fateful commitment to enter the war against the Serbs'. Similarly, responding to Thatcher's call for action, the paper's 14 April editorial cautioned against emotional reactions, again describing proposed action as a 'fatal ... commitment' and asking whether Britain should 'get sucked in'.

Caution about using force because it was dangerous did not amount to opposition in principle and in other editorials the *Mail* implied that using force ought at least to be considered. The paper's 1 April editorial said that while peacekeepers and aid workers had offered 'alleviation of suffering', there had been 'no curb on the unbridled savagery of the aggressors'. Asking 'Could we – should we – have gone in hard and early with air strikes?', the *Mail* suggested that to have done so 'might have cauterised the bloody conflict before a whole people were driven into exile'. The article concluded that 'Posterity may judge our ineffectuality to be as shaming as their suffering was piteous'. Similarly, the paper's 7 April leader asked 'Should we, even now, resort to armed intervention to put an end to the carnage?' Although it suggested that 'All the options have nightmarish consequences', the *Mail* said that 'one thing is sure: a sense of impotence in the face of such pain and cruelty is leading to a growing sense of shame in the West'. This editorial, appearing on the same day as an article by the paper's regular Bosnia commentator, Mark Almond, forcefully arguing for military intervention to end the humiliation of being 'idle spectators [to] genocide', was the nearest the *Mail* came to endorsing military action. By the end of the month, the paper was arguing that 'Impatience for action by the new incumbent in the White House [Clinton] can be no substitute for a coherent war aim and an agreed strategy to achieve it' (27 April).

The *Guardian* also emphasised the 'agonising questions' raised by the 'dismal failure' of the West (6 April). Dismissing Nato enforcement of the no-fly zone as a 'dangerous distraction' (13 April), the paper argued that 'Air action is not only a dubious step into the unknown but a diversion from the hard graft of peace-keeping' (22 April) and that 'bombing a few bridges' would be 'at best a diversion, at worst a disaster' (24 April). Unlike the *Mail*, however, the *Guardian* was dubious about such measures because it wanted Western leaders to go much further. While describing Thatcher's proposals as 'flawed' (15 April), the paper nevertheless welcomed the debate about using force, arguing that 'The fact that the argument is out in the open at long last is the important thing' (19 April). The *Guardian's* preferred option was to put 'many more peace-keepers on the ground' and to explore 'the ideas for a UN protectorate or trusteeship' (13 April). These proposals were further elaborated by senior columnists Hugo Young and Martin Woollacott. Arguing that 'to bomb or not to bomb should still be an open question', Young advocated 'the introduction of massive numbers of ground troops to separate the combatants, create protectorates behind the old republican frontiers, and remain there for the necessary years to ensure they are respected' (22 April). Woollacott, meanwhile, aimed not just at a UN takeover of Bosnia but at bringing about regime change in Serbia. Europe and America should, he said, be 'ready to use ground forces offensively in Bosnia', in the service of the 'only objective which ultimately makes sense', which was 'to create the conditions, through appropriate military action in Bosnia, likely to lead to a change of government in Belgrade' (17 April).

As this suggests, some commentators were concerned to draw out the implications of the Bosnian conflict for the wider framework of post-Cold War international relations. Thus the *Guardian* warned that 'a defeat for the United Nations' would 'obliterate any remembrance of the talk about a New World Order' (15 April) and suggested that 'The longer-term answer lies in developing new institutions both at the UN and regionally which are capable of dealing with the much greater demand now faced for peace-keeping and – almost certainly before long – for peace-making' (13 April). Young pursued this line of argument vigorously, calling for a 'new grammar of international relations', which would involve a 'willingness to intervene, and a language capable of explaining, defining and justifying such a new rule of international conduct' (13 April). The core problem, he suggested, was that 'people no longer know what to think about the purposes of military policy'. With the end of the Cold War, the 'legitimising basis for military policy has all but vanished', he said, but the choice was between 'let[ting] the genocidal slaughter continue' or 'Defining a world order that regards military intervention as a legitimate expedient through which the UN agrees to prevent a greater evil' (15 April). Returning to the theme on 22 April, Young noted that, while 'Douglas Hurd has been a solitary voice, pressing to reconsider the doctrine that internal affairs should never attract outside intervention', such a reconsideration would be required to deal with 'future struggles' in the former Soviet Union and elsewhere. 'Preemption', he concluded, 'is the name of the future game'.

The *Independent* also emphasised the wider implications of the Bosnian war, recalling promises of a New World Order:

> This, remember, was to have been the new era in which the Soviet veto would no longer hobble international action, in which pan-European institutions would come into their own, expanding their civilising influence eastward to teach less-fortunate areas how to shed the outdated concepts of nationalism. (13 April)

Western policy toward Bosnia, however, had failed to live up to these expectations: 'There can seldom have been a worse betrayal of everything the West claims to stand for' (13 April). The shame of failure was taken by the *Independent* as an argument for escalating intervention. Welcoming Nato enforcement of the no-fly zone as an 'achievement that deserves welcome' (2 April) because 'hope attaches to even the smallest advance' (13 April), the paper argued in a series of editorials that the next step must be bombing. Calling for 'bold thoughts on Bosnia', the *Independent* warned that the Serbs had 'deep contempt for the West's inability to assert itself' and urged that plans for bombing them should be 'pursued with more vigour' (15 April). On 19 April the *Independent* announced that it was 'Time to show our anger', and again suggested that, since the Serbs regarded Nato and other international institutions with 'contempt' and had 'run rings around Western diplomats and politicians', it would at some point 'become necessary to fire a shot in anger, since mere threats to do so no longer carry any weight'. By 23 April the *Independent* had decided that 'Only force will do in Bosnia', because 'the only thing that will impress the Serbs is direct experience of Western military power'. Like the *Guardian*, this editorial also floated the possibility of a 'protectorate imposed by UN forces that would take over communications, utilities and borders ... [and] remain a decade or more to rebuild a multi-ethnic democratic state'.

The *Times* also welcomed enforcement of the no-fly zone as 'the first visible military challenge to Serbian power' (9 April) and went on to call for further action. Arguing that Thatcher's 'shame at the West's failure to stop the carnage is widely shared', the *Times* urged 'a dramatic escalation of the West's military commitment' (15 April). The Serbs should be given an ultimatum to sign up to a Western-sponsored peace agreement, backed by 'a willingness to use air power in the event of Serb non-compliance; and, in the event of success, a readiness to position 50,000 or more Nato troops in Bosnia speedily' (15 April). While this editorial suggested the deployment of Nato troops only in the event of a settlement being reached, within days the *Times* was arguing for ground troops to be used offensively. On 17 April the paper suggested that lesser measures, such as lifting the arms embargo, were only a way to avoid the 'critical option', which was 'to declare outright war on Serbia, aimed at enforcing a peace settlement'. No irony appeared to be intended in the suggestion that 'outright war' was the best way to bring about peace. Two days later the *Times* returned to the theme, arguing that the Serbs would 'heed only one language, the roar of a bigger gun' and again suggesting a ground war: 'the bombing of military targets alone may not impress the Serbs, unless it is backed up with a forthright commitment to move on to ground warfare if necessary' (19 April).

Interestingly, arguments about the need to 'impress the Serbs' often seemed to have more to do with preserving the credibility and prestige of the West than with saving the Bosnian Muslims or achieving peace. The *Times* editorial just cited, for example, argued that failure to stop the Serbs would mean that '"the international community", as comfortably conceived by so many, will … be near to extinction' (19 April). Note that it is the extinction of the 'international community', rather than of Bosnian Muslims, which is said to be at stake. Similarly, the same day's editorial in the *Independent* suggested that 'bombing supply lines to Serb forces' was 'the most promising option', even if it did not end the fighting, since 'The Serbian leadership must be given a reason to revise its hitherto justified contempt for the West' (19 April). The *Independent* also argued that Bosnia was 'the first major test' of Europe's 'response to the new environment emerging from the rubble of Communism' (20 April). As such, proving the 'credibility' of Europe or the West sometimes seemed to be the main objective, as when the paper suggested that Western leaders could not pull out of Bosnia 'without doing huge damage to their own credibility and that of the international order they claim to represent, not to mention the suffering people of Bosnia' (23 April). The thinking behind the *Independent*'s position was drawn out by columnist Andrew Marr, who attempted to show that Britain had a direct national interest in Bosnia because turning away would do 'terrible damage to the international order on which, ultimately, we also depend for our security' (20 April). But it sometimes appeared that helping the 'suffering people of Bosnia' was almost an afterthought and that saving Western prestige was the primary concern.

1994: reactions to Nato bombing

The editorial positions established in 1993 on the use of force were maintained in press reaction to Nato bombing of Bosnian Serb forces around Gorazde in April 1994. The *Mail* said the Serbs 'had it to coming to them', but added, in keeping with its earlier emphasis on the 'fateful' quality of greater military commitment: 'let there be no doubt, something momentous has happened … something imponderable in its consequences' (11 April). The *Guardian* said the bombing was 'inevitable' because 'The Serb bluff had to be called', but bemoaned the lack of ground troops, arguing that 'A substantial garrison of the type now proposed could have deterred Serb attacks and saved lives' (11 April). For the *Independent* there was 'no realistic alternative to bombing the Serbs' because they had 'directly challenged the United Nations' (12 April); and for the *Times* 'a mere ceasefire [would] now be insufficient' if 'the UN's credibility is to be restored' (12 April).

Nato airstrikes failed to have the desired effect and instead prompted the Bosnian Serbs to take a number of UN personnel hostage. This induced further soul-searching about the failure of the West. As the *Guardian* noted in an 18 April editorial, 'Sections of the Western political establishment have been working themselves into a fine hysteria of self-loathing'. Dismissing this as a 'silly, self-indulgent response', the *Guardian* argued that 'extended bombing' would be effective only 'if there were thousands of American troops on the ground, so that the path of escalation was clear' (21 April). Since no such deployment seemed likely, however, the *Guardian* advised that the West should simply admit its failure but 'stick in and do everything we can'. Other papers were somewhat prone to the 'hysteria' identified by the *Guardian*. The *Independent* worried about the 'battered credibility of the United Nations, Nato and the United States' (12 April) and described the episode as 'probably the worst of the many defeats in this war that the Western powers have inflicted on themselves' (18 April). For the *Times*, the West was 'on the run' (16 April) and the 'catastrophe in Gorazde' presaged 'appalling consequences for the credibility of the United Nations and of Nato' (19 April). For the *Mail*, the hopes of a 'New World Order' had been 'crushed in the wreckage of Gorazde'. The 'catastrophic weakness of the liberal democracies' meant that 'the world is left rudderless' and 'there is no leadership in the civilised world' (20 April).

As these comments suggest, Western credibility continued to be a major concern. Pondering the 'shame and despair evoked by Western policies', the *Independent* said the Serbs had 'played on the international community like a violin' (18 April) and Marr characterised the clash with the Serbs as 'a contest between a lady missionary and a tiger' (19 April). Arguing that 'the West [had] put its prestige and its security on the line in Bosnia', in the *Mail* Almond said Nato had allowed the Serbs to 'tweak its nose' (12 April). Similarly, the *Mail*'s Ann Leslie bemoaned the West's 'incalculable loss of face' (19 April), describing the Serbs as a 'little Balkan rabble' who were 'making fools of the world' (25 April). Given that bombing had already been tried, however, commentators were somewhat more circumspect about what should be done. The *Mail* was the most downbeat, arguing that while humanitarian aid should continue 'There is little we can do now for the people of Bosnia' (20 April) and that the best available option was to 'lift the Western embargo on the sale of arms to the Moslems' (25 April). The *Guardian*, as noted above, advised the West to 'stick in and do everything we can', but also acknowledged that 'The UN can't stop a war that the Serbs (or the Muslims) decline to end' (21 April). Similarly, the *Independent* wondered whether the UN was 'going down the drain as a peace-keeping organisation' (19 April) and resorted to polling its readers on what would be the best course of action (22 April). The fact that most responses endorsed the option of deciding 'that the Serbs must be defeated' seemed to give the paper some heart, however, and it commissioned an article outlining 'a strategy for peace through intervention' (26 April). Finally, the *Times* proposed that the West 'keep the economic tourniquet on Serbia', deploy further UN troops and continue to pressure Serbia to accept a peace deal, but the emphasis was now as much on diplomacy as on force (19 April).

Criticism of Western policy

As we have seen, the newspapers generally took a highly critical editorial line on Western policy, often denouncing the shameful failure of governments and international institutions, but this criticism tended to be limited by the presumption that further intervention was desirable. Berating Western leaders for their weakness or indecision was usually the accompaniment to calls for tougher action. Other articles voicing criticism of Western policy, making up 22 per cent of all coverage, tended to be similar. This may be illustrated from our 1994 sample, which contained both the greatest number of articles containing criticism (87) and the highest proportion of such articles (28.5 per cent of coverage for the period).[22] Of the 87 articles containing criticism of Western policy in our 1994 sample, 13 were editorials, already discussed above, 21 were comment pieces by columnists or guest writers, and a further 24 articles were reporting criticisms made by others (although in some instances journalists also elaborated on their sources' views). This leaves 29 articles, a third of those voicing criticisms of Western policy, in which journalists aired their own opinions on the news pages.

The *Times* and the *Mail* were the most cautious about blurring the line between news reporting and commentary, but did so occasionally. In the *Mail*, for example, Doughty described UN Special Representative Yasushi Akashi as 'a man floundering and out of his depth', who had been 'made to look weak and foolish' and who showed 'familiar helplessness in the face of Serb bullying'. The point of these loaded descriptions was to urge the West to adopt a tougher attitude: Doughty thought that 'The UN and Nato have again been made to look fools…. All the stirring words about the West's determination to make the Serbs pay for their defiance melted into doubt, confusion and bickering' (25 April). Similarly, in the *Times* Eve-Ann Prentice and Michael Evans, respectively the paper's diplomatic and defence correspondents, argued that 'The West has in many ways seemed like a chess player failing to take account of the likely consequences of the moves it makes and then looking nonplussed when the opposition manoeuvres into a strong position' (18 April) and James Bone described the UN as 'harvesting the bitter fruit of its earlier weakness' (19 April). Such reporting reinforced editorial judgements that Western policy was too weak.

The news pages of the *Guardian* and *Independent* were more often peppered with the opinions and judgements of reporters. In the 18 April 1994 edition of the *Guardian*, for example, Traynor described the siege of Gorazde as 'the biggest humiliation in the war to date for the UN, Nato and the Western powers'; reporting on Clinton's decision not to launch 'punitive or wider military action' beyond the initial airstrikes around Gorazde, Simon Tisdall said that despite 'many humiliations' the Clinton administration had 'reverted … to its preferred Balkan posture: it ducked'; and defence correspondent David Fairhall said the UN had 'opted for the half-hearted use of air strikes' with 'disastrous results'. These reports all implied that tougher military action would be preferable. Similarly, in the *Independent*, Barber described a 'shameful week for the West in Bosnia' (16 April) and in a joint article with the paper's defence correspondent, Christopher Bellamy, said there was 'a question mark over the credibility of Western policy' (18 April). Some days later Andrew Marshall and Emma Daly said 'Western involvement in Bosnia' was characterised by a 'mixture of farce and tragedy' (*Independent*, 25 April).

While most criticism was narrowly circumscribed, in that it assumed Bosnia's problems ought to be solved by further Western intervention, some articles challenged this view and took an anti-interventionist stance. All papers published some articles which argued against Western intervention, but the *Times* offered the most, the majority of them (five out of seven) by columnist Simon Jenkins. Jenkins challenged the views of 'armchair strategists' who were urging greater intervention (14 April 1993), for example describing such commentators as wanting 'somebody else to die to show how much we care' (17 April 1993). Military intervention would 'serve only to satisfy a lust for blood' (24 April 1993), the West 'should never have got into Bosnia' and unless it withdrew 'the war [would] be further prolonged' (20 April 1994). Jenkins argued this case consistently and forcefully, but was a minority voice. Only 17 articles argued against Western intervention in Bosnia – less than 2 per cent of total coverage – and such views were always confined to the comment pages.

It may also be noted that there was very little critical reflection on whether media coverage of the war was adequate. Of a total of 12 articles which included some comment on the role of the Western media, two were simply reports of a complaint by Martin Bell, the BBC's correspondent, that his organisation had 'glamorised war by failing to show the real pain and bloodshed' (*Guardian* and *Times*, both 13 November 1995) and one was a feature praising female reporters for 'writing wrongs' by 'bringing home the human story' of war (*Guardian*, 30 March 1993). There was also some discussion of the role played by the 'armchair generals' and 'laptop bombardiers' in the media (again, Jenkins was a mordant critic).

Conclusions

The Bosnian war tended to be understood as the result of Serbian aggression, contrary to the claim that 'ethnic hatred' explanations dominated media coverage. The preferred explanation, reinforced by the descriptive terms used for Serbian leaders and dissimilar media treatment of 'ethnic cleansing' by different parties to the war, followed the views of official sources and indicated a degree of anti-Serb bias on the part of press commentators and journalists. Proposed solutions to the conflict usually involved urging greater and more forceful Western action, while any fundamental questioning of intervention was confined to the margins.

As we might expect, Western sources were most prominent, with 63.2 per cent of coverage citing at least one such source (any of those in Figure 3.1 apart from Russia), as compared with the 36.4 per cent which cited at least one local source (any of those in Figure 3.2). The relative prominence of Bosnian Muslim sources no doubt reflects the fact that, as several critics have observed, Western reporters tended to congregate in Sarajevo and report from the Bosnian Muslim side, and is also indicative of the greater attention paid to the suffering of some victims rather than others (Gowing 1994, 1997). The prominence of British sources confirms the often-observed tendency of news

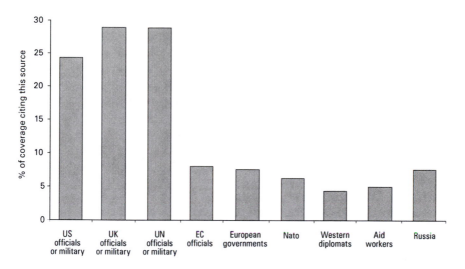

Figure 3.1 Prominence of the different types of international source, Bosnia coverage.

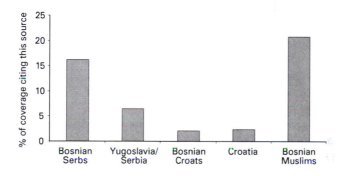

Figure 3.2 Prominence of the different types of local source, Bosnia coverage.

to adopt a national or ethnocentric perspective. A relatively large number of articles adopted a specifically British news angle, usually focusing on the role of the country's military.[23] Such articles: focused on the effects of the war on British troops (for example 'Scenes of brutality scar British forces', in the *Times*, 22 April 1993); assessed developments in terms of British prestige (General Michael Rose, for instance, was the 'Man who restored Britain's good name'; *Guardian*, 12 April 1994); and highlighted clashes between British and local forces ('Coldstream Guards give trigger-happy Serbs a taste of steel'; *Guardian*, 18 April 1994). While no doubt reflecting the prominent role played by British commanders in two of the periods examined (Colonel Bob Stewart in 1993, General Rose in 1994), as well as newspapers' generally national-centred perspective on international events, such stories are perhaps also indicative of a broader trend, whereby events were often presented in terms of a confrontation between the Serbs and the West.

As discussed above in relation to the prescriptions offered in editorial columns, the West was often seen as humiliated and shamed, a preoccupation which sometimes even overshadowed professed concern with saving Bosnian Muslims. Indeed, in some reports of the 1994 Nato airstrikes it sounded as if the West had been the target of the Bosnian Serbs. According to a report in the *Mail* (18 April 1994), for example, 'UN credibility [was] blown away' by 'Serb tanks' and the Bosnian Serbs 'blew apart the West's best peace efforts'. The *Times* discovered the UN's 'credibility ... buried in Gorazde's rubble' (23 April) and the *Independent* described British officials as 'sift[ing] through [the] wreckage of Western policy' (18 April). The *Guardian* reported that 'a savage Serbian onslaught' had 'left UN and Nato credibility in shreds' (25 April) and Woollacott argued that 'the Muslims ... are in effect bystanders' because 'This fight is about the effectiveness of the UN' (12 April). Although particularly marked in relation to the confrontation over Gorazde, similar formulations were also evident in other periods. In 1993, for example: the international community was said to face 'the effective destruction of its entire Bosnian strategy' (*Guardian*, 17 April 1993); the UN was described as 'tak[ing] a beating over Bosnia' (*Independent*, 10 April); and the *Times* wondered whether Britain's relationship with America might 'join the long casualty list of the Balkans conflict' (23 April). This view of the war as a struggle to assert Western credibility could be used as an argument for tougher action, but it was also a perspective shared by influential sources. UN commander Philippe Morillon said an attack on Srebrenica would constitute 'an attack on the entire world' (*Times*, 19 April 1993) or 'a declaration of war on the world' (*Mail*, 23 April), for example; US Secretary of State Warren Christopher said the fall of Gorazde would be a 'blow to American and UN credibility' (*Times*, 7 April 1994); and America's UN ambassador Madeleine Albright said that events in Bosnia went 'beyond war to the brutalisation of law and civilisation itself' (*Mail*, 20 April 1994).

As suggested in our discussion of the use of the term 'ethnic cleansing', while official Western sources were evidently able to influence coverage, journalists also sought to shape how national and international actors understood and responded to the conflict. It is difficult to unpick the patterns of mutual influence retrospectively, but from the start of the war, when Western recognition of Bosnia cast Serbia as an international aggressor, there was a complementary relationship between the perspectives of the media and Western officials.

CHAPTER 4

Rwanda, 1994

Around 800,000[1] people were killed in Rwanda between 6 April 1994, when President Juvenal Habyarimana was assassinated, and 18 July 1994, when the Rwandan Patriotic Front (RPF) declared victory and formed a new government. Some 10,000–50,000 Hutu supporters of opposition parties were targeted, but the vast majority of those killed were civilians from the minority Tutsi community. The perpetrators of the violence included state forces such as the Presidential Guard, political militia groups such as the Interahamwe, and Hutu civilians. There was already a United Nations presence in Rwanda in April 1994, but that month the UN decided to reduce its forces from 2,500 to 270 following the killing of 10 Belgian troops. In May, as the violence continued, the UN Security Council agreed a larger international force to protect civilians, but its deployment was endlessly delayed. Instead, the UN sanctioned a unilateral French military intervention, Operation Turquoise, which established a 'safe area' in part of the country at the end of June. On 18 July the RPF, an organisation composed mainly of Rwandan Tutsis who had been exiled to Uganda, declared victory, having captured the capital, Kigali, and taken control of most of the country. International attention now focused on the huge refugee camps which had developed on Rwanda's borders. Around two million people fled the violence and the RPF advance, most taking refuge in Zaire (Democratic Republic of the Congo), but with substantial numbers also in Tanzania and Burundi. A cholera epidemic among refugees prompted further calls for international action, but since the camps also housed the remnants of the defeated Hutu regime responsible for the mass killings, humanitarian aid increasingly came to be seen as problematic. In autumn 1996 the new government established by the RPF intervened to close the camps, forcing most refugees to repatriate.

Context

Much discussion of Rwanda focuses on how the mass killings of 1994 should be explained: as systematic genocide or as an outbreak of spontaneous 'tribal' violence. In the literature there is near-universal agreement that it should be understood as genocide, but many critics have found that 'tribal' explanations were preferred in media reporting. This point is most often made in relation to early coverage (Livingston and Eachus 2000: 218), although a study of British (mainly television) reporting during 1996 and 1997 suggests that, while explanations improved somewhat, ideas about 'tribalism' persisted even in later coverage (Beattie et al. 1999: 260, 266). Commentators have suggested a number of reasons for this, including the fact that, with experienced regional correspondents in South Africa to cover the elections there, most reporting in April 1994 was done in difficult conditions by 'parachutists' who had less experience and specialist knowledge (Dowden 1995b: 87). The use of stock ideas about 'tribalism' probably reflected broader thinking at the time about the renewed importance of 'ethnicity' in the post-Cold War world (Livingston and Eachus 2000: 215) as well as established stereotypes about Africa (Philo et al. 1999: 219–20).

Whatever the reasons for its adoption, the 'tribalism' framework was misleading. The difference between Hutu and Tutsi cannot be understood in 'tribal' or 'ethnic' terms, since the two groups occupy the same territory and share a common language, customs and religious traditions. As Mahmood Mamdani (2001: 42) observes, even in the specialist literature, Western discussion of the distinction has been shaped, and often distorted, by colonial or anti-colonial attitudes, some writers emphasising differences, others sameness. This problem has been further complicated by the fact that the former emphasis is now identified with the old Rwandan regime and the latter with the new government established by the RPF (Pottier 1995). Nevertheless, there is broad agreement that, although a social division between ruling Tutsis and subject Hutus had already been established by the late 19th century, it was the arrival of Europeans, and particularly the system of colonial rule organised by Belgium in the 1920s and 1930s, which racialised Hutu and Tutsi identities. Whereas in the past there was some possibility of social mobility (becoming a Tutsi through accumulation of wealth), the system of identity cards introduced by the Belgian authorities fixed these categories. The Tutsis were seen by Europeans as a non-indigenous and superior race, who had had a civilising influence on the backward Hutus and whose continuing privileges were essential to maintaining order. There was certainly conflict between Hutu and Tutsi in Rwanda (and in neighbouring Burundi) in the past, including large-scale massacres – notably in the period around the country's achievement of independence in 1962 and again in the early 1970s – but this was the product of post-colonial politics rather than of centuries-old tribal hatred. As Mamdani (2001: 131) argues, by the time of independence, both groups had internalised the racial identities of colonialism, using these as the basis of their claim to power – either as a 'traditional' privilege which ought to be restored, or as the birthright of the truly 'indigenous' population. Philo et al. (1999: 221) suggest that news coverage failed to take account of this history, a problem which they attribute to a reliance on official Western sources, who were 'unlikely to dwell on the misdeeds of the former colonial powers'.

As we have seen in other chapters, questions of explanation are almost always linked to prescriptions for action. Part of the objection to the 'tribal' framework is that it 'contributed to international indifference and inaction, and hence the crime itself', in the words of the Joint Evaluation of Emergency Assistance to Rwanda (JEEAR 1996: study II, section 4.3). It has been argued that an emphasis on incomprehensible and irrational hatreds depicted Rwanda as different and distant (Myers et al. 1996; Wall 1997), making it easier for Western governments, particularly the US, not to respond (Livingston and Eachus 2000: 226). US officials avoided using the term 'genocide' publicly – despite reportedly characterising the killing as such in internal discussions (Peterson 2000: 295) – and according to Samantha Power (2004: 9) this in turn made journalists reluctant to use it. A now declassified internal US Defense Department discussion document from 1 May 1994, for example, raised the issue of whether to call for an international investigation of 'possible violations of the genocide convention', but warned: 'Be Careful.... Genocide finding could commit [the US government] to actually "do something"'.[2] In fact Secretary of State Warren Christopher did call the killing 'genocide' on 21 May 1994, but the UN force which was agreed in principle around the same time was subject to interminable delay, mainly due to obstruction by the US.

A related criticism is that even when Western governments and media gave greater attention to Rwanda, during the huge refugee exodus in July 1994 and the ensuing cholera epidemic in the camps in Zaire, their response was, at best, inadequate. On 22 July, shortly after the RPF's victory, US President Bill Clinton announced an 'immediate and massive' aid operation, but critics complained that this brought relief not only to refugees but also to the perpetrators of genocide who had fled the country. For some commentators, indeed, the estimated two million people in the camps were not genuine refugees at all and the international response was 'counterfeit humanitarianism' (de Waal 1997: 195). Western governments later came to share similar views; for instance, British Development Minister Clare Short argued that 'humanitarian assistance strengthened the evil forces which had brought about the genocide in Rwanda' (quoted in Fox 2000: 24) and Madeleine Albright, America's UN ambassador at the time of the crisis, condemned the use of humanitarian aid to 'sustain armed camps or to support genocidal killers' (quoted in Gourevitch 2000: 350). The experience intensified debate among aid agencies over whether the traditional neutrality of humanitarianism should be abandoned (Halvorsen 2000; Fox 2000, 2002; Terry 2002), a discussion which paralleled contemporary arguments about media neutrality.

With the onset of the refugee crisis, critics have found that media coverage did become orientated to encouraging international involvement, but have objected that, in effect, too much sympathy was shown, as distancing reports of 'tribal' violence were replaced by coverage which simplistically called for aid but still failed to explain events. Greg Philo et al., for example, object that news reports describing refugees as fleeing 'from killing' were 'unclear in the sense that the Hutu refugees were fleeing from the *consequences* of a genocide which they had themselves perpetrated. They were afraid of retribution for the acts which they had committed.' The argument is that, having justified non-intervention, the media now justified the wrong sort of intervention (Philo et al. 1999: 215, 226). For some analysts, the problems with this phase of the coverage were due to naivety or practical considerations; Livingston and Eachus (2000: 223), for instance, suggest that when the scale of the killing became obvious news organisations wanted to cover it, but access to the refugees was easier. Others, such as Mel McNulty (1999: 268, 270), argue that the media colluded in Western governments' pursuit of a 'neo-colonial' agenda in the region. Similar criticisms were made of the earlier Operation Turquoise: while the French presented this as a purely humanitarian inter-vention, many suspected that it was designed to prop up the remnants of the old regime, long supported by France, and to prevent an outright RPF victory (Callamard 2000; Prunier 2000).

Despite general acceptance that the killings of 1994 should be understood as genocide, a few writers have drawn attention to problems which arise from this framework, or some versions of it, in terms of both explanatory blind-spots and prescriptive implications. The massacres have been exten-sively documented, and evidence of official planning and preparation for the extermination of Tutsi civilians has been gathered by journalists, human rights groups and others (Keane 1995; Prunier 1995; African Rights 1995; Human Rights Watch 1999; Melvern 2000). What seems more difficult to explain is the extensive civilian participation: indeed, as Mamdani (2001: 8, 18) observes, many analysts have 'shied away from this troubling fact'. Whereas ideas about spontaneous 'tribal' or 'ethnic' hatred downplay the extent of direction and planning from above, accounts which emphasise top-down organisation have more difficulty explaining popular participa-tion in the killings. Perhaps the most common explanation offered is that Rwandan culture produced citizens who were so indoctrinated with hatred and so obedient to authority that they obeyed orders to kill (Prunier 1995: 57, 245; Gourevitch 2000: 23). As some critics have pointed out, however, this explanation is not only implausible, since it overlooks evidence of 'a growing defiance of authority' in early 1990s Rwanda (Mamdani 2001: 199–200), but it also implies a 'cultural' version of the very tribalist framework it seeks to avoid. Claims of 'ethnic difference' between Hutu and Tutsi are discounted in this approach, but the cultural difference of Rwandan society as a whole is emphasised. Similarly, when the NGO African Rights characterises 'Rwandanese society' as suffering from a 'pathological condition', or when Fergal Keane describes 'tens of thousands' of Rwandans as 'infected … by an anti-Tutsi psychosis' (both quoted in Collins 1998: 6), the invocation of mental illness brings this type of explanation closer to the idea of irrational ethnic hatreds than might first appear. Although explaining the massacres as genocide would seem to imply a political understanding of motivations and actions, this is not always the case.

A related criticism is that, in their concern to confirm that the killings should be characterised as genocide, some analysts tend to abstract it from its context. In particular, there is a tendency to downplay any relationship between the genocide and the civil war which was fought between the government and the RPF from October 1990. Alain Destexhe (1995: 68), for example, maintains that 'genocide has nothing to do with war'; and Philip Gourevitch (2000: 98) argues that 'although the genocide coincided with the war, its organization and implementation were quite distinct from the war effort'. Failure to make this separation is seen as a failure to put the killings in their proper moral context, yet the civil war had a close bearing on what followed. The rapid expansion of the army (from 5,000 to over 30,000) and the organisation of armed civilian 'self-defence forces' after 1990, for example, were in direct response to the conflict with the RPF. Furthermore, each RPF offensive produced greater waves of internally displaced refugees – around 80,000 in 1990, 350,000 in 1992, and 950,000 following its February 1993 offensive – so that by 1994 one in every seven Rwandans was displaced. Compounding Rwanda's already severe economic problems, the successive refugee crises created 'widespread hunger and starvation' (Mamdani 2001: 187, 203, 206). It seems likely, in other words, that the willingness of many Rwandans to join in with the killing in 1994 had more to do with their experience of civil war over the previous three years than with any cultural peculiarity.

A third, again closely related, criticism is that the negative impact of international intervention prior to 1994 tends to be underestimated or ignored by most analysts. The RPF's 1990 invasion was repulsed with French help, but although France had been a staunch supporter of Habyarimana's one-party state during the Cold War, Western priorities in Africa had already begun to change. The watchword was now 'democratisation', as Rwanda came under pressure from Western donors and international financial institutions to allow the formation of opposition parties, and to reach a compromise with the RPF through a peace process which culminated in the 1993 Arusha Accords. The international pressure for reform in Rwanda is generally seen as positive, even by writers explicitly seeking to emphasise the negative role of West (Melvern 2000; Power 2001), but some commentators, particularly Barrie Collins, have highlighted its divisive effects as a key factor in pushing Rwandan society further toward violence. From the perspective of the Habyarimana regime, the power-sharing arrangements envisaged by the Accords promised to reward the aggressive strategy of the RPF with vastly disproportionate influence under a proposed new government. The RPF, meanwhile, must have been acutely aware that democratisation would eventually leave it as a minority party with no hope of overall electoral success. Although they signed the Accords, both sides were preparing for conflict (Collins 2002: 163–70; see also Musabyimana 1995: 95–6; Mugabe 2000). The recent experience of Burundi – where the democratisation process collapsed in a serious outbreak of violence in which over 50,000 people were killed and 200,000 fled to Rwanda following the October 1993 assassination of the elected Hutu president of Burundi – no doubt also led many Rwandans to expect further conflict. When Habyarimana was killed, along with the new Burundian president, on 6 April 1994 it is not surprising that many took it as the signal that the moment of confrontation had arrived (see Mann 2005: 470).

Similar arguments can be extended to the later refugee crisis and eventual closure of the camps. Analyses which emphasise Hutu cultural difference and deference to authority, and which take little account of the circumstances of civil war and international intervention which polarised Rwandan society, tend to see the refugees in a wholly negative light. Either they are seen as collectively guilty, as in the comments by de Waal and Philo et al. cited above, or they are seen as in thrall to the organisers of the genocide, who encouraged people to flee and then tried, through intimidation and propaganda, to prevent returns. As Fiona Terry (2002: 174) argues, however, contrary to the 'generalized notion that all the camp inhabitants were brainwashed "hostages" of the deposed government', the actions of the RPF had given refugees 'a genuine reason to flee'. A UN investigation led by Robert Gersony uncovered evidence of 'clearly systematic murders and persecution of the Hutu population in certain parts of the country' carried out by the RPF. According to Human Rights Watch (1999), Gersony's team estimated that 25,000 to 45,000 people had been killed by the RPF between April and August 1994, including women, children, the elderly and the handicapped. Reluctant to undermine the new RPF government, the UN suppressed the report, claiming it did not exist and forbidding Gersony himself to speak about it. As the Joint Evaluation of Emergency Assistance to Rwanda commented:

> it appears that some of those involved in ensuring [the] implementation [of the repatriation strategy] were prepared to suppress evidence that all was not well in Rwanda, also that the fears of the refugees about their safety on returning may well have been justified. (JEEAR 1996: study III, chapter 6)[3]

With little credence given to their reasons for flight, the reluctance of refugees to return to Rwanda was taken as evidence of their guilt, or their allegiance to those who were guilty. The RPF, meanwhile, tended to be seen as a benign force, to be praised for ending the genocide. Yet, as Human Rights Watch (1999) notes, RPF strategy in 1994 was designed to secure overall military victory, rather than to rescue the maximum number of Tutsi civilians, and the RPF strongly opposed UN proposals at the end of April 1994 to send 'a larger peacekeeping force … with a broader mandate to protect civilians'. According to Wayne Madsen (1999: 125), the US officially began providing military training to the RPF in January 1994, and indirect training and support began earlier, when the organisation was exiled in Uganda. RPF leader Paul Kagame interrupted a training course at Fort Leavenworth in order to assume command of the 1990 offensive. US reluctance to intervene in Rwanda 1994 is often seen largely as a consequence of America's recent experience in Somalia (Power 2001), but it may also indicate that the US had calculated that the best outcome would be a decisive RPF victory. The 1 May 1994 Defense Department document quoted earlier also stated plainly what US policy was at the time: 'sanction the ongoing aid to the RPF'.

When the RPF's new regime later invaded Zaire and attacked the refugee camps, it did so with US approval. At a meeting of regional African leaders in October 1996, Secretary of State Christopher called for the camps to be closed, effectively encouraging the attacks on what Washington described as 'centres of terrorism'; and the US provided training to the RPF military, supposedly simply to 'professionalise' it, but which in fact included instruction in psychological warfare and special forces operations (*Washington Post*, 16 August 1997, 14 July 1998). The largest camp, Mugunga, which had already absorbed thousands of refugees fleeing attacks on other sites, was shelled for six hours on 15 November 1996 with heavy mortars and artillery, and mass killings continued over several months as the refugees were, in the words of Refugees International, 'herded and hunted' across Zaire. By April 1997 it was estimated that 10,000 refugees had been killed since the previous November, and UN official Roberto Garreton reported 'indubitable evidence of mass graves and massacres' (Refugees International 1997: 82, 58). Some humanitarian organisations continued to highlight the plight of around 700,000 who had not been repatriated, but the US provided over-flight data which drastically underestimated the number who had fled. Announcing the data at the US embassy in Kigali, the American military briefer referred to the refugees as 'targets of opportunity' and identified some groups as Interahamwe militia, despite having no way of knowing this; some aid workers believe that information on the location of these 'missing' refugees was passed to the RPF government and its allies in Zaire (Gowing 1998: 59–60).

By this stage, however, many journalists (and aid workers) had come to regret their earlier sympathy for the refugees. According to Oxfam's director of emergencies, Nick Stockton, many journalists failed to question the low estimate of the number of missing refugees, and thereby gave the misinformation a 'legitimacy that US official information managers could barely have dreamed of' (quoted in Gowing 1998: 42). Furthermore, he argues, journalists helped to legitimise the attacks on the camps:

> some of the best British correspondents who knew the region and its politics rapidly promoted a consensus that here, at last, was the chance to deal with an entirely murderous group [the Hutus] who had been foolishly succoured by aid. (Quoted in Gowing 1998: 36)

The criticisms of earlier coverage for failing to associate the refugees with the perpetrators of genocide had an effect on later reporting (Beattie et al. 1999: 231). Ironically, a concern to adopt a more 'morally correct' position appears to have legitimised attacks on refugees, as 'all Hutus were often implicitly written off as "killers" or "extremists"' (Gowing 1998: 40–1). The longer-term destabilisation of the region which the RPF offensive, carried out in concert with local rebels seeking to overthrow the Zairian regime, helped to precipitate is outside the scope of this study, but the November 1996 attacks on the refugee camps are important to consider from the point of view of the media's role. Arguments will no doubt continue over whether a different style of reporting could have influenced the policies of Western governments in April 1994, although this seems unlikely. In 1996, however, Gowing's pioneering study suggests that the media played an important role in legitimising and justifying the attacks on the refugees.

Questions

The main questions addressed in this chapter are:

- How were the mass killings of 1994 explained? How far did explanations improve or change over time?
- How were the refugees portrayed? Did perceptions of the refugees change over time?
- What solutions were proposed and how was Western involvement evaluated?

The core samples for this case study are the two four-week periods spanning Habyarimana's assassination on 6 April and the victory of the RPF on 18 July 1994. Given the importance, in terms of both Western involvement and changes in media reporting, of the refugee crisis and eventual closure of the camps, a sample of coverage from this later period was also included: 1–30 November 1996 was chosen, since the main movement of refugees back to Rwanda occurred mid-month, with the attack on Mugunga camp. In order to provide continuity, a sample from 1995 was also included: following the procedure set out in Chapter 3, the period chosen was the same as that for the first sample (30 March–27 April), thereby incorporating the first anniversary of Habyarimana's death and the onset of violence. Attention was also focused on Rwanda during this period both because of renewed violence in Burundi, which led tens of thousands of the Rwandan refugees there to seek sanctuary in Tanzania, and because of the new Rwandan regime's forcible closure of camps for 'internally displaced' Hutus inside Rwanda. Of particular significance was an RPF attack on Kibeho camp, which left between 4,000 and 8,000 dead.[4] The total coverage[5] for the periods selected was as shown in Table 4.1. The overall quantitative pattern for the first two sample periods conforms to that found in US coverage (Livingston and Eachus 2000) and in British television coverage (Philo et al. 1999), in that there was a substantially greater quantity in July

Table 4.1 Numbers of articles about Rwanda

	Habyarimana assassination (30 March– 27 April 1994)	RPF victory (27 June– 25 July 1994)	First anniversary (30 March– 27 April 1995)	Closure of camps (1 November– 30 November 1996)	Totals
Guardian	27	57	27	50	161
Independent	28	41	17	49	135
Times	21	30	14	64	129
Mail	7	11	3	N/A[a]	21
Totals	83	139	61	163	446

[a] The *Mail's* coverage for November 1996 was not available on the LexisNexis or ProQuest databases.

1994 than in April, and no coverage at all before the 6 April assassination of Habyarimana. The *Mail*'s coverage for November 1996 was not available on the LexisNexis or ProQuest databases.

Explanations

Articles attempting to explain the violence in Rwanda accounted for 9.2 per cent of all coverage examined. Overall, 17 articles took the causes of violence as their main focus, and a further 24 articles mentioned causes in passing.[6] This echoes the findings of Philo et al.'s (1999: 219–20) study of television news on Rwanda. The limited quantity of explanatory material is not exceptional: the proportion of overall coverage devoted to explanations is comparable to that for Bosnia, and the proportion in our April 1994 sample (25.3 per cent) is similar to that for Somalia. As we would predict, most explanations appeared in April 1994 (21 articles, eight of them taking the causes of violence as their main focus), and far fewer in the later sample periods.[7] The *Guardian* and *Independent* offered the greatest amount of explanatory material, respectively carrying 16 and 14 such articles, as compared with only five in the *Mail* and six in the *Times*. The quantity for the *Times* is strikingly low, given that the paper devoted far greater attention to Rwanda than did the *Mail*: explanatory articles accounted for only 4.7 per cent of total coverage in the *Times*, the lowest of any of the papers examined.[8]

Tribal war

'Tribal' explanations were relatively prominent in April 1994, appearing in just over half of all explanatory articles during this period.[9] Sometimes this view was attributed to sources, as when the *Times* reported that UN officials feared a 'new eruption of tribal violence' (7 April), or when the *Guardian* quoted a business colleague of Britain's former honorary consul as saying 'This sort of thing has happened before.… All the problems are tribal' (16 April). More often, journalists themselves adopted the idea in news reports and features. The *Mail* reported 'bloody tribal violence' between people 'locked in conflict for decades' (9 April), for example, and in the *Independent* Robert Block suggested that Rwanda and Burundi 'straddle perhaps Africa's most gory ethnic faultline', describing their histories as 'marked by ethnic hatred and tribal violence' (8 April). Both the *Independent* and the *Times* also offered 'tribal' explanations in their editorial columns, the former arguing that 'the ancient enmity between the Hutus and Tutsis, which is at the heart of the conflict in Rwanda, is beyond hope of early resolution', and the latter describing 'a history of slaughter between the minority Tutsi and the majority Hutu tribes', which had given rise to 'bloodthirsty mobs fuelled by atavistic enmity' (both 11 April).

Even setting aside the fact that the distinction between Hutu and Tutsi cannot be understood in terms of conventional ideas about 'tribal' or 'ethnic' difference, invoking notions of 'atavistic enmity' or 'ethnic faultlines' is not much of an explanation. Rather, it implies that conflict is simply a given – an inevitable product of difference. This was illustrated in Geoffrey Wheatcroft's article on what he perceived as a resurgence of 'tribal conflict' since the end of the Cold War, discussed in Chapter 3 for its comments on Bosnia. Regarding Rwanda, he argued that the 'veritable bloodbath ... presages the breakdown of the continent and the final collapse of all the bright hopes for "decolonisation" of a generation ago' (*Mail*, 11 April). Much like his argument that communist repression had contained ethnic conflict in the Eastern bloc, Wheatcroft suggested that in Africa 'as long as the age of empire lasted, tribalism was held in check', but that after the withdrawal of the colonial powers 'the old tensions and rivalries flared up'. The attainment of modern statehood, he argued, was 'always a fantasy' for Africa because the territories carved out by colonists 'bore no relation whatsoever to the boundaries between peoples, or tribes, or ethnic groups'. This was inaccurate as a description of the case in hand, since the kingdoms of Rwanda and Burundi, each populated by both Hutus and Tutsis, pre-dated colonial rule, but Wheatcroft's intention was clear: to suggest that the primal forces of tribalism had overwhelmed modern political settlements, either in a sudden post-Cold War explosion in the case of former communist countries, or in a slow disintegrative process in former African colonies. In this perspective, tribal hatred festers beneath the surface of 'sophisticated modern civilisation', and different conflicts are all understood as 'a recrudescence of something old, of something deep inside human nature'. Such an approach begs the question of why violence should have erupted when it did. Only one explanatory article adopting the 'tribal' framework attempted to address this question, and it did so by bringing in other factors as contributory causes. This article, an obituary of Habyarimana in the *Independent*, framed Rwanda in terms of 'the ... disease [of] perpetual ethnic conflict between the once dominant minority Tutsi tribe and the majority Hutu', but it also noted that colonial rule had intensified this division and suggested that 'renewed tribal tensions' had been precipitated by 'the dire state of the economy, exacerbated by the collapse of coffee prices' (8 April).

The acknowledgement in this last article that colonialism was at least partly to blame for sharpening divisions is worthy of further comment. Wheatcroft's argument implied that imperial rule had been a necessary check on tribal hatreds in Africa, a view which was echoed in another *Mail* commentary, from 23 July 1994, by Myles Harris, a London doctor who had spent some years working in Africa. Contending that the 'hatreds run deep and far back into unrecorded history', and that the 'two tribes ... have been killing each other for as long as anybody can remember', Harris argued that 'this frightfulness has been going on all over the continent since the colonial powers fled it so precipitously in the Sixties'. For Harris, it was not imperialism but decolonisation that led to violence and 'savagery': previously, Africa had been 'flourishing under colonial rule'. These views, however, did not appear to be typical. More often, the colonial era was viewed in a wholly negative light in the articles sampled for this study. In the *Guardian*, for example, Victoria Brittain wrote that 'The Belgian colonialists, like all other colonial powers, ruled by playing on ethnic stereotypes and exacerbating the sense of ethnic difference' (28 June 1994) and a 23 July 1994 editorial observed that the 'meddling colonial powers, Germany, France and Belgium, made a malevolent hash of Rwanda, with their social engineering and military calculations'. In the *Times*, Matthew Parris described Belgium as 'one of the greediest, nastiest, most corrupt and reckless little powers in history', with a 'direct responsibility for the mess her rapacity left in Zaire, Rwanda and Burundi' (11 April 1994) and in the same edition of the *Mail* as Wheatcroft's commentary a news report explaining the problem as tribal also noted that the 'minority Tutsi ... were promoted into an elite by Belgian colonists' (11 April). Across all the coverage examined, 21 articles mentioned Rwanda's colonial past as a negative factor in exacerbating division and conflict, almost twice the number of explanatory articles which adopted a 'tribal' framework.

While the idea of 'tribal war' was clearly important in the April 1994 coverage, it was far less prominent in the later periods examined and had disappeared by November 1996. In fact, the only explanatory article framing the causes of violence in terms of 'tribal hatreds' outside our April 1994 sample was Harris's comment piece in the *Mail* quoted above. A similar pattern emerges if we look at the far greater number of articles (183 in total) which included a description of the violence. These were mostly news reports which, while they did not offer any sort of developed explanation, implied a particular understanding of the violence through their choice of descriptive terms. Typical examples of 'tribal' descriptions in early articles were Mark Huband's *Guardian* report on 11 April 1994 mentioning 'a four-day tribal bloodbath', 'tribal fighting', 'tribal slaughter' and 'an orgy of killing by ... Hutu tribesmen'; or a Reuters report in the *Independent* (8 April 1994) which characterised the killings in terms of 'tribal violence', 'continuing tribal slaughter' and 'another outbreak of ... ethnic slaughter'. As shown in Figure 4.1, the theme of 'tribal war' was prominent as a description of violence in April 1994 (accounting for 16 out of 39 descriptive articles in this period), but sharply declined thereafter and disappeared entirely by the final period of our study.

Considering coverage overall, ideas about 'tribal war' were not dominant, occurring in 11 out of 41 explanatory articles (only one more than the number which explained the killing as genocide), and in only 23 of the further 183 articles containing a description of the violence (as compared with 121 describing it as genocide). Even in April 1994, the 'tribal' framework was not as overwhelming as might be expected from the literature. For one thing, there was a greater variety of descriptions than in the other periods. Six of the 16 articles describing the violence in terms of 'civil war' occurred in April 1994, as did seven of the 12 articles containing descriptions classified as 'mixed'. In most cases, mixed descriptions in April 1994 (though not in later periods) contained the idea of 'tribal violence' but also suggested that the killing was politically motivated. In the *Guardian* (13 April 1994), for example, John Palmer wrote of 'inter-tribal fighting', but also noted that 'much of the fighting in Kigali appears to have been among Hutu factions which are either for or against negotiations

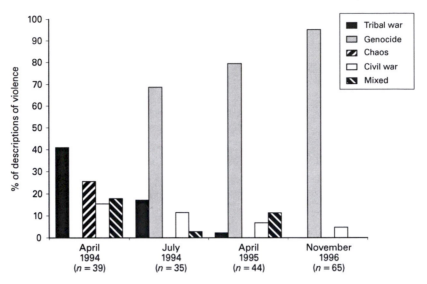

Figure 4.1 Descriptions of violence by period, Rwanda coverage.

to establish a multi-ethnic democracy with the Tutsi opposition'. Similarly, the *Independent* reported 'tribal and political butchery' (9 April) and in the *Times* Catherine Bond said it was 'impossible for outsiders to identify who is murdering who' but suggested that 'most of the killing is probably not random but carried out along ethnic and political lines' (12 April). Such articles were attempting to distinguish different sorts of violence in a fluid and confusing situation. Towards the end of April, for instance, Lindsey Hilsum reported that killings had initially been political, targeting 'both Hutu and Tutsi politicians and supporters of parties opposed to the late president', but now, she suggested, 'the massacres appear to be purely ethnic' and were organised by 'local officials … working with the police and military' (*Guardian*, 26 April).

A further important feature of descriptions of violence in April 1994 was that around a quarter of them (10 out of 39) emphasised ideas of generalised chaos or anarchy, as in a 9 April *Times* report of 'gunmen … killing and looting, as anarchy in the Rwandan capital deepened'. Similarly, in the *Guardian* Hilsum reported that Kigali had 'descended into chaos', quoting an unnamed diplomat who described 'Various clans … murdering others' in a process of 'general score settling' (8 April). Hilsum's report is a particularly striking example because she later co-authored a study which was sharply critical of confused early news coverage (Philo et al. 1999). Although such criticism is most often aimed at journalists' unthinking use of misleading ideas of 'tribal hatred', this was clearly not the only factor which gave rise to confusion. It would seem that even experienced and capable reporters produced confusing reports of the violence because the situation itself was genuinely confusing and chaotic. In another report, on 16 April, Hilsum highlighted contextual political factors, such as the stalled implementation of the Arusha Accords, past political assassinations and the recent arming of civilians, and described the current violence in terms of both battles between rebels and government forces and an 'orgy of ethnic violence between the majority Hutu and minority Tutsi tribes'. She also continued to characterise the violence as an 'anarchic situation' and 'an orgy of violence'. As Scott Peterson (2000: 253) admits, his own early reports 'described a "free-for-all" and "chaos"' because he simply could not tell what was happening.

A final factor which should be taken into account in assessing the importance of 'tribal' explanations is that a few articles explicitly challenged this framework. There were only six such articles in our sample, but four of them appeared in April 1994 (the other two, both in the *Independent*, were from November 1996). A feature article in the *Independent* (22 April 1994) on the escape from Rwanda of Oxfam representative Anne Mackintosh described her as 'insist[ing] that the fighting is not tribal'. Mackintosh was quoted as saying that 'It is not nearly as simple or as mindless as tribal fighting'. Rather, she suggested, the violence was 'unleashed' by those in the government and army who 'stood to lose from the [Arusha] peace agreement', and was largely perpetrated by 'young men who are unemployed, disaffected, and poorly educated ... no-hopers with a kind of bottled-up hatred of the have-nots for the haves'. Similarly, the *Guardian* (23 April) quoted an 'aid agency source' as saying: 'This is not a tribal war ... the causes of this conflict are colonial and social. To refer to it as a tribal war suits the purposes of those who want to turn their backs on Rwanda and leave it to cut its own throat'. The rejection of a 'tribal' explanation on the grounds that it justified non-intervention also featured in two further *Guardian* articles in this period. One was a brief item entitled '"Non-Ethnic" Killings', about Amnesty International's call for intervention to stop the violence, which reported the organisation as having 'said the killings were mistakenly characterised as ethnic infighting' (27 April). More significantly, the other article was an editorial, on 8 April 1994, which argued that 'it is important from afar not to explain this away as the result of inevitable "ethnic savagery" nor to regard it as an excuse for not getting more involved'.

Overall, while there was a misleading emphasis on 'tribal hatred' in early reporting, this was not an overwhelming theme in the coverage. Rather, there were a variety of explanations and descriptions, an element of genuine confusion about how events should be understood, and even in early coverage a few voices challenging the 'tribal' framework. It may be that, in much the same way as the extent of 'ethnic' explanations in coverage of Bosnia appears to have been exaggerated, if critics are apt to overstate the significance of 'tribal' explanations in coverage of Rwanda this is in part because they wish to suggest that a different style of reporting could have pressured Western governments to respond more forcefully. By July 1994 a different explanation had already become the dominant one: that the killings were genocide.

Genocide

Whereas all except one of the explanatory articles adopting the 'tribal' framework appeared in April 1994, the first articles explaining the violence as genocide did not appear until our June/July 1994 sample. The term 'genocide' was occasionally used in April 1994, but not in a way which contradicted 'ethnic' or 'tribal' explanations. When Richard Dowden wrote of 'the genocide of Hutu and Tutsi', for example, this was simply another way of describing what he also referred to as mutual 'ethnic hatred' and a 'pathological rivalry between the two ethnic groups' (*Independent*, 11 April 1994). Similarly, a news item in the *Times* mentioned 'past genocides' but in the context of reporting current 'tribal violence' (7 April); and in the *Guardian* Jerry Gray said that there had been 'genocidal orgies' in the past, but understood the present violence as part of a 'centuries-old African feud' which was fuelled by competition for land (12 April). The 10 articles explaining the killing as genocide were not evenly distributed across the coverage: six of them appeared in our June/July 1994 sample, and all 10 were from either the *Guardian* or the *Independent*, which carried six and four such articles, respectively. The difference across periods, with only three explanatory articles of this type in April 1995 and one in November 1996, did not mean that this framework declined over time, since in other articles, as shown in Figure 4.1, genocide became increasingly common as a description of the violence. More probably, an understanding of the killings as genocide was firmly established by the time of the first anniversary, whereas in July 1994 writers felt they had to argue for this explanation against rival interpretations. The difference between papers is probably also less significant than it appears. As shown in Figure 4.2, descriptions of the violence in other articles were similar in all four publications, and the absence of explanatory articles framing the violence as genocide in the *Times* and *Mail* is more a reflection of the very low quantity of explanatory articles of any sort in these two papers.

The main point made by articles explaining the killing as genocide in June/July 1994 was that the violence was planned and systematic, rather than spontaneous and chaotic. By 28 June, Victoria Brittain was able to suggest in the *Guardian* that 'No one can any longer doubt that the extermination of the Tutsis was planned', for example. Other articles described 'systematic operations to hunt down and kill Tutsis' (*Independent*, 1 July) and 'government … orchestration' of the genocide (*Guardian*, 9 July). This point continued to be emphasised in explanatory articles from later periods, as when a *Guardian* editorial on 24 April 1995 argued that 'it remains wrong to regard the Rwandan genocide as a spontaneous ethnic war'. The issues identified earlier, of how to explain the relationship between the genocide and the civil war, and how to explain popular participation in the killing, were very rarely addressed, perhaps not surprisingly given the small quantity of explanatory material overall. Only one article explaining the killing as genocide from our July 1994 sample tackled the first of these issues. In a piece for the *Guardian* based on interviews with Hutu refugees, Hilsum struggled to understand how 'Hutu ideology justifies genocide' (11 July 1994). The interviewees – two educated young men, and another man whose Tutsi wife and mother had been killed – seemed unapologetic about the killing and maintained that it had been justified. Citing a Rwandan proverb, 'You would do to us what we are going to

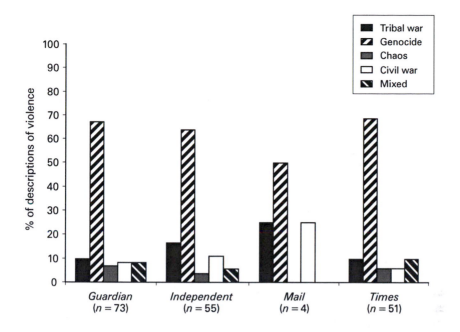

Figure 4.2 Descriptions of violence by newspaper, Rwanda coverage.

do to you', Hilsum suggested that their professed fear of Tutsis was irrational paranoia, and concluded that people had been led to kill by 'the Hutu extremist ideology professed by Rwanda's rump government and disseminated by state radio and a private station, Mille Collines'. Her comment that it was 'hard to tell when people are merely mouthing the ideology or when they believe what they say' indicated the difficulty she had in understanding their views and motivations.

The later periods examined in this study also each featured only one article in which the author attempted to understand why people had participated in or supported the killing: an article on the first anniversary by Dowden (*Independent*, 7 April 1995) and a 'guide to the Zaire crisis' in 1996 by Mary Braid (*Independent*, 16 November 1996). Braid also gave a decisive role to propaganda when she wrote that: 'Just as the Nazis disseminated propaganda against the Jews, the Interahamwe was fed – and fed others – a diet of anti-Tutsi propaganda'. Such propaganda, she noted, 'played on deep-seated fears', but she located these fears in the colonial era, when 'Under Belgian ... rule the minority Tutsis were the educated elite and the Hutus mostly second-class citizens'. The genocide was a response to the Arusha 'power-sharing agreement', as the government talked peace but strengthened the militias while 'the country's radio stations ... foster[ed] hate warning that the Tutsis, or "cockroaches", were conspiring to once again enslave Hutus'. Dowden's article, one of the fullest attempts at explanation in our samples of coverage, also described planning and preparation for genocide, but noted that 'Although the killings began with lists and targets, the genocide spread through the country like a whirlwind'. The Hutu, he suggested, were 'driven by fear that they would be subjected to traditional Tutsi domination', and unlike Braid he located these fears in the present as well as the past. Observing that 'The extermination of the Tutsis was carried out while the civil war raged', Dowden also noted that the Arusha Accords had been signed under 'heavy pressure' from Western governments and financial institutions following the RPF's 1990 invasion. This was the nearest that any article came to discussing the relationship between the civil war and genocide.

Although the concept of genocide featured in around a quarter of all explanatory articles and two-thirds of all articles containing a description of the violence, this does not necessarily imply that the quality of this explanation was particularly high. Beattie et al. observe that in television reporting of Rwanda in 1996, despite the numerous references to 'genocide', in most cases explanations 'did not go beyond the image of tribal conflict'. The missing element, they suggest, was an explanation of 'the sophistication of the Rwandan state … [and of how] the genocide was part of a calculated political programme … planned and instigated with an appalling efficiency'. Instead, television coverage continued to play upon stereotypical ideas about Africans as primitive and irrational (Beattie et al. 1999: 251, 254, 258). The first of these points does not really apply to our samples of press coverage: as noted above, although they were few in number, when explanatory articles began discussing the killings as genocide it was precisely this element of planning and organisation that tended to be emphasised. In descriptions of the violence, the term 'genocide' was rarely qualified or elaborated but, when it was, the most common theme was again its planning and organisation. In our July 1994 sample, both the *Guardian* (5 July) and *Independent* (16 July) used the term 'systematic genocide', for example; and in their April 1995 descriptions, these papers used terms such as 'politically organised extermination' (*Guardian*, 6 April) or 'planned massacres' (*Independent*, 5 April).

The exception was the *Times*, which referred to a 'genocidal frenzy' on four occasions during these periods, twice in editorial columns (on 20 and 24 July 1994), a term which suggested a loss of control rather than planning and organisation. The turn of phrase illustrates the point made earlier that an explanation of the killings as genocide can, in some versions, come close to ideas about irrational violence and psychosis. In its November 1996 coverage the *Times* also diverged in the way suggested by Beattie et al.'s second point, in that it did perpetuate stereotypical views of African difference in a number of articles, for example describing refugees as 'trapped in the heart of darkness' (15 November 1995). As we shall see, this was closely related to the paper's editorial stance on what should be done about the refugee camps in Zaire. For now, it might be suggested that while explaining the violence as genocide tended not to emphasise 'ethnic' or 'tribal' differences within Rwandan society, it did not preclude a view of Rwanda, or even Africa as a whole, as defined by difference.

Prescriptions

April 1994: pessimistic prognoses

The three broadsheets each ran one editorial about Rwanda in April 1994, all referring to how an understanding of the violence as 'tribal' could be an argument against intervention. As noted above, the *Guardian* (8 April) refused to 'explain this away as the result of inevitable "ethnic savagery" nor to regard it as an excuse for not getting more involved'. The problem in both Rwanda and Burundi, it suggested, had been 'how to shift towards Hutu majority rule with sufficient safeguards for the Tutsis'. The paper was downbeat about the possibility of success in this effort, concluding that developing 'political structures' which could reconcile divisions would be 'difficult at best and may become impossible in countries which are among the poorest in Africa'. Nevertheless, the *Guardian* said that both countries 'desperately need more aid – for development as well as for their refugees – as much as they now need a serious UN peace-keeping effort'.

The *Independent* (11 April) also posed the problem in terms of the 'tendency to equate the right of self-determination with the right to form an ethnically homogeneous state', arguing that this was 'a recipe for continuing conflict'. The crisis in Rwanda was, in this perspective, part of a larger problem of 'containing the pressures of ethnicity within existing frontiers', and the answer lay in 're-examining the doctrine of self-determination and developing more flexible approaches to concepts of state sovereignty and inviolable frontiers'. This was in keeping with arguments the paper had made about the need to revise principles of state sovereignty in relation to the intervention in Somalia. In this case, however, the *Independent* did not advocate forceful intervention. The editorial began by saying that violence in Rwanda and Burundi 'will, sadly, reinforce a widespread view that Africa is a lost continent, so barbarous, so deeply sunk in tribal conflict and so remote from our concerns that nothing can be done to help it'. Although apparently rejecting this view – the editorial was headlined 'Africa Is Not a Lost Continent' – the *Independent* in fact endorsed it, arguing that it was 'uncomfortably near the truth where some African countries are concerned', including in the case of Rwanda, where the 'ancient enmity between the Hutus and Tutsis' was 'beyond hope of early resolution'. Rwanda's potential to 'benefit from outside help' was low, and in any case the position of the international community was one of 'helplessness'. Arguing that, in general, 'peace in many areas will depend less on the presence of blue berets than on constitutional arrangements, election systems and even frontier changes' to overcome ethnic divisions, the paper implied that peacekeepers should be sent in only once there was a peace to keep.

Taking a similar line, the *Times* (11 April) also described the violence in such a way as to bolster arguments against further Western involvement. Using terms such as 'ethnic hatred', 'atavistic enmity' and 'blood frenzy', it argued that 'It is for the Rwandans themselves to cure their malaise'. Comparing Rwanda with Somalia, the *Times* said that 'the analogy is flawed' because 'There is no method in Rwanda's madness'. This was a somewhat curious argument, given that the *Times* had also characterised the conflict in Somalia in terms of anarchy and chaos. Rejecting the option of 'armed international intervention', the *Times* echoed the *Independent*'s view of the UN's role, recommending that the Security Council should call for a return to the Arusha Accords and then possibly send more peacekeepers to 'supervise the plan's implementation'.

July 1994: atoning for past failure

Despite some differences of emphasis, there was general editorial agreement among the three broadsheets in July 1994 (the *Mail* again ran no editorial on Rwanda during this period). Firstly, all were highly critical of past Western failure and sceptical of France's Operation Turquoise. For the *Guardian* (6 July), the French intervention was 'mischief-making' and a 'dubious flourish' which had 'give[n] peace-keeping a bad name'. The *Independent* agreed that Operation Turquoise was 'a classic opportunity ... to cloak the pursuit of national interest in lofty humanitarian garb', but took it as symptomatic of the 'inability of the United Nations to muster the political willpower and military muscle to enforce a credible international order – except where the interests of its most prominent members are directly threatened' (6 July). Similarly, in a 20 July editorial the *Times* said the UN's role had been 'a dishonourable one, in betrayal of its own principles', and that by withdrawing most of its troops in April 1994 it had left a 'moral and institutional vacuum which was to be filled much later and unsatisfactorily by the French'. For all three papers, criticism of past international failure was the prelude to arguing for greater future intervention. Criticising previous UN inaction, the *Guardian* argued that 'a real UN presence with really impartial aims' was now needed, while the *Independent*, also condemning the record of 'international dithering' on Rwanda, called on the UN to address 'the need for preventive diplomacy and a rapid intervention force' (both 6 July); and the *Times* said that 'The UN has betrayed the country once: it must not do so again' (20 July).

Secondly, all three papers agreed on why the refugees had fled. According to the *Guardian*, it was the 'vicious broadcasts' of 'radio stations still controlled by the former ... regime' which had 'panic[ked] the Hutus into flight'; the *Independent* said that refugees had fled because of the 'shrill radio broadcasts of the extremists' (both 23 July); and the *Times* (20 July) said the 'surge of frightened refugees has been attributed directly to broadcasts urging Hutus to flee to Zaire, as "the RPF are going to come and kill you"'. The unattributed source of this information was Sylvana Foa, a spokesperson for the UN High Commissioner for Refugees (UNHCR).

Thirdly, all three papers argued that, although such fears were largely unfounded, action should be taken to reassure refugees it was safe to return. The *Guardian* (23 July) recommended various measures, including: sending 'Tutsi envoys, and other African emissaries ... among the refugees'; deploying military observers to 'buttress security' in Rwanda; and silencing the former regime's radio stations. The *Independent* suggested that 'the Hutus may need the additional reassurance of a UN force to protect them' (23 July) and the *Times* proposed 'a large presence of UN peace-keepers, perceived as neutral and acting in a supervisory capacity', to be drawn from other African countries (20 July). The *Times* also called for the establishment of a UN war crimes tribunal so that 'by seeking to punish the architects of genocide it can atone for its earlier sins of omission, and for its failure to comprehend the horror of Rwanda'.

These prescriptions for action to atone for past failure suggested a need for the UN and Western governments to restore their own lost moral authority, but they also implied support for the new RPF government's promises of national reconciliation: according to the *Times*, the UN could 'redeem itself by strengthening the hand of the new government' (20 July). The *Guardian* objected that Operation Turquoise had undermined the RPF, by 'encouraging ordinary Hutus' not to trust it (6 July). The *Independent* said that 'Most of the evidence supports the credibility of the RPF' (23 July) and the *Times* (20 July) praised the RPF as being 'determined to assemble a broad-based government of ethnic reconciliation', having 'defeated the forces of the genocidal Hutu "interim government"'.

While the *Guardian* and *Independent* emphasised the need for immediate humanitarian relief, all three broadsheets agreed that the longer-term goal of Western policy should be the return of refugees. In fact this was already the orientation of Western policy: on the same day (23 July) as the *Guardian* argued in its editorial column for the 'overwhelming wisdom' of persuading refugees 'to return home as quickly as possible', a report on its foreign news page noted Clinton's promise to support 'an immediate deployment of UN peacekeepers in Rwanda to help persuade the displaced people that it was safe to go home', a suggestion the report described as 'rapidly emerging as the only long-term strategy for dealing with the crisis'. Also on 23 July the *Times* reported the UNHCR adopting the same stance. Spokesman Ray Wilkinson said: 'We feel convinced enough from what we heard (from the RPF military leader) to put our reputation on the line and encourage people to go home'. At least in terms of their editorial stance, then, there was no evidence that the newspapers simply called for humanitarian aid for the refugees in the way that Philo et al. (1999) found in television news. Rather, all three broadsheets argued that the refugees' fears of the RPF were largely unfounded and called for international action to encourage their return.

In terms of news reporting, the picture was less clear-cut, in that some reports did include calls for a greater international humanitarian operation in the refugee centres outside Rwanda. Six articles in July 1994 featured explicit calls for military intervention in support of the aid effort, but in all cases these articles were reporting the opinions of others, usually aid workers. The *Guardian*, which carried three such articles, came closest to endorsing this view itself, with a front-page report headlined '"Only Military" Can Save Rwandan Millions' (22 July). A further 17 articles criticised the aid operation as too slow or too limited and called directly or indirectly for a greater effort. Again, this theme was most prominent in the *Guardian*, which carried seven such articles; all these articles, however, were based on the opinions of aid agencies and other sources. Taken together, articles highlighting demands for a greater humanitarian operation accounted for 16.5 per cent of total coverage during this period, but aid agencies were leading the call for greater intervention rather than the press.

One further issue which needs to be addressed here is how news articles explained the refugee exodus. Very little evidence was found to support the argument of some critics (for example Melvern 2000: 218) that news reports gave confusing accounts of refugees fleeing 'from genocide'. In July 1994 one article did offer a somewhat confusing explanation, in that it described 'internally displaced' Hutu refugees in Rwanda as 'an army of civilians uprooted from their homes by fighting and murderous ethnic militias', which may have given the impression that the 'ethnic militias' were Tutsi (*Independent*, 8 July 1994), but across all of our sample periods only one article described the refugees as having 'fled the genocide' (a 2 November 1996 *Guardian* report). Where press reporting might be faulted is that it was often vague about the reasons for the refugees' flight. Of the 86 articles in our July 1994 sample which dealt with the refugee crisis, around a third (29 articles, or 33.7 per cent) gave no explanation of why they had fled. Yet these reports should be seen in context: given that two-thirds of articles over a short period did offer explanations for the refugee crisis, journalists could justifiably assume some understanding of ongoing events. Where reasons for the flight of refugees were given, the most common explanation was that they were fleeing the advance of the RPF (32 articles, or 37.2 per cent). News reports were therefore somewhat out of step with editorial opinion on this issue. Only nine articles (10.5 per cent) said that refugees had fled because they were persuaded or forced to by the old regime – the explanation favoured in editorial columns – although, as discussed below, this was to change in later coverage.

It should also be noted that, contrary to what is implied by those who criticise the media for advocating a naive humanitarianism, around a quarter of all articles about the refugee crisis (21 articles, or 24.4 per cent) stated explicitly that the refugees included people who were guilty of the massacres. This sometimes involved reporting the views of sources, as when the *Guardian* (12 July 1994) noted that aid agencies had said 'that they knew hundreds, if not thousands, of those they were helping were murderers', and quoted a senior UN official as saying:

> we may actually be legitimising the actions committed by the Rwandan people and legitimising their view that they are victims. But they are not victims. The victims are the 500,000 to one million people who are dead.

But often journalists voiced the same view themselves. The *Guardian*'s Chris McGreal, for example, said that:

> Rwandan refugees do not win sympathy easily…. The men invite special scrutiny for the look that seemed to shine from the eyes of those who manned the murderous militia roadblocks. These are a people who slaughtered their neighbours. (25 July)

April 1995: dealing with ambiguity

Only the *Times* and the *Guardian* ran editorials about Rwanda in April 1995, each commenting, at the beginning of the month, on both the first anniversary of Habyarimana's assassination and on current events in Burundi, where many of the estimated 200,000 Rwandan refugees who had been in the country since the previous year were now trying to cross into Tanzania because of attacks on Hutus by the Burundian army and Tutsi militias; and towards the end of the month on the forcible closure of the Kibeho camp for 'internally displaced' Hutus in Rwanda. Both developments raised questions about the earlier assumption that it was safe for Hutu refugees to return to Rwanda.

Before examining the editorials, it is worth noting that the events of April 1995 prompted a slight shift in the explanatory framework. In the *Independent*, for example, reporting on the killing of Hutu civilians by the Burundian army, David Orr commented that: 'Westerners who have come to view the Hutu ethnic group as the only perpetrators capable of such infamy after last year's genocide in Rwanda are having to refashion their understanding'. Whereas in Rwanda 'the Tutsi minority emerged as the largely innocent victims of atrocities' and the RPF were 'hailed as saviours', he argued, in Burundi it was 'now clear that neither ethnic group is blameless and that Tutsi soldiers and militiamen are killing with the same ferocity as their Hutu counterparts in Rwanda' (5 April). This reassessment of the black-and-white view of the two groups was also signalled in other ways. Six articles highlighted the plight of the thousands of Hutu prisoners in Rwanda. The *Times*, for example, reported Amnesty International's claim that up to 50,000 were being held in prisons and 'torture centres' (6 April). In the *Guardian*, a number of articles in April 1995 reframed Rwanda in terms of a 'spiral' or 'cycle' of violence, an idea which appeared in five of the paper's articles during this period, but only once outside it (on 21 July 1994, also in the *Guardian*). This was quite distinct from the idea of ancient 'ethnic' or 'tribal' hatreds: indeed, the paper's editorial on 24 April 1995 explicitly challenged 'stereotyped views of the ethnic antagonism between Hutus and Tutsis as being so deep-seated as to be unstoppable' and insisted that it was 'wrong to regard the Rwandan genocide as a spontaneous ethnic war'; rather, the 'cycle of violence' idea was an acknowledgement of current Tutsi abuses against Hutus in both Rwanda and Burundi, and was usually linked to comments on the prospects for justice and reconciliation. A 7 April report in the *Guardian*, for example, said that problems with the first Rwandan trials of those accused of genocide threatened 'efforts to build confidence in the law and break Rwanda's cycle of killing'. Later in the month, it suggested that it was the killings at Kibeho which 'bludgeoned hopes of ending Rwanda's cycle of ethnic violence' (*Guardian*, 24 April).

In an editorial on 5 April 1995 the *Times* explained that Hutu refugees in Burundi had initially fled 'fearing retribution from the Tutsi-led Rwandan Patriotic Front Government', but they had not returned home because of 'the grip in which they are held by Hutu extremists'. This implied that it was safe for the refugees to return but that their extremist leaders were not allowing them to do so. The article then contradicted this by arguing that 'International efforts to rebuild Rwanda must be pursued with increased vigour, so that Rwandan Hutu refugees can leave Burundi at an early date', suggesting that it was the failure of such rebuilding efforts which had so far prevented the refugees from returning. The contradiction stemmed from the paper's attempt to skirt round evidence that refugees had well founded reasons to be afraid of returning to Rwanda. These reasons were highlighted in the *Guardian* the next day, when it wrote of the refugees' 'real apprehension of lawlessness' (6 April). Also referring to Rwanda's need for 'urgent help to build an infrastructure', the *Guardian* made it clear that the main target of such help should be the country's judicial system. The paper said that the 'UN operation to protect human rights in Rwanda must move speedily into higher gear' and alluded to the mistreatment of Hutu prisoners in 'secret camps and chaotic prisons'. A similar point was made in the same day's edition in a commentary by Francoise Bouchet-Saulnier of Médecins Sans Frontières, who called for greater progress in the work of the UN war crimes tribunal. Also highlighting the plight of '30,000 detainees … piled up in the country's overcrowded prisons', most of whom had been arrested without charge, and who had 'little chance of a fair hearing', Bouchet-Saulnier called for international action to bring 'the thousands guilty of genocide to justice' and to stop 'the revenge killings that are tearing apart what remains of civil society'. Both Bouchet-Saulnier and the *Guardian* thus sought to combine expressions of concern about revenge killings and the ill-treatment of prisoners with a suggestion that, in the words of the paper's editorial, 'the victims of genocide … [taking] action unilaterally' was an understandable result of international failure to deliver justice.

The evident discomfort over how far to criticise the new Rwandan regime was heightened by the killings at Kibeho. Subsequent commentary has been sharply divided both on this event and on the media's handling of it. De Waal (1997: 200–1), for example, says the media 'faithfully reproduced' the accounts given by NGOs, which were overly critical of the RPF government (he says one aid agency's statement 'could have been drafted by the extremists themselves'), unlike the more balanced assessment by the International Independent Commission of Inquiry set up to investigate the incident. Terry (2002: 209–12), in contrast, argues that the Commission's report was a 'flagrant sham' which came close to justifying the attack on the camp, and criticises the 'tragic' acceptance of this 'overtly flawed' report by journalists, as well as by donor governments, the UN and NGOs. Terry's view appears to be the more accurate one: both editorials about Kibeho in our sample found reasons to explain the attack on the camp and implied that it was understandable, if not justified.

The *Times* was the most forthright, claiming that 'the Government soldiers were menaced by the mobs of machete-wielding Hutu extremists present in the camp' (25 April). The *Times* said this was 'neither excuse nor justification for the subsequent killing', but appeared to treat it as exactly that when it described Kibeho as 'the last redoubt of the interahamwe – the Hutu death squads in Rwanda'. The *Times* called for 'a full investigation … and exemplary punishment for those soldiers found guilty of murder', but endorsed the British government's view that 'Kibeho had been in the grip of Hutu extremists' and that Britain should continue supporting the RPF regime.[10] The *Guardian's* 24 April leader was more equivocal but reached similar conclusions. The article acknowledged the 'understandable' fears of refugees outside Rwanda, but argued that the 'large numbers' who had returned suggested that 'many of those who remain are controlled or influenced by Hutu extremists'. This was 'no excuse' for the mistreatment of the refugees at Kibeho, the *Guardian* said, but appeared to treat it as such, suggesting that 'this and other camps are still dominated by extremist Hutu militia who have played their part in the latest violence'. Like the *Times*, the *Guardian* blamed the 'tactics of the Tutsi soldiers' and criticised the Rwandan government only for having 'exercised little control' over its troops; it argued that for international donors 'the lesson is … that more, not less, needs to be done'.

Terry (2002: 213) argues that, in the aftermath of Kibeho, the RPF 'skilfully deflected attention away from its strong-arm tactics and laid the blame on the aid community for supporting the structure'. In that sense, it was 'a dress rehearsal for the refugee camps in Zaire eighteen months later'. The way this worked can be seen in both reporting and commentary in April 1995, particularly in the *Times*. In a *Times* report on 24 April which described Kibeho as 'a permanent threat to the … army', Sam Kiley quoted a 'long-serving European diplomat based in Kigali' who commented that, while there was 'absolutely no excuse' for the behaviour of the RPF:

> they have been begging for the international community to help them to break up the Hutu militias inside Rwanda and in the refugee camps in Zaire and Tanzania, and we have done absolutely nothing except make sure that those responsible for the genocide are fed, watered and sheltered.

It was therefore 'no great surprise' that the RPF had 'finally cracked'. This perspective was in line with editorial arguments that donor support for Rwanda's judicial system and greater efforts to advance the progress of the UN's international tribunal were necessary not only to prosecute those guilty of genocide but also to prevent further revenge killings or 'loss of control' by the RPF. The paper's 25 April editorial concluded by criticising 'the slow pace at which the trials for genocide are proceeding', arguing that there could be 'no reconciliation in Rwanda until the Hutu extremists are tried and punished'. These arguments carried the unfortunate implication that, so long as the international community failed to deal with the guilty Hutus, it was understandable and perhaps even justifiable if the RPF dealt with them by force. Hence, as Terry (2002: 211) argues, 'It was only a small step from "resolving" the [internally displaced persons] problem at Kibeho to "resolving" the refugee problem in Zaire'.

November 1996: 'dawn of hope' in the 'heart of darkness'

In November 1996 the *Times* and the *Guardian* were again the only papers in our study to devote editorials to Rwanda, and again, despite some differences between them, they shared a fundamentally similar understanding of what the problem was and how it should be resolved. The focus of editorial discussion was a proposed humanitarian military intervention to ensure the delivery of aid to Hutu refugees and to establish safe corridors for their return to Rwanda. It initially appeared that the refugees were simply caught up in fighting between Zairian government and rebel forces, the latter including local ethnic Tutsis backed by the Rwandan RPF government; but it gradually became clear that the RPF was intervening with the purpose of dispersing or repatriating the refugees. French proposals for multilateral military action were slow to gather support but by mid-November the dispatch of a Canadian-led UN force seemed a real possibility, the US (and Britain) having agreed to contribute troops. No sooner had the force been agreed, however, than its deployment was thrown into question by the mass repatriation of refugees as the RPF broke up the last, and the largest, camp, at Mugunga, on 15 November. The question was now whether to intervene in order to help those refugees who had fled deeper into Zaire instead of returning, but their number was disputed. While the UN estimated that up to 700,000 had fled, the US claimed that the number of 'missing' refugees was nearer to 200,000 and decided an armed intervention was no longer necessary.

Of the two papers, the *Guardian* was the most favourably disposed to the idea of international armed intervention. Its 5 November editorial accused the UN of 'sit[ting] on its hands' while what was needed was 'effective intervention on a much wider scale'. A few days later, commenting on an Anglo-French agreement that the refugees had to be 'assisted to return voluntarily', the *Guardian* complained that current plans were 'sadly short on specifics' and lacked 'more than a token sense of urgency', arguing that despite the difficulty of repatriating the refugees, 'no cost is too high and no effort too great' (9 November). Similarly, on 15 November the paper said the UN should send a larger force than the 10,000–20,000 now proposed; it warned that there could be no 'quick fix' and argued for a longer deployment than the four months envisaged by the UN. The *Times* took a much more negative view of proposals for international action. Describing the region as 'Africa's black hole', the paper's 2 November editorial advised only diplomacy, rather than military intervention, to 'try to prevent a regional war'. On 8 November the *Times* rejected the French proposal for an international force, claiming that 'almost every official in Britain' viewed it as 'ill-conceived, impractical and designed more to boost the faltering position of France in Africa than to address the underlying causes of the fighting'. Similarly, its 15 November leader, entitled 'Congo Fever', objected to the way that Britain had been 'Chided by the French [and] chivvied by the Americans' into agreeing to contribute troops to the UN force, and highlighted the 'fierce challenges', 'serious risk' and 'horrors' awaiting British troops in 'this rain-drenched Tropic'.

A striking feature of the *Times*' coverage in November 1996 was its emphasis on Africa's primitiveness, difference and danger, often couched in cliches. The paper's 2 November editorial, for example, described Zaire as 'a black hole in the heart of Africa' and as 'Africa's hate-consumed heart', and wrote of the 'Fear of catching the Zaire disease'. On the same day, diplomatic editor Michael Binyon described the 'heart of Africa' as 'impenetrable' and as populated by 'turbulent tribes'; and articles on 15 and 23 November referred to Zaire as 'the heart of darkness'. Reports which emphasised horror, disease and chaos reinforced the sceptical view of intervention taken in the paper's editorial columns. So, for example, Kiley described the 'grim conditions awaiting British troops' in terms of 'horror' and 'satanic violence' (15 November). After suggesting this 'satanic violence' would break the 'hardest hearts of paratroopers', Kiley said 'The only thing systematic here is violence – and the spread of disease'. He also developed a particular fascination with a local Zairian people, the Mai Mai (in our sample he was the only reporter to mention them), whom he described as 'tribes-men, in monkey skins and coated with white paint, [who] wave their penises at their enemies and think they are bullet-proof' (15 November). These 'naked voodoo warriors' were rumoured to 'practise cannibalism' and were 'apparently driven by little else but blood-lust' (13 November). In similar vein, a feature by Richard West asked 'What horrors await us in the Congo?' and described the 'dread of mysterious illnesses from countries surrounding the Congo basin' as 'an old nightmare' (23 November). An interpretation of these lurid accounts as reinforcing an anti-interventionist stance is supported by the fact that the only article not from the *Times* to use the 'heart of darkness' idea did so in a similar fashion: to emphasise the dangers facing Western troops. This was a report in the *Independent*, entitled 'Aid Force Aims for the Heart of Darkness', which explained the 'hot welcome' and 'stiff challenges' faced by the proposed force by saying that: 'The situation in eastern Zaire is much as depicted in Joseph Conrad's *Heart of Darkness*, a century ago' (14 November).[11]

Articles in the *Times* signalled the paper's opposition to intervention in other, less coded, ways too. Kiley did not simply report the international debate about intervention but opined that 'Military intervention is not needed' and 'would be criminal' since it would 'safeguard the killers' (8 November). Similarly, his 15 November report argued that 'Military intervention now is a crazy idea. East Zaire's rebels should be left to sort out the refugees.' Kiley took a cynical view of aid agencies, predicting a 'funding frenzy' among organisations which had 'become known as "the agony industry", the multimillion-pound business of giving' (12 November). Earlier experiences of intervention were also recalled to caution against precipitate action. Defence correspondent Michael Evans argued that US experience in Somalia stood 'as a permanent warning to all the countries now suddenly jumping on the "must-do-something" bandwagon' (15 November), while the paper's 8 November editorial said that 'France should know from Bosnia how foolish it is to rush in troops on the assumption that "something must be done"'. It was no surprise to find Simon Jenkins warning against 'another fatal adventure by the West' (16 November) or Conor Cruise O'Brien urging the West to 'let Zaire fall apart' (19 November), since such commentators had consistently taken an anti-interventionist stance. That the paper's editorial column should disparage the sentiment that 'something must be done', however, appeared to be something of a departure, since the *Times* had argued forcefully for military intervention in Bosnia and Somalia.

Despite the differences between newspapers, however, there was also considerable common ground. Most importantly, there was a consensus that action must be taken to close down the camps, deal with the 'extremists' and repatriate the refugees: the disagreement was over how this ought to be accomplished. The *Guardian*'s 15 November editorial, for example, while generally supporting the dispatch of a UN force, objected that there was no plan for how 'the Rwandan extremists could be disarmed and separated from the rest of the refugees' or for how to 'avoid setting up permanent camps'. Quoting a spokeswoman for the World Food Programme, the paper argued that 'without separating "the bad guys with the guns from the people who need to live today," little can improve'. On the same day, the paper ran a comment piece by Alex de Waal arguing that there were 'strict limits' to what could be achieved by a humanitarian intervention. The 'central challenge', he said, was the 'presence of Hutu extremist forces', whose 'genocidal ideology ... makes fascism seem moderate' and who 'must be removed from the political scene'. De Waal said it was futile trying to disarm these extremists and that there could be 'no bloodless political solution': 'If we are not prepared to go and destroy the Hutu militias, we should not stand in the way of the people who are prepared to do so'. Taken together, these two articles effectively defined the parameters of the debate: whether the West should deal with the 'extremists' directly or let the RPF attack the refugee camps.

The fine line separating these positions was evident from the *Independent*'s coverage. Although the *Independent* ran no editorials, its correspondent in the region, Mary Braid, freely offered her own views on what should be done, but she shifted from support for international protection of refugees to an endorsement of the RPF's attack on the camps in a matter of days. On 9 November Braid thought 'Outside military intervention looked certain to be needed to save 700,000 Rwandan refugees trapped by fighting in eastern Zaire'. By 14 November she was arguing that the point of international action was not so much to save the refugees but to disarm the 'extremists', a task which would 'prove impossible if those sent to do the job are deprived of the right to use force'. Two days later, Braid argued that proposals for intervention which did not include separating and disarming the Interahamwe would 'miss the point', since 'Without that separation there is little hope for the region'. By this stage, Mugunga had in fact already been closed by the RPF, a development which, in another article in the same day's edition, she welcomed as 'Some good news from Africa'. Euphemistically describing the deliberate attack on the camp as 'unexpected spontaneous combustion', Braid said it was 'the outcome everyone wished for' and that it had 'saved [the UN] from a mission that already had failure written all over it' (16 November). Similarly, in the *Times* Kiley predicted that 'Our poor soldiers will have a United Nations mandate which ... will be weak and muddled.... British soldiers will be asked by the UN ... to give succour to Hutu extremists who will live on to kill' (15 November). The next day, the *Times* hailed the violent break-up of Mugunga camp as a 'Dawn of Hope' (the title of its 16 November editorial).

This highly positive view of the RPF's attacks on refugee camps outside Rwanda's borders was underpinned by a transformation in how the refugees had come to be viewed. In contrast to the way that most explanations of the refugees' flight in July 1994 cited their fear of the RPF, by November 1996 their failure to return home was most often explained as a result of their being forced by extremist leaders to stay in the camps. In this period, three out of every four articles which explained why the refugees had not returned cited this reason.[12] The most common terms used to describe the refugees were 'hostages' (in 15 articles) and 'human shields' (in 14 articles). Hence, the camp closure could be presented as a liberation; the *Times*, for example, said the refugees were 'Free at last' (15 November). The acknowledgement, in some of the reporting from April 1995, that refugees might have good reasons to fear returning to Rwanda was now largely forgotten. Only one article mentioned the earlier RPF attack on Kibeho camp, and even that did so in such a way as to minimise its significance: Kiley recalled that RPF soldiers had 'lost their cool' at Kibeho when they were 'stampeded by the Hutus' and had killed 1,500 people (*Times*, 8 November). He gave no source or explanation for his unusually low estimate of the number killed. As noted above, the logic of the argument developed in relation to the attack on Kibeho in April 1995 was followed through in the autumn of 1996: if the international community failed to deal with the extremists, then the RPF was justified in doing so. Braid, for example, said the attack on Mugunga was 'spurred by the news that the world would not do what was necessary: disarm the militia men and separate them from the refugees' (*Independent*, 16 November). Similarly, the suggestion in some reporting in April 1995 that the inhabitants of Kibeho were the threat, rather than the soldiers attacking the camp, was repeated and amplified in the November coverage. Despite the fact that it was the RPF and its local allies who were mounting an assault on the camps in Zaire, nearly a third of articles dealing with the refugees in November 1996 described the refugee camps as a military threat to Rwanda (30 out of 101 articles). Yet, as Terry (2002: 169–70) observes, the rout of the former government's army and militia in 1996 demonstrated that their strength 'in the minds of international observers' was 'not matched by the reality on the ground'. Rather, the new RPF government 'exaggerated the [former regime's] level of military preparedness in order to legitimise its own future actions against the camps by convincing international public opinion that the [former regime] constituted a formidable threat'.

In their treatment of those refugees who fled into the interior of Zaire instead of returning to Rwanda when Mugunga was broken up, the newspapers again diverged. The *Guardian* and *Independent* showed some concern for their situation. McGreal, for example, noted that the US and UN had drawn 'entirely contradictory conclusions' from satellite photos, the UN spotting '750,000 miserable souls being driven in circles' while 'The Americans saw almost nothing'. The RPF and its allies, he noted, 'appear ever more willing to write them off' (*Guardian*, 25 November). In the *Independent*, Orr said the plight of missing refugees had been 'described as a "hidden holocaust"' and reported the view of aid agencies that 'hundreds of thousands of Rwandan refugees had been driven deep into the country's interior, beyond the reach of help', although he also noted that 'no real evidence has emerged of the predicted humanitarian disaster' (21 November). In the *Times*, however, Kiley maintained his former stance, describing the refugees as 'heading deeper into the interior of the country to fulfil a military plan to establish a "safe and sure base" for a future invasion of Rwanda' (19 November) and dismissing aid agency estimates of the number of remaining refugees as 'wild speculation' (23 November).

Criticism of the West's role

The main criticism emphasised by most writers on Rwanda – that the West did not intervene to stop the killing – received little contemporary attention in press coverage: it featured in only 22 articles. Half of these appeared in April 1994 (with five in July 1994, four in April 1995 and two in November 1996), when the criticism was most often directed at the UN. This view was some-times attributed to sources such as aid agencies or British Labour MPs, but was also often voiced by journalists themselves, particularly in the *Guardian*. Huband, for example, described how 'UN troops [stood] by and watch[ed] the carnage' (12 April); and Hilsum said the UN's 'moral failure' had 'once more battered its image' (16 April).

The issue which attracted the most critical comment was the role played by France. Overall, 66 articles featured criticisms of the French, 36 of them in July 1994, at the time of Operation Turquoise. In this period the view was more mixed than in later coverage, however, with 16 articles highlighting positive aspects of the French action. A front-page report in the *Independent*, for example, described a 'daring French mission ... to evacuate 600 Rwandan orphans and displaced children, and 100 nuns and priests, including Europeans, Hutus and Tutsis' (4 July). In November 1996, when 29 articles mentioned critical views of French involvement, criticism was rarely mitigated in this fashion. When a source was cited for this criticism, it was usually either the RPF or anonymous 'critics', as in a 5 July 1994 *Guardian* report which said that 'Critics suspect the French of planning to divide Rwanda or using its safe haven to preserve the current administration'. In other articles, the problematic character of France's role was stated as the reporter's own view or simply as a matter of fact, as when McGreal said the French were 'compromised by collaboration' and described 'French army commanders ... working closely with officials implicated in the murder and persecution of Tutsis' (*Guardian*, 1 July 1994).

Yet criticism of France was easy for British newspapers and was accompanied by no wider questioning of Rwanda's relationship with the West. Dowden, for example, describing Operation Turquoise as a 'military adventure ... rooted in imperial tradition', argued that 'It is a principle of diplomacy, universally recognised, that just as there are no friends, only interests, so there are no humanitarian motives – only longer-term interests'. This prompted him to ask 'what is the reason for France sending 2,500 troops to Rwanda?', but he did not think to ask similar questions about the involvement of other countries in Rwandan politics – indeed, Dowden suggested France's relationship with

Africa was 'a unique and complicated one that it is hard, maybe impossible, for British people to understand' (6 July 1994). Only two articles took a similarly critical view of US and UN intervention prior to April 1994. In the *Times*, Simon Jenkins challenged the 'myth that "the world" … [had] ignored Rwanda' and suggested that Western diplomatic intervention since 1990 had 'coincided with a rise in political and economic instability, assassination and genocide'; and in a commentary for the *Independent*, Kenan Malik noted that 'Western powers have put intense pressure on Rwanda … to democratise itself', that the International Monetary Fund's structural adjustment programme for the country had 'tied economic aid to political reform', and that these twin pressures had resulted in 'the devastation of an already fragile economy and an intensification of internal power struggles' (both 20 July 1994).

In July 1994 there were 23 articles which either called explicitly for military intervention in support of the aid effort or criticised the international humanitarian operation as too slow or too limited. Over time, however, views of the aid operation changed, with growing criticism that humanitarian relief was being given to killers. In July 1994 only two articles, both in the *Guardian*, raised this issue: Hilsum reported that the refugees included 'hundreds of members of the notorious Hutu militia' but it was 'impossible for foreign workers to know who is who' (4 July); and Huband reported a statement issued by aid agencies which said it was 'difficult to provide humanitarian assistance' for people who 'may have instigated mass murders' and which called for them to be 'brought to trial' (12 July). Seven articles mentioned such problems in April 1995 and 13 in November 1996. The greater prominence of this theme in 1996 was, of course, closely related to arguments that the camps had to be closed and that the RPF attacks on the camps were justified. As we saw, these arguments also entailed criticism of planned international action as too limited, either because it would fail to close the camps or because it would not involve disarming the Hutu militia, yet although coverage was often critical of proposals put forward by France and the UN, it was in line with US policy. The US government said in June 1996 that while voluntary repatriation remained the 'preferred option', it was also time to 'look at other options … no matter how difficult it is to reconcile those options with refugee conventions' (quoted in Terry 2002: 185). At a time when it was providing military training to the new Rwandan government, the US effectively sanctioned the attack on the camps. Only one article drew attention to collusion between the US and the RPF: a report by McGreal which noted that RPF opposition to international intervention in aid of refugees who had not been repatriated after the closure of the camps had 'strong backing from the Americans, who helped stall proposals for intervention at the UN Security Council, and vacillated when asked to help track the refugees by satellite' (*Guardian*, 25 November 1996).

Given the limited character of most critical commentary, it is not surprising that there was little critique of the media's own role: only three articles addressed this topic. In a 25 July 1994 commentary for the *Guardian*, Germaine Greer railed against coverage of the refugee exodus, describing the media as a collective 'parasite' and accusing them of 'stripping the Rwandan refugees of their last shred of dignity'. In comments which echoed the criticisms sometimes made of coverage of Somalia, Greer characterised news reports as offering 'the pornography of war, genocide, destitution and disease'. Yet although she was dismissive of the 'pretence that we do it so that the Rwandans may at last be assisted', Greer called for those in the West to 'accept ... global responsibility' and to 'organise and fund a ... secular, professional disaster brigade, with the right to requisition supplies and logistical support, and to cross frontiers' in order to avert future catastrophes. On the same day, the *Times* ran an article by John Simpson which took a more positive view of the role played by the media. Contrasting Western inactivity in April 1994 with the current humanitarian intervention, Simpson argued that 'Now the Western powers are vying with each other to show how much they are doing, because they know that people have seen the pictures, and want action to be taken'. Although he argued that this 'unspoken compact' between the media, aid agencies and governments could be 'extraordinarily effective' in prompting international action, he also expressed some unease with new demands that reporters should be seen to care, noting that 'a line has been crossed' as the 'observers ... become full participants' in the events they cover. Simpson was referring to what later became known as the 'journalism of attachment', a topic which received further attention when Martin Bell coined the term in a speech in November 1996. The *Guardian* reported the speech (23 November) and ran a comment piece by Linda Grant (25 November) discussing Bell's views in relation to Rwanda. Grant objected that emotive reporting of the refugee situation was misleading, in that it implied a false equivalence between the 1996 attacks on the camps and the 1994 massacres: 'It was very easy for television viewers to miss a crucial distinction between these two sets of powerful images. The Rwandans who died in the mass slaughter and those who were in the camps were not the same people.' However, she did not reject the 'attached' approach as such – she argued that 'We still desperately need what Martin Bell calls "journalism of attachment"' – suggesting rather that reporters had shown too much sympathy for the refugees. Her implication was that emotive or 'attached' reporting was acceptable so long as it was for the right cause.

Fergal Keane's emotive reporting from Rwanda for the BBC attracted some praise in the press: Tom Sutcliffe said that Keane had 'importantly added what reporters too dismissively refer to as "colour"' (*Independent*, 29 June 1994); and Victoria Brittain said he had told the 'brutal truth about Rwanda' and conveyed his 'undisguised rage and disgust for the perpetrators of these killings' (*Guardian*, 28 June 1994).

Conclusions

The story about the media's reporting of Rwanda which emerges from the literature is that, having contributed to international indifference by characterising the violence as 'tribal war' in April 1994, journalists sought to compensate for this failure by highlighting the plight of refugees in July, thereby committing the further error of encouraging international sympathy for the perpetrators of genocide. Some analysts add that in 1996 journalists again sought to correct past mistakes by legitimising the attacks on the refugee camps. As a broad description of changes in the tone of coverage this story contains some truth, but in certain respects it is also something of a caricature.

'Tribal' explanations and descriptions of violence were indeed prominent in early reporting but this was in the context of coverage which was quite varied and which even included a few articles explicitly challenging the 'tribal' frame. The explanatory framework did change over time, with genocide becoming the dominant idea, but this did not imply that there was any great improvement in media explanations. The quantity of explanatory material in later periods was very low and the more complex aspects of the genocide were rarely explored. There is some justice in the accusation that a simplistic idea of 'tribal massacres' was replaced with an equally simplistic idea of 'genocidal massacres', although the problem was not so much a failure to emphasise organisation and planning as a failure to understand the killings as political. This meant that, in some later coverage, references to genocide and to the continuing threat posed by extremists became simply another way to emphasise the difference and danger of the region.

It is not quite true to say that coverage in July 1994 simply encouraged sympathy for refugees: news reports relayed aid agency calls for military intervention and a greater aid effort, but a quarter of all articles about refugees in this period also said that the refugees included the perpetrators of genocide, while editorials said refugees had fled because they were under the control

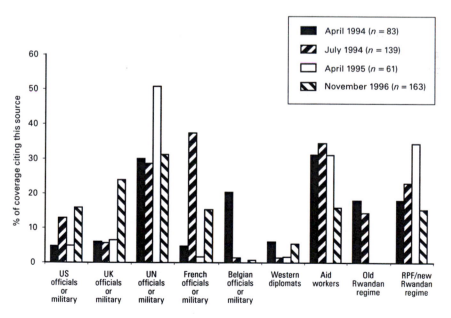

Figure 4.3 Prominence of the different types of source, Rwanda coverage.

of their leaders, and called for their repatriation. There is little evidence that press reporting conflated the refugees with the victims of genocide at any stage. Although events in 1995 prompted some reconsideration of simplistic categorisations of 'good Tutsi' and 'evil Hutu', press reporting tended to maintain a positive view of the RPF while attitudes to Hutu refugees hardened.

The pattern of news sources indicated in Figure 4.3, which shows the percentage of articles in which sources were cited in each of our sample periods, bears out McNulty's contention that reporters relied heavily on 'fellow Westerners'. It does not, however, support her further argument that reporting 'adopted ... much of the Habyarimana regime's agenda ... unquestioningly' (McNulty 1999: 277). Strikingly, the RPF was cited as often as representatives of the then Rwandan government or military in April 1994, with the RPF overtaking the old regime as a source by July and even surpassing aid workers in 1995. The relative prominence of the RPF as a source probably contributed to media acceptance that attacks on Kibeho in 1995 and the camps in Zaire in 1996 were a legitimate, or at least understandable, response to the international community's failure to deal with the Hutu refugees.

Finally, while there were many complaints about international responses to Rwanda, most of this 'criticism' was curiously uncritical. Although journalists were generally suspicious of France's proclaimed 'humanitarian' motives in Rwanda, few questions were asked about the role played by the international diplomatic and economic intervention in Rwanda immediately prior to April 1994, nor about continued US support for the RPF in 1996. There has been much criticism of the media for failing to raise the alarm about genocide, although it is doubtful that a different style of reporting would have produced different policies in Western capitals. Less remarked is the fact that a desire to correct past mistakes and to adopt a more 'moral' stance led in 1996 to reporting that actively legitimised further violence, in which, as Terry (2002: 192) notes, 'hundreds of thousands died or disappeared' over the following months.

CHAPTER 5

Kosovo, 1999

The focus of this chapter is Operation Allied Force, the Nato air campaign against Yugoslavia from 24 March to 10 June 1999. Nato's intervention was in response to ongoing conflict in the Serbian province of Kosovo and was triggered by the Yugoslav government's failure to sign a peace agreement with representatives of Kosovo's ethnic-Albanian majority. Nato's declared aim was primarily humanitarian – to protect Kosovo Albanians from attacks by the Yugoslav security forces and prevent a 'humanitarian catastrophe' – although in the event such attacks intensified during the bombing and there was a huge refugee exodus from Kosovo. The Nato campaign moved through different phases, initially targeting air defences, then Serbian forces in Kosovo and then, from early April, broadening the target list to include infrastructure in the rest of Serbia. Various diplomatic initiatives also accompanied the bombing campaign, which ended with a plan brokered by Germany with the assistance of Russia (Gowan 2000: 44–7). After this agreement had been signed, Nato ground forces moved in to police the territory, now administered as an international protectorate under the authority of the UN. Although Kosovo formally remained part of Yugoslavia, its protectorate status meant that in practice it was removed from Yugoslav state sovereignty and in the months following the conflict most of the province's non-Albanian population fled or was forced out. At the same time, ethnic-Albanian ambitions for independence also remained frustrated (see Chandler 2000b: 204–11).

Context

Nato's Kosovo campaign was conducted without UN authorisation, although it claimed the authority of Resolution 1199, drafted by Britain and adopted by the Security Council on 23 September 1998, which called for a ceasefire and warned of an 'impending humanitarian catastrophe' in Kosovo. No more explicit authorisation was sought because of the likelihood that Russia and China would have vetoed it. Since Yugoslavia had attacked no other state, Nato was not acting in self-defence and was therefore arguably in violation of its own charter also. It was not only critics of the bombing who argued that it was illegal (for example Littman 2000): its supporters have also acknowledged that it lacked legal authority. The Independent International Commission on Kosovo (IICK) conceded that 'the intervention was … not legal' (IICK 2000: 289), for example, and the House of Commons Foreign Affairs Select Committee (2000) said that the bombing was of 'dubious legality'. However, these assessments both argued that the Nato campaign was nevertheless legitimate. For the IICK (2000: 289), the bombing was 'legitimate because it was unavoidable: diplomatic options had been exhausted', while for the Foreign Affairs Select Committee (2000) it was 'justified on moral grounds' because there was a 'humanitarian emergency … before Nato intervened, and … a humanitarian catastrophe would have occurred … if intervention had not taken place'. There are grounds, though, for doubting both these claims.

The claim that Nato action was a last resort, launched only after diplomatic efforts to resolve the conflict between the Yugoslav government and ethnic-Albanian separatists had failed, is true in the sense that there were numerous diplomatic initiatives prior to the onset of bombing. The status of Kosovo had been raised as an international issue at the time of the Bosnian war, but Western interest in Kosovo greatly increased from late 1997. Over the course of 1998 the US and European governments, Nato, the Contact Group (established in 1994 for international mediation in Bosnia), the UN, the Organisation for Security and Co-operation in Europe (OSCE), the G8 and the European Union all took a growing interest in Kosovo, variously passing resolutions, sending diplomatic missions and envoys, and imposing economic sanctions.[1] Nato repeatedly indicated its willingness to take military action before it actually did so, deploying an 'air verification mission' and stationing an 'extraction force' in Macedonia, intended to support the OSCE's Kosovo Verification Mission (KVM), which monitored a ceasefire in 1998–99. Diplomatic pressure for a settlement culminated in talks at Rambouillet, near Paris, in February 1999. The original deadline for reaching agreement on a plan for settling the conflict was extended, the talks being finally adjourned only on 19 March, and even after that US envoy Richard Holbrooke made a further last-ditch attempt to secure Yugoslav agreement to the plan on 22 March. It would appear, then, that great efforts were indeed made to explore all diplomatic options and avoid military action.

However, critics have suggested that the diplomatic effort was less genuine than it seemed. The Rambouillet negotiations presented a draft agreement which both sides were asked to sign, but the expectation was that if the Kosovo Albanians agreed to the plan and the Serbs refused then Nato bombing would be seen as a legitimate response. As Tim Judah's account of the negotiations makes clear, US Secretary of State Madeleine Albright wanted the Kosovo Albanian delegation to sign and the Serbs not to, in order to 'trigger the bombing' (Judah 2000: 214). According to State Department spokesman James Rubin, the aim was 'to create clarity … as to which side was the cause of the problem … and that meant the Kosovar Albanians agreeing to the package and the Serbs not agreeing to the package'.[2] Rubin even spelled this out to reporters at the time, explaining at a 21 February 1999 briefing that 'in order to move towards military action, it has to be clear that the Serbs were responsible' for the failure of the talks (quoted in Judah 2000: 212). Initially, however, the ethnic-Albanians refused to sign, since the plan did not offer full independence for Kosovo, whereas the Yugoslav side accepted the political agreement, although arguing that it should be implemented by UN rather than Nato troops. This presented a conundrum for the Western brokers of the talks. While they worked on persuading the Kosovo Albanian delegation to accept the draft agreement, its terms were changed in ways which ensured its unacceptability to the Yugoslav side: Kosovo's future as part of Serbia was left uncertain, a Nato force was insisted on and an appendix was inserted that gave Nato troops unrestricted access to the whole of Yugoslavia, including territorial waters and airspace, and immunity from local law (Johnstone 2002: 244–7). As a State Department official reportedly told US journalists, the US had 'deliberately set the bar higher than the Serbs could accept' because the Serbs 'needed … a little bombing to see reason' (quoted in Kenney 1999). Seen in this light, the diplomatic process seems to have been a way to legitimise Nato bombing rather than a genuine attempt to prevent further conflict.

The claim that Nato intervention was legitimate on moral grounds – as an extreme but necessary measure in response to a humanitarian disaster – also has a surface plausibility but begins to look less credible the more we examine the evidence. In a speech a year after the bombing, then Nato Secretary General Lord George Robertson (Britain's Defence Secretary at the time of the conflict) asked 'Was the intervention in Kosovo moral?' He suggested that 'the only possible answer is yes', because: 'By March of 1999, Serb oppression had driven almost 400,000 people from their homes'. According to Robertson, 'this was ethnic cleansing – plain and simple', because 'before the air campaign … the atrocities being committed by Serb forces against the Albanians were organized, systematic, and dictated by a centrally directed strategy' (Robertson 2000). It is true that the conflict had created around 400,000 refugees and 'internally displaced persons' during the year preceding the bombing. However, according to the UN, by March 1999 many had returned home 'in places where there is no violence, and especially where KVM has a continuing presence' (UNHCR 1999a). Furthermore, in contrast to Robertson's retrospective assertion that 'this was ethnic cleansing – plain and simple', contemporaneous assessments suggested various different reasons for the flight of refugees, including 'clashes between Government security forces and the KLA [Kosovo Liberation Army], kidnappings, street violence and, more recently, military exercises by the Yugoslav army' (UNHCR 1999a). German Foreign Ministry reports in early 1999 stated that:

> explicit political persecution linked to Albanian ethnicity is not verifiable … actions of the security forces [are] not directed against the Kosovo-Albanians as an ethnically defined group, but against the military opponent and its actual or alleged supporters.[3]

It should also be noted that the refugees included around 55,000 who fled to other parts of Serbia or to Montenegro (UNHCR 1999b), the majority of whom were presumably Kosovo Serbs. This evidence suggests refugees fleeing the conflict between Serbian forces and KLA guerrillas rather than a one-sided campaign of 'ethnic cleansing'.

It is no doubt true, of course, that Serbian 'counter-terrorist' operations involved attacks on civilians, and sometimes targeted whole villages in a campaign against 'actual or alleged supporters' of the KLA. The OSCE's KVM was designed to mitigate this, and apparently had some success. However, the ceasefire it monitored was one-sided, in that it restricted the activities of the Yugoslav security forces while allowing the KLA to 'get organised, to consolidate and grow', in the words of KLA commander Agim Ceku.[4] The result was that, in the months before the Nato airstrikes, the main cause of violence in Kosovo was KLA activity. Just before the bombing, the US Committee for Refugees reported:

> Kosovo Liberation Army … attacks aimed at trying to 'cleanse' Kosovo of its ethnic Serb civilian population. UNHCR said, 'Over 90 mixed villages in Kosovo have now been emptied of Serb inhabitants and other Serbs continue leaving, either to be displaced in other parts of Kosovo or fleeing into central Serbia.' The Yugoslav Red Cross estimates there are more than 30,000 non-Albanian displaced currently in need of assistance in Kosovo, most of whom are Serb. (US Committee for Refugees 1999)

At the time, even Nato privately acknowledged the real cause of continuing conflict: according to minutes of the North Atlantic Council, the KLA was 'the main initiator of the violence' and had 'launched what appears to be a deliberate campaign of provocation'.[5] Publicly, however, the Serbs were blamed for the violence, while behind-the-scenes support was provided to the KLA. KVM monitor Roland Keith later described the head of the OSCE mission, US diplomat William Walker, as 'part of the American diplomatic policy … which had vilified Slobodan Milosevic, demonised the Serbian Administration and generally was providing diplomatic support to … the KLA leadership'.[6] In addition to 'diplomatic support', it later transpired that the US had also provided more practical assistance: in 2000 the US Central Intelligence Agency (CIA) admitted that its agents had been among the OSCE monitors, 'developing ties with the KLA and giving American military training manuals and field advice on fighting the Yugoslav army and Serbian police'.[7]

Despite evidence that the violence in Kosovo was not simply the result of one-sided 'ethnic cleansing' by the Serbs, the retrospective claim that the bombing was the only 'moral' response to a humanitarian crisis gained credibility from the established view of the Bosnian war and from the refugee crisis which occurred during the Kosovo campaign. As discussed in Chapter 3, in coverage of Bosnia 'ethnic cleansing' was widely understood as a mainly, or even exclusively, Serbian practice. Yet in their study of US news coverage Seth Ackerman and Jim Naureckas found that the earliest usage of the term in Yugoslavia applied it to the actions of ethnic-Albanian nationalists. The first reference to the concept of 'ethnic cleansing' occurred in 1982, when the *New York Times* reported the comments of a Yugoslav government official in Kosovo (an ethnic-Albanian) describing nationalists in the province as aiming 'first to establish what they call an ethnically clean Albanian republic and then the merger with Albania to form a greater Albania' (quoted in Ackerman and Naureckas 2000: 98–9). During the 1980s 'ethnic cleansing' was used exclusively to refer to the programme and activities of Kosovo Albanian nationalists, who 'encouraged' Serbs and Montenegrins to leave the province both through peaceful means, such as buying up property, and through violence and intimidation.[8] It was the activities of ethnic-Albanian nationalists in driving Serbs out of Kosovo during the 1980s which allowed Slobodan Milosevic to assume the mantle of protector of the Serbs when he told them, during a 1987 visit to the province: 'No one should be allowed to beat you' (quoted by Hudson 2003: 70). Yet while Milosevic's nationalist identification with Kosovo Serbs has been widely condemned, much less attention has been paid to the growth of ethnic-Albanian nationalism in the province (see Johnstone 2002: Chapter 5; Vickers 1998: Chapter 11).

The Nato airstrikes were initially justified as a measure to prevent a refugee crisis. On the first day of the bombing, Rubin insisted that if Nato had not acted, 'you would have had hundreds of thousands of people crossing the border'; and the following day Prime Minister Tony Blair declared: 'fail to act now … [and we] would have to deal with … hundreds of thousands of refugees.'[9] Once the bombing began, and hundreds of thousands did indeed flee, Nato aims had to be quickly redefined: now the objective was to halt and ultimately to reverse the exodus of ethnic-Albanian refugees. Logically, it might be expected that the refugee crisis would be seen as a failure of Nato's strategy, yet political leaders attempted to head off criticism with two related claims. Firstly, it was maintained that no refugees were fleeing the bombing: all were being either deported or terrorised into leaving by Serbian forces and paramilitaries. This argument was bolstered by the ICTY's indictment of Milosevic and other Yugoslav leaders for crimes against humanity, on 27 May 1999. Secondly, it was claimed that this 'ethnic cleansing' of Kosovo Albanians was not a response to Nato action but was the result of a premeditated policy and would therefore have happened anyway. Documents outlining a secret Serbian plan for 'ethnic cleansing' – codenamed Operation Horseshoe – were revealed by the German government at the beginning of April. After the war, however, Brigadier General Heinz Loquai, a former OSCE advisor, exposed the supposed blueprint for genocide as a fake concocted by the German intelligence services.[10] The alleged existence of Operation Horseshoe did not explain why around 60 per cent of Kosovo's Serbs and Montenegrins – 100,000 people – fled during the Nato bombing campaign (Binder 2000).[11] The fact that large numbers of non-Albanians fled Kosovo during the bombing suggests that the Nato action was at least a contributory factor in causing the refugee crisis; and although it is undoubtedly the case that violence and intimidation by Serbian forces also caused large numbers of people to flee, the failure to substantiate claims that this was part of a premeditated strategy leaves the suspicion that Nato intervention escalated the violence in Kosovo.[12]

Critics have accused mainstream Western media of acting as little more than propaganda mouthpieces for Nato during the Kosovo campaign. After the conflict, the *Independent*'s Robert Fisk said his fellow reporters had behaved either as 'sheep', who passively accepted official claims, or as 'frothers', who strongly identified with the proclaimed morality of the bombing.[13] Subsequent revelations certainly suggest that official claims about both Nato military successes and alleged Serbian atrocities were exaggerated. A confidential US Air Force report revealed that 'the number of targets verifiably destroyed was a tiny fraction of those claimed' by Nato, and an internal inquiry by the Royal Air Force put the number of tanks hit by Nato at around seven, rather than the 93 claimed at the time.[14] Claims of large-scale 'systematic' killing or even 'genocide' committed by the Serbs were also exaggerated: post-war forensic investigations failed to corroborate claims that 10,000 – let alone claims of 100,000 or even more – had been killed. The true figure appears to have been closer to 5,000 – a number which does not distinguish between civilians and combatants, nor between Albanians and Serbs.[15]

While such revelations support Fisk's view that there was a lack of scepticism, some analysts have emphasised that there was a degree of critical questioning on the part of journalists. Surveying British television news coverage, for example, Greg McLaughlin (2002: 122) argues that 'there was real media counterweight to Nato spin ... in the news rooms back in London'. In particular, he points to scepticism about the explanations offered by Nato when bombs hit the wrong targets and when the bombing caused 'collateral damage'. There is no doubt that Nato was sensitive to criticism over this issue, and it was a source of friction with journalists: Blair's press spokesman, for example, complained that: 'the Western media got itself into a mindset that the only show in town was "Nato blunders"' (Campbell 1999). However, Piers Robinson's study of US coverage suggests that while such criticism was relatively common, it was generally circumscribed by reporters' underlying agreement with the aims of Nato action. Criticism of Nato accidents was often related to the broader question of whether high-altitude bombing was the most effective strategy, whether it in fact made 'accidents' inevitable and whether the aims of the campaign would be better served by a ground assault. As Robinson (2002: 109) puts it, criticism remained within the sphere of 'legitimate controversy', in that critical coverage 'operated within a certain set of boundaries, primarily concerning whether the air war was working or whether there should be an escalation to the use of close air support and/or ground troops', but rarely questioning 'the underlying legitimacy of Nato's action'.

Questions

The main questions considered in this chapter are:

- How was the conflict between Serbs and Albanians in Kosovo explained?
- How was the Nato action explained, and how far was it seen as legitimate?
- To what extent was coverage critical of Nato action and sceptical of official claims?

Table 5.1 Numbers of articles about Kosovo

	Start of Nato bombing (17 March–14 April 1999)	End of Nato bombing (20 May–17 June 1999)	Totals
Guardian	349	244	593
Independent	357	283	640
Times	328	250	578
Mail	174	121	295
Totals	1,208	898	2,106

The sample periods for this study are: the week leading up to the start of the Nato action, on 24 March 1999, and the following three weeks; and the three weeks prior to the end of the bombing campaign, on 10 June 1999, and one week afterwards. Although there was conflict in Kosovo both before and after the Nato campaign, the key focus of the study is on Operation Allied Force and the large quantity of coverage during these two core periods precluded the addition of further samples. The total coverage[16] for the periods selected was as shown in Table 5.1.

Explanations

In this case study, 'explanation' could refer to one of two things: the history and origins of the conflict between Serbs and Albanians in Kosovo; and the reasons for the Nato intervention. As we will see, the way the internal conflict and external intervention were explained usually had prescriptive implications in terms of what international response was seen as appropriate. In this section we will also return to the issues raised in Chapter 3 about anti-Serb bias and the use of the terms 'ethnic cleansing' and genocide. Although the proportion of coverage devoted to explanations was low (around 9 per cent of the total), there was a large number of explanatory articles: 186 overall, comprising 35 which were mainly devoted to explanations and 151 in which explanations featured more briefly. As would be expected, most explanatory material appeared during our first sample period (137 articles compared with 49 for the second period), and most focused on the reasons for the Nato intervention (119 articles, compared with 67 focusing on the conflict between Serbs and Albanians in Kosovo).[17]

The Serb/Albanian conflict

Explanations of the conflict in Kosovo can be divided into two broad types, both of which rehearsed themes familiar from earlier chapters. Some articles understood the conflict in terms of long-standing ethnic hatreds, usually seen as typical of the Balkans, while others explained the conflict as the product of aggressive nationalist policies deliberately pursued by the Serbs and their leaders. As would be expected from our findings on Bosnia in Chapter 3, it was the second type of explanation which predominated: 49 articles explained the conflict in these terms, whereas only 18 explained the conflict in Kosovo as typical of the mutual ethnic hatreds of the Balkan region.

One of the most fully developed 'ethnic' explanations of the conflict was a *Times* feature by Michael Binyon entitled '1,000-Year Story Written in Blood' (29 March 1999). Claiming that 'the peoples of the Balkans have been feuding for 1,000 years … turning on their ethnic rivals in periodic massacres', Binyon suggested that relationships between the peoples of the region were shaped by 'vendetta politics' because 'tight-knit clans' had long memories of their 'blood-soaked history'. After the Second World War, Binyon argued, 'the heavy hand of communism' had 'suppressed local nationalisms', but had not resolved the underlying problem, which he identified as the fact that 'nowhere was a homogeneous people able to create a state where ethnic, religious and geographic borders corresponded'. In this perspective, conflict is understood as the inevitable outcome of different ethnic groups laying claim to the same territory (Binyon compared Kosovo with Palestine in this respect, as another 'intractable crisis'). Binyon saw the role of Milosevic in stirring up nationalism as a problem, but only insofar as he had helped to awaken 'the latent resentments of the earlier Balkan wars': a process which to some degree, Binyon implied, happened spontaneously anyway, as older generations passed on resentments and 'visceral suspicions', keeping alive 'the feuds of the past'. A similar view was put forward by Roger Boyes, who identified Milosevic and the Serbs as the immediate cause of conflict but argued that 'Mr Milosevic … is only part of the overall Balkans problem' (*Times*, 5 June). This larger problem, Boyes suggested, was ingrained in the region's geography and history: the Balkans had seen 'centuries of bloodshed' because of being situated 'on the outer cusp of modern Europe, on the faultline of empires', and had suffered historically from 'an inability to integrate minorities or to progress much beyond clannish political structures and corrupt self-serving economic management'. This view of the Balkans as a backward region on the outer limits of 'modern Europe' could be understood to have been a matter of choice: Richard Beeston (*Times*, 17 June), for example, argued that 'The Serbs had the choice of becoming another boring, prosperous Western European nation like those around them, but instead chose the well-worn path of Balkans tribalism'. More often, however, Serbia's political backwardness was understood to be the product of cultural factors – as, for instance, when Tom Walker argued that the Serbs' 14th-century clash with the Ottoman empire had had a long-lasting effect on the 'Serbian national psyche'. The Serbs were 'taking on Nato' in 1999, Walker suggested, because they were 'haunted by the ghost of Lazar', the Serbian prince defeated by the Turks at the 1389 battle of Kosovo Polje (*Times*, 25 March).

In the *Mail*, this type of explanation was often linked to doubts about the wisdom and efficacy of international intervention. A long feature by Edward Heathcoat-Amory and Steve Doughty, for example, described Kosovo as a

'Timebomb with a 600-year fuse', a 'cauldron of ethnic and religious rivalry' and a 'horrendously complicated tangle of ancient religious and ethnic hatreds', which presented the West with a 'dangerous dilemma' (*Mail*, 25 March). Announcing that 'Today's troubles in Kosovo began in 1389', they noted that, despite the West's apparent success in ending conflict in Bosnia, 'deep hatreds' still existed there and Nato peacekeepers worked against a 'background of mistrust, revenge and racial hatred'. Heathcoat-Amory and Doughty pushed this argument to its logical conclusion, wondering whether the only real solution might be simply to allow the strongest side to win: 'if the West's only concern was to build a lasting peace in the Balkans, it should perhaps have had the moral courage to stand aside as Milosevic behaved like a butcher, and allow the Serbs to take over Kosovo, after all'. The same day's editorial argued, also in the context of emphasising the 'doubts and risks as NATO goes to war', that 'this is a part of the world which has for centuries been consumed with seething hatreds' (*Mail*, 25 March), while the following day's leader column again raised questions about the Nato action, arguing that there was 'little prospect yet that this conflict can be brought to a speedy conclusion' and describing Kosovo as a 'seething cockpit of nationalist hatreds' (26 March). Similarly, shortly after the end of the war, *Mail* reporter Ross Benson characterised the Balkans as a region where 'blood feuds are a way of life [and] where atrocity begets retribution'. This was in the context of reporting the flight of Kosovo Serbs, and carried the suggestion that the underlying dynamic of conflict had simply been reversed rather than resolved: 'hatred still courses violently through this troubled land', said Benson: 'First the Albanians. Now the Serbs. More graves to be discovered' (15 June).

Articles such as these often made exactly the connection between 'ethnic explanations' and a non-interventionist policy stance which critics have identified in relation to Bosnia and other conflicts. Indeed, the connection seems clearer in the *Mail*'s early stance on Kosovo than it was in the coverage of Bosnia examined in Chapter 3. Yet the significance of this explanation should not be overstated. Firstly, an emphasis on 'horrendously complicated ethnic hatreds' and the like did not necessarily imply a non-interventionist stance, particularly when it appeared outside the pages of the *Mail*. The article by Boyes cited above, for example, was headlined: 'Europe Cannot Afford to Wash Its Hands of the Balkans Mess' (*Times*, 5 June). Despite arguing that 'In the Balkans, peace is merely a lull between combats', Boyes maintained that a commitment to exporting 'democracy and prosperity' by integrating the region into the European Union could bring a better future. In the *Guardian* (23 March), Hugo Young anticipated that Nato would have to try to 'keep apart visceral ethnic enemies never likely to surrender their mutual hatred', and he described the prospect of war as 'ominous', predicting that 'it will be hell'. Yet this did not imply that he was against it: Young argued in favour of intervention in 'defence of a community being treated so hideously'. Indeed, even in the *Mail* an emphasis on 'centuries-old hatreds' did not, as we shall see later, imply outright opposition to the war: it was more a way of highlighting doubts and dangers than of arguing for disengagement.

Secondly, 'ethnic' explanations were not incompatible with blaming Milosevic and/or the Serbs for causing the war. Two days after his article emphasising the alleged impact of medieval history on the contemporary Serbian 'national psyche', for example, Walker returned to the theme, describing Kosovo as 'Europe's faultline' and again rehearsing the story of 1389, but this time focusing on how, in the more recent past, Milosevic had used a sense of historical grievance to present himself as 'the messiah of a rekindled Serb nationalism' (*Times*, 27 March). Similarly, in the *Independent* (3 April) James Dalrymple recalled hearing 'the language of the Balkans' during a conversation with a Macedonian taxi driver: 'The words and the thoughts that fester into hatreds that lead inevitably down the road to ethnic cleansing and mass murder'. While this rather fanciful leap from minicab drivers to mass murder implied some peculiarity in the culture of the Balkans, Dalrymple also laid the blame squarely on 'Milosevic and his brand of ruthless barbarism', and suggested that the Serbs were 'using the same techniques that the Nazi oppressors employed nearly 60 years ago'. The invocation of the Nazis, discussed further below, implied that the conflict should be understood in terms of one-sided oppression rather than mutual ethnic hatreds, but despite their apparent incompatibility the two sorts of explanation were also used simultaneously by Nato leaders. As Jonathan Freedland noted in the *Guardian* (7 April), the Clinton administration encouraged 'comparisons of the current catastrophe with the Nazi slaughter of the 1940s' at the same time as the President explained the conflict in Kosovo as the product of 'old, even primitive hatreds'. While there was a strand of 'ethnic' explanation in the coverage sampled for this study, it was largely overshadowed by explanations which blamed Serbian nationalist aggression for the conflict.

This second type of explanation – accounting for 73.1 per cent of all articles which offered some explanation of the Serb/Albanian conflict – understood 'ethnic hatreds' to be the product of recent political circumstances, not the inevitable result of some centuries-old feud. In this perspective, violence was seen to result from the Serbs' pursuit of a deliberate policy (of 'ethnic cleansing' or genocide) rather than as the spontaneous product of old animosities between different ethnic groups. This type of explanation identified Milosevic as responsible for starting the conflict in Kosovo, and often all the wars of Yugoslavia's break-up during the 1990s. As Rosemary Righter put it in the *Times* (2 April): 'The touch-paper of the Balkan conflagration was lit in Kosovo, by the inflammatory rhetoric of one man, Slobodan Milosevic'. This position was adopted in editorials in all three broadsheets examined for this study: the *Times* said the Kosovo conflict was 'a war started by a man suspected of atrocities' (28 May); the *Independent* described Milosevic as the 'architect of a decade of misery in the Balkans' (10 June); and the *Guardian* called him 'the architect of this historic calamity' (11 June). This strand of explanation sometimes entailed a close focus on Milosevic's personal biography and psychology. In the *Mail* (24 March), for example, Mark Almond described Milosevic as a 'psychopath' and trawled through his family history to suggest that the 'emotional backdrop' of 'a family bent on self-destruction' had given him a 'relentless drive for survival, no matter who or what might suffer as a consequence'. Similarly, in the *Guardian* (27 March) Ian Traynor argued that Milosevic was driven by 'the death wish that haunts his family', while in the *Times* (3 April) Janine di Giovanni identified Milosevic's wife, Mirjana Markovic, as 'the driving force behind her husband's ruthless quest for power'.

Other articles focused less narrowly on Milosevic's family and persona, instead arguing that the problem was the Serbian government and/or the Serbian people. One version of this explanation, which appealed particularly to writers in the *Guardian*, understood the problem in terms of colonialism and racism. Jonathan Steele, for example, described Kosovo as having suffered from 'Ten years of apartheid' and said that the current conflict was best understood as 'racism run riot' (*Guardian*, 13 April). The apartheid theme had already been advanced by the *Guardian*'s Ian Traynor, in a 25 March article arguing that Milosevic had 'erected a police state built on ethnic apartheid in Kosovo'; and it was taken up a few days later at a press briefing by the Foreign Secretary, Robin Cook, who accused Milosevic of 'trying to recreate a new apartheid in Europe'.[18] The day after Cook's briefing, the *Times* ran an interview with him making this point ('I cannot accept apartheid through ethnic cleansing in Europe') and in another article in the same day's edition Michael Evans said that Milosevic was attempting to 'fulfil his vision of an apartheid state in Europe' (30 March). Steele also suggested that 'The Serbs have always treated Kosovo like a colony', implying that the province was not really part of Serbia; this idea was echoed on the same day by Ian Hunt, who claimed that 'The situation that has led to war is a semi-colonial one' (*Guardian*, 13 April). Steele's suggestion of racism is also notable, in that he evidently intended to accuse Serbs in general rather than only Milosevic and his regime; indeed, he claimed that 'the racism which most feel towards Albanians cannot be overestimated'. Similarly, Hunt wrote of the 'Serbs' failure to understand ... that their own security depended on treating all "citizens" as equals' (13 April).

The blaming of the Serbs and/or Milosevic specifically for the conflict was reinforced by a number of descriptive devices used across the coverage as a whole. Box 5.1 indicates that descriptions of Milosevic tended to emphasise his guilt, either directly, by characterising him as a criminal and as the cause of the war, or indirectly, by describing him as a brutal dictator. There was some disagreement over how to describe him, most obviously regarding his success or failure as a politician: David Aaronovitch, for example, argued that 'the legend of Super-Slobba, the Belgrade Machiavelli' was one of the 'great myths of the Kosovan war' (*Independent*, 8 April), while other writers characterised him in just these terms. There was also some disagreement over how far to demonise Milosevic. In its 12 April editorial, for example, the *Guardian* argued that 'the Government should be cautious about demonising Slobodan Milosevic too aggressively', since he would likely be a necessary negotiating partner, while the *Independent* argued to the contrary that 'The invention of the monster "Slobba" of Belgrade is a justified use of tabloid techniques to portray a tyrant in vivid colours' (editorial, 3 April).

The papers did agree, however, on Milosevic's criminality and welcomed his indictment by the ICTY. The *Mail* (4 June) and *Guardian* (11 June) both

Box 5.1 Descriptions of Milosevic

Tyrannical dictator
- 'a dictator' (President Bill Clinton)
- 'a dictator' (Prime Minister Tony Blair)
- 'a nationalist dictator' (Tony Blair)
- 'a dictator' (UNHCR spokeswoman)
- a 'ruthless dictator' (General Sir Charles Guthrie, Chief of the Defence Staff)
- 'the Serbian dictator' (Alex Salmond, MP)
- rightly described [by Blair] as a dictator
- a dictator
- the dictator
- the Serb dictator
- The Serbian dictator
- the Yugoslav dictator
- the brutal dictator
- a brutal and thuggish dictator
- a brutal dictator with much innocent blood on his hands
- a brutal dictator who cares more about Kosovo than life itself
- a stubborn Balkan dictator
- elusive dictator
- an isolated and bankrupt dictator
- defeated Yugoslav dictator
- a great dictator with all the trademarks of one: madness, cruelty and longevity
- 'tinpot dictator' (historian Nikolai Tolstoy)
- the increasingly popular ruler of an increasingly dictatorial regime
- a tyrant
- the tyrant
- this tyrant
- A mad, bad tyrant
- tyrant who thrived on war
- loves power and has a mighty security apparatus
- the Yugoslav strongman
- the Serb strongman
- the Serbian strongman
- the Belgrade strongman
- Serbia's strongman
- the 57-year-old strongman who has teased and toyed with the West for eight years
- [portrayed by Britain's Defence Secretary George Robertson as] genocidal
- a leader who has revived all the horrific images of the worst excesses of the Nazis in the Second World War
- 'Adolf Hitler Jr.' (US official)
- Belgrade's own little Hitler
- 'he reminds me of Hitler' (Ilona Rothe, founder of Mothers Against the War)

- 'an evil man … Hitler in a different country' (Falklands veteran Simon Weston)
- Slobodan Milosevic and Saddam Hussein of Iraq, perhaps the world's most reviled dictators
- Saddam's new friend
- Like Saddam Hussein the man is a monster
- 'another Saddam Hussein … an evil man who is putting two fingers up to everyone else' (UK taxi driver in vox pop)
- a nasty job of work but … not Hitler or Stalin
- 'a ruthless ruler' (Bishop of Oxford)
- an utterly ruthless ethnic cleanser

Brutal
- the butcher
- the Butcher of Belgrade
- the Butcher of the Balkans
- butcher of the Balkans
- the loveable Butcher of the Balkans
- 'This Balkan butcher' (KLA spokesman)
- painted [by Nato governments] as a bloodthirsty Balkan monster
- 'barbaric'
- Warlord
- a warlord
- Serbia's hard man
- the old brute
- blood-soaked
- 'callous' (senior Nato diplomat)
- Callous Milosevic
- 'a playground bully' (Madelaine Albright)
- Like the bully in the school yard
- a bully
- 'not Hitler but a Balkan thug' (Henry Kissinger)
- thug
- Psychopath who duped the West
- 'a man-made psychopath' (expatriate Yugoslav doctor)
- the 'madman'
- may be both mad and bad
- Like his equally crazy sidekick Dr Radovan Karadzic in Bosnia, he casts himself as a persecuted genius, a Serbian hero … [with a] by now highly developed martyr complex
- 'a very evil man who is willing to take horrendous steps against civilians' (Julian Brazier, MP)

Criminal
- 'an indicted war criminal' (Tony Blair)
- 'an indicted war criminal' (Foreign Secretary Robin Cook)
- 'an indicted war criminal' (Labour MP)
- 'a prime candidate for trial [for war crimes]' (human rights lawyer Geoffrey Bindman)
- 'a criminal' (Kosovo Albanian journalist)
- 'a war criminal' (Kosovo Albanian lawyer)
- a man [Nato] brands a war criminal
- a man accused of being a war criminal
- eminently indictable [by the ICTY]
- Indicted criminal
- indicted war criminal
- an indicted war criminal
- the indicted war criminal
- the first serving head of state to be indicted as a war criminal
- the architect of this historic calamity, and now an indicted war criminal
- the first sitting head of state to be charged with crimes against humanity
- as an indicted war criminal … an impossible leader for a self-respecting country
- the Yugoslav President and indicted war criminal
- a moderate war criminal
- an indicted but unconvicted leader
- a man suspected of atrocities
- a war criminal
- the war criminal
- now officially a war criminal
- an international outlaw
- a criminal political leader
- the man who heads the tribunal's wanted list
- a man of criminal mind and zero compassion

Cause of war
- 'a dictator who has done nothing but start new wars' (Bill Clinton)
- 'a man who has devastated [the Serbs'] country' (Tony Blair)
- a man who has brought 'so much death and barbarism' to the Balkans (Tony Blair)
- 'hell bent on war' (George Robertson)
- a man intent on destabilisation after a year of broken promises

(paraphrasing Nato spokesman)
- a man who has caused four wars and thousands of deaths yet managed to stay in power for almost 10 years
- 'a man accused of war crimes, a man who has been responsible for so many wars before this one' (Kosovo Albanian refugee)
- 'he is the problem' (KLA leader Hashim Thaci)
- 'the problem, not the solution' (attributed to British ministers)
- by far the greatest barrier to peace in the Balkans
- the aggressor
- a territorial expansionist
- the author of [the] crisis
- architect of a decade of misery in the Balkans
- the cause of Yugoslavia's agony
- the man who is the agent of the old federation's collapse
- 'The instigator of Serbia's misery' (Montenegrin government spokesman)
- the man who humiliated the [Yugoslav] army three times in a decade
- the malign survivor of the mayhem he launched on the Balkans
- an addict seeking out ever more powerful enemies to satisfy his craving for confrontation and crisis
- a violent interloper on the stage of European history
- the most dangerous and ruthless man in Europe
- the arch-villain

Unsuccessful leader
- a man whose time has passed
- probably the least successful national leader since Baby Doc Duvalier led Haiti
- head of a shrinking, beleaguered, increasingly impoverished nation
- a disastrous leader of Serbia
- the Serbian Nero who fiddled while his country burned
- as callous about the fate of his fellow Serbs as about the lives of Croats, Moslems or Albanians
- at last begins to look like the loser that he must, at

whatever cost, be eventually proved to be
- the most brutal and unsuccessful leader [Yugoslavia] has ever had
- Like a desperate poker player
- a leader who has led his country into war, isolation and increased economic depravation

Cunning politician
- The master of Belgrade
- The master of Machiavellian statecraft
- Wily ruler who thrives on political turmoil
- a brilliant politician
- equipped with the finest of political noses
- shrewd, manipulative leader
- wily
- the old fox
- a cunning operator
- cunning operator
- consummate survivor
- unlikely survivor
- a master escapologist
- 'a great operator, a great talent, but ... ideologically empty' (Serbian political commentator)
- 'a brilliant negotiator' (former US ambassador Warren Zimmermann)
- this tough and cunning operator whose capacity to trick, delay and dissemble will not be ended by military action alone
- one of the wiliest, toughest, most treacherous, canny, tricky, ruthless and resourceful human beings Madeleine Albright had ever encountered
- a master of procrastination and exploiting divisions among his opponents
- like a Serbian Brutus
- 'a rotten strategist but a good tactician' (Professor Michael Clarke)
- a master tactician
- a tactically shrewd opponent
- the master of the weasel phrase
- a master manipulator of ethnic and national feeling in the former Yugoslavia
- 'a man who had used the worst evil possible to rise

to political power' (Ken Livingstone, MP)
- a 'serial breaker of promises' ('senior [British] government sources')
- a man who has broken so many promises
- 'a liar' (KLA spokesman)
- a liar (attributed to refugees)
- a liar and a cheat
- a proven liar
- 'power-mad' (expatriate Serb)
- 'a genius of evil' (Serbian painter)

Personalised descriptions
- Monstrous
- a disgusting creature
- a vile and wicked man
- this appalling man
- unquestionable villain ... bloodstained individual without any redeeming feature: a walking argument for the existence of hell
- dour and always smartly dressed
- stocky, baby-faced, misty-eyed and sharply dressed
- tidy, methodical
- a man of extraordinary reticence
- A depressive and reclusive man
- cigar-smoking, brandy-drinking
- unpredictable and Byzantine
- 'has a death wish' (Western diplomat)
- suicidal, on a mission to destroy everything he touches
- 'capable of anything' (OSCE observer)
- nothing but trouble
- the prisoner of his personal and tribal history
- an enigmatic mixture of bravado and cowardice
- fears strength as much as he exploits weakness
- The defiant Yugoslav leader
- faintly absurd
- [with Yevgeny Primakov, Russian Prime Minister] two slab-faced heavyweights
- 'that bastard' (Crown Prince Aleksandar Karadjordjevic)
- Uncle Slobodan
- Slobba

Descriptions of Milosevic were too numerous to include all of them here: we counted 229 different terms. The descriptions omitted are: 17 which focused on his politics (ranging from 'unreconstructed communist', through 'fascist-communist boss' and 'nationalist bigot' to 'cynical opportunist'); 12 describing how he was viewed by Serbs (mostly as 'a hero'); and six describing him as having been tolerated by the West (as, for example, 'a man we could do business with' or 'a necessary evil').

Descriptions are in quotation marks where they appeared that way in the original; attributions are given where the article attributed a phrase.

described him in their editorial columns as 'an indicted war criminal': a formulation which, as discussed in Chapter 3, violated the usual presumption of innocence. Writing in the *Independent*, Steve Crawshaw took the indictment as confirmation of guilt, announcing that 'Mr Milosevic is now officially a war criminal' (17 June), an assumption that would not be made in an ordinary criminal case. The *Times* correctly noted that any presumption of guilt 'must now be officially suspended', but clearly implied that Milosevic was indeed guilty of war crimes, observing in an editorial headlined 'Indicted Criminal' that 'There are few governments that do not privately presume Slobodan Milosevic to be guilty of the most monstrous atrocities in Kosovo' (28 May). Before any indictment had been issued, the *Independent* expressed its 'hope that … Milosevic and his fellow war criminals will be brought to justice', asserting that its own news reporting 'should be enough to convict the Serbian leadership of crimes against humanity' (editorial, 1 April). This stance closely followed that of Nato leaders, who inadvertently undermined the claimed independence of the UN tribunal by issuing their own threats to prosecute Milosevic and others via the ICTY. In what appeared to be a coordinated series of statements in late March and early April, British ministers announced that they were gathering evidence to pass to the ICTY, naming individual political and military leaders who would be, in Cook's words, 'liable to face indictment before the international war crimes tribunal' (*Guardian*, 30 March). Similar statements were made by the Nato Secretary General, by the Nato press spokesman and by representatives of other Nato governments. Critics have argued that such statements – coupled with the fact that leading Nato governments were providing both the funding and enforcement capacity of the ICTY – suggest that the tribunal was acting politically (Skoco and Woodger 2000: 34–6). In any case, the effect of the indictment was undoubtedly to reinforce and legitimise Nato's claim to be fighting a criminal enemy.

Comparisons between the Serbs and the Nazis combined this theme of criminality with the idea that the conflict in Kosovo should be understood in terms of racism and colonialism. The Nazi comparison did not constitute an explicit and developed explanation of the conflict between Serbs and Albanians. Rather, the parallel was usually suggested in terms of images, echoes or precedents: reporters described 'pictures and stories … [which] recall the dark days of the second world war' (*Guardian*, 9 April), 'scenes reminiscent of the Nazi holocaust' (*Mail*, 3 April), or 'the most savage act of ethnic cleansing in Europe since the Second World War' (*Independent*, 10 June), for example. The closest any article in our samples came to developing such parallels into an explanation was a report on 9 April in the *Times* by Susan Bell on Operation Horseshoe, which claimed that this 'chilling document' was derived from an earlier proposal – drawn up in the 1930s by Serbian intellectual Vaso Cubrilovic and advocating the forcible expulsion of ethnic-Albanians from Kosovo – which had 'overtones of the run up to Hitler's Final Solution'. Bell's report was misleading in every way: in its comparison of Cubrilovic's text with Nazi ideology (see Johnstone 2002: 205–8); in its suggestion of continuity between the 1930s and the 1990s (Bell wrote that 'the blueprint for President Milosevic's ethnic cleansing was drawn up shortly before the Second World War'); and in the fact that, as noted earlier, the 'blueprint' supposedly discovered by the German government was a fake. In this she was not alone: in our samples of coverage, no report expressed any scepticism about Operation Horseshoe.

There was some questioning of the Nazi comparison more generally, however: in our samples of coverage, 20 articles – including, significantly, three editorials – questioned or rejected comparisons between Milosevic and Hitler or between the actions of the Serbs and those of the Nazis. Such articles were written from a variety of perspectives. To Simon Heffer in the *Mail* (27 March), for instance, the comparison seemed 'ludicrous' because he favoured a 'far more complex' explanation: 'the savagery that has been happening in what used to be Yugoslavia for the past eight years is simply part of a historical continuum stretching back to the Dark Ages'. For Jeremy Hardy in the *Guardian*, meanwhile, the parallel was rejected from the perspective of opposing the war: he argued that 'Hitler is mentioned, in order to suggest that anyone asking exactly what are the aims of this war, is a closet Nazi' (3 April). Objecting to the propagandistic use of the Nazi parallel did not necessarily imply opposition to the war, however: Vanora Bennett, for example, argued that it was clearly inaccurate and therefore made for ineffective propaganda, commenting that 'The case for intervention is not helped by exaggeration' (*Times*, 2 April). This seemed to be the spirit in which the *Guardian* (5 April, 26 May) and *Independent* (12 April) questioned the comparison in their leader columns. The *Guardian* argued for an escalation of the war, while bemoaning the fact that 'We practically ring up the Serbs to tell them attacks are on the way so that they can get everybody out of the buildings', but nevertheless said that what Yugoslav forces were known to have done was 'bad enough … without adding atrocities which may or may not have taken place in any number' (5 April) and that 'We do not yet know enough about what has happened in Kosovo to throw about words like "genocide"'(26 May).

Yet more often the Nazi parallel was adopted uncritically in news reports and commentaries: as against the 20 articles questioning the comparison, 147 reproduced it. In adopting this descriptive frame, journalists imitated and elaborated the rhetoric of Nato leaders, who freely used terms such as 'genocide' and 'genocidal' in their daily press briefings (Hume 2000: 71–2). In our samples, around half the articles drawing parallels with the Nazis were simply reporting the views of sources (69 articles, or 46.9 per cent); the rest of the time, journalists adopted the idea as their own. To illustrate how this worked, we can look at coverage on 1 April, when the newspapers reported a number of statements evoking the Nazi comparison. White House spokesman Joe Lockhart said that 'We're beginning to see evidence of potential genocide' (*Independent*) and Rudolf Scharping, the German Defence Minister, claimed there were 'concentration camps' in Kosovo (*Times*). The *Guardian* reported similar claims by German Foreign Minister Joschka Fischer and KLA leader Hashim Thaci, while in the *Mail* Paul Harris paraphrased the views of a Kosovo Albanian refugee, who was 'part of the biggest exodus in Europe since World War II': 'How, she asks, can a world approaching the 21st century be capable of genocide?' In the same day's editions, reporters and commentators also adopted this viewpoint themselves. The *Guardian*'s front-page story described 'scenes reminiscent of the treatment of the Jews in the second world war', while on page 3 Ian Traynor and Jonathan Steele discovered 'grim new echoes of Nazi horrors', a 'chilling echo of the pogroms and camps of the Nazi era' and 'eerie reminders of Nazi methods'; and in a further article Traynor said that 'Serbian forces [were] rampag[ing] through Kosovo in an ethnic cleansing blitz and a genocidal cull of Kosovan males'. That day's *Times* editorial wrote of 'the genocidal operations in Kosovo', while in the *Independent* Emma Daly and Marcus Tanner reported 'Serbs try for "final solution"', and columnist David Aaronovitch said that 'when you examine the views of the man and woman on the Belgrade tram, it is easier to see how so many Germans in the Thirties bought the Joseph Goebbels version of the world'. The *Independent*'s Robert Fisk visited the site where, 'by an awful coincidence, Nato's first salvo of this new Balkan war landed only a few hundred metres from the mass grave of 7,000 Yugoslav civilians, victims of the worst Nazi atrocity of the Second World War'; looking at pictures of the 1941 massacre of Serbs he 'could not help thinking … of what was happening on the other side of the mountains to the south, in Kosovo'. In the *Mail*, David Williams reported the same story and drew out the same 'haunting similarities' between the current actions of Serbian forces and those of the Nazis, while his colleague, David Hughes, also heard an 'echo of the Holocaust', and wrote that the Serbs were engaged in 'an Orwellian attempt to wipe [Kosovo Albanians] from history' (the adjective was taken from the previous day's Nato press briefing, when the spokesman had described 'a kind of "Orwellian" scenario').[19]

These examples are by no means untypical. It may seem rather odd, therefore, that at the same time as newspapers featured 'echoes of the Holocaust' on their news pages, they also questioned the comparison in their comment pages and even in editorial columns. There seems to have been an element of bad faith in some of the commentaries and reports drawing parallels with the Nazis. It is notable, for example, that while there was no explicit questioning of the German government's claims about Operation Horseshoe, neither did this story receive the kind of attention we might expect had journalists believed it to be genuine. This was, after all, supposed to be documentary proof of Milosevic's 'genocidal' intent, yet apart from four articles in the *Times* the story featured only briefly in one report in the *Independent* (8 April) and the other two papers in our sample ignored the story. Moreover, in addition to the 20 articles challenging the Nazi comparison, a further nine articles treated it in a highly self-conscious way. Richard Norton-Taylor, for example, noted that the vocabulary used by British government officials in discussing Kosovo contained 'many deliberate echoes of Hitler's regime' (*Guardian*, 3 April); Michael Binyon observed that media coverage conveyed 'intentional echoes' of the Holocaust, although he said that this was because of the use of 'emotive language and images' rather than a matter of 'deliberate distortion' (*Times*, 3 April). Most strikingly, journalists sometimes drew attention to the deliberate use of the comparison by Nato leaders but then pressed ahead and used it themselves. The *Guardian*'s Ian Traynor, for example, observed that the German government had 'opted for a propaganda offensive likening Slobodan Milosevic to Adolf Hitler' while the German media featured 'calculated echoes of the Nazi era' (3 April). Yet a week later Traynor himself wrote of 'a grim echo of the Nazi deportations of European Jews' (10 April). He did not say whether this too was 'calculated' and part of a 'propaganda offensive'. His colleague, Jonathan Freedland, developed the knack of both repudiating and embracing the Nazi comparison within the space of a single article. In a 26 March commentary he wrote that 'No one is saying that the Serb war against the ethnic-Albanians compares with [the Holocaust]', but in the next breath warned that 'when confronted with state-run mass murder we cannot go on doing nothing':

> Unless we want to see the same old story played out once more, we have to act. The alternative is to sit through the Oscars of 2020, watching Steven Spielberg pick up Best Picture for Jovanovic's List: Slaughter in Kosovo – adding that benighted place to the roll-call of Cambodia, Rwanda and all the other theatres of hate where we shamed ourselves by doing nothing. (*Guardian*, 26 March)

Similarly, in a 14 April article Freedland drew attention to the way that Cook had 'ratcheted up the rhetoric, identifying Serbia with fascism three times in a single flourish', but then added a flourish of his own, arguing that 'Just as the US scholar Daniel Goldhagen has shown how it was impossible for ordinary Germans to be ignorant of the Final Solution, so today's Serbs can hardly claim to be in the dark'. Judging from the tone of some of the coverage, it appears that journalists not only were well aware of the propaganda value to Nato of drawing comparisons between the Serbs and the Nazis, but also suspected that the comparison was not really justified. Many nevertheless invoked the Holocaust, closely following the rhetoric of Nato leaders and further reinforcing the dominant explanation of the conflict between Serbs and Albanians, which understood the problem in terms of Serbian aggression.

Nato intervention

Given the pattern of explanations in relation to the conflict between ethnic-Albanians and Serbs, it is not surprising that most explanatory articles focusing on the Nato bombing framed it as legitimate and necessary. Of the 119 articles which offered an explanation of Nato action, around a fifth simply followed the lead of Western governments in presenting it, without further elaboration, as an attempt to prevent (15 articles) or to halt and reverse (nine articles) the humanitarian disaster and the Serbian campaign of 'ethnic cleansing' which had caused it. Other explanatory articles revolved, in one way or another, around the question of whether intervention was driven by Western values or interests, or both. As noted earlier, presenting Nato action as 'moral' was central to its claimed legitimacy, given its at best ambiguous legality. Yet while the accent, in official pronouncements, was certainly on morality, Nato leaders also often claimed that there was in fact a convergence of Western values and interests. In a major speech during the conflict, Blair even elaborated this into a 'doctrine of international community', based on a 'subtle blend of mutual self interest and moral purpose'.[20]

Initially, Western interests were explained in terms of what intervention would prevent from happening – further violence, a refugee crisis and regional instability. On the eve of bombing, for example, Nato Secretary General Javier Solana explained that: 'Our objective is to prevent more human suffering and more repression and violence against the civilian population of Kosovo. We must also act to prevent instability spreading in the region' (*Guardian*, 24 March). As violence in Kosovo escalated and the refugee crisis developed, the argument was not tenable in quite this form. Official claims about the bombing's moral purpose became grander and centred increasingly on what the military action implied about the values of Europe and the West. In a 14 April article for the *Mail*, for example, Solana described Nato as 'an Alliance based on values which its member countries hold in common' and argued that 'Kosovo is a defining moment not only for Nato, but for the kind of Europe we wish to live in at the beginning of the 21st century'. Even more sweepingly, Blair argued that the war had been in defence not only of European values but also of civilisation itself, describing it as a 'battle for the values of civilisation and democracy everywhere' (*Independent*, 24 May), and afterwards declaring that 'Good has triumphed over evil, justice has overcome barbarism and the values of civilisation have prevailed' (*Guardian*, 11 June).

At the same time as the moral rhetoric escalated, the discussion of claimed values coinciding with Western interests continued, although after the initial rationale of preventive action collapsed this had to be framed somewhat differently, with the emphasis now on containing conflict and preserving Nato's own prestige. While Blair's 'biggest motivation' was said to be his 'strong moral sense', for example, he also reportedly had 'no difficulty in convincing himself that war … is in Britain's national interest' and was motivated by both 'fear of a Balkans war eventually convulsing the Continent and the potential damage to Nato's credibility' (*Times*, 2 April). The bombing's seemingly ever-larger moral purpose could also be cast in terms of a convergence of interests and values, in the sense that spreading Western values would lead to future peace and security: hence Blair argued that 'The spread of our values makes us safer'.[21] The invocation of interests can be understood partly as a sign of real anxieties – no doubt the concerns over Nato credibility were genuine, for example – and also as providing another string to the bow of those arguing in favour of intervention.

For supporters of the bombing, explaining it as a matter of self-interest as well as of moral values provided an answer to the criticism of double standards. That is to say, when critics pointed out that the West's proclaimed 'values' had not led to intervention in other cases, it could be argued that Kosovo was different because it also directly engaged Western interests. 'This is realpolitik, not a Blue Peter appeal', said Freedland, for example, dismissing such critics as naive. If self-interest 'converges with an urgent, humanitarian imperative, as it has in Kosovo, the left should not whine', he said, 'It should celebrate' (*Guardian*, 26 March). His fellow *Guardian* commentator Hugo Young, having initially taken the view that Nato's main motivation was 'humanitarian impulse', merely 'propped up by a thin strategic view of what might or might not otherwise happen in the wider Balkans' (1 April), later argued that 'Realpolitik, though absent at the start, now wholly occupies the scene' (13 April). Nato had to continue bombing because it 'cannot afford to lose', maintained Young: 'If it does, the stability of southern Europe will be mortally in peril'. Strikingly, while 21 articles took up the 'convergence of interests and values' idea, almost all of them were based around an exposition of the views Nato leaders. Only in the *Guardian* did journalists take on and develop the argument themselves. The paper's 26 March leader column acknowledged that 'Double standards abound' in Western foreign policy, but argued that 'there is nothing dishonourable in the idea of national interest nor in the practical judgment that in the circumstances, the balance of right and interest tips in one direction'.

About the same number of articles, mostly written from a critical perspective, identified some sort of tension between interests and values (23 articles, or 19.3 per cent of those explaining Nato intervention). These were of two quite different types. Around half of them (12 in total) cast doubt on the sincerity of all the 'values' talk. Anti-war commentators argued that the moral claims were propagandistic cover for hidden interests. Tariq Ali, for example, identified 'much more sordid' motives, to do with redefining Nato 'from a defensive alliance into a zapping organisation' which could 'hit a target state anywhere in the world to defend the interests of the United States' (*Guardian*, 1 April). Similarly, Serbian writer Srdja Trifkovic said the US was pursuing 'selfish interests' and hoping to establish an 'American military and political powerbase in southeastern Europe' (*Times*, 18 March). Others made the different but related point that Nato politicians were motivated by a desire to demonstrate their own righteousness. *Mail* columnist Lynda Lee-Potter said that politicians had 'embarked on a dangerous bombing mission to prove to us that they were intrepid and fearless' (31 March), for example, while in the *Times* Ben Macintyre suggested that Clinton had wanted to put the scandals of his presidency behind him and 'end his term in office in the glow of martial victory and moral rectitude' (20 May). The other half of these articles (11 in total) questioned the 'values and interests' formula from the opposite perspective, contending that Nato leaders had become carried away with their own emotions and moral fervour. Arguing that intervention had made the situation worse, for example, the *Independent*'s Robert Fisk suggested that bombing was 'about getting our own back' for 'the years of Western humiliation in Bosnia' (30 March). Somewhat similarly, Simon Jenkins said that Western troops were being 'marched into battle by fidgety leaders to get nasty pictures off the television screen':

> A wild compulsion appears to have seized Western liberalism as it gazes ogle-eyed at whatever atrocity the networks have selected for the nightly 'grief pornography' slot. It is as if, with the Cold War over, liberals now want their turn at playing war games. They want to feel the surge of power, the roar of the chopper blade, the thrill of 'bombs away'. (*Times*, 9 April)

Here the criticism was not that the professed values were not sincerely held, but that to construct a foreign policy around them was irresponsible and dangerous. 'Non-intervention in foreign civil wars', noted Jenkins, 'has been normal British policy in the past' (*Times*, 14 April).

While Jenkins was critical of the Nato action, five further *Times* articles argued from a pro-war position that more weight should be given to considerations of strategic interest. In a series of editorials at the beginning of the campaign, the *Times* highlighted the danger of seeing 'the region once again perilously destabilised' if Nato did not act (24 March), contended that one of the 'most powerful arguments for NATO's engagement' was the fear of 'a wider Balkan war' (25 March) and urged the government to 'stress the consequences of regional instability to the whole of Europe' (26 March). This line partly expressed the paper's conviction that emphasising matters of national, strategic interest would bolster the argument for intervention, but it also perhaps indicated a certain nervousness about the precedent being set. As its 25 March editorial pointed out, 'Nato has departed dramatically from its original founding purpose.... It was no part of Nato doctrine to wage war against a sovereign European state other than in self-defence.' This theme was pursued by Peter Riddell, who also sought to make the case for intervention on strategic rather than ethical grounds, and who argued that there had been 'too much moral outrage and not enough candour' from politicians. Riddell drew attention to the way Nato action seemed to herald 'the creation of a new doctrine of intervention', but approvingly noted the view of the former Conservative Foreign Secretary Douglas Hurd that 'this doctrine of the humanitarian duty to intervene is regional, not universal' (26 March, 31 March). The preference for an emphasis on interests more than values was both a pro-war argument and a way to set limits on the otherwise boundless possibilities for ethical interventionism. In this, the *Times* sought to answer the concerns of Conservative Party supporters who 'cannot see ... a compelling national interest ... and fear that the humanitarian reasons for action ... might set a dangerous precedent' (26 March).

However, the most common explanation for Nato bombing was that it was moral: this theme featured in 46 (38.7 per cent) of the articles seeking to explain the intervention. The morality of the bombing could be explained in various ways. Particularly toward the end of the war, writers sometimes assumed that Nato's moral credentials were beyond debate and simply asserted that this was 'a war launched for humanitarian purposes' (*Guardian*, 8 June), that Nato had 'good intentions' (*Guardian*, 9 June) or that 'This was among the very few wars fought not in pursuit of national interests but for reasons of simple humanity' (*Independent*, editorial, 10 June). Articles which elaborated a fuller explanation of the moral character of Nato action did so in two main ways. One key idea – implicitly reinforced by the dominant explanation of the conflict within Kosovo as the product of Serbian aggression – derived the morality of the bombing from the evil it was trying to stop. Francis Wheen, for example, argued that 'we are right to bomb the Serbs' in order to stop 'genocide' (*Guardian*, 7 April) and the *Times* explained the purpose of the war as 'the comprehensive reversal of Mr Milosevic's criminal drive to uproot and destroy an entire society' (editorial, 11 June). This type of explanation was offered by only 17 of the 119 articles explaining Nato intervention, but was given added weight by the sorts of explanatory frames and descriptive devices used across all coverage in relation to the conflict within Kosovo. As Steven Barnett observed in the *Guardian*, media reporting of 'pitiful, oppressed, degraded and sometimes brutalised refugees' provided 'precisely the evidence of ethnic cleansing and Serbian atrocity that we needed to convince us of the moral rectitude of this "humanitarian" war' (7 June).

The other key strand of explanation, appearing in 29 articles (24.4 per cent of explanations of the intervention) and again following the lead of official statements, framed Nato action as moral in terms of the West's or Europe's self-definition. *Independent* columnist Anne McElvoy, for example, argued that intervention in Kosovo would uphold 'Western ideals' and would help to create 'a wider sense of what it means to be a European, as bestowing some basic values and duties of care for one another' (24 March). Here, Western ideals were held to be the reason for intervention at the same time as the intervention was understood to confirm and consolidate such ideals. This is somewhat reminiscent of coverage of Bosnia when, as discussed in Chapter 3, concern for the West's or the UN's authority sometimes overshadowed professed concern for the victims of the war. As the *Guardian*'s Hugo Young put it: 'The testing of Europe is as great, in its way, as that of the brutalised Kosovars' (23 March). Indeed, the shameful experience of failure in Bosnia was sometimes recalled in order to explain why intervention was necessary. In the *Guardian*, for instance, Martin Woollacott said that the war was 'the terrible pay-off for years of circling the problem rather than confronting it' (3 April) and that action was necessary because of 'all the prevarications, wrong decisions, and wilful refusals to face the facts, over the years, of Western policy making in the Balkans' (27 March). Similarly, the *Times* said that 'The West must remember that it has been its piecemeal reactions to successive evils perpetrated by Mr Milosevic that forced Nato in the end to take up arms' (editorial, 5 June) and the *Independent* recalled that 'For years we forced our troops in the Balkans to scuttle around in armoured personnel carriers, dealing out charity rather than tackling the root cause of conflict: Serb aggression' (editorial, 25 March). 'Now', the paper hoped, 'that humiliation may be over'. The point of the contrast with Bosnia was thus to suggest that intervening in Kosovo proved or tested the West's resolve and commitment to its values. The *Mail* said the suffering of refugees was 'an indictment of European values and of civilisation itself' (editorial, 3 April), while for the *Guardian* Kosovo was 'a test for our generation' (editorial, 26 March); columnist Polly Toynbee, describing the Nato bombing as an act of 'chivalry' which could usher in a 'new ethical world order', said the war was 'the test of our resolve to lay new foundations for policing tyranny' (*Guardian*, 12 April).

Explanations of the conflict in Kosovo and of Nato action were not uniform but they did tend to draw the same conclusion: that the intervention was legitimate. As this implies, there is a close relationship between explanations and the prescriptions advanced in editorial columns and elsewhere, to which we turn next.

Prescriptions

The Kosovo conflict attracted 66 editorials in our first sample period and 43 in the second.[22] It was often observed at the time that divisions in the public debate about the war crossed traditional left/right lines. A *Guardian* editorial on 27 March, for example, argued that 'old battle lines have become blurred and confused' and noted in particular that 'The *Daily Mail* is deeply sceptical of the Nato operation; the *Guardian* more supportive'. As will already be apparent from our discussion of how newspapers explained the Kosovo conflict, they all supported Nato intervention,[23] although there were some interesting differences of emphasis. The discussion below explores these differences, concentrating mainly on our first sample period, when newspapers devoted more attention to tackling potential objections to and doubts about Nato action.

Initially it was the left-of-centre broadsheets, the *Guardian* and *Independent*, which took the most bellicose line, probably because they were most in sympathy with the moral framework presented by Blair, Clinton and other Nato leaders. On 19 March the *Guardian* announced that if Milosevic failed to accede to Nato demands, 'There will have to be a military intervention in Kosovo'; and by 22 March the *Independent* had decided that 'the use of force is justified and necessary'. While arguing for military action on the grounds of what it would do for Kosovo – the *Guardian* said that 'Kosovo must be saved' (23 March) and the *Independent* welcomed 'military action against a regime that has systematically attacked the rights of the people of Kosovo' (25 March) – both papers also explained the necessity of bombing in terms of upholding the honour of the West. For the *Guardian*, using force was the 'only honourable course for Europe and America', because otherwise a 'humiliated Europe might even have to bargain with Milosevic' in order to deliver humanitarian aid to Kosovo (23 March); for the *Independent*, it was important to 'show that Nato's threats aren't empty' (22 March) and to prove the 'credibility of the Western alliance' (25 March).

As noted earlier, the *Times* acknowledged 'widespread uneasiness about departing from Nato's defence-orientated doctrine, to attack a sovereign state which has not directly threatened the security of an Alliance member' (20 March). Yet the paper was in no doubt that intervention was needed and it argued, like the other broadsheets, that 'Nato's credibility is on the line; so are Kosovan lives'. The *Mail* was the least convinced of the case for war at the outset and emphasised the 'risks' of a 'dangerous enterprise' (24 March) and 'doubts about this risky enterprise' (27 March). These doubts were not allayed by the initial impact of the bombing: the *Mail* observed that 'the air strikes seem to be in danger of making a bad situation even worse' (27 March) and that 'in the short-term at least, the plight of the Kosovars has been worsened by Nato's action' (31 March). The latter editorial, however, declared that 'We have a moral duty' to help the refugees. The *Mail* launched its own charity appeal that day and began to shift its attitude to the war. The following day's editorial, headlined 'Why Britain Must Offer Sanctuary', acknowledged that sympathy for refugees 'may seem an unusual view from a newspaper which has campaigned so long and so hard for a more robust approach to bogus asylum seekers'. Yet these were 'unquestionably genuine refugees fleeing in terror', not 'economic migrants seeking simply to exploit Britain's generous welfare system' (1 April). Indeed, within a week the *Mail* was describing them as 'our fellow Europeans' (8 April), although by June its usual preoccupations seemed to have returned, as it reported 'concerns that it will be impossible to keep track of [Kosovo refugees], particularly if they find jobs and stop claiming benefit, leaving the door open for many to stay on after it is safe to return home' (1 June).

The fact that bombing provoked rather than prevented a refugee crisis evidently demanded an explanation. The *Times* argued robustly that violence by Serbian forces was 'not a response to airstrikes' but was 'long-planned, and would have gone ahead without a Nato decision to act' (30 March), and described the violence as 'deliberate and premeditated' (31 March). The *Independent* accepted that the situation was 'a disaster' (1 April) and that, in the short term, 'the war has only made the lot of the Kosovo Albanians even worse' (2 April). However, it countered these concerns with a number of arguments: first it claimed that 'the assault on the Kosovo Albanians began … before the war started' (30 March); then it conceded that 'it was the British Government's attempt to protect these people that provoked their enemies and forced them to head for the exits' but took this to mean that Britain now had a 'moral obligation' to help the refugees (1 April); and then it argued that 'the 'wholesale slaughter and "ethnic cleansing" provides the most vivid possible reminder of why it was necessary to take tough action against Milosevic in the first place' (2 April). The *Guardian* also acknowledged that intervention 'may be self-defeating, actually increasing the pain of Kosovo's Albanians, not soothing it' (30 March) and that 'the humanitarian crisis has turned into a catastrophe' (6 April), but it was in no doubt that the cause of the refugee crisis was 'fear of the Serbians rather than fear of the bombing' (8 April) and it saw no reason to question Nato's redefined objective: 'the aim of this war is the safe return of every Kosovo Albanian to their homes' (6 April). The *Mail* was most forthright in its criticism of Nato, arguing repeatedly that 'Nato's air strikes have worsened the plight of the Kosovars' (3 April), and it persisted with such criticisms even after the end of the war, reminding readers that bombing 'itself produce[d] an awesome tide of human suffering' (11 June).

As indicated above, however, with the onset of the refugee crisis the *Mail* actually shifted to a much firmer pro-war stance. Like the *Independent*, the *Mail* argued that 'we have a moral obligation to these huddled masses … because Nato air strikes have certainly worsened their plight' (1 April). More importantly, where the *Mail*'s early emphasis on doubts and risks appeared to be tied to its understanding of Kosovo as, in the words of the paper's 26 March editorial, a 'seething cockpit of nationalist hatreds', from early April it framed the conflict quite differently, adopting the 'Serbian aggression' explanation and drawing comparisons with the Holocaust. The key turning point was its 2 April editorial, which said that 'Nothing on this scale of human misery has been seen in Europe since the end of the Second World War' and described 'a grisly echo of Nazi horrors'. Later editorials took the same tone, linking denunciations of Serbian 'barbarism' with calls for tougher action. The paper's 5 April leader said that 'For once, the feeling that "something must be done" cannot be dismissed as facile sentiment', and urged that the 'Serbian killing machine' be 'halted and destroyed', for example; and its 7 April editorial, headlined 'Why the West Must Keep on Fighting', argued that the actions of 'Milosevic and his pack of murderous savages' meant that 'Nato must continue and intensify its campaign', even if it became 'increasingly difficult to avoid civilian casualties'.

Having overcome its initial doubts, the *Mail* even began calling for the use of ground troops. The paper started off asking nervously, 'Will we be dragged into a ground war?' (26 March) and in its 2 April leader comparing Kosovo with the Holocaust it still only wondered whether Nato might be forced 'to think the unthinkable and consider launching a ground war'. The *Mail* seemed to follow public opinion, noting on 29 March that 'the public ... does not wish to risk a single British life on the ground', but discovering on 10 April that 'polls in Britain, America and France suggest a shift in favour of using troops'. By 13 April, with more opinion poll evidence of public support, the *Mail* was 'Starting to think the unthinkable', even criticising 'the refusal to countenance the use of ground troops'. Later in the war the paper reinterpreted its own early doubts as having stemmed from politicians' reluctance to commit ground troops from the start. It commented that 'this is a conflict the West should never have engaged in unless it was prepared to go all the way which means ground action' (28 May), and maintained that it had been the decision to rule out ground forces which had 'provoked deep unease among those who supported Nato's aims' (5 June). The *Times* urged Nato 'to think the unthinkable' earlier, arguing in its 1 April leader for the use of ground troops, on the basis that it was 'even more unthinkable' that Nato should fail. Raising the prospect of Western 'humiliation' (5 April) if airstrikes did not work, the *Times* returned to the theme repeatedly, arguing for a ground invasion in seven further editorials.

Given their early pro-war stance, it is not surprising that the *Guardian* and *Independent* took a forceful line on ground troops. The *Independent* broached the question fairly cautiously in its 22 and 25 March editorials but argued on 30 March that 'Nato cannot delay sending in troops' since it was clear that 'the war has become a potentially genocidal conflict', and continued the theme in nine further editorials. The *Guardian* argued as early as 19 March that 'Air strikes are not enough' and called for a 'full-scale use of conventional force'. Having decided in advance that bombing alone would not be sufficient, the paper continued calling for the use of ground forces throughout March and April, and raised the issue in seven further editorials during our first sample period. As the war neared its end, however, the *Guardian* adopted a more critical tone. Whereas the *Mail* recast its initial doubts as wise foreknowledge of the need to threaten a ground invasion, the *Guardian* reinterpreted its recommendation of ground troops as a critique of the bombing, noting in its 4 June editorial that although air power seemed to have 'worked', it had done so only because it had been 'brutal beyond belief', widening targets to include civilian infrastructure and deploying indiscriminate munitions such as cluster bombs. Having called for a ground campaign even before the first bomb fell, the paper now said that, given the 'penchant for high-tech overkill' demonstrated in the airstrikes, a Nato invasion could have led to 'fearful bloodletting' (4 June). Perhaps the paper had forgotten its 5 April advice that Nato should conduct the war in a 'less conversational' fashion, so as not to allow the Serbs to 'get everybody out of the buildings' before they were bombed.

All the newspapers in this study called for Kosovo to become an international protectorate. The *Independent* recommended this solution on 30 March; it noted that the terms of the Rambouillet agreement were 'already moribund' and called on Nato to 'send in ground troops to establish a protectorate'. By 8 April the other papers had followed suit. The *Independent* also hinted at the possibility of making Kosovo an independent state, arguing that the objective was not only to 'restore Kosovo to the Kosovars' but to 'put an end to the ambitions of Milosevic for a Greater Serbia' (3 April), perhaps forgetting that Kosovo was already part of Serbia. The *Guardian* explicitly advocated an independent Kosovo, suggesting 'recognition of Kosovo's independence' (5 April) and 'a more or less autonomous Kosovan entity' (12 April). Indeed, the *Guardian* wished that the war aims could be extended to the regime in Belgrade, and argued from the start that, although 'Milosevic's fall from power cannot be a formal aim', the ultimate objective was 'a general settlement in former Yugoslavia, and such a settlement is hard now to envisage if Milosevic is still in power' (25 March). The *Times* voiced similar hopes, suggesting that the only chance of peace was if 'Nato's bombing alters the balance of power in Belgrade' (7 April) and advising that Nato should not allow Milosevic to retain his 'brutal hold on Kosovo, and with it political power in Serbia' (8 June).

The fact that Nato intervention meant interfering in the internal affairs of a sovereign state was not perceived as a major problem by most press commentators. The *Guardian*'s Ian Black, for example, simply noted that 'since the end of the cold war, the case for humanitarian intervention inside sovereign states has gained ground, beginning in Kurdistan in 1991' (25 March), while the *Independent* argued that 'Morally, the old doctrine that the internal affairs of nation states are inviolate ended with the Holocaust in Germany' (editorial, 3 April). As this suggests, it was the moral arguments for intervention which were thought to justify ignoring the principle of non-interference. Identifying somewhat less closely with the politicians making these 'moral' arguments, columnists in the *Times* and *Mail* sometimes sounded a note of caution and criticism. In the *Mail*, for example, Stephen Glover argued that 'Age-old international law is being challenged' and objected that the logic of 'ethical' intervention was an argument for perpetual war: 'Britain would become a war machine, a martial state with a single end in view' (13 April). In the *Times*, Riddell observed that one of the lessons drawn from Bosnia was that 'the international community could, and should, intervene in what had previously been regarded as internal conflicts' (5 April) and James Landale said that 'Establishing the principle that outside countries can intervene in a sovereign state to halt "ethnic cleansing" would mark a radical shift in the basic norms of international relations' (12 April). *Times* commentators seemed to have forgotten their own newspaper's enthusiasm for just such a 'radical shift' at the beginning of the 1990s in Somalia (see Chapter 2).

What *was* different in 1999, however, was that intervention was launched without explicit UN authority. This is of particular interest because a similar situation arose before the invasion of Iraq in 2003: then it was France which threatened to veto any UN resolution authorising war; in 1999 it was Russia and China which, as the *Mail* noted, were 'bitterly opposed to Nato's plans' (24 March). The *Mail* said that there would be 'questions in the UN over the legality of the action' but refrained from raising such questions itself and in fact never mentioned the issue again in its editorials during our sample periods. The *Times* observed matter of factly that 'Nato did not seek explicit approval from the UN Security Council, partly because Russia, one of five permanent members, would have used its veto' (26 March), but the paper sought to quash objections about the lack of UN mandate and supported Nato's claim to be acting on the basis of Resolution 1199, passed the previous year. Besides, argued the *Times*, Nato bombing was 'within the spirit of the Charter, to preserve peace and security', and not acting 'would have done far graver damage to international law' (25 March). This was broadly the argument advanced in 2003 over Iraq: that acting as a 'coalition of the willing' would uphold UN authority rather than undermine it. Indeed, in 1999 the *Independent* cited Blair's rationalisation of earlier bombing raids on Iraq to justify similar action against Yugoslavia, in particular his point that '"when the international community agrees certain objectives and then fails to implement them, those that can act, must"' (26 March). Similarly, the paper pointed to 'the lesson of Bosnia', namely that 'the only way to face down the bullies of Belgrade is by the threat of force' (22 March), and recalled how in Rwanda the 'feebleness of UN-led military forces [had] been demonstrated, with tragic consequences' (26 March). The *Guardian* also recalled past failures, arguing that the UN's 'constitution is a recipe for inaction' (26 March) and that the 'Cambodias and Rwandas of recent history were possible only because the strong governments of the West did nothing' (27 March). The sort of worries that arose about the lack of UN authority in 2003 seem to have been easily put aside in 1999.

Criticism

Overall, 313 articles (14.9 per cent of total coverage) voiced some criticism of the Nato campaign. The majority of these articles (232) appeared in our first sample period, when they also made up a greater proportion of coverage (19.2 per cent, compared with 81 articles, or 9.0 per cent in the second period). The *Guardian* carried the most critical articles (98), but it was in the *Mail* that criticism accounted for the greatest proportion of coverage: the paper carried 74 such articles, making up 25.1 per cent of its total coverage.[24] This is less than the proportion of critical coverage in the other case of 'humanitarian military intervention' in this book – Somalia – but still it is a substantial amount. The main limitation, as with Somalia, was not so much the quantity of criticism as its quality.

The issue which attracted most critical comment (94 articles) was Nato's reliance on air power. Both the *Guardian* and the *Times* began warning of the limitations of air power even before the first bomb fell. On 23 March, for instance, the *Guardian*'s Martin Walker raised the prospect that the Serbs might 'not bow to Nato air power, and force the alliance into a ground operation to take Kosovo and establish a Nato protectorate'; and in the *Times* Peter Riddell said there were 'questions about what bombing would achieve on its own', and noted that 'None of the Western allies … is willing to commit ground troops and risk the likely large casualties'. Very occasionally, the conclusion drawn from the apparent ineffectiveness of the bombing was that Nato should abandon the war, as when Norman Mailer wrote in the *Guardian* (25 May) that 'If the bombing is done with the notion that our own blood is not to be shed, it is obscene' and concluded that the only option now was to 'make peace'. More usually, however, criticism of the reliance on air power was linked to calls for ground troops to be deployed, or for greater support to be given to the KLA. The *Independent*'s Rupert Cornwell, for instance, argued that 'the West has a seemingly inescapable moral obligation to send in ground troops to provide the deliverance for the Kosovo Albanians it promised – but which its bombs could not deliver' (9 April) and the *Mail*'s regular military commentator on the conflict, Gulf war commander Sir Peter De La Billiere, repeatedly argued along the lines that 'the Allied task is to convince Milosevic that we really will – if necessary – move beyond air strikes' (2 April). Criticism of the reliance on air power, in other words, was generally an argument in favour of escalating the war.

The topics which attracted the second and third greatest amounts of criticism were that bombing was making the situation worse for Kosovo Albanians (59 articles) and that there was insufficient effort to provide aid and asylum for them (54 articles). These points potentially had more critical purchase, but the emphasis on the suffering of ethnic-Albanian refugees generally bolstered the case for war rather than challenged it. This was, as we saw, the editorial stance of the *Mail*, which argued that 'Nato's air strikes have worsened the plight of the Kosovars. We have an absolute moral obligation to them' (8 April). Similarly, Martin Kettle reported that in the US there had been 'increases in support for the bombing campaign, even though most Americans also believe it triggered the humanitarian cataclysm in Kosovo' (*Guardian*, 10 April); and Janine di Giovanni said that among the refugees themselves there was 'anger and resentment as the Nato airstrikes meant to save them have caused even more damage and heartache', but observed that 'They want ground troops to protect them' (*Times*, 31 March). As this suggests, criticism of the bombing for having worsened the plight of Kosovo Albanians could again lead to calls for a ground invasion. In the *Mail*, for example, Lynda Lee-Potter said that bombing had 'made things savagely worse for the Albanians', but since it was 'too late to stop now' the only option was 'the deployment of land troops' (31 March); and in the *Independent* Fisk said that, in terms of Nato's original objectives, 'we have already lost this war', and he went on to ask 'why, for God's sake, did no one ... realise the bombing must be supported by ground troops?' (5 April).

This is not to say that all criticism ended up in a call for an escalation of the conflict. Although not the *Independent*, the three other papers had regular contributors who took a clear anti-war stance – such as Mark Steel in the *Guardian*, Simon Jenkins in the *Times* and Corelli Barnett in the *Mail* – and all four papers reported the views of MPs, such as Tony Benn, who opposed the war. Some of this criticism was far-reaching, challenging the basis and legitimacy of Nato intervention. In the *Mail*, for example, Barnett noted that 'This sovereign state has been offered a choice between a foreign army of occupation on her soil if she did sign a deal, or being bombed if she did not' (23 March), while in the *Guardian* Richard Gott said that establishing a protectorate 'would amount to a new colonialism' (10 April) and described Blair as 'an old-fashioned imperialist' (20 May). However, presentation of a clear anti-war argument was rare, amounting to only 32 articles, or 1.5 per cent of total coverage.

In assessing the extent to which the newspapers took a sceptical and critical view of the war, it is also useful to consider how they reported Nato 'accidents' and 'collateral damage'. Despite official complaints of a media fixation with 'Nato blunders' (see above), in our sample periods only 143 articles discussed accidents and 'collateral damage' caused by the bombing: less than 7 per cent of total coverage. Moreover, these articles varied in terms of tone and the prominence they gave to the negative effects of the bombing. Just over half of them (76 articles, or 53.1 per cent) were either brief summary reports or were mainly concerned with another aspect of the war and mentioned 'accidents' only in passing. There were 44 articles which could be classified as critical, either because they explicitly criticised Nato or because they drew attention to the human effects of the bombing. *Times* journalist Eve-Ann Prentice was herself injured in an airstrike in Kosovo and gave a vivid account of what it was like to be under Nato bombardment (1 June), for example, and Fisk's reports from Belgrade and Kosovo for the *Independent* tended to take a highly emotive tone, focusing on individual victims and challenging Nato claims that it was going to 'extraordinary lengths' to avoid civilian casualties (for example his report of 14 April). While such articles may well have had an emotional impact, they cannot be said to have dominated the coverage.

The sort of scepticism about Nato justifications of 'collateral damage' shown by Fisk and a few others was the exception rather than, as McLaughlin (2002: 122) suggests, the rule. Sometimes writers seemed to go out of their way to exonerate Nato, as when Woollacott complained that 'The Serbs don't appreciate how carefully the force against them is being deployed' and described the Serbs' failure to 'grasp ... the efforts now made to limit Serb casualties' as 'part of the general problem of consciousness in that country' (*Guardian*, 27 March); or when Marcus Tanner argued that the Serbs were to blame for the deaths of 80 refugees in a Nato airstrike because they had deliberately used them as 'human shields' in an effort to provoke 'an international outcry against a Nato "massacre'" (*Independent*, 2 June). Robinson's (2002: 109) assessment, that criticism was largely limited by the presumption that Nato action was legitimate, is accurate. This did not mean that there was no critical commentary, but that most of it was arguing for an escalation from air war to ground invasion.

Conclusions

Press coverage of the Kosovo conflict closely followed Nato's agenda in many respects. In terms of explanations, some writers (such as Corelli Barnett in the *Mail*, quoted above) pointed out that Yugoslavia had been given an ultimatum which any sovereign state would find unacceptable, but there was little discussion of the recent background of conflict in Kosovo. Instead, a few articles explained the conflict in terms of 'ancient ethnic hatreds', while the majority portrayed it as a case of one-sided, quasi-colonial Serbian aggression, despite the fact that, as indicated in the introduction to this chapter, the KLA was known to be the main instigator of violence in the period immediately before Nato intervened. Newspapers generally welcomed the indictment of Milosevic, prejudged his guilt and demonised him as criminal, tyrannical and the cause of the war. There was criticism of Nato 'accidents', but this was not as prominent as official complaints suggested, and while there was also criticism of Nato for having exacerbated or precipitated the refugee crisis, the effect of coverage of refugees was generally to consolidate support for the bombing rather than to detract from it, since it was understood as confirming that Nato was acting for 'moral' reasons. Explanations of Nato action differed in the emphasis they gave to values and interests, but the most common explanation of the intervention endorsed the moral claims, which, because of the questionable legality of the bombing, were central to its legitimacy. The main theme of 'critical' coverage was that Nato was not going further and launching a ground war.

As Figure 5.1 indicates, Nato sources dominated coverage. Reporters reproduced Nato spin even when they were aware that certain themes – particularly 'genocide' – were being deliberately promoted by official spokesmen as part of a propaganda strategy.

One further category of criticism which is worth mentioning here is those articles which reflected on the quality of media coverage itself. Overall, 29 articles pursued this theme – only 1.4 per cent of total coverage. Indeed, Nato propaganda was sometimes discussed in positive terms, as when Charles Bremner, in an article headlined 'Britannia Rules the Airwaves', praised the Britons conducting Nato briefings, Air Commodore David Wilby (a 'smooth media operator') and Jamie Shea ('the star of the show'). As Bremner noted admiringly, 'A sentence [from Shea] on Sunday on Europe's worst humanitarian disaster since the Second World War made the world's front pages' (*Times*, 30 March). As we have seen, other terms picked up directly from Nato briefings included descriptions of events in Kosovo in terms of 'apartheid' or an 'Orwellian scenario'.

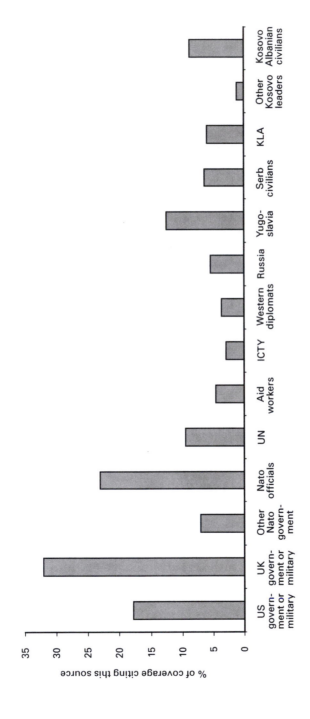

Figure 5.1 Prominence of the different types of source, Kosovo coverage.

One further example which illustrates the adoption by journalists of the vocabulary of official spokesmen is the term 'machine'. Nato leaders and spokesmen habitually described the Serbs in terms of machinery, no doubt with the intention of both dehumanising the enemy and supporting the comparisons drawn with the Nazis by suggesting industrial efficiency. The British Defence Secretary, George Robertson, for example, said at one briefing that airstrikes were inflicting 'considerable damage on the Serb war machine', that nowhere in Yugoslavia would be 'immune from the attacks on the military machine', and that Nato would hit any target 'related to the war machine of Milosevic' (*Times*, 1 April). Other officials used similar terms, but it was a particular favourite of Robertson: one reporter later described him as 'using his pet phrase – "Milosevic's murderous machine" – again and again' (*Independent*, 9 June). In our samples, 26 articles used phrases such as 'killing machine', 'war machine', 'ethnic cleansing machine' and 'propaganda machine' when quoting the phrases used by Nato leaders and officials. In a further 66 articles, however, journalists used similar phrases themselves, without quotation marks, and even invented their own variants, such as 'pogrom machine' and 'anti-PR machine'. The idea became so well worn that an understanding of shorthand phrases such as 'The Serbian machine' (*Independent*, 29 March) or simply 'Milosevic machine' (*Mail*, 7 June) could be assumed.

In terms of their explanation of the conflict, their endorsement of the 'moral' character of Nato bombing, their editorial support for the war and their adoption of Nato vocabulary even when they were well aware that it was part of a coordinated propaganda effort, the newspapers examined in this study clearly failed to offer any challenge to official claims.

CHAPTER 6

Afghanistan, 2001

This chapter focuses on Operation Enduring Freedom: the US-led military action in Afghanistan, undertaken in response to the 11 September 2001 terrorist attacks on the US. In justifying its military response, the US cited both the authority of the UN Security Council, which passed a resolution on 12 September 2001 describing the terrorist attacks as a 'threat to international peace and security' and affirming an 'inherent right of individual or collective self-defence', and the support of an international coalition, which was assembled prior to launching military action on 7 October 2001. Britain was the main contributor of military assistance; other countries mostly offered diplomatic or in some cases logistical support. Military action was primarily directed against the al-Qaeda network responsible for 9/11 but also entailed overthrowing the Taliban government of Afghanistan, which had failed to hand over the network's leader, Osama bin Laden. US Defense Secretary Donald Rumsfeld formally announced an end to 'major combat operations' in Afghanistan on 1 May 2003, but in a sense this was both belated and premature. It was belated because, even though the US and its allies failed to kill or capture bin Laden, military operations were widely seen as having succeeded long before: al-Qaeda forces in the country had effectively been destroyed, the Taliban ousted and a new government installed, on 22 December 2001. At the same time, it was also a premature declaration of victory, since conflict continued long afterwards: in 2007 'major clashes' were still being reported between 'insurgents' or 'remnants of the Taliban regime' and the International Security Assistance Force deployed since December 2001.

Context

The war in Afghanistan was justified primarily as an act of self-defence. Since US action was clearly taken in response to the attacks on New York and Washington, it may seem that the question of explanation is straightforward. However, simply to say that the war was a response to 9/11 leaves open, for example, the question of whether it was a matter of attempting to bring the organisers of terrorism to justice, as official statements tended to suggest, or whether it was more a case of exacting revenge or carrying out punishment – alternatives which could imply different judgements about the legitimacy of the military intervention.[1] Two main considerations complicate the picture: firstly, that, while the main target was bin Laden and his network, the operation also took on the task of defeating the Taliban government; and secondly, the fact that Operation Enduring Freedom was part of the wider 'war on terrorism' announced by the Bush administration after 9/11.

Western leaders sent somewhat confusing and contradictory signals regarding their intentions toward the Taliban. Some official statements suggested that the Taliban were the enemy just as much as al-Qaeda, and that overthrowing the Afghan government would be justified in its own right. In his 20 September 2001 address to Congress, for example, President George W. Bush highlighted human rights abuses in Afghanistan and said that 'we condemn the Taliban regime'.[2] Similarly, Rumsfeld reportedly said the Taliban 'had no right to be in power regardless of any involvement in terrorism', arguing that 'the world did not believe that violence against women and children ought to be tolerated' (*Times*, 1 October 2001). If this gave the impression that effecting 'regime change' in Afghanistan was a Western objective, however, other statements implied that the West had no quarrel with the Taliban as such, and that it was only being indirectly targeted insofar as it presented a barrier to bin Laden's capture. Bush emphasised that 'we're not into nation-building',[3] for example, and a week into the campaign he told the Taliban 'You still have a second chance': 'If you cough [bin Laden] up … then we'll reconsider what we are doing to your country' (*Mail*, 13 October).

What gave rise to these vicissitudes was both a degree of genuine uncertainty and indecision, and an element of political calculation. Bush reportedly backtracked on early statements that removing the Taliban was an objective of the war because Pakistan, formerly the main supporter of the Taliban but now America's key regional ally in the 'war on terror', was alarmed at the prospect that Afghanistan's internal opposition force, the Northern Alliance, would take over (*Guardian*, 29 September). The US itself was not particularly keen to see an outright Northern Alliance victory either, given that the groups which comprised it had a disastrous record of violence and infighting: at one point the US was reportedly holding back from bombing Taliban positions around Kabul in case the Northern Alliance took the capital (*Independent*, 12 October 2001). On the other hand, the Taliban regime was not recognised by the UN as the legitimate government of Afghanistan, and even before the start of military action the US was actively supporting moves to establish a new head of state and interim government for the country (*Guardian*, 3 October). A strategy document drawn up by the British government shortly after 9/11 stated that, assuming the Taliban did not relinquish bin Laden, 'we require sufficient change in the leadership to ensure that Afghanistan's links with international terrorism are broken' (*Guardian*, 11 October). The coalition launched the war wishing to see the Taliban overthrown, but without any agreed strategy for replacing it.

In response to Western demands that they hand over bin Laden, the Taliban leadership made several offers to negotiate his extradition, eventually even dropping their initial requests to see the evidence against him. Yet neither the US demands nor the Taliban offers can be taken at face value. Given the failure of the Anglo-American forces and their local allies to find bin Laden, it seems doubtful that the Taliban would have been able simply to 'hand him over', even had they wished to do so: their offers were no doubt attempts to avert and then to halt the US-led assault. For its part, the US had no expectation that its demands would be met and in fact rejected all Taliban offers out of hand, declaring that there was nothing to negotiate. As Rahul Mahajan (2002: 16–17) points out, the US did not approach the problem of gaining access to al-Qaeda in Afghanistan as a normal matter of legal extradition. Rather, Bush made a general demand that the Taliban 'hand over every terrorist, and every person in their support structure', and threatened that states which harboured terrorists would be considered hostile to the US and therefore legitimate military targets.[4] This had the advantage that the coalition could present the war as a last resort after its demands had not been met, thereby legitimising a military campaign which would likely involve 'regime change' but without having to construct any further justification for overthrowing a government which had played no direct part in the 9/11 attacks. At the same time, drawing the Taliban into the frame was also politically useful, in that it allowed a potentially diffuse and unfocused 'war on terror' to assume the more traditional form of war against a state. A few days before the start of the campaign, the *Guardian* reported that some British government ministers wished to 'widen the coalition focus' in order to provide a kind of get-out clause so that, in the event that bin Laden was not killed or captured, 'the mission … would not be seen as a failure' (2 October). This is indeed what happened, although the impression of success was short-lived.

Additionally, this 'widening of the focus' provided an extra dimension to the justification for war, in that the Taliban regime was already known in the West as one which, through its extreme interpretation of Islamic law, violated human rights. This aspect of the case for military action was particularly highlighted by Prime Minister Tony Blair, who invested the 'war on terrorism' with a broader humanitarian, moral purpose. His October 2001 speech to the Labour Party conference, for example, set the Afghan war in the context of 1990s human rights interventions, when he pointed to successes in Kosovo and elsewhere, and also claimed that 'if Rwanda happened again today … we would have a moral duty to act'. For Blair, the response to 9/11 showed 'the power of community', which, he argued, had the capacity to 'heal' Africa, to 'defeat climate change' and to bring peace to the Middle East, among other things. Specifically in relation to Afghanistan, Blair described the Taliban regime as 'founded on fear and funded on the drugs trade' and said that narcotics production was 'another part of their regime that we should seek to destroy'. He said he wanted the 'world community' to show 'as much its capacity for compassion as for force', and promised that: 'We will not walk away, as the outside world has done so many times before'; and 'we will assemble a humanitarian coalition alongside the military coalition so that inside and outside Afghanistan, the refugees ... are given shelter, food and help'. The war, he argued, could become 'a fight for justice', bringing 'values of democracy and freedom to people round the world'.[5]

What appears at first glance, then, as a straightforward response to the 9/11 attacks could also encompass other issues, including the promotion of human rights, the advancement of global justice and a clamp-down on narcotics production. While such considerations were clearly intended to boost support for military action, however, they raised problems of their own. Highlighting the issue of drugs, for example, backfired when some reports cited UN sources pointing out that 'Almost all Afghan opium this year came out of territories controlled by America's ally in the assault on Afghanistan, the Northern Alliance', and that the defeat of the Taliban, who had 'completed one of the quickest and most successful drug elimination programmes in history', would probably 'result in a surge in opium production' (*Independent*, 19 October 2001). More problematic than this peripheral issue was the insistence that the campaign would be accompanied by humanitarian action – an idea given concrete expression in America's decision to drop food aid as well as bombs over Afghanistan – which focused attention on the plight of refugees and heightened worries that the military action might in fact be making matters worse. In mid-October, the UN Commissioner for Human Rights, Mary Robinson, called for a 'pause' in the bombing to allow aid to be delivered, and relief agencies criticised the aerial food drops as a stunt which was of little or no help. Similarly, criticism of the Taliban regime for its record of human rights abuse may have inadvertently helped to give credence to idea that the West was waging war on Islam, since the features of the regime that Western politicians found objectionable – particularly the oppression of women – all flowed from its claim to be a 'pure' Islamic state (Karim 2002: 107). Some analysts have suggested that radical Islam has been drafted in as a 'replacement for communism' in the post-Cold War era: a development which, it is argued, was 'influenced by the discourse of the "clash of civilizations" and strengthened by the events of 11 September 2001' (Thussu and Freedman 2003: 2). The idea that the 'war on terror' was really a 'crusade' against Islam was taken up both by bin Laden himself and by some Muslim critics of the war, so that Western leaders felt obliged to insist repeatedly that they were not at war with Islam.

Moreover, while Bush's explanation of the war as a fight against 'evildoers' sought moral clarity, Blair's emphasis on human rights and global justice could be taken as an implicit acknowledgement that previous Western policy was in some sense the root cause of the 9/11 attacks. At the least, the crisis in Afghanistan could be understood as a case of 'blowback': the unintended consequences of earlier policies. During the Soviet occupation of Afghanistan in the 1980s, America poured billions of dollars into the country to support the Mujahideen resistance (Rashid 2001: 18). Working both directly and through Pakistan's intelligence service, the CIA helped to turn Afghanistan into the premier international centre for armed radical Islamists, including bin Laden (Cooley 2000: 226). Blair's pledge that this time the West would not 'walk away' was an admission that previous Western involvement had left the country in chaos. Some critics broadened this argument to suggest that it was not just previous interference in Afghanistan which was problematic but the history of Western imperialism throughout the Muslim world and elsewhere. Blair's emphasis on the need for global justice seemed to acknowledge that, while the 11 September attacks were not legitimate themselves, they might be an expression of legitimate grievances. Both Blair and Bush implicitly gave credence to bin Laden's claim that the attacks had been, in part, a blow against injustice in the Middle East, by promising renewed efforts to resolve the Israeli/Palestinian conflict and declaring their support for a Palestinian state.

The question of Western policy in the Middle East was also raised by those who sought to challenge official explanations of the war by uncovering hidden motivations. John Pilger, for example, argued that 'a primary reason for the attack on Afghanistan is the installation of a regime that will oversee an American-owned pipeline bringing oil and gas from the Caspian basin' (Pilger 2001; see also Mahajan 2002: 32–3). Critics tended to complain that these sorts of alternative explanations were not explored by the mainstream media. Pilger (2001) remarked that some news coverage contained 'little more than fables straight from the Pentagon and the Ministry of Defence' and that the 'Real reasons for the actions of great power are seldom reported'. Similarly, Robert McChesney (2002: 92–4) argued that US media coverage was basically propagandistic, with no debate about whether to go to war and no commentary on the 'very powerful interests in the United States who greatly benefit politically and economically by the establishment of an unchecked war on terrorism'. McChesney (2002: 98) also pointed to a lack of 'meaningful context and background' in media reporting of the war, a concern echoed by Karim H. Karim (2002: 106), who said that previous US involvement in Afghanistan was 'hardly ever mentioned in the media, which instead presented the US as a savior for the long-suffering Afghans'.

A number of critics have also drawn attention to official attempts to control and censor news during the war, by restricting the movements of Western journalists (Mahajan 2002: 88; Gordon et al. 2003) and seeking to limit the output of the Arab satellite channel Al Jazeera. Secretary of State Colin Powell asked the Emir of Qatar to 'restrain' the station's activities, including its coverage of statements by bin Laden (Mahajan 2002: 89–92); and the coalition bombed Al Jazeera's offices in Kabul, claiming this was unintended but providing an explanation which, as Nik Gowing (2003: 234) observed, was full of 'deeply worrying inconsistencies'. Gowing (2003: 236–7) argued that, despite restrictions, in some cases journalists on the ground were able to challenge the official version of events, for example with photographic evidence that the US had bombed a Red Cross warehouse in Kabul. In the main, however, critics have charged the media with complicity in minimising the effects of the bombing. Some US journalists argued that civilian casualties were not particularly newsworthy, or that reports of deaths caused by coalition bombing ought to be 'balanced' by reminders that the Taliban were harbouring terrorists (Mahajan 2002: 83–6). At the same time, the media have also been accused of taking a largely uncritical view of coalition claims to be providing humanitarian assistance: US media critic Norman Solomon said that many news organisations were 'eager to play along' with what he described as a cynical exercise in 'media manipulation'.[6]

Of course, official attempts at 'information management' during wartime are nothing new, although Phillip Knightley (2001) argues that the level of restriction was such that reporting effectively reverted to the situation which existed before the emergence of war correspondence in the Crimean war, in that the Western military was again basically able to report its own war. However, control of the 'information space' has arguably assumed a new and greater importance in recent conflicts, as governments have used the media as a forum for conducting 'public diplomacy' (Brown 2003a, 2003b). This was given an extra prominence in relation to the war in Afghanistan because, as the first visible manifestation of the 'war on terrorism', it signalled what many analysts have understood as a major ideological shift. That is to say, the 'war on terror' discourse which developed in the wake of 9/11 was more than just a way of framing the conflict in Afghanistan: commentators have suggested that it was more like the Cold War framework, in that it purported to explain a host of domestic and international developments, and offered a comprehensive model for making sense of diverse events (Norris et al. 2003: 15; Moeller 2004: 63). While Western leaders were successful in establishing what Montague Kern et al. (2003: 283) describe as a 'consensual frame' around the idea of a 'war' on terrorism – as opposed, for example, to explaining their response as a law-enforcement response to a criminal act – it is argued that news coverage of the conflict in Afghanistan was to some degree characterised by competing frames, as bin Laden and opponents of the war sought to frame it as a war on Islam (Brown 2003a: 94–7). Videotapes released by bin Laden could also be considered a form of 'public diplomacy', directly challenging Western interpretations of events. When, in October 2001, the British government summoned broadcasters to Downing Street in order to advise them, somewhat absurdly, that video statements by bin Laden might contain 'coded messages', it was a sign of nervousness about the coalition's ability to secure agreement with its own 'war on terror' frame.

Kern et al. (2003: 299) argue that, in the long run, the power of the 'war on terrorism' frame was such that it legitimised pre-emptive military action against Iraq in 2003, despite the absence of evidence linking Iraq with the 11 September attacks. This argument is made with the benefit of hindsight, however, and may not necessarily describe how events were understood at the time. As noted above, some critics have suggested that the idea of a 'clash of civilisations' informed official discourse (Thussu and Freedman 2003: 2) or that Western media coverage demonised Islam (Karim 2002). The evidence for these claims is far from clear-cut, however: a study of US news coverage of American Muslims and Arab Americans found that their public image actually improved after 9/11 (Nacos and Torres-Reyna 2003), while the BBC issued guidelines instructing journalists that they 'must avoid giving any impression that this is a war against Islam'.[7] Potentially more significant, perhaps particularly in a British context, is the way that, as discussed earlier, in addition to the idea of military action in Afghanistan being part of a 'war on terrorism', leaders also invoked human rights and humanitarianism, continuing themes familiar from interventions of the 1990s.

Questions

The main questions considered in this chapter are:

- How was Western military action in Afghanistan explained? Is there evidence of competing news frames? Was Western action seen as legitimate and, if so, on what grounds?
- How far did press reporting examine the wider context and historical background of the war? Were alternative explanations of Western actions explored?
- To what extent did coverage take a critical view of Western military action and official claims, for example in relation to civilian causalities?

The first sample period examined in this study is the week leading up to the start of military action on 7 October and the following three weeks. Two alternatives were considered for a second sample: the accession of a new government in December 2001, or the announcement by Rumsfeld of the end of 'major operations' in May 2003. The former was chosen, taking the three weeks preceding and one week following the installation of the new Afghan government on 22 December as our sample. There were two reasons for this: firstly, while this event did not mark the end of conflict, it was widely interpreted at the time as the conclusion of the main coalition military effort; and secondly, Rumsfeld's official announcement on 1 May 2003 – which also did not in fact signal the end of conflict – was overshadowed by the similar announcement made about Iraq by Bush on the same day, and consequently there was far less coverage of Afghanistan in April/May 2003 (297 relevant articles as opposed to 666 for the period chosen).[8] The total coverage[9] for the periods selected was as shown in Table 6.1.

Table 6.1 Numbers of articles about Afghanistan

	Start of military action (1–29 October 2001)	Inauguration of new government (1–29 December 2001)	Totals
Guardian	750	164	914
Independent	479	197	676
Times	501	219	720
Mail	211	86	297
Totals	1,941	666	2,607

The large total for the *Guardian* in the first sample period merits some comment. The *Guardian*'s archive differed from those of other papers, in that its running strap-lines in both periods incorporated our search term, 'Afghanistan' ('Attack on Afghanistan' in October; 'War in Afghanistan' in December), and the *Guardian* included a diverse range of material under these headings. Stories on Israel or Iraq in the other newspapers examined, for example, would be caught by our LexisNexis searches only if they mentioned Afghanistan, where-upon they could be assessed for relevance. For the *Guardian*, by contrast, such stories would be included by virtue of the strap-line even if the body of the story did not mention Afghanistan. Rather than judging each of these articles for relevance in terms of its content, it was felt that since the *Guardian* had signalled that they were in some sense part of the same overall story, our data should reflect this. Newspapers' choice of strap-lines is of course an interesting framing device in itself, to which we shall return below.

Explanations

The proportion of coverage devoted to explaining the war in Afghanistan was low, accounting for only 5.7 per cent of the total. The three broadsheets examined each carried a similar number of articles focusing mainly on explanations – 23 in the *Guardian*, 24 in the *Independent* and 22 in the *Times* – while the *Mail* ran eight: together these 77 articles made up just 3 per cent of total coverage, with 71 further articles offering brief explanations (148 articles in total). A greater quantity of explanatory material appeared during the first period examined than in the second (108 and 40 articles, respectively), but the proportion of total coverage was similar across both samples (5.6 and 6.0 per cent, respectively). Two main reasons may be suggested for the low level of explanatory material. Firstly, since the conflict was part of the wider 'war on terrorism', the overall story was a very big one, encompassing a huge variety of events and develop-ments, from anthrax attacks in the US, through the implications of the war for Western policy in the Middle East, to worldwide reactions to the terrorist attacks and America's response. The number of articles dealing with causes and explanations was in fact higher than in many of the other case studies examined, but the sheer size of the story meant that they still accounted for only a small proportion of total coverage. Secondly, it seems probable that the modest pro-portion of coverage devoted to explanations reflected an assumption that, since it was obviously being conducted in response to 9/11, the war did not really require much explanation. Where military action *was* seen as requiring explana-tion, this was often linked to some dissatisfaction with official accounts. Hence a significant portion of all explanatory material (65 articles, or 43.9 per cent) involved some critique of the war, and overall the most common explanatory theme, as we shall see, was that the deeper causes of the war involved some form of 'blowback' from previous Western policies. It should also be noted that articles which did not develop explanations nevertheless often framed the war in particular ways through the use of strap-lines or brief statements describing

Table 6.2 Numbers of occurrences of phrases describing various targets of the military action, Afghanistan coverage

	'Terror(ism)'	Al-Qaeda/ bin Laden	Taliban	Both Taliban and al-Qaeda	Revenge/ reprisal
Guardian	245	20	20	16	32
Independent	218 (513[a])	29	16	29	33
Times	246	18	25	24	27
Mail	156 (178[a])	14	19	20	19
Total	865 (1,182)	81	80	89	111

[a] Total including strap-lines.

the conflict, and these are examined too, since they are indicative of the taken-for-granted assumptions about the reasons for military action.

War aims and targets

Announcing the start of military action, Bush told US and allied forces 'Your mission is defined. Your goal is clear' (*Times*, 8 October 2001). In fact, however, the aims and objectives of the mission were far from clearly defined. Four days before the beginning of the campaign, for example, a British government spokesman was quoted as saying: 'We are consciously not saying we want to overthrow the Taliban. That is a matter for the internal politics of Afghanistan' (*Guardian*, 3 October). Yet three days later Blair was reportedly 'putting the finishing touches to plans to replace the Taliban with a democratic government' (*Mail*, 6 October). This ambiguity about whether the Taliban regime was being directly targeted was echoed in journalists' statements about who or what the war was against, but it was also a major focus for critical comment.

Table 6.2 shows the number of brief descriptive statements, across all coverage examined, about who or what was the target of the war. Figures in parentheses for the *Independent* and *Mail* include strap-lines which defined the action as a war or campaign on or against terror(ism), while the first figures indicate the number of times such phrases featured in the body of articles.[10] Either way, it is clear that 'war on terrorism' was, as would be expected, the overwhelmingly dominant frame.

In terms of those articles which actually developed an explanation of the war, however, the picture is less clear-cut. Of the 148 articles which included some explanation of the war, 39 explicitly discussed the targets and objectives of military action, and of these only nine explained it in terms of the 'war on terrorism', usually in the context of arguing that this global framework had to be made clearer. William Rees-Mogg, for example, said that Bush was doing 'what has to be done in the offensive against terrorism' and noted the importance of 'maintain[ing] the world recognition that this is a war against terrorism' (*Times*, 8 October). This emphasis chimed with the official US perspective: two days later the *Times* reported that the administration was 'emphasising the wider scope of its war on terror' and, rather than concentrating only on bin Laden, was attempting to ensure that 'the US public is focused on the wider war aims of defeating terrorism for years to come' (10 October). The *Times* also took up this theme in its editorial columns, arguing that 'the military operation in Afghanistan is one facet only of a campaign which, the US is determined, will reach and destroy terrorist organisations and their infrastructure and supporters wherever they operate' (11 October) and stressing that 'Afghanistan is only one corner … [of] a worldwide canvas' (8 October) or that 'The Greater Game extends far beyond Afghanistan' (9 October). Strikingly, all nine articles explaining the aims of the action in Afghanistan in terms of a wider war on terrorism appeared in the *Times* (and all during our first sample period), suggesting that, of the four papers examined, the *Times* identified most closely with the official 'war on terror' frame.

It is notable that, as indicated in Table 6.2, about the same number of articles described the conflict as a war against the Taliban as described it as a war against bin Laden and/or al-Qaeda, while an only slightly larger number of articles described it as targeting both. A similar pattern is evident in terms of those explanatory articles which addressed war aims and targets: four explained the war as targeting the Taliban, two explained it as a war against bin Laden or al-Qaeda, and three explained it as targeting both the Taliban and al-Qaeda. While this suggests that press coverage reflected official ambiguity about whether and to what extent the Taliban regime was being directly targeted, the striking feature of explanatory articles is that many of them (16 of the 39 discussing the aims and targets of the war) were highly critical of this vagueness on the part of coalition leaders. In the *Mail*, for example, Stephen Glover described the coalition's war aims as 'extremely vague and ill-defined', and he suggested that attacking the Taliban rather than concentrating only on al-Qaeda 'seems pointless and possibly unjust' (16 October); and the same day's editorial column, headlined 'Campaign Needs a Clear Strategy', asked 'What is the point of bombing a benighted, backward people who bear little culpability for the events of September 11?' In the *Guardian*, Jonathan Steele suggested that the target had been widened to include the Taliban because coalition leaders had realised that 'finding Bin Laden might prove impossible' (11 October) and so that 'any hit on the dartboard [could] be trumpeted as proof we've scored' (6 October). In the *Times*, columnist Mick Hume characterised the bombing as 'a war shaped by propagandist considerations that is bereft of consistent aims' (22 October), while in the *Independent* two editorial columns took issue with the 'war' framework itself, arguing that 'the model of law enforcement' would be 'morally superior to the model of war' (5 October) and that 'talking about a war against all terrorists only causes confusion', since the causes of, and appropriate responses to, terrorism were quite different in different contexts (6 October). As these examples suggest, the 'war on terror' frame was not accepted without question.

Newspapers' choice of strap-lines is also interesting in this respect. The *Mail* made least use of them, running features under the heading 'The War Begins' soon after the start of bombing and switching to 'War on Terror' later in the month. In December the *Mail* had no continuing strap-line for its Afghan reporting, but for a few days in the first half of this period it did run features under the headings 'Rout of the Taliban' and 'End of the Taliban'. The *Times* consistently used 'War on Terror' in both periods, aside from a few days in December.[11] The *Independent* was similar to the *Mail* in October, using 'War on Terrorism' for most of the month but adopting 'Air Strikes on Afghanistan' for just over a week following the start of the war. In December, however, the *Independent* chose the less bellicose 'Campaign Against Terrorism', perhaps implying some distance from the official decision to frame the West's response in terms of 'war', as in fact had been indicated in its editorials of 5 and 6 October mentioned above. The *Guardian*'s choice of 'Attack on Afghanistan' is also striking, since it implied that the military action was an act of aggression on the part of the US and its allies, although in December the paper chose the more neutral line 'War in Afghanistan'.

Finally in terms of war aims, it is notable that after 'terrorism' the largest number of brief descriptive statements about the war characterised it in terms of retaliation, reprisal, revenge/vengeance, retribution or punishment for 9/11. Five articles explaining the aims of military action also framed the war in these terms, and in all but one case this was linked to some criticism of the war. In the *Times*, for example, Simon Jenkins argued that this was 'essentially a war of revenge' (5 December) or of 'punitive retaliation' driven by 'America's rage and need for reprisal' (28 December); in the *Guardian* Charlotte Raven said that 'The US needs blood in the sand to appease public opinion' and that it was attempting to satisfy 'its desire for revenge' (9 October). The extent of the implied criticism should not be overstated: both these commentators argued that the West should devise smarter ways to tackle terrorism, and Jenkins also emphasised in his column on 7 December that 'America sincerely seeks a wider justice and a wider security in the world'. Although the execution might be 'hamfisted', he argued, 'the goal is noble'. The *Independent*'s 9 October editorial also explained the war as 'retaliation' for the events of 11 September, but argued forcefully that this was entirely legitimate: 'it is disingenuous and unnecessary to dress up what is eminently justified retaliation and reprisal as something else'.

This last example was in fact more typical of the way that the terms 'retaliation', 'reprisal', 'retribution' and 'punishment' (although almost never 'revenge')[12] were used in the larger number of articles which included brief descriptions of the war. Of the 111 articles describing the war in these terms, only 30 did so in a way which implied criticism. George Monbiot, for instance, argued that since the military action was a matter of 'retaliation' rather than self-defence, it could not claim UN sanction (*Guardian*, 16 October); and peace activists were reported as campaigning 'for restraint and against US retaliation' (*Independent*, 4 October). Yet in most instances terms such as 'retaliation' and 'punishment' were either used neutrally or were employed in the context of endorsements of the war, including in official statements. European governments, for example, were widely reported as giving 'their backing for "legitimate" US retaliation' (*Guardian*, 20 October) or as stating 'their "wholehearted support" for the US reprisals' (*Independent*, 9 October). Donald Rumsfeld reportedly 'said that the bombing was also meant to be punitive' (*Guardian*, 8 October) and told American forces that 'the US needed to send a message that terrorist acts would not go unpunished' (*Mail*, 17 October). If anti-war writers and peace campaigners quoted in news reports assumed that describing the war as 'retaliation' or 'reprisal' challenged its legitimacy, they were evidently mistaken.

It is also worth noting here that, as Knightley observed at the time (*Guardian*, 4 October), a number of articles characterised the war as 'inevitable'. In our sample, 21 articles used the terms 'inevitable' or 'unavoidable' to describe the war, which signalled some acceptance of America's right to retaliate for 9/11.

A humanitarian war?

While terms such as 'retaliation' and 'reprisal' could all be used approvingly, 'revenge' was almost always used in a way that implied criticism. Indeed, official statements sometimes explicitly rejected any suggestion that revenge was a motive. In a statement to the House of Commons on 4 October 2001, for instance, Blair promised that 'We will not act for revenge'; and in his address to the Labour Party conference in Brighton that year he made the point that relatives of the 9/11 victims 'don't want revenge' (*Times*, 5 October and 3 October, respectively). This was because, while 'revenge' implied base emotions, coalition leaders wished to suggest that they were acting from higher motives: the 9/11 relatives 'want something better in memory of their loved ones', argued Blair. This loftier purpose was embodied in the humanitarian claims made for the campaign. Of 148 explanatory articles, 26 explained the war in terms of humanitarian or human rights goals (17.6 per cent). Following Blair's conference speech, for example, the *Guardian*'s Martin Woollacott endorsed the Prime Minister's attempt to 'place the expected military action in Afghanistan within the context of recent humanitarian interventions' and argued that he was 'right to revive the idea of a "new world order"' (5 October); in the same paper Jonathan Freedland observed that the 'anti-war camp came to Brighton to shake their fists – and ended up clapping their hands' because Blair 'came on like a speaker at an NGO fringe meeting, hitting every one of their pet causes: interdependence, climate change, renewable energy, aid, debt relief as well as the wars in Rwanda, Congo and the plight of the Palestinians'. The effectiveness of such rhetoric in galvanising Labour Party support for the war, Freedland suggested, was evidence that 'this crisis could still prove to be the progressives' moment' (*Guardian*, 3 October).

Although the 'humanitarian' explanatory theme was by no means dominant, it was relatively prominent in our first sample period (when all but three of the articles explaining the war in these terms appeared), accounting for 21.3 per cent of all explanatory articles during October, and it was the third most common category of explanation overall. It is significant insofar as it was indicative of a certain convergence between the position set out in early October by Blair and that adopted by the newspapers: two of the 26 articles were written by government ministers (Jack Straw and Peter Hain) and six were editorial columns. In its 6 October leader, headlined 'Mercy Mission', for example, the *Times* suggested that the worsening humanitarian crisis in Afghanistan was an argument in favour of military action: 'the humanitarian emergency is one more reason why there is pressure on Washington to act soon'. The paper also judged that Western military action would make it 'likely that this terrible crisis will be turned to the Afghan people's benefit' by ending the Taliban's 'sickening' oppression of women. The *Independent*'s 3 October editorial enthused over Blair's 'statesmanlike and mature' conference speech (also described here as 'deft', 'affecting', 'intellectually coherent', and as making arguments 'persuasively' and with 'great clarity'), which had 'provided a clear and often inspiring vision'. This was in marked contrast with the stance taken in the paper's 9 October leader, quoted above, which argued that it was unnecessary for 'eminently justified retaliation and reprisal' to be 'covered with the veneer of a humanitarian operation'. The *Independent* tried to square this circle in its 22 October editorial, which maintained that 'Dealing with the humanitarian crisis is part of, not a diversion from, the campaign', but chiefly in that doing so would help in the 'war for world opinion'. The US should 'attend to the refugee crisis', the paper argued, because this would strengthen the West's position in the 'propaganda war for … Muslim and Arab opinion'. This suggested a purely instrumentalist approach, in which humanitarian efforts were important in terms of their propaganda value rather than for their own sake, and indeed, as discussed further below, the *Independent*'s editorial line was somewhat inconsistent and cynical in this respect.

The claimed humanitarian dimension of the campaign was particularly important for the *Guardian*, although in that paper's case it worked rather differently from how it did in the other papers. The *Guardian* also welcomed the 'version of the campaign against terrorism which Mr Blair has so energetically promoted', according to which the military action could be understood as 'the embodiment of … "the moral power of a world acting as a community"' (10 October leader, quoting Blair). But the paper made its support conditional on the war living up to promises made by both Blair and Bush, that coalition strategy would involve a 'three-pronged approach', whereby the military action would be accompanied by equal efforts on the diplomatic and humanitarian fronts, advancing prospects for peace in the Middle East and relieving the suffering of Afghan civilians. As the *Guardian*'s 19 October editorial explained, it was 'on the understanding that these three policy elements would be given equal weight' that 'many people in this country, including this newspaper, decided that the overall strategy could be supported'. Thus, while the *Guardian* identified most closely with the Blairite vision, the paper was inclined to assess the conduct of campaign critically when it appeared that humanitarianism and diplomacy were not being sufficiently prioritised. As we shall see below, much criticism of the war centred on just this issue, although such critique did not imply outright opposition. In this editorial the *Guardian* wondered 'what has happened to the integrated, three-pronged approach' but simply urged Blair to 'knit together far more closely … the military and humanitarian elements of the campaign', and predicted that, as the coalition gained control of more territory, the 'military and humanitarian imperatives [would] exactly coincide'.

As noted above, official statements about the humanitarian case for war included the claim that it would end injustices and human rights abuses in Afghanistan. This issue was kept in view through a steady trickle of reports and commentaries highlighting the abuses committed by the Taliban. Such articles were not very numerous – there were 52 in total – but they might be considered significant in that they added an extra dimension to the 'humanitarian' justification for military action. When Robert Fisk remarked caustically that 'we did not go to war in Afghanistan to make the world free for kite flyers or cinema lovers or women in veils' (*Independent*, 8 December), it was this type of article he had in mind. In fact, a report by Anthony Loyd in the same day's edition of the *Times* provided an excellent example of the genre, describing the Taliban's 'crank aspirations and bigoted assumptions' and detailing the brutal law-enforcement regime of the Afghan Department of the Promotion of Virtue and Prevention of Vice, which included not only public executions, amputations and the imposition of extreme restrictions on women, but also a stipulation that men wear 'beards of the requisite length' and bans on 'kite-flying and chess'. Not all articles about Taliban repression took such an obvious pro-war stance as Loyd's, which compared the Taliban with 'other extremist powers in history's hall of infamy', including the Nazis, the Khmer Rouge and 'Milosevic's Yugoslav war machine', and which expressed some surprise that 'neither the international community nor the United Nations … undertook any significant act against the … regime' until 1998. Yet the implication of most reports and commentaries cataloguing the regime's abuses was that action against the Taliban was desirable. Also on the same day, a feature in the *Guardian* noted that 'The Taliban's brutal treatment of women has been one of the justifications for the west's campaign'.[13]

It is notable that 'humanitarian' explanations were relatively neglected by the *Mail*. The paper ran only three articles explaining the war in these terms, the most substantial of which was a freelance comment piece by Oxford academic Niall Ferguson (on 13 October, arguing for a new, politically correct version of 'The White Man's Burden'), and the idea was never taken up in editorial columns. Similarly, the *Mail* devoted only four articles to discussing Taliban human rights abuses – a theme it had dropped altogether by December – while the *Independent* carried 13 such articles, the *Guardian* 14 and the *Times* 21. The *Mail*'s political orientation perhaps made it generally less sympathetic to Blairite 'moral' justifications for war but, more particularly, any concern with humanitarianism and human rights was tempered by the paper's stance on asylum seekers. An 8 October article by Steve Doughty, for instance, highlighted how 'saving the lives of millions of refugees' was a 'key war aim', since only 'massive Western aid can help the victims of 22 years of war and brutality in Afghanistan', but, tellingly, Doughty wrote that 'War in Afghanistan threatens the West with the biggest humanitarian crisis since World War II', presenting the crisis as a problem for the West rather than for Afghans. This was because, he explained, 'Britain and Europe, already under pressure from asylum seekers and migrants from south Asia, will quickly feel the push of millions travelling westwards in hope of survival and a better life'. This perspective on the humanitarian crisis took its cue directly from Blair: the report simply elaborated his argument that humanitarian action was necessary 'to deliver stability so that people from that region stay in that region'. Similarly, the *Mail*'s 7 December editorial welcomed the 'destruction of the fanatics' in Afghanistan, but went on to complain about Britain's lax asylum policy, and expressed the hope that the '19,000 Afghans [who] have sought asylum in Britain to escape the Taliban' would be 'sent home, now the regime is destroyed'.

In the broadsheets, some commentators followed Blair's lead in linking action in Afghanistan with other humanitarian crises of the 1990s. This was a particular theme of writers in the *Independent*: defending the idea of 'liberal imperialism' in Afghanistan, for example, columnist David Aaronovitch said that his former support for the principle of non-intervention in sovereign states had changed during the Bosnian war, and he also cited Rwanda as a case where non-intervention was unsupportable (5 October). Similarly, Anne McElvoy asked: 'What would Kosovo be like today without an intervention against its oppressor Slobodan Milosevic? What future would Afghanistan have had with the Taliban still in charge?' (*Independent*, 19 December). The current action in Afghanistan was also sometimes used to suggest the need for greater commitment in countries which had previously seen Western intervention. Anticipating an American return to Somalia as part of the 'war on terrorism', for instance, Bruce Anderson described the country as 'an African Afghanistan, in which nominal control by a barbarous regime provides a cloak for anarchy and terror' (*Independent*, 10 December). In the *Guardian*, Henry Porter hoped to see the West acting with greater determination and 'retributive force' than it had in Bosnia, arguing both that the victims of 9/11 'must receive the justice denied the men of Srebrenica' and that the West ought to do more to apprehend those accused of war crimes in the former Yugoslavia.

Altogether, 16 articles made these sorts of connections between Afghanistan and past crises in Bosnia, Kosovo, Rwanda and Somalia in the context of arguing in favour of the current campaign. Twice as often, however, such comparisons were drawn negatively (in 32 articles). Bosnia tended to be remembered for the failure of the UN and the ongoing demand for peacekeeping troops; for example, the *Mail*'s 11 December editorial warned of 'mission creep' and its 20 December leader cited Britain's commitments in Bosnia as a reason not to send peacekeepers to Afghanistan. The Kosovo conflict was recalled by those condemning the use of cluster bombs and the accidental bombing of civilians; the *Guardian*, for instance, reported that mounting casualties in Afghanistan might 'usher in the feared "Kosovo moment"' as public support began to 'wobble' (29 October). Past experience in Rwanda was cited by the UN's Mary Robinson to draw attention to the suffering of Afghan refugees: she called for a 'pause' in the bombing in order to avert 'a Rwanda-style humanitarian catastrophe' (*Guardian*, 15 October). And Somalia was remembered chiefly because of America's ignominious withdrawal, Richard Dowden arguing against 'Another clumsy, ill-informed American intervention' in the country (*Guardian*, 13 December). Although there was some support for Blair's attempt to cast the crisis in Afghanistan in the mould of 1990s-style humanitarianism, then, past examples of interventionism could just as easily be mobilised by those critical of the current war.

A clash of civilisations and a war on Islam?

The article by Loyd quoted above was also notable for the way it presented the Taliban as exotic and strange. Afghanistan's rulers, he said, were 'detached … from any sense of reality' and 'on initial encounter they looked like a joke'. Loyd recalled meeting the Taliban governor of Herat in 1996:

> A pot-bellied dwarf of a man, with lizard green eyes surrounded by charcoal rings and topped by a huge, teetering turban, he sat on a throne barefoot.
>
> Too short to touch the ground, his legs swung above the floor as he spoke, painted toes twirling distractingly as they did so. Seated beside him his entourage of teenage catamites and vacant-eyed fighters were no less hilarious. (*Times*, 8 December)

Loyd's textbook Orientalism was not typical of all articles highlighting Taliban human rights abuses, but it was indicative of a certain overlap between criticism of the regime as violating standards of civilised behaviour and a conception of the Taliban as radically 'Other'. This is also suggested by the range of descriptions of the Taliban present across all our sampled coverage, set out in Box 6.1. Descriptions of the Taliban as brutal and repressive, as (harbouring) terrorists and as being generally unpleasant and evil can readily be understood in terms of support for official justifications for the war as helping to defeat terrorism and, as an added benefit, removing a regime guilty of human rights abuses. Yet more or less equal weight was given to descriptions depicting the Taliban as backward, strange, fanatical and psychotic, while the most common descriptive device was to highlight the Taliban's Islamic fundamentalism or extremism.

Of course, this is largely what we would expect. The most obviously notable feature of the Taliban was indeed its extreme interpretation of Islam, and the regime's supporters also understood it in this way, as offering a 'pure' form of Islamic government. It is more the combination of descriptions of the regime as 'Islamic fundamentalists' with conceptions of 'fanatics', 'lunatics', 'feudal', 'strange' and 'bizarre' which might be understood as evidence of a 'clash of civilisations' or an anti-Muslim framework. The terms 'fanatic' or 'fanatical', suggesting a mixture of religious extremism and irrationality, are particularly interesting, in that they were used (in relation to both the Taliban and al-Qaeda, as well as their sympathisers) in all papers but with marked differences in frequency. While the *Guardian* and *Independent* used these terms only five and eight times, respectively, they appeared 50 times in the *Times* and 55 times

Box 6.1 Descriptions of the Taliban

Religious fundamentalists
- fundamentalists
- religious fundamentalists
- fundamentalist movement
- fundamentalist regime
- fundamentalist rulers
- fundamentalist Taliban rulers
- the fundamentalist Taliban
- fundamentalist Islamic regime
- Islamic fundamentalist regime
- Islamic fundamentalist Taliban
- Afghan fundamentalists who sheltered Osama bin Laden
- Moslem rulers
- Moslem fundamentalist rulers
- hardline rulers
- hardline regime
- 'hardline regime'
- hardline Islamist regime
- extremist regime
- extremist Afghan regime
- the world's most implacable Islamic movement
- rag-tag army of Islamic zealots
- extremist religious bigots with guns and four-wheel-drive Jeeps
- desperate mullahs
- 'At the core of the Taliban are groups of religious fanatics' (British minister Jack Straw)
- the fanatically Sunni Muslim Taliban
- mysterious army of fundamentalist students
- puritanical
- 'extremely puritanical' (British academic John Baily)
- Cromwellian
- obscurantists
- theocrats
- 'a crude form of theocratic dictatorship that is as cruel as it is arbitrary' (Tony Blair)
- a theocratic system of government so harsh it took Afghanistan back to the dark ages
- an unworldly version of their co-religionists in the rest of the Islamic world, more interested in applying sharia law than in resisting the more obvious manifestations of Western oppression
- Fired with the certainties of the most simplistic interpretation of the Koran and angered by the corruption of an older generation of mojahedin leaders
- an extraordinary experiment

in Islamist fundamentalism which brought Afghanistan to the brink of destruction
- initially offered a sense of stability ... [but] imposed a brutal mix of strict Koranic interpretations and tribal customs, alien to many Afghans, who became horrified by the regime
- plain-living, devout warrior-priests, living an austere life which is not just monastic but, when it is not celibate, predominantly homosexual
- extremist force drunk on its own fundamentalist ideology
- a regime that defines itself by Islam, albeit of a twisted variety
- proud and suspicious, alert for religious infringements
- for all their faults, they painfully recall a time when religious faith in Europe was also strong
- not monsters ... a wild mixture of religious fundamentalism, puritan ideology, Pashtun nationalism and the social norms of the Afghan village, common to every Afghan ethnic group
- 'the only government that actually provides Islamic law' (US Talib John Walker Lindh)
- a 'pure' Islamic government (Taliban Radio)

Fanatical/mad
- the berserkers who govern [Afghanistan]
- a psychotic cult
- psychopathic, woman-hating lunatics
- 'fanatics' and 'murderers' (Israeli foreign minister Shimon Peres)
- a fanatical enemy which glories in bloody self-sacrifice
- [Omar's] fanatical followers
- Fanatics who long for their 'hour of destiny'
- brutal and destructive to the point of insanity
- rather ill-disciplined though fanatical tribal fighters
- monstrous fanatics

Primitive/backward
- 'They are barbaric and hate women' (British journalist Christina Lamb)

- an army of fanatical bumpkins
- '[lacking] the knowledge or management skills to run a government' (Afghan refugee)
- 'no educated people in this administration ... all totally backward and illiterate [with] ... no idea of the history of the country and, though they call themselves mullahs ... no idea of Islam' (Taliban defector)
- monstrous, Iron Age regime
- ragtag Talibans
- PR mutts
- barbarians
- feudal Afghan army
- medieval warriors

Alien/strange
- Their culture ... is strange and hostile not just to us, but to Kabul ... and to pretty well the entire Islamic world
- an occupying force, even though they were Afghans
- 'no longer a part of Afghanistan' (Afghan leader Hamid Karzai)
- distinctly odd, as well as frightening
- 'out of this world' (Egyptian journalist Mohamed Heikal)
- an unrelenting and totally unwesternised 'enemy'
- a bizarre utopian experiment that went wrong
- a leadership which, publicly at least, has succeeded in expunging virtually all traces of human personality
- indoctrinated Taleban robots
- an obscurantist sect that smashes television sets and hangs videotapes from trees

Brutal/authoritarian
- repressive regime
- a brutal and oppressive regime
- intolerant regime
- the most arbitrary regime in the world
- 'an extraordinary, exceptional, oppressive set of people' (British minister Peter Mandelson)
- seems an oppressive regime
- 'the oppressive Taliban regime' (Donald Rumsfeld)
- eccentrically brutal regime
- 'brutish regime' (Afghan NGO worker)

- dictatorial
- 'a regime sustained by brutality and violence' (Jack Straw)
- the brutal and bigoted regime
- brutal regime
- 'butchers' (former opposition fighter)
- 'vicious group' (CIA director George Tenet)
- Mullah Omar's thugs
- brutal regime

Terrorists
- 'terrorist regime' (Russian President Vladimir Putin)
- 'terrorist regime' (Afghan refugee)
- 'a group of gunmen who took our nation hostage' (Afghan exile)
- 'very dangerous, they are terrorists' (Northern Alliance boy soldier)
- stealthy bands of terrorists
- a rogue power
- [al-Qaida's] political sponsors
- [bin Laden's] accomplices in crime
- of the same breed as the suicide bombers in New York
- 'a regime ... that was one of the most brutal anywhere and was training thousands of terrorists' (Tony Blair)
- 'world class harbourers' of terrorists (Donald Rumsfeld)
- 'a regime which sponsors and harbours terrorists' (Blair's press secretary, Alastair Campbell)
- 'an example of state-sponsored terrorism' (US politician Newt Gingrich)
- terrorist-sponsored state

Generally unpleasant/evil/ criminal
- thoroughly rancid
- ignominious
- deeply disagreeable
- vileness incarnate

- predators
- the criminal government of Afghanistan (Afghan women's organisation)
- the ostracised regime
- one of the most horrible regimes on earth
- 'an appalling regime, unelected and unsupported' (Oxfam's policy director, Justin Forsyth)
- a brutal regime
- a disruptive regime
- the pariah regime
- One of the nastiest, cruellest and most dangerous regimes in the world
- the murderous Kabul regime
- 'the most evil administration since the Nazis' (Richard Ferguson QC)
- 'like Nazis and one cannot deal with them' (attributed to Jack Straw)
- Similar to Germany's first Nazis of the 1930s
- Atrocious Taleban regime
- a regime beyond any pale
- a rabble of sadistic torturers and drug-pushers
- 'world-class liars' (Donald Rumsfeld)
- a regime that is built on massive fraud and raw force that considers itself virtuous, ruling a land without song, laughter, or women's faces

Tough fighters?
- 'very tough people' (Donald Rumsfeld)
- 'dogged opponents' (Donald Rumsfeld)
- 'tough warriors' (US Rear Admiral John Stufflebeem)
- an enemy with only limited military assets but a lifetime of guerrilla fighting experience
- 'If you push them hard they aren't so tough' (Northern Alliance fighter)

- never been as invincible as their myth suggests

Stabilising force
- 'harsh, but they brought peace to Afghanistan' (Afghan refugee)
- horrible ... [but] did impose a kind of order on Afghanistan
- a repressive regime which at least has brought some stability to 95% of Afghanistan

Creation of others
- a monster created by our two 'Alliance' friends Pakistan and Saudi Arabia
- a perfect product of the rapine and pillage of the Northern Alliance's years of terror
- in many ways the creation of our very own friends in the Northern Alliance

Other descriptions
- the perfect adversary for Tony Blair
- like the Vietcong
- finished as a political force
- 'a regime with no rules ... makes policy as it goes along ... can be very arbitrary' ('experienced Taliban observer')
- a government [the UN] does not recognise
- 'a mix of good and bad' (Taliban defector)
- 'extremely respectful' (Channel 4's Tristana Moore)
- 'most of them are fairly ordinary, just trying to get through life' (BBC producer Gordon Adam)
- 'just country guys on a bandwagon' (social anthropologist Andrew Skuse)

Descriptions are in quotation marks where they appeared that way in the original; attributions are given where the article attributed a phrase.

in the *Mail*. Given that the latter's volume of coverage was less than that of the broadsheets, the *Mail*'s use of these terms particularly stands out, and it was also the paper most given to emphasising Afghanistan's cultural difference.

Despite the weight of descriptions highlighting the Taliban's religious fundamentalism or extremism, the regime was not generally portrayed as typical of either Islam or of Afghanistan. Rather, as is evident from many of the descriptions listed in Box 6.1, the Taliban were seen as perpetrating a peculiarly 'hardline', 'strict', 'simplistic' or 'twisted' version of Islam, and as imposing unwanted restrictions on ordinary Afghans. Some of the *Mail's* coverage, however, took a different view, largely through the contributions of its correspondent on the ground during the first two weeks of October, Ross Benson. His dispatches from Northern Alliance territory frequently emphasised Afghanistan's otherness, usually presented in terms of its backwardness and culture of violence. Afghanistan, said Benson, was a 'wild', 'barbarous', 'fractured', 'benighted' and 'Godforsaken' land, where 'time has gone backwards'. The landscape was both 'medieval' and 'a Mad Max, post-apocalyptic nightmare' (13 October) and to enter it was 'to step into the Middle Ages' (1 October). It was a country with a 'time-honoured tradition of unmentionable cruelty' (1 October), where 'killing has always been a way of life' (4 October), where the 'inhabitants have been fighting either the outside world or each other for centuries', and which 'has always been locked in its savage past' (1 October). This past had 'given it ... a present of bigoted, hopeless poverty and intolerance' (4 October), in which a Western-run hospital stood as an 'island of sanity and decency' amid the 'squalor of the Panjsher Valley' (6 October). Benson did highlight what he called 'the Taliban's perverted, profane interpretation of the Koran' (1 October), but generally saw this as simply the latest expression of Afghan backwardness. When he said, for example, that 'The mullahs ... regard what we call "progress" ... as an attack on their beliefs', he also suggested that 'This has been their attitude ever since the first European ventured into these forbidding mountain ranges in the early 19th century' (13 October).

The point of Benson's colourful accounts was to argue that there was a kind of fit between the extremism of bin Laden and the Taliban, and the wider culture of Afghanistan. Hence, for instance, he claimed that 'if the notion of eternal salvation as a reward for mass murder is incomprehensible to the modern mind, it does not seem in the least out of place here', and that 'Only in a country like Afghanistan could a fanatic like Osama Bin Laden flourish' (1 October). On this basis, Benson suggested that the war could be understood in terms of a clash of civilisations. Highlighting the Taliban's subjugation of women and other abuses, he repeatedly claimed that 'It is this way of life the Taliban government is trying to impose on all of us by force of terror' (4 October) and that 'the iron grip religion exerts on these men of war means they will forever detest the West and all that it stands for' (13 October). Ultimately, Benson concluded, this was a religious and cultural war: 'It comes down to a question of outlook, of aspiration and, when you get right down to it, of faith' (13 October).

Interesting though Benson's reports are, however, their significance should not be exaggerated: outside the pages of the *Mail*, few commentators agreed with the 'clash of civilisations' idea. In the *Times*, film-maker Nick Danziger saw 'hauntingly similar parallels' between Afghanistan and Kosovo, both of which had 'been in flames throughout their histories', and he argued that 'The roots of both [conflicts] were clashes between the Christian West and Islam, between affluence and poverty and a society with a multiplicity of choices and others with deeply ingrained traditions' (29 October). In the *Independent*, Francis Fukuyama framed the conflict in terms of his concept of the 'end of history', arguing that 'the struggle we face is not the clash of several distinct and equal cultures', but rather merely 'a series of rearguard actions from societies whose traditional existence is ... threatened by modernisation' (11 October). However, Fukuyama did appear to concede some ground to Samuel Huntington's (1993) 'clash of civilisations' thesis, arguing both that there was a Christian cultural basis to Western ideas about 'the universalism of democratic rights' and that 'there does seem to be something about Islam, or at least fundamentalist Islam, that makes Muslim societies particularly resistant to modernity'. Overall, there were only 10 explanatory articles which framed the war in terms of a 'clash of civilisations' or a conflict between the West and Islam (6.8 per cent of all explanatory articles). Supporters of the military action generally followed the lead of coalition politicians in rejecting such ideas.

On the opposite side of the argument, anti-war critics sometimes challenged official statements that the war was not an attack on Islam or a 'clash of civilisa-tions'. Reported statements by bin Laden, other al-Qaeda spokesmen and the Taliban frequently included the claim that the West was at war with Islam, and similar views were reportedly held by the Deputy General Secretary of the Muslim Council of Britain (*Independent*, 25 October) and other critics of the war. Only the *Guardian* gave this case a full airing, however, in a comment piece by Faisal Bodi entitled 'Of Course It's a War on Islam' (17 October). Bodi argued that the US had 'inflicted another wound on the bleeding body of the Muslim *ummah*, or nation, in the name of a war against international terrorism' and that the coalition was 'attempting to deal once and for all with those who refuse to yield to the American world order'. The 'clash of civilisations' thesis was also sometimes raised by critics of the war. Freedland said he felt 'deeply ambivalent about this war' because, although coalition leaders had attempted to 'trash the idea' of a clash of civilisations, 'they never paused to wonder how Islam felt about the west' (*Guardian*, 10 October). The US and its allies, he argued, had 'played directly into Bin Laden's hands ... inadvertently proving that America and Islam are locked in an epic clash of civilisations after all'. Similarly, Madeleine Bunting criticised Blair's talk of a 'battle of values' because it came 'perilously close to a clash of civilisations' (*Guardian*, 4 October).

Bunting's comments again suggest the potential for some convergence between 'humanitarian' justifications for war (war would put an end to Taliban abuses) and an emphasis on the cultural difference of the Taliban or of Afghan society generally. While this study does not support the claim made by some critics that the 'clash of civilisations' explanation became widely influential in the aftermath of 9/11, there is evidence that Afghanistan was sometimes seen in press coverage as backward and primitive, a perception which could be conveyed without referring to Islam or the human rights record of the Taliban. In particular, the notion of 'tribalism' was used routinely in descriptions of the country (and of the border areas of Pakistan) and its people. The terms 'tribe' or 'tribal' appeared in 311 articles overall (11.9 per cent of total coverage), in a variety of contexts. The country, for example, was described as 'riven by tribal and ethnic division' (*Times*, 29 December) and as characterised by 'ethnic and religious complexity ... [and by] intense tribalism' (*Times*, 5 October). Hamid

Karzai, who headed the new interim government installed by the coalition, was described in three separate *Times* articles on 6 December as a 'tribal chief', an 'important Pashtun tribal leader' and a 'Westernised tribesman'. Similarly, the *Independent* recounted how Karzai 'sat cross-legged with other tribal leaders' (13 December) and described the 'Tribal elders and warlords who had come to the capital for the inauguration of the new interim government' as sporting 'flowing beards and robes' (26 December). As these examples indicate, an emphasis on Afghan 'tribalism' persisted after the overthrow of the Taliban.

'Blowback', oil and American aggression

The notion of 'blowback' – explaining the war as the product of previous Western policy – was the most common theme, appearing in 47 of the 148 articles which offered an explanation for the war (31.8 per cent). This type of explanation was most favoured in the *Guardian* and *Independent*, which carried 23 and 18 such articles respectively, as compared with only four in the *Times* and two in the *Mail*. These were also the only two papers to take up this explanation in their editorial columns, five times in the *Guardian* and three times in the *Independent*. 'Blowback' is discussed here together with the more minor explanatory themes of oil (10 further articles) and US aggression (eight further articles), since articles in all three of these categories tended to highlight similar points about Western, particularly US, policy.

The explanations classified under the heading of 'blowback' may be divided into two types. The first, accounting for 14 articles, focused on the West's record in Afghanistan. In the *Independent*, for instance, Fisk's reports from the region frequently mentioned the role of the CIA and Pakistan's intelligence service in arming the Mujahideen and helping to create both the Taliban and bin Laden's organisation (see, for example, his articles on 8, 11, 26 and 27 October). A second type of 'blowback' explanation, featured in 33 articles, set the conflict in the larger context of the history of imperialism and injustices caused by Western involvement in the Middle East. In the *Guardian*, for example, Paul Foot argued that while 'the vast wealth of the irresponsible and greedy few and the indescribable poverty, hunger and thirst of the many' did not excuse terrorism, it did help to explain it. Foot predicted that 'if the gap between rich and poor is allowed to grow, terrorism will grow too' (16 October). Similarly, the *Guardian*'s Seamus Milne said that 'What powerful states call terrorism may be an inevitable response to injustice', and argued that groups such as al-Qaeda were 'unquestionably the product of conditions in the Arab and Muslim world for which both Britain and the US bear a heavy responsibility' (25 October). The same day's edition of the *Independent* carried a comment piece by Kaizer Nyatsumba arguing that 'At the heart of the problem is the duplicitous nature of American foreign policy, which has been responsible for thousands of deaths around the world over the years'. Highlighting the 'arrogance and hypocrisy' of the US, Nyatsumba suggested that America would 'continue to have enemies in the developing world' as long as it 'continues to be a bully'. When Pilger accused the mainstream media of 'disassociating the September 11 atrocities from the source of half a century of American crusades, economic wars and homicidal adventures', he may have had a point about some of the coverage but as far as explanatory articles are concerned he was by no means the only writer drawing attention to Britain and America's 'blood-soaked historical record' (*Guardian*, 4 October).

Two key issues were particularly emphasised in this type of explanation: Western support for Israel and Americans' purported general ignorance. Complaining that Bush and Blair were pretending that 9/11 was 'not connected to other atrocities America committed years ago', for example, Gary Younge said it was now 'widely accepted that without a just settlement in the Middle East, networks like al-Qaida will always be able to prey on disaffection in the Arab world' (*Guardian*, 15 October). Similarly, in the same day's edition of the *Independent* Tariq Ali argued that 'Unless the Palestinians are guaranteed a viable, sovereign state, there will be no peace'. Also in that day's edition, Andrew Gumbel reported from the US on how 'the attacks of 11 September exposed the United States as a politically unaware nation'. The current 'global crisis [was] born largely of ignorance', argued Gumbel: 'Americans' ignorance of the sheer anger and resentment that their government's policies have stirred up around the world, and, arguably, the ignorance of desperate people in the Islamic world who have turned to radical fundamentalism as the answer to their problems'. Although the ignorance of people in the Islamic world was also seen as a factor here, the accent was on the failings of the US: the report was headlined 'Americans Wake Up To Ignorance' (*Independent*, 15 October). Also criticising the US for 'cosset[ing] Israel's refusal to make a reasonable settlement with Palestine' (as well as for abandoning Afghanistan after the Soviets' defeat), the *Guardian*'s Hugo Young was another who broadened the argument to include what he called 'America's mono-cultural incomprehension' of the rest of the world. Arguing that 9/11 was 'not a random flailing', Young suggested that the underlying problem was US 'domination' and 'insensitivity' (9 October).

Although journalists and commentators were usually careful to point out that they wished to understand, rather than to excuse, the attacks of 11 September, these sorts of arguments bore a disconcerting similarity to those of al-Qaeda. In a videotape released just after the start of military action, for example, bin Laden said that 'America will never dream of security or see it before we live it and see it in Palestine', while an al-Qaeda spokesman claimed that 'What happened in the United States is a natural reaction to the ignorant policy of the United States' (*Guardian*, 8 October). Such views apparently had some resonance. On 23 October the *Guardian* reported the finding of a poll in Italy which showed that 'About a quarter of Italians justify the September 11 attacks by saying they were, at least to some extent, the result of US foreign policy, in particular in Muslim countries' and in December a global opinion survey reportedly found that 'most think America brought [the] terror attacks on itself'. The latter poll, conducted among 'people of influence in politics, media, business and culture' in 24 countries, showed a 'barely disguised resentment at America's massive power in the world', prompting the *Independent*'s Rupert Cornwell to ask 'Did America somehow ask for the terrorist outrages in New York and Washington?' (21 December).

Even more surprisingly, similar ideas were taken up by a number of establishment figures, including coalition leaders. The First Sea Lord, Admiral Sir Nigel Essenhigh, acknowledged that sympathisers of al-Qaeda had 'legitimate grievances' (*Guardian*, 13 October), for example, and the Bishop of Winchester, Michael Scott-Joynt, argued that 'This terror is a judgment upon us', because Western electorates had 'encouraged, supported or at least allowed our governments, over so many decades, to develop our standard of living at the expense of millions in the southern hemisphere' (*Guardian*, 28 December). Development Minister Clare Short said that the US 'had to consider why it attracted so much criticism around the world' and she suggested that 'One major cause is the unresolved conflict in the Middle East' (*Times*, 26 December), while at the other end of the political spectrum Conservative MP Nicholas Soames argued that 'the grievances of Palestinians must be addressed to avoid future conflict' (*Times*, 5 October). This stance was in fact written into the British government's official strategy document for the war on terrorism, which signalled the need to tackle the 'underlying causes of terrorism', including 'the Arab–Israeli conflict' (*Independent*, 11 October). Hence, despite having said that Blair was 'withering about those who insist on trying to understand the causes of terrorism' (3 October), the *Mail* later reported him as saying: 'We need to understand the real sense there is here in the Arab world and different parts of the world about the injustice of the conditions in which the Palestinians live' (11 October). Similarly, Bush said it was necessary to 'combat evil with understanding' (*Times*, 27 October), while James Dobbins, the US Special Envoy sent to Afghanistan in December, said that America was among those responsible for 'a decade of abuse and neglect' in the country, and that 'on September 11 the international community and the United States ... paid a price' (*Times*, 18 December). As these examples suggest, criticising America's past record and viewing al-Qaeda's terrorism as an expression of legitimate grievances in the Middle East did not necessarily imply an anti-war stance. Elements, at least, of the 'blowback' explanation were also voiced by pro-war writers and by elite coalition figures.

There was a similar ambiguity about explanations which highlighted Western oil interests. Of the 10 articles featuring this theme, only three did so in the context of making (or citing a source making) an explicitly anti-war case. In the *Guardian*, Bunting argued that, for coalition governments, concern about Afghanistan's future was 'secondary to western interests – getting rid of Bin Laden and installing a regime more likely than the Taliban to facilitate oil and gas development in Central Asia' (22 October). In the following day's edition, Monbiot conceded that the US was engaged in a 'genuine' if 'misguided' attempt to 'stamp out terrorism by military force', but suggested that the war was also a 'late colonial adventure' designed to further the interests of the US oil company Unocal, which wanted to build oil and gas pipelines through Afghanistan. 'Given that the US government is dominated by former oil industry executives', noted Monbiot, it would be 'foolish to suppose that such plans no longer figure in its strategic thinking' (*Guardian*, 23 October). In December, the *Guardian* carried an interview with Gore Vidal, who, among other points, observed that 'We have a bunch of oilmen running the country', and suggested that Bush family oil interests were driving policy (6 December).

Three further articles, while not taking an anti-war stance, did imply some criticism of US policy through their emphasis on the importance of oil. Andy Rowell argued that, in first supporting and then ousting the Taliban, America had been guided by oil interests, and Mark Seddon criticised the Bush administration for prioritising 'America's economic and strategic interests ahead of tracking down Islamist terrorists' prior to 9/11 (*Guardian*, 24 October, 18 December). A related point was made in the *Times* by Anatole Kaletsky, who argued that, in the longer term, the West 'must break its addiction to oil', partly because 'American foreign policy has become a "hostage" to oil dependence' but mostly because 'Oil money is the main source of financing for terrorism and religious fanaticism throughout the Islamic world' (18 October). The *Times* was the only paper to take up the issue of oil in its editorial columns, where it was argued that there was a tension between 'the West's two fundamental priorities in the Middle East, secure access to the Gulf's oil, and Israel's existence within secure borders' (12 October). While the US had a 'moral requirement to protect Israel', the paper suggested, the 'strategic requirement to secure access to oil' meant that America had to gain the support of Arab allies and promote stability the region, even if that meant 'putting unprecedented pressure on Israel' (13 October). In this view, the objective of defeating terrorism was understood as related to the West's need for oil, but this did not imply a critical or anti-war position. Indeed, oil could also be seen as a good reason to fight the war: in the *Mail* (12 October), Anthony Sampson said that oil was the 'ultimate prize Bin Laden is fighting for', suggesting that al-Qaeda had to be defeated in order to maintain oil exports from the Middle East.

Whereas articles which explained the war by pointing to oil interests or the legacy of past Western policies did not necessarily imply criticism of the military action, the same cannot be said of those which understood the war in terms of American aggression. For the most part, however, this idea was confined to the *Guardian's* December 2001 coverage, indicating a more critical understanding of Western policy as it became clear that the Taliban would soon be overthrown and discussion increasingly turned to where the 'war on terrorism' might go next. A number of *Guardian* writers highlighted the influence of what Julian Borger (17 December) called 'super-hawks' within the US government, and criticised the emerging 'Bush doctrine'. Younge explained that 'Relying exclusively on the use of force, the Bush doctrine maxim is: "To every action there should be an unequal and disproportionate reaction"' (10 December), for example, and Bunting called it a 'new US doctrine of terror' (17 December). Outside the *Guardian*, the bullish mood in Washington tended to be discussed in a less critical way. In the *Independent*, for example, Bruce Anderson described the US as 'a superpower stung to anger and then to action, determined to exert its strength and to minimise its future vulnerability' (17

December). Altogether there were eight articles discussing the war in terms of US belligerence, all but two of them in the *Guardian*'s December coverage.

Failed states: making sense of competing frames

The explanations discussed above are highly varied and even somewhat contradictory. In part, the diversity of explanations derives from differences between papers (*Mail* writers taking up the 'clash of civilisations' idea and *Times* journalists emphasising the context of 'war on terrorism', for example) or from the fact that assessments of the war changed over time (as with the *Guardian*'s shift of emphasis from an early endorsement of the coalition's 'humanitarian' purpose to a more critical view in December). Yet in other respects conventional political dividing lines seem to be blurred, so that explanatory categories and descriptive themes which we might logically associate with a critical or anti-war stance – describing the military action as 'retaliation', for example, or explaining it by reference to the negative effects of past Western policies – could also be advanced by supporters of the war. On the one hand, in shorthand descriptions of the conflict, the 'war on terrorism' frame was clearly dominant; yet, on the other hand, this idea was not accepted unquestioningly in explanatory articles, which from the outset often featured criticism of confused Western war aims. Rather than simply seeing this mixed picture as evidence of the existence of competing frames, however, it might be suggested that in fact there was more common ground than first appears among the various explanations offered in press coverage.

This common ground is captured by the idea of 'failed states', which could be viewed as a kind of 'master concept', flexible enough to incorporate most of the other strands of explanation sketched out above. The concept's broad scope was suggested by Foreign Secretary Jack Straw, who argued that:

> Terrorists are strongest where states are weakest … [and] find safe havens in places – not just Afghanistan – where conflict, poverty, ethnic and racial tensions, exploitation, corruption, poor governance, malign interference from outside or just plain neglect have brought about the collapse of responsible government and civil society…. If there is one common denominator which links Cambodia in the Seventies to Mozambique and Angola in the Eighties to Yugoslavia, Rwanda, the Democratic Republic of the Congo and Sierra Leone in the Nineties to Afghanistan today, it is this: that when we allow governments to fail, warlords, criminals, drugs barons or terrorists will fill the vacuum. (*Guardian*, 22 October)

Straw makes the 'failed states' concept do a lot of work here, by suggesting it can encompass such different contexts as Cambodia, Rwanda and Afghanistan, and can explain the problem of 'warlords' and 'drugs barons' as well as terrorists. Its elasticity in Straw's hands derives from the political purpose to which it is put: attempting to legitimise present action by drawing in a host of other issues, including poverty, ethnic conflict, exploitation and poor governance. Reporting Straw's speech for the *Times* (23 October), Michael Binyon noted that it was 'clearly intended to silence critics on the Left, who blame the Government for neglecting humanitarian aid in favour of the war effort', and indeed the most important connection made by Straw – pointing to what he regarded as recent international successes in Sierra Leone, Bosnia, East Timor and elsewhere – was between Afghanistan and the 'humanitarian' interventions of the 1990s.

This connection is significant because of the argument that since 'failed' states do not, by definition, possess full sovereignty, international intervention is both necessary and legitimate. As we saw in Chapter 2, this was precisely the argument made about intervention in Somalia in the early 1990s. In the present context, emphasising that 'For the last five years [Afghanistan] has not even existed as a functioning state' and that 'there are no state institutions worth speaking of in Kabul', Straw argued that 'the global order, as conceived in the wake of the second world war', had now fundamentally changed. He meant that the principles of non-interference and equality between sovereign states which had underpinned the post-1945 order were no longer relevant because 'nowadays, conflicts arise where no functioning state exists'. The direct inspiration for Straw's views was Robert Cooper, the British government's envoy to the talks establishing the new Afghan government in December (see Cooper 2004). At the time of Straw's speech, Peter Riddell also elaborated on Cooper's ideas in the *Times*, in arguing that Afghanistan was 'the most extreme, and destabilising, example so far of the chaos produced by failed states' (22 October) and that 'familiar ideas about national sovereignty and non-intervention look irrelevant in the face of such instability' (23 October). Similarly, in December Giles Whittell drew on Cooper's ideas to characterise both Afghanistan and Somalia as '"failed states", quagmires where the rule of law has given way to that of warlords, and the apparatus of government has collapsed' (*Times*, 12 December).

Although only eight articles explicitly elaborated an explanation of the war in terms of 'failed states', this idea was often implicit in other sorts of explanation. Most obviously, it provided a basis for arguing for the necessity of 'regime change': thus, while Straw said that 'Removing the Taliban regime is not an aim of the military action', he also argued that the ultimate objective of intervention was to install 'a stable, durable, representative government, committed to eradicating terrorism … with which we can work on the humanitarian crisis, drugs, human rights and longer-term development' (*Guardian*, 22 October). Similarly, on its own the claim that military intervention in Afghanistan was led by humanitarian or human rights concerns was bound to seem questionable, since the core issue was obviously terrorism and the need to respond to 9/11. When combined with the idea that Afghanistan was a 'failed state', however, the larger 'moral' claims made by Blair and others could be made to look more credible: describing Afghanistan as a 'failed state' encompassed both the idea that the Taliban regime had allowed terrorism to flourish and the idea that it was an illegitimate government guilty of abuses against its own citizens. As Kaletsky argued in the *Times* (11 October), the Taliban was both intertwined with al-Qaeda (it 'could not have been sustained without the support of bin Laden's military and financial network') and had perpetrated 'many crimes' of its own, including 'enslav[ing] all the women and millions of the men in Afghanistan'. Describing the Taliban as 'a rabble of sadistic torturers and drug-pushers', Kaletsky noted that it had 'never been recognised by the UN as the legal government of Afghanistan' and argued that it 'cannot claim the privileges of an internationally recognised sovereign state.'

The 'failed states' concept did not, of course, encompass the ideas of a clash of civilisations or a war against Islam, which were always repudiated by coalition leaders. However, it does allow us to understand the emphasis, in much reporting, on Afghanistan's backwardness and 'tribalism' in a new light: these characteristics were not so much markers of religious, cultural or civilisational difference as indicators that Afghanistan lacked proper statehood. Again, Somalia provides an illuminating comparison: as we saw in Chapter 2, an emphasis on 'clan hatreds' or a 'culture of blood revenge' tended to be seen as bolstering the case for international intervention. From the 'failed states' perspective, it also becomes clear how pro-war writers and even coalition leaders could incorporate the idea of 'blowback' into their account of the war's causes: past neglect had contributed to state breakdown and the task now was to intervene more. McElvoy summarised the official British view as being 'that the West bears responsibility for allowing Afghanistan – and other failed states – to get into such a dire condition in the first place and is thus obligated to stay around to clear up the mess when it does intervene' (*Independent*, 19 December). The history of imperialism and the importance of oil interests could also be seen in a similar light: as holding back the development of proper democratic states in the Middle East and thereby creating the conditions which had given rise to terrorism. Aaronovitch, for instance, mounting a staunch defence of the war, said that the 'long-term reason for the [11 September] attack[s]' lay 'in the poisonous legacies of colonialism, the Cold War and the terrible failure of secular Arab governments' (*Independent*, 27 December). Although he said it would be 'crudely reductionist' to 'lay all this ... at the feet of the United States', he also suggested that if the Western coalition did not engage in 'nation-building' in Afghanistan it would be 'doomed to repeat the same errors that helped to put us here in the first place'.

Even the critical view of the war as driven by White House 'hawks' appears differently in light of this discussion. This explanation emerged in the context of a debate in December about future priorities: while the US seemed ready to move on to other targets, Britain and other European countries were keen to emphasise the importance of peacekeeping and nation-building operations in Afghanistan, in which their own forces would have an important role. As Lawrence Freedman argued in the *Independent* (18 December), the Americans were 'disinclined to volunteer for humanitarian operations and "nation-building"', while Blair's view was that 'unless the West engages fully in the political and economic life of states such as Afghanistan then they will continue to fail and continue to cause trouble for the rest of the world'. Similarly, McElvoy cited a 'senior advisor to the Prime Minister' (probably Cooper) as complaining that 'the Americans want to fight and then go, the Europeans don't want to fight but want to come in afterwards so that it looks as if they're doing something, and Britain is in the middle' (*Independent*, 19 December). To be fair, explanatory articles which emphasised US aggression in December were mostly written by commentators, such as Bunting and Younge, who had been critical of the war all along. But there seemed more scope for such airing views in December because they chimed with official British concerns over whether the US would simply move on to pursue the 'war on terrorism' elsewhere, or would give sufficient priority to nation-building (and over whether British troops would be allowed to lead such efforts). Again, it is worth recalling the US-led intervention in Somalia, when worries about a lack of American 'staying power' appeared as a criticism but in fact constituted an argument for more extensive and longer-term intervention.

Prescription and critique

Overall, 268 articles contained some criticism of the war, while a further 86 news reports focused on civilian 'collateral damage' caused by coalition bombing, and in December an additional 18 articles focused on the mistreatment of prisoners, particularly at the Qala-i-Jhangi fortress, where hundreds of Taliban captives were killed. Together, these 372 articles accounted for only a modest proportion (14.3 per cent) of total coverage, but this has to be weighed against the sheer size and diversity of the overall story. The *Guardian* carried by far the most critical articles (142 altogether, 112 of them during October), but the large quantity of *Guardian* coverage counted in our sample meant that this still accounted for only 15.5 per cent of the paper's total output.[14] The main limitation of the critique offered by the papers sampled for this study was that it tended to focus quite narrowly on the effects of the military action, rather than questioning whether the action was justified in principle. As Riddell remarked in the *Times* (18 October), reporting parliamentary debate about the war: 'Doubts and dissent are often confused; uncertainty is not the same as opposition'. Much of the criticism voiced in the press fell into the category of doubts and uncertainties, rather than dissent and opposition. To appreciate this, it will be helpful first to examine the editorial stance taken by each newspaper before returning to look in more detail at the main criticisms they offered.

Guardian

The *Guardian* supported the war, but with little enthusiasm and much caution. 'Hold your fire' called the paper's leader column on the eve of the bombing, arguing that it would be 'truly tragic if, impatient for results and eager for revenge, the US opened fire precipitately' (6 October). The US in fact opened fire the very next day, but the *Guardian*'s doubts did not translate into opposition, largely, as we saw earlier, because of Blair's humanitarian claims about the war. According to the paper's 'Readers' Editor', Ian Mayes

(20 October), a minority of *Guardian* leader writers did oppose the war but the overall editorial stance was to offer 'qualified support'. This was premised, Mayes explained, 'on the understanding that [military action] is accompanied by continuing diplomatic and humanitarian efforts'. The nearest the *Guardian* came to opposition was in its 26 October editorial, which raised a number of 'pressing questions' about the war's 'conduct and aims', including whether killing bin Laden was 'the best way of ensuring justice for the September 11 victims and of upholding international law', and why military action had 'so far focused on the Taliban, whose overthrow is not a stated war aim'. The core issue, for the *Guardian*, was that the public was being asked to 'take an awful lot on trust', an objection it had already raised in editorials on 5 and 15 October. On 5 October, the *Guardian* posed this issue in terms of the evidence against bin Laden, arguing that, in the absence of publicly available proof of his guilt, 'Mr Blair's case comes down to two words: trust me'. This was not because the paper thought bin Laden was innocent – this same editorial said it was 'simply perverse to pretend that anyone … [else] is responsible' – rather, the *Guardian* argued that the absence of firmer evidence 'narrows the moral high ground … provides ammunition for those who want to accuse the US of arrogance, and … narrows the scope for error and bad judgment in the US-dominated response'. The curious implication of this argument – that the provision of more evidence would widen the scope for error and bad judgement – captured the *Guardian*'s position nicely: unconvinced that the coalition's claim to the moral high ground was entirely secure, and suspecting the US of arrogance, the paper did not welcome the prospect of defending a war which might involve errors and misjudgements.

The *Guardian* was more confident in opposing a war that was not happening, declaring in comparatively unequivocal terms its opposition to any widening of the 'war on terror' to Iraq. 'Such a move would be unsupportable' proclaimed the paper's 10 October leader (at least, it would be so 'in current circumstances', without 'very clear proof' and without the US having 'proper recourse to the international community'). Regarding the present war, the *Guardian*'s expression of reservations came across as carping criticism, often about secondary and sometimes quite peripheral issues. The paper complained repeatedly about the lack of media access (on 9, 13, 15, 16 and 26 October), for example, and about Blair's high-handed leadership style (on 1, 23 and 24 October). As we saw above, the *Guardian* also raised questions about whether the 'humanitarian' aspects of the campaign were being sufficiently prioritised but did not oppose the bombing on these grounds either; it described the aerial food drops as 'smart' (6 October) and professed itself reassured by Clare Short, whom the paper described, without apparent irony, as 'a sort of socialist pit canary in the war cabinet' (24 October).

In terms of diplomacy, the paper urged greater efforts to resolve the Israeli/Palestinian conflict, but it appeared that at least part of this issue's importance for the *Guardian* lay in the implication that past Western policy in the Middle East had caused the grievances which led to 9/11. The paper's 9 October editorial described bin Laden as 'disingenuously linking his evil cause with that of Palestine', but the *Guardian* itself had already firmly linked bin Laden's cause with Palestine, demanding on 2 October that 'US thinking on Palestine must now change forever', and advising Bush that if he hoped to 'strike at the roots of the anti-western anger that feeds terrorist violence' he should 'invite Yasser Arafat [the Palestinian leader] to Washington'. On 11 October, looking for 'The roots of the rage', the *Guardian* advised that both 'Islam and the West must … look inwards', but the emphasis was on the misconduct of the West, particularly the US. Rejecting the idea of a 'clash of civilisations', it said that 'al-Qaida is not a uniquely Muslim phenomenon, nor is Islam especially prone to nurturing terror'. Rather, the 'roots of rage' lay in what had been done to the Islamic world by the West: this was a 'dysfunctional relationship' which carried a 'destructive colonial legacy' into the present as Western governments 'blunder on to repeat the mistakes of the past'. The *Guardian* hoped for a 'shared search for justice sensitive to both traditions', but left little doubt that the main barrier to this was the US, which had 'projected its influence, its values and its interests with little understanding of its consequent obligations' and which 'wages war with impunity, making the rules, bending the law, ignoring consensus and bullying its friends'. Identifying closely with Blair's emphasis on the global 'power of community', the paper reserved its most stinging criticism for what it saw as American arrogance. The *Guardian*'s 24 October editorial, responding to Bush's statement that 'This conflict is a fight to save the civilised world' and his suggestion that 'those who support terrorism are just as bad as the terrorists themselves', was particularly scathing. Incensed by Bush's 'apparently narrow understanding of a complex, contradictory, inter-connected planet where there are no simple definitions and no easy answers', it poured scorn on the 'challenging idea' that 'Mr Bush is the man best qualified to be the judge of human progress and the guardian of global culture', and said that while some might see Afghanistan as outside the civilised world, 'others might nominate west Texas'.

In December the *Guardian* was still bemoaning the lack of attention to humanitarian need, but now in the context of reconstruction and nation-building. The paper was initially quite upbeat about the fall of the Taliban, arguing that the military campaign had been 'largely vindicated' (8 December). However, this editorial – headlined 'George Bush, Not Tony Blair, Is the Victor' – complained of a lack of US effort on the 'humanitarian and diplomatic fronts', observing that 'George Bush has done little to suggest that he shares these priorities'. The *Guardian* still saw some hope that the future direction of international intervention in Afghanistan might follow a more Blairite 'humanitarian' agenda, however, noting that Britain was best placed to take the lead role in peacekeeping operations, which, though difficult, 'could make an important contribution to the rebuilding of Afghanistan' (11 December). Supporting the 'hard but necessary task' of nation-building, the *Guardian* remained highly critical of the US, and argued that the Pentagon was 'crassly ignor[ing] Afghanistan's political, humanitarian and reconstruction imperatives' and, by its 'disdain for peacekeeping', was increasing the risks to British troops (20 December).

Independent

Judging from the contradictions of tone and stance which characterised the *Independent*'s leader columns during October, it seems likely that the internal debate at the paper was similar to that which Mayes described at the *Guardian*. The inconsistency concerned the 'humanitarian' claims for the war, which, as we saw, the paper first welcomed enthusiastically, then dismissed as an unnecessary 'veneer' and finally decided were worthwhile but only for their propaganda value. In its 3 October editorial, the paper said of Blair's 'power of community' speech: 'there will also be criticism that his vision, however commendable, is impossibly ambitious ... [but this] criticism is surely misplaced'. Two days later, the paper voiced such criticism itself, mocking Blair as the 'Moraliser to the World ... trying to fight all the evils of the globe at once' (5 October). The following day's editorial argued, as if in reply, that Blair was 'trying to rally support for a nobler cause, which has been decried as "trying to solve all the world's problems at once", but which deserves a more thoughtful reception' (6 October). Whatever internal disagreements lay behind this editorial to and fro seem to have been resolved by recognising the importance of 'humanitarian' claims to the propaganda war.

Just as it did with the issue of humanitarian aid, the *Independent* also supported calls for a bombing 'pause' but only in order to help the propaganda effort. While actually agreeing that the government was 'right to dismiss' the arguments of aid agencies, it also noted that 'the weapons of persuasion and propaganda need to be deployed with more sophistication' (20 October). In this context, the *Independent* argued, 'the political imperative to make a gesture becomes overwhelming'. The paper therefore endorsed calls for a pause in order to deliver aid, fully expecting this 'gesture' to be futile ('no doubt any food which did get in would be stolen by the Taliban'), but arguing that it would make for good publicity. Similarly, the *Independent*'s 26 October editorial raised the issue of civilian casualties and expressed worry about the 'damage being done to the US and its allies in the propaganda war'. The paper refrained from criticising the coalition for killing civilians and highlighted 'the Taliban's culpability in using them as human shields or in preventing outside aid from reaching them', but objected that 'The more Afghan civilians suffer ... the more squeamish world opinion will become'. Evidently the paper also considered 'collateral damage' a matter of presentation rather than principle. This editorial was also dismissive of what it called 'the cop-out tendency of the stop-the-war movement', which objected to the campaign on the grounds that it was not being conducted through the UN. This criticism, the paper noted, was 'simply ill informed', since the UN had effectively sanctioned action against al-Qaeda by passing resolutions 'recognising the US's right [to] self-defence'. Yet having demolished the argument for greater UN involvement, the *Independent* then conceded that it would be better if the Americans were to 'recognise the importance of invoking the UN' because, predictably, it would help 'in the propaganda war'.

The *Independent* also attacked anti-war protestors in its editorials on 1 and 22 October and was generally more bullish than the *Guardian* in its support for the war. The paper did raise criticisms about the campaign's conduct but rejected any insinuation that this meant it lacked 'moral fibre' (29 October). This attitude may seem odd given that, as we noted above, the *Independent* questioned the 'war' framework, suggesting that a law-enforcement model would be better. In fact, while by no means such a reluctant warrior as the *Guardian*, the paper repeatedly warned against widening the focus of the war, initially advising the coalition to focus only on al-Qaeda, and not to take on the task of overthrowing the Taliban (5 October), and then cautioning against taking on other targets, such as Iraq (9 and 12 October) or Somalia (12 and 20 December). This caution meant that, by December, the positions of the *Guardian* and *Independent* had converged around support for British-led peacekeeping efforts and criticism of the US. 'America must build peace as well as wage war' announced the paper's 20 December editorial, which argued that 'with power comes responsibility'. Criticising Washington's 'apparent willingness to embark on new military adventures in Somalia and in Iraq' and its proposals for 'morally deplorable and politically senseless' military tribunals to try terrorist suspects at the same time as it refused to support the International Criminal Court (12 December), the *Independent* echoed the *Guardian*'s view that British and American priorities had diverged. Noting that 'the total of unintended casualties in Afghanistan alone may approach, or even exceed, the 3,000-plus who died on 11 September', the paper warned that a 'reckless prosecution of the anti-terror offensive beyond Afghanistan would invite the risk that the war will be perceived in many parts of the world simply as one of terror against terror' (27 December). Although this was couched in terms of the *Independent*'s customary concern with perceptions and presentation, the criticism was now more far reaching. The following day's editorial declared that Bush had 'revert[ed] to type' in abandoning the 'coalition-minded diplomacy of the campaign against terrorism' in favour of a return to 'isolationism' (28 December).

Times

Of the four newspapers examined, the *Times* was by far the most bellicose, repeatedly urging tougher action. Almost as soon as hostilities had started, the *Times* advised that 'targeting must not be so cautious that the Taleban can shrug off the attacks as a mere irritation' (9 October) and it continued in the same vein, stressing the 'need … to keep up the military momentum' (16 October) and demanding that '[ground] operations inside Afghanistan must now accelerate' (22 October). The paper thought the US was 'pulling its punches' (19 October) and described the bombing as 'almost desultory' (27 October). The *Times* also raised the 'spectre of nuclear terrorism' (26 October) as another reason to step up the campaign. Whereas other papers warned against extending the war on terror to Iraq, the *Times* saw it as inevitable that 'the logic of this conflict [will put] Iraq and the West on collision course' and, despite accurately forecasting the political divisions such a confrontation would cause, the paper did not rule it out, instead urging Blair to consider the option (25 October).

In contrast to the *Guardian*'s criticisms of the West's 'destructive colonial legacy' in the Middle East, when the *Times* wrote of the need to 'crush the roots of terrorism … [by addressing] the political and cultural troubles that blight the Arab world' (12 October) this did not imply any Western responsibility for creating such troubles. Rather, the fault was seen to lie with Arab regimes, whose 'bad behaviour' the coalition was temporarily obliged to tolerate. Thinking particularly of Saudi Arabia, the paper argued that:

> The West may be fighting the good fight, but it is forced to court as allies in this struggle some of the most reactionary and discredited regimes around, regimes which give terrorists purchase by their failures to provide proper education, skills and economic opportunities.

Similarly, while the paper recommended that Western strategy should aim at achieving a 'peaceable cohabitation between Israel and the Palestinians' (13 October), it also argued that 'no claim, including those of the Palestinians, can be properly addressed' until 'the terror networks and the stranglehold that they have over Muslim opinion' had been eliminated (17 October).

Compared with the liberal broadsheets, the *Times* was more sceptical about Blair's 'ethical' claims for the war; although it conceded that 'strong moral purpose is in these days an undoubted strength', it warned the Prime Minister against 'the temptation of the running sermon' (3 October). From the outset, it preferred a traditional emphasis on Britain's 'national interests' (8 October) and an Atlanticist foreign policy orientation. Accordingly, in December the *Times* was highly critical of the government's support for a new European Security and Defence Policy, preferring Britain's freedom to flex its own 'military muscle' over official enthusiasm for 'sharing sovereignty' with the European Union (3 December). It was also dubious about the government's eagerness to lead 'peacekeeping' operations in Afghanistan and instead echoed the US view that the priority should be military operations against remaining al-Qaeda and Taliban units (11 December). However, this did not mean that the paper rejected the idea of 'nation-building' in Afghanistan. In October the *Times* noted ominously that 'this violent country reeks of the blood of outsiders – Persians, Moguls, British, Russians – who tried to stop it making trouble', but criticised the US for having 'left this broken country to its own murderous devices' after arming the Mujahideen in the 1980s and argued that 'the West must show now that it has at least some eye to the future' (16 October). As the paper accurately noted, despite the apparent differences between Bush and Blair over the importance of nation-building, both agreed that 'terrorists thrive in war-torn, incoherent states as mosquitoes do in swamps'.

While it expressed some initial doubts over whether it was 'necessary, or wise, to declare war on Afghanistan' rather than targeting only bin Laden (2 October), the *Times* itself sometimes presented the war in terms of a moral obligation to liberate the Afghan people and to reconstruct the country. This editorial, entitled 'Against Evil', described Afghanistan as 'a primitive, terror-ridden, travesty of a state' and urged the coalition to declare 'that they are ready to fight for Afghans, not against them – for their release from medieval horrors whose cruelty, even in Afghanistan's violent history, has been surpassed only by Genghis Khan's enemy hordes'. A week later, the *Times* had decided that the 'dismemberment' of the Taliban was 'certainly an objective' of the campaign, since the West had a 'clear, if subsidiary, interest in the political and economic stabilisation of Afghanistan' (9 October). Thus, while the *Times* expressed scepticism about the International Security Assistance Force, saying that the government had 'committed Britain to a risky and uncertain venture', this did not represent any opposition in principle. Rather, the *Times* was anxious to emphasise the 'overriding need for proper co-ordination with Washington' as against German arguments that 'the peacekeeping force must be independent of the American command' (20 December). Whereas the *Guardian* and *Independent* were very critical of America's prioritising of military objectives over peacekeeping, the *Times* continued to identify British interests with those of the US.

Mail

While the *Guardian* was generally unsympathetic to the conservative Bush administration and made its support for the war conditional on it being couched in Blairite terms, the *Mail* generally disliked New Labour and supported the war as strengthening Britain's alliance with the US. Hearing what it wanted to hear in Blair's October 2001 conference speech, the *Mail* said:

> Not since the Second World War has a Prime Minister committed himself so openly and irrevocably to the transatlantic alliance. Whatever happens now in this unfolding crisis, Britain is in it alongside the Americans, no matter what. (3 October)

Despite the difference of political emphasis, in one sense the *Mail* and *Guardian* were not that dissimilar: each supported the war while signalling its doubts by raising criticisms of secondary issues. The *Mail* complained about Blair's 'presidential' style of leadership (3 October), denounced government 'attempts to impose censorship on the broadcasters' (15 October), warned against any 'widening [of] the conflict' to Iraq (11 October) and particularly highlighted the issue of 'trust', pointing to government advisor Jo Moore's advice to use 9/11 to 'bury bad news' as evidence of New Labour's 'sickness and cynicism' (10 and 12 October). The underlying reservations which these criticisms indicated were stated most sharply in the *Mail's* editorials of 16 and 27 October. The first of these asked 'Is there anything useful to be gained from reducing [Afghans'] already devastated towns to even smaller rubble?' and argued that to continue the bombing 'simply increases the chances of killing more innocent civilians and adding to the flood of refugees – tragedies that are propaganda gifts for Bin Laden and the Taliban'. As with the *Guardian*, however, such objections did not imply opposition to the war: the *Mail* said that to raise 'hard questions' was 'emphatically not to deny that this war has to be fought' (27 October).

The most distinctive feature of the *Mail's* editorial stance was its hostility to British leadership of international reconstruction efforts in Afghanistan. The tone of its December editorials became increasingly harsh, describing the proposed deployment as confusing 'well-meaning humanitarianism with the defence of core national interests' (11 December), then as an 'extremely risky operation' and a 'dubious enterprise' (18 December) and finally as 'an operation that is already beginning to resemble a dog's breakfast' (20 December). The *Mail* sugared the pill, hailing the 'brilliant victory' over the Taliban and repeatedly praising the 'courage, professionalism and skill' of British troops (11, 18 and 20 December). Yet there was no doubting the paper's 'considerable unease' about the commitment of British forces to the mission, a stance which echoed the 'deep misgivings' expressed by Conservative Party leader Iain Duncan Smith around the same time (reported in the *Mail* on 18 December). There may have been more to the *Mail*'s position than simply its party-political orientation, however. The paper's overriding attitude throughout was one of fear: fear that, in the words of its 27 October editorial, 'our troops are in harm's way and Britain is a target for terrorist retaliation'.

Despite its political sympathies, the *Mail* was not entirely averse to casting the war in Blairite terms: its editorial of 26 December, for instance, argued that after the 'stunning' military success in Afghanistan there was 'a new sense of community and shared values among many nations', a sentiment that could have come straight from one of the Prime Minister's speeches. The paper tended to laud Blair when it thought that his influence would limit the war and lessen the dangers. The *Mail* hoped he would use his 'influence in Washington' to dissuade Bush from pursuing a confrontation with Iraq (11 October), for example, and urged the President to 'listen to Mr Blair as the honest broker' and refrain from 'any new demonstration of American military power' (7 December). When it looked at the war's wider context, the *Mail* did not see legitimate grievances caused by the West and/or repressive regimes in the Middle East, as depicted in the broadsheets. Rather, it saw 'anti-American mobs' (5 October), who were 'attracted by fundamentalism', threatening 'the more moderate Arab states', such as Saudi Arabia (9 October). This fear of the mob informed the paper's preference for the 'clash of civilisations' explanation, which was less a confident espousal of Western or Christian values than an exaggerated fear of the 'Other'. As the paper's leader of 18 October put it: 'Anti-Western mobs rage from Iran to Nigeria'. When it came to the question of British involvement in the international stabilisation force, therefore, the *Mail* could not understand 'Mr Blair's boy-scout eagerness' and instead emphasised the risks to British troops in 'fiercely inhospitable bandit-country' (20 and 18 December). In fact this had been the *Mail*'s attitude from the start: even when it called for 'strong nerves' in its 9 October leader, the paper could not help fearing the 'potentially horrendous consequences' of opening 'a Pandora's Box' in 'one of the world's most unstable regions', and wondered whether coalition leaders were 'really aware of the terrible complexities involved'.

Criticisms

The official emphasis on the claimed 'humanitarian' dimension of the campaign may inadvertently have served to heighten concern about the impact of the bombing: the two biggest categories of critique were the humanitarian/ refugee crisis (55 articles) and civilian casualties (47 critical articles plus 86 news reports on this topic). As noted in the introduction to this chapter, these are both areas where analysts of US news coverage have accused the media of being uncritical. On the evidence of this study, the British press cannot be faulted on these grounds, although some qualifications have to be made. Firstly, most criticism of the coalition for aggravating, or at least failing to address, the humanitarian crisis was reported critique: that is to say, in 45 of the 55 articles raising this issue, criticism of the coalition bombing came not from journalists but from the sources they chose to cite. In most cases, these sources were relief agencies or UN representatives who, ostensibly because of their 'neutral' position, limited the extent of their criticism and avoided making overtly political points. The most prominent critic was Mary Robinson, who called only for a temporary 'pause', not for the bombing to be abandoned altogether. Secondly, none of the newspapers examined endorsed this call in their editorial columns. Even the *Guardian*, which had attached most importance to the 'humanitarian' claims for the war, and which carried 30 of the 55 articles criticising coalition strategy on these grounds,[15] echoed the British government's opposition to demands for a pause in the bombing (in its 24 October editorial).

The issue of civilian casualties is slightly different, in that while, again, many articles on this topic were based around the views of sources (27 out of 47 critical articles), journalists themselves also played an important role in bringing the issue to public attention in news reports. Overall, the coverage examined in our study did not shy away from exposing the destructive effects of the bombing, although there were differences between papers in this respect, with the quantity of articles criticising the bombing because of the civilian casualties it caused corresponding to the quantity of news reports on this topic. The *Independent* carried both the most critical articles (19) and the greatest number of reports (32) about 'collateral damage'; the *Guardian* was a close second, with 15 critical articles and 25 news reports on the issue. At the other end of the scale, the *Times* carried half the *Independent*'s total, with 10 critical articles and 16 news reports, and the *Mail* carried only three articles criticising the war on these grounds and 13 news reports focusing on civilian casualties. This division is not surprising, given the newspapers' different political sympathies and the fact that, as we have seen, 'ethical' considerations were most important to the liberal broadsheets (even if the *Independent* tended to explain this in terms of their propaganda value). However, it bears repetition that raising these concerns rarely implied outright opposition to the war.

Looking more closely at news reports of civilian casualties, it is apparent, firstly, that even writers who generally took a pro-war stance could produce highly emotive and critical reports of particular events. Loyd's 29 October dispatch for the *Times*, for example, focused on the killing of a 22-year-old woman whose house was 'vapourised' by a 500-pound allied bomb, and remarked that her death was 'unlikely to trouble State Department minds' and that Afghan villagers found it hard 'to stomach ... the death of civilians in an apparently haphazard bombardment that fails to inspire hopes of a lasting peace'. Notwithstanding his critical tone here, by December, as we saw above, Loyd was depicting the war in black-and-white moral terms, comparing the Taliban with the Nazis.

Secondly, journalists whose reporting of civilian deaths and suffering did reflect their own critical view of the war nevertheless also tended to accept the need for Western intervention to overthrow the Taliban. Jonathan Steele, for example, wrote in the *Guardian*'s news pages of 'the agony of the air strikes which has sent an estimated 400,000 civilians fleeing in terror' (7 December) and a few days later argued in the comment section that the 'air strikes have driven at least 600,000 people from their homes', bringing 'misery to ... many innocent Afghans' (11 December). Yet although he described himself as an opponent of the war, Steele conceded that 'Toppling the Taliban may eventually give Afghanistan the chance of good government' and 'may eventually prove to be the best thing to have happened in Afghanistan for a decade'. Similarly, the *Independent*'s Robert Fisk wrote that 'hundreds – let us be frank and say thousands – of innocent civilians are dying under American air strikes in Afghanistan' and that 'the "War of Civilisation" is burning and maiming the Pashtuns of Kandahar and destroying their homes because "good" must triumph over "evil"' (10 December). These comments come from a quite extraordinary article in which Fisk recounted how he had been severely beaten by Afghan refugees but argued that they were justified in attacking him because of the suffering civilians had endured under US bombardment. 'If I was an Afghan refugee', he concluded, 'I would have attacked Robert Fisk'. Yet even Fisk was not opposed to Western intervention as such, and suggested that in some respects it did not go far enough. Describing the Northern Alliance as 'a bunch of ethnic gangs steeped in blood', he argued that 'What Afghanistan needs is an international force ... to re-establish some kind of order' (3 October), for instance, and complained that 'a mere 50 Royal Marines' were being sent to join a force of 'only a few thousand men who will need the Kabul government's permission to operate' (22 December). The fact that approval of the peacekeeping and 'nation-building' aspects of the intervention could lead to calls for greater Western intervention weakened criticism of the effects of the bombing.

After the humanitarian crisis and civilian casualties, the topic which attracted most critical comment was media coverage itself: 38 articles focused on the media, all but five of them during October. They raised a variety of issues. Seven articles were directed wholly or mainly against the US media, and either directly or by implication exempted their British counterparts from similar criticism. Roy Greenslade, for example, contrasted the subservience of American journalists with the 'persistent questioning of motive, strategy and tactics levelled at Blair's government by the British press' (*Guardian*, 3 December). The foundation for this self-satisfaction was questionable: Knightley (*Guardian*, 4 October; *Mail*, 9 October) and others offered some hard-hitting criticisms of the British media's acceptance of official disinformation and propaganda. It is also notable that five articles drew a similar contrast, not between the US and British media, but between mainstream Western news organisations and the more credible coverage provided by alternative outlets such as Al Jazeera (*Independent*, 11 October) and various websites (*Guardian*, 16 December). However, Greenslade did have a point, in that, as we have seen, the overall tenor of much coverage was indeed critical, at least of the tactics and effects of the war. At the other extreme, complaints that the government and media were stifling dissent appeared wide of the mark: when Monbiot complained of a 'new McCarthyism' (*Guardian*, 16 October) in both the US and Britain, for example, the fact that he and other *Guardian* writers did not appear to be subject to any such restrictions rather undermined his argument. In the same day's edition, Jeanette Winterson protested that 'artists, writers and actors have a right to speak out against war', yet it turned out that the only person she identified as discouraging them from doing so was *Sunday Times* restaurant critic A. A. Gill.

The fourth most frequent criticism was that the war would create more terrorism rather than defeating it. This argument featured in 33 articles, distributed fairly evenly across all four papers, although with differences of emphasis.[16] In the broadsheets, this criticism was raised by anti-war writers such as Foot (*Guardian*, 16 October) and Ali (*Independent*, 15 October), and was often linked to an understanding of terrorism as 'blowback' from previous policy. In the *Times*, Jenkins warned that the bombing was likely to provoke 'a violent response', and he argued that the West should instead address its 'decades of mistreatment' of the Muslim world (10 October), for example, while Matthew Parris predicted that the war would cause 'more sorrow for the future' and advised the coalition to focus instead on the real grievances which led 'millions' to feel some sympathy with al-Qaeda (*Times*, 20 October). For the *Mail*, however, the emphasis tended to be on the fear of reprisals. Columnist Peter McKay, for example, asked 'Are we setting ourselves up for years and years of reprisals, stifling security measures and morale-sapping uncertainty?' (8 October), suggesting the war might expose Britain to 'more rather than less terrorism' (29 October), and Andrew Alexander argued that while America had no choice but to respond to 9/11, 'Britain had ample choice, since we were not targets of the terrorists' (26 October). While Alexander saw Britain's decision to offer military support as rash and dangerous, Cambridge academic John Casey argued that 'the Americans are doing what they have to do, and so is Britain in supporting them', but still felt 'anxious about the future', predicting that the war would 'set large parts of the Moslem world on fire' and that the US might end up 'in a quagmire' (*Mail*, 10 October). The fear of 'turning all Moslems into enemies' highlighted by Casey was also articulated by Stephen Glover in an article entitled 'Are We Waking a Monster We Can't Control?' (*Mail*, 9 October). Glover said that 'behind the zealots are thousands, millions more, whose hatreds may now be harnessed', and he worried that 'our leaders have set something in motion which they may not be able to stop'. Although, for some writers, the argument that military action would create more terrorism was intended to bolster the anti-war case, for others it merely expressed fear and uncertainty.

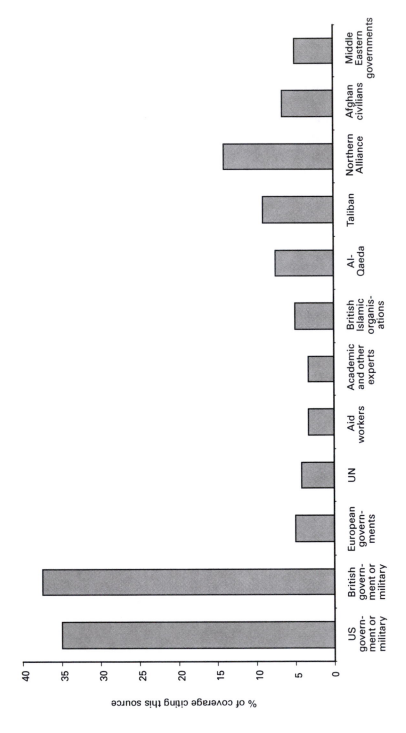

Figure 6.1 Prominence of the different types of source, Afghanistan coverage.

Conclusions

As indicated in Figure 6.1, the US and Britain dominated the news in terms of sources cited, and the official 'war on terrorism' frame was, as would be expected, the dominant idea. The perceived legitimacy of the intervention no doubt stemmed largely from this counter-terrorist framework, in which coalition action was seen as a justifiable response to the attacks of 11 September. Other sources were relatively marginal, including those who offered criticism, but in any case key Western sources of criticism – the UN and aid agencies – largely confined themselves to apolitical comment on humanitarian issues. Such concerns were probably heightened by the claimed 'humanitarian' aspects of the campaign, which may also have encouraged coverage of civilian casualties of the bombing. Contrary to what has been found in other studies, there was no shortage of criticism of the effects of the bombing, and there was also much critical discussion around issues of political trust and censorship. These criticisms were quite narrow, however, and there was very little fundamental questioning of the legitimacy of the intervention.

While, for the US, ideas of retaliation and self-defence may have seemed sufficient explanation, British leaders had to work harder at justifying military action, since Britain had not been attacked. The 'moral' and human rights arguments offered by Blair had only limited impact in terms of explanatory articles, and attempts to legitimise action by drawing parallels with earlier 'ethical' interventions were not always successful. The importance of the 'military humanitarianism' of the 1990s was indirect, in that it had established the idea that a moral imperative to intervene could override principles of non-interference and sovereign equality. The idea that the West's own security interests converged with its humanitarian and human rights values – already articulated in relation to Somalia and, most clearly, Kosovo – was adapted for the war on terrorism via the 'failed states' concept. This allowed apparently critical strands of explanation – especially the idea of 'blowback' from previous Western mistakes – to be incorporated into mainstream accounts, rather than, as some critics have suggested, simply ignored.

At the same time, of the newspapers in our study, only the *Times* was prepared to argue a robust pro-war case. The *Independent* tended to dodge issues by focusing on questions of presentation rather than principle; the *Guardian* offered conditional support hedged about with minor complaints and suspicion of American arrogance; and the *Mail* betrayed its own calls for 'strong nerves' with its nightmare visions of anti-Western hordes. It was this pusillanimity that gave much of the coverage its apparently 'critical' tone. In fact there was considerable underlying agreement on the desirability of extensive, long-term Western intervention, and no substantive criticism of international 'nation-building' efforts.

CHAPTER 7

Iraq, 2003

The last of our case studies concerns another conflict which, at the time of writing, is still ongoing: the invasion and occupation of Iraq. Military action was launched by a US-led coalition on 20 March 2003 as a 'pre-emptive' strike, justified mainly through allegations (subsequently proven to be false) that Iraq possessed 'weapons of mass destruction' (WMD). A secondary justification presented intervention as part of the 'war on terrorism', in that it was claimed that Saddam Hussein's regime had connections with al-Qaeda (a claim which was also subsequently found to be untrue). As suggested by the name given to the US mission – Operation Iraqi Freedom – a third line of justification was that the war would liberate the Iraqi people and install a democratic government, thereby setting a positive example for the wider region. As with the intervention in Afghanistan, although the war had a long and violent aftermath, it was generally perceived at the time as having been concluded swiftly and successfully. President George W. Bush declared the 'end of major combat operations' on 1 May 2003, but even before that most contemporary commentators took the toppling of a statue of Saddam in Baghdad on 9 April, broadcast live around the world, as signalling the victory of the coalition.

Context

After its defeat in the 1991 Gulf war, Iraq was subjected to international economic sanctions, which caused large-scale suffering. The UN Children's Fund estimated that rising mortality rates after 1991 had resulted in 500,000 excess deaths of infants under the age of five by 1998 (Pellett 2000: 161), for example, and Denis Halliday, the UN official in charge of coordinating humanitarian aid for Iraq, described the sanctions regime as a 'genocidal attack on a whole society' (quoted in Pilger 2004: 30). Additionally, in enforcing the 'no-fly zones' established over northern and southern Iraq after the Gulf war, the US and Britain regularly bombed the country. The most intensive and high-profile action was the Operation Desert Fox air campaign of 16–19 December 1998 but, as Anthony Arnove (2000: 9) notes, Anglo-American airstrikes continued throughout the following year and beyond, hitting Iraq almost every other day of 1999. Arnove goes on to observe that then, too, the main justification for Western policy was the prevention of WMD proliferation and Iraq's alleged failure to comply with international demands for its disarmament after the 1991 war. In 1998, according to former UN weapons inspector Scott Ritter, the US used the inspections programme to gather intelligence and to provoke a conflict by demanding greater access than that agreed between Iraq and the UN (Ritter and Rivers Pitt 2002: 51–4).

Given this recent record of conflict, it is not surprising that the attacks of 11 September were widely understood at the time to have put an all-out war against Iraq on the agenda. The first impulse of the US administration seems to have been to seize on 9/11 as an opportunity to deal with Iraq (Shaw 2005: 100). Former US officials subsequently revealed, for example, that the immediate reaction of Bush and other senior figures was to frame their response in terms of retaliation against Saddam (Sirota and Harvey 2004). Yet by October the US was reportedly attempting to 'quell mounting expectation that President Bush is poised to widen America's war on terrorism by taking military action against Iraq' (*Times*, 25 October 2001), because of worries that it would undermine international support for the war in Afghanistan, and by the end of the year British Foreign Secretary Jack Straw had stated unequivocally that there was 'no evidence to support any link' between Iraq and the attacks of 11 September (*Independent*, 21 December 2001). In spring 2002, however, with the Afghan campaign apparently brought to a successful conclusion, the US had decided on war with Iraq, Bush announcing on 5 April: 'I made up my mind that Saddam needs to go' (quoted in Kampfner 2003: 167). According to John Kampfner's account of the decision-making process, Prime Minister Tony Blair reached an agreement with Bush in August 2002 that, before taking any action, they should first seek a mandate from the UN, on the understanding that if the UN proved unwilling or unable to deal with the problem supposedly posed by Saddam, Britain would be part of a 'coalition of the willing' and join a US-led invasion (Kampfner 2003: 196–8).

From autumn 2002, the British and American governments worked hard to show that Iraq posed a threat. As David Sirota and Christy Harvey (2004) observe, from September onwards US leaders made repeated public claims that there were links between Iraq and al-Qaeda, although these appear to have been largely for domestic consumption.[1] The main focus was on WMD, with dossiers of evidence about Iraq's weapons programmes being produced by both the US and British governments in September 2002.[2] According to US Deputy Defense Secretary Paul Wolfowitz, the WMD issue was emphasised for pragmatic reasons: it seemed to be 'the one issue that everyone could agree on.'[3] In the short term, this tactic worked: the US and Britain gained unanimous agreement for Security Council Resolution 1441, passed on 8 November 2002, threatening Iraq with 'serious consequences' if it did not cooperate fully with a new round of weapons inspections. Yet this consensus soon began to disintegrate. While Britain and the US claimed that

Iraq was failing to comply properly with the demands of Resolution 1441 and that military action was therefore justified, opposition to war grew both domestically and internationally, with France, Germany and Russia signalling their unwillingness to support a war. In response, the WMD threat was talked up even more – Britain issued another dossier on 3 February 2003, and Secretary of State Colin Powell made an elaborate presentation of evidence to the UN two days later[4] – and agreement on a second resolution, proposed by the US and Britain on 25 February, was sought at the UN.

Three aspects of the debate in the run-up to the war are particularly interesting in relation to this study's focus on the legitimacy of international intervention. Firstly, while the prospect of war gave rise to deep divisions and disagreements, opening a diplomatic rift between Europe and the US and provoking increasing anti-war sentiment in domestic politics, at the same time there seemed to be considerable agreement on the need for the international community to deal in some way with the problem presented by Saddam's regime and its alleged WMD. The position of European governments opposed to war was not, of course, that war was wrong in principle, but that UN weapons inspectors should be allowed to complete their work and that action short of an all-out invasion could bring Iraq into line. In February 2003 France and Germany agreed a plan for a 'peaceful invasion', involving reconnaissance flights, triple the number of inspectors and UN troops backed up by 150,000 US soldiers stationed on Iraq's borders (*Guardian*, 10 February). Media commentators also sometimes combined an anti-war stance with an emphasis on the need for tough intervention. The *Independent*, for example, advocated 'intrusive inspections backed by the threat of limited force' (editorial, 7 February 2003) and *Guardian* columnist Jonathan Freedland (19 February) argued that 'the peace camp has to set out its own, alternative method of ridding Iraq of its oppressor', such as 'muscular rights inspectors' backed by 'a military presence' (see further Hammond 2004). Mainstream British political figures who aligned themselves with the anti-war cause tended to imply that under different circumstances they would be pro-war. Charles Kennedy, for example, the leader of the Liberal Democrats, on 15 February 2003 told an anti-war demonstration in London that he had 'yet to be persuaded as to the case for war against Iraq', objecting that force should be used only with UN authority and after all other options had been exhausted and weapons inspectors had completed their work.[5] Similarly, in resigning from government over the war on 17 March, Robin Cook said he agreed with those who 'want inspections to be given a chance, and [who] suspect that they are being pushed too quickly into conflict'. His main objection seemed to be that Britain was 'going out on a limb on a military adventure without a broader international coalition'.[6] When Kennedy emphasised that his party could not support war 'without a second UN resolution' and Cook insisted on the importance of getting 'agreement in the Security Council', they implied that with such a resolution they would be happy to support the war. All this suggests that, despite pronounced public disagreements over the war, in media coverage we would expect to find a degree of common ground on the question of whether intervention in Iraq was legitimate and desirable.

Secondly, it appears from previous studies of media coverage that doubts over Anglo-American claims about Iraqi WMD were aired before the war but put aside during the invasion itself. In Britain, the controversy surrounding government claims emerged most fully after the war, when BBC journalist Andrew Gilligan said in a 29 May 2003 broadcast that officials had 'sexed up' the September 2002 dossier by including a claim that Iraq could deploy WMD within 45 minutes, even though they knew this to be false. However, the credibility of the British 'evidence' had already been contested long before this. Within two days of the February 2003 dossier being published, Cambridge academic Glen Rangwala revealed that it was not a summary of new high-level intelligence but a clumsy cut-and-paste job plagiarising an old PhD thesis and other unacknowledged sources.[7] For this reason it became widely known in the media as the 'dodgy dossier'. In fact, the government's September 2002 document had been described in the same terms (O'Neill 2002) and Rangwala had challenged that one too, even before it was published, preparing a pre-emptive 'counter-dossier' with Labour MP Alan Simpson.[8] Thus, although there were widespread complaints after the event that politicians had led Britain to war on a 'false prospectus', the falseness of their case was actually widely known and discussed beforehand. Nevertheless, in their detailed study of British television coverage during the invasion, Justin Lewis and Rod Brookes (2004: 135) found that of those reports referring to WMD, 86 per cent suggested that Iraq possessed such weapons, compared with 14 per cent voicing doubts about their existence or possible use. Only one television news report stated unequivocally that there were no WMD. Similarly, a study of British press and television coverage by Howard Tumber and Jerry Palmer (2004: 140) indicates that reports during the invasion emphasised fears of an imminent chemical-weapons attack. It would appear that questions about the coalition's WMD claims were for some reason forgotten during the war itself, re-emerging only afterwards. This may also indicate some underlying agreement on the desirability of intervention and/or a willingness to suspend critical judgement during wartime.

A third striking aspect of the pre-war debate was the argument that an invasion would 'liberate' the Iraqi people. Faced with mounting domestic opposition – as manifested in the huge anti-war demonstration on 15 February – and with its WMD evidence increasingly called into question, the British government shifted ground shortly before the war to emphasise what Blair called 'the moral case for removing Saddam' (Kampfner 2003: 273). Around the same time, Bush began foregrounding similar themes, arguing in a 26 February speech that a 'liberated Iraq' would 'show the power of freedom to transform' the Middle East.[9] As the invasion began, this was the argument which was emphasised. Bush told the Iraqis: 'The tyrant will soon be gone.... The day of your liberation is near' (*Times*, 18 March 2003); and Blair promised them: 'we will liberate you. The day of your freedom draws near' (*Guardian*, 28 March). This was evidently an attempt to argue that, as in Kosovo, a 'coalition of the willing' was justified in taking military action on moral grounds even if it lacked explicit UN authority, and indeed an anomaly of the debate about Iraq was that the US and its allies were sharply criticised for acting without a

UN mandate despite the fact that this had not been seen as a barrier to military intervention in Kosovo. Although it came to the fore too late in the day to mend international divisions over the war, the 'moral' argument may have had some impact on domestic debate and on media perceptions of the invasion. A number of commentators had already signalled their preference for a justification based on human rights. Arguing in support of war, for example, the *Independent*'s Johann Hari wrote that:

> We do not need Bush's dangerous arguments about 'pre-emptive action' to justify this war. Nor do we need to have the smoking gun of WMD. All we need are the humanitarian arguments we used during the Kosovo conflict. (10 January 2003)

It seems likely that such arguments encouraged support for the war, even though the explicit justification for action was WMD. Lewis and Brookes (2004: 135–6) found that television news during the war was almost twice as likely to suggest that Iraqis were happy about being 'liberated' (26 per cent of references to the Iraqi people) than to depict them as being hostile or suspicious toward the invasion (14 per cent of references). At the same time, however, they also noted that an even greater number of references to Iraqis concerned the death or injury of civilians (37 per cent). It is possible that, as in Afghanistan, the emphasis placed on the 'moral' aspects of the invasion may have helped to draw attention to evidence which called such claims into question.

One of the key questions about media coverage concerns the extent to which it was pro- or anti-war. Several analysts have drawn attention to the media's propagandistic role, describing this in terms of 'mass deception' (Edwards and Cromwell 2004) or 'psychological warfare against the public' (Curtis 2004). Most of this critique has focused on the false claims about WMD and, as a secondary theme, about Iraq's links to al-Qaeda. A related criticism is that media coverage failed properly to explore the views of those opposed to war. Studies of US coverage found that television news was dominated by pro-war sources (Rendall and Broughel 2003) and that while anti-war protests attracted much press attention, they were largely depicted as marginal and irrelevant (Bishop 2006). Critics of the war have also put forward alternative explanations of why the US wished to invade Iraq, arguing that it was about oil and/or that it was about asserting American imperial dominance, having been planned long in advance by neo-conservatives at the think-tank Project for the New American Century, who had now risen to power in the Bush administration (Rampton and Stauber 2003; Rowell 2004; Klare 2005).

Other analysts, however, have instead highlighted what Nick Couldry and John Downey (2004: 280) call a 'legitimation of dissent' in the mainstream British press. Tumber and Palmer (2004: 164), for example, suggest that anti-war protests were 'given space and prominence in the media', while Des Freedman (2003) draws attention to the campaigning anti-war stance taken by the *Daily Mirror*, which abandoned its usual diet of tabloid trivia in favour of front-page articles by radical journalist John Pilger. These critics are all careful not to overstate their case – noting that criticism generally became more muted or disappeared entirely once the war started, and that the *Mirror*'s opposition ultimately proved weak and inconsistent – but the picture they present is quite different in emphasis from writers who see the media as having played an overwhelmingly supportive, propagandistic role. The evidence of these studies suggests both that there was a clear left/right split in press coverage and that 'elite media and political discourse … was deeply divided' (Couldry and Downey 2004: 280; see also Tumber and Palmer 2004: 93–4). It was uncertainty and divisions among the elite themselves, they suggest, which allowed greater room for dissenting opinions to be aired, at least in the period leading up to war.

Questions

The main questions addressed in this chapter are:

- How did newspapers treat the allegations about Iraq's WMD and links to terrorism? To what extent were these taken at face value? Were questions put aside once the war started?
- How important were 'moral' or 'humanitarian' arguments in establishing the legitimacy of intervention in Iraq? How far was its legitimacy questioned?
- To what extent did media coverage encompass the views of anti-war critics and protestors? Were alternative explanations for the war explored?

Since the main invasion phase of the Iraq war was so short, utilising the same sampling method as in other case studies produces a continuous eight-week period of coverage, from one week before the invasion until one week after Bush's announcement of the end of 'major combat operations' (13 March–8 May 2003). Rather than dividing this sample into two four-week blocks, it was approached in terms of pre-invasion, invasion and post-invasion periods, as set out in Table 7.1.[10]

Explanations

There were 253 articles in our samples of coverage which offered some explanation of the war, comprising 28 mainly concerned with explanations, 164 in

Table 7.1 Numbers of articles about Iraq

	Pre-invasion (13–19 March)	Invasion (20 March–1 May)	Post-invasion (2–8 May)	Totals
Guardian	155	1,134	65	1,354
Independent	128	1,022	50	1,200
Times	183	1,233	61	1,477
Mail	87	530	27	644
Totals	553	3,919	203	4,675

which the reasons for war were a minor theme and 61 articles reporting official statements which offered a rationale for war. Together these accounted for 5.4 per cent of total coverage, although explanations were most prominent before the start of hostilities, accounting for 10.5 per cent of coverage, and diminished sharply in our post-invasion sample, when they constituted only 2.5 per cent.[11] The two most common explanatory themes were, firstly, that the invasion was being undertaken in order to assert American hegemony (78 articles, or 30.8 per cent of all explanatory material) and, secondly, that it was a war of liberation (66 articles, or 26.1 per cent). If we leave aside those articles which simply reported official explanations and focus only on the 192 articles in which journalists or guest writers developed their own ideas, these themes are even more prominent, accounting respectively for 40.6 per cent and 34.3 per cent of such articles.

The *Mail* devoted the greatest proportion of its coverage to explanations (7.6 per cent) and the *Times* the least (3.8 per cent), with the *Guardian* and *Independent* in the middle (5.7 and 5.9 per cent, respectively). The sorts of explanation favoured by the different papers divided clearly along political lines, so that the most common explanatory theme in both the *Times* and the *Mail* was that the war was an attempt to liberate Iraq and bring democracy to the Middle East (33.9 per cent of explanations in the *Times* and 48.9 per cent in the *Mail*), while the *Guardian* and *Independent* favoured the idea that the invasion was an assertion of American power (42.9 per cent of the *Guardian*'s explanations and 36.6 per cent of the *Independent*'s).[12] Yet it is striking how evenly balanced the two main strands of explanation were, both in terms of the quantities of articles devoted to them and in terms of how they framed the reasons for war. This will become apparent in the discussion below, but first we examine the rationales for war in reported official statements and speeches.

Official explanations

Coalition leaders usually framed the need for military action in terms of the liberation of Iraq: just over 75 per cent of their reported statements claimed this justification for war. The ostensible reason for war – the disarmament of Iraq – was somewhat less prominent, featuring in 66 per cent of reported statements, while links between Iraq and international terrorism were mentioned in 25 per cent of such articles, almost always in tandem with the theme of WMD. As this suggests, the most common formula was to combine the 'liberation' and 'disarmament' arguments. Initially, the British government identified 'regime change' as an explicit campaign objective only insofar as it was a corollary of the main aim of removing the threat from WMD: Blair was reported to have 'spelt out the policy of regime change for the first time' by stating that 'If the only means of achieving the disarmament of Iraq of weapons of mass destruction is the removal of the regime, then the removal of the regime of course has to be our objective' (*Independent*, 20 March). Yet both British and American leaders frequently presented disarmament and liberation as twin objectives of the war: Bush said he had 'a strategy to free the Iraqi people from Saddam Hussein and rid his country of weapons of mass destruction', for example, and Blair said that 'Iraq will be disarmed of weapons of mass destruction and the people of Iraq will be free' (*Independent*, 25 and 28 March).

The argument that the invasion was simultaneously a war of liberation and a pre-emptive act of self-defence drew on similar ideas to those discussed in Chapter 6 in relation to the notion of 'failed states', whereby military action was understood in terms of both interests and values. Iraq was not a failed state but a 'rogue' state, which had allegedly failed to comply with international demands for disarmament and therefore presented a threat both in itself and in its potential to aid terrorists. At the same time, as a tyrannical regime which oppressed its own citizens, the Iraqi government was seen to lack legitimacy: it both violated norms of democracy and human rights at home and presented a threat to an 'international community' which was understood to embody such values. Hence, for example, in announcing the start of military action Bush described Iraq as 'an outlaw regime that threatens the peace with weapons of mass murder' and promised both to 'defend our freedom' and to 'bring freedom to others' (*Times*, 21 March). Similarly, a joint statement by the British, American and Spanish governments at a summit in the Azores shortly before the war claimed the coalition would simultaneously 'support the Iraqi people's aspirations for a representative government that upholds human rights and the rule of law as cornerstones of democracy' and ensure that Iraq would 'never again be a haven for terrorists of any kind', as well as disarming Saddam of his 'nuclear, chemical, biological and long-range missile capacity' (*Independent*, 17 March).

Reporting a speech by Bush which framed the war as a fight for 'freedom', Roland Watson noted that 'after months of emphasising the threat of Iraq's weapons of mass destruction, Mr Bush barely mentioned the issue' (*Times*, 1 April). The President 'concentrated on the drive to bring "freedom and dignity" to the Iraqi people', Watson commented, because he was 'Mindful that US coalition forces have yet to find any chemical or biological stocks'. No doubt Watson was correct to suggest that the importance of claims about 'liberation' increased as the likelihood of discovering any WMD seemed to diminish, but, as noted above, before the invasion there was already a shift of emphasis from WMD and terrorism to liberation and democracy, in response to growing opposition to war. Recasting the invasion as liberation was not only a way to bypass mounting controversy over evidence of Iraq's WMD: it also sought to answer suspicions about US motives and objections that the intervention lacked UN authority. Blair was described as 'Rounding on critics who question the motives of the war' by claiming that 'the brutality of the Iraqi dictator is justification in itself', while Bush said that America and Britain were 'acting together in a noble purpose' (*Mail*, 28 March). Similarly, Blair was said to have 'challenged' his critics by emphasising 'the nature of this regime':

> When people read the details of the torture chambers, the prisons, the thousands upon thousands of people that Saddam killed, even those who disagreed with the war should see that the Iraqi people have greater freedom and hope than they ever had in the years under Saddam. (*Times*, 24 April)

As we shall see below, Blair's invitation to rally round the 'ethical' results of the war was at least partially successful.

Where critics complained that action without an explicit Security Council mandate would be illegitimate, coalition leaders attempted to turn the argument around by claiming that they were acting to uphold UN authority. According to the joint Azores summit statement, it was Saddam's defiance of Security Council resolutions which had 'undermined the authority of the UN' (*Independent*, 17 March). The argument recalled earlier debates about humanitarian military intervention: if the UN was unable or unwilling to act decisively, a 'coalition of the willing' was justified in enforcing the will of the 'international community'. 'Remember Rwanda or Kosovo', said Bush, when 'The UN didn't do its job' (*Guardian*, 17 March). In reporting these comments, the *Guardian*'s Nicholas Watt described Bush as adopting 'the language of the toughest hawks in Washington, who would love to see the UN consigned to the history books'. Yet, however disingenuously, Bush was also drawing on arguments developed by advocates of 'ethical' intervention in Kosovo and elsewhere, that a moral imperative to intervene should override questions of legality or UN approval. In a parliamentary debate on the war, Blair also voiced concerns that inaction would 'turn the UN back into a talking shop' and would 'do the most deadly damage to the UN's future strength, confirming it as an instrument of diplomacy but not of action' (*Times*, 19 March). Arguing that acting without explicit UN authority was the best way to uphold that authority may have been paradoxical, but it was no more contradictory than the claim that bombing Yugoslavia in 1999 was simultaneously illegal and legitimate (Chapter 5). The problem for coalition leaders in 2003 was convincing their critics that might coincided with right. In the parliamentary debate just mentioned, Blair obliquely acknowledged this by arguing that, if others failed to act, the US would be 'forc[ed] … down the very unilateralist path we wish to avoid' and urging that Britain should use its 'power to influence for the better'. The unspoken assumption was that, if left to its own devices, the US would not act as ethically as it would if influenced by coalition partners.

Liberation and democracy

The pro-war papers took their cue from coalition leaders, most often framing the war in terms of the liberation of the Iraqi people. Describing Saddam as 'a psychopath hell bent on controlling the world', *Mail* columnist Lynda Lee-Potter argued that 'The aim of this war is peace not destruction … young men and women will be fighting for peace, justice and the future stability of the world' (19 March), for example; and in the *Times* (14 April) William Rees-Mogg hailed the US as an 'engine of global liberation', which spread 'the idea of liberty, of human freedom, of self-government and of democracy'. Yet although it was conservative newspapers which most favoured this view of the war, such explanations were elaborated in ways which crossed traditional left/right divisions. The *Times* featured comment pieces by Labour MP Ann

Clwyd and Conservative MEP Baroness Emma Nicholson, for example, which explained the necessity of regime change in very similar terms. For Clwyd, it was 'essential to liberate the people of Iraq' from an 'evil, fascist regime' for 'humanitarian reasons alone' (18 March), while Nicholson said that the 'hundreds of thousands of victims of [Saddam's] genocide' had led her to advocate 'regime change to alleviate human suffering' (9 April).

Several writers drew out the implicit parallel with the arguments made for 'humanitarian' military intervention in Kosovo and elsewhere. Describing the Iraqi government as a 'violent and genocidal regime', Rees-Mogg argued that 'Kosovo is the nearest comparable case to Iraq' and concluded that 'genocide, ethnic cleansing and torture are not protected by national sovereignty, when committed by a government against its own people' (*Times*, 17 March). Similarly, historian Antony Beevor argued that the lesson of Bosnia was that 'It is not white Toyotas and UN flags you need, but war-fighting troops with armoured fighting vehicles' (*Times*, 29 March). As noted above, some liberal or leftist commentators advocated intervention on ethical grounds, even though they distrusted Bush and doubted the evidence on WMD. *Guardian* columnist David Aaronovitch described himself as 'Agnostic on the threat of weapons of mass destruction', professed himself to be 'sceptical on alleged Iraqi links with new Osama bin Laden-type groups' (1 April), acknowledged that 'You can complain as much as you like (and often correctly) about the Bush administration' and wished there had been a second UN resolution, but still supported the war on the grounds that it would 'have the effect of removing one of the worst and most violent tyrannies in the world' (18 March). Similarly, the *Independent*'s Johann Hari began one pro-war column by announcing: 'George Bush is terrifying'. He spent most of the article criticising Bush's policies before concluding: 'If he listens to the people around him pressing for Iraqi democracy, not least our own Prime Minister, then even those of us who detest him will toast him' (21 March). 'Our job on the left is not to try to stop America from ever acting', chided Hari in another piece: 'one of the great tragedies of the 1990s, the Rwandan genocide, wasn't caused by too much America but by its failure to act'. Recalling that the US had 'acted in Kosovo to prevent ethnic cleansing', he suggested that 'our job is to try to steer this colossus towards spreading the values of its own American revolution: the overthrow of tyranny and the birth of democracy' (11 April).

Hari's idea of prodding America in the right, ethical direction echoed Blair's justification of support for the US. Yet even in this respect the political dividing lines were not clear-cut. In the *Mail*, Max Hastings said that while he had 'little faith in the judgment or understanding of the world of George Bush and those around him', Blair had 'taken a brave decision, that the only hope of influencing American behaviour is to share in American actions' (22 March). Columnist Stephen Glover rubbished most official justifications for war, maintaining that 'No evidence has been produced which proves that Iraq possesses weapons of mass destruction which could cause damage to the US, Britain or the rest of Europe', and scorning the 'Wholly unproven connections between Saddam and al-Qaeda' (*Mail*, 18 March). Referring to the government's plagiarised dossier,

Glover said 'We have undoubtedly been misled' and complained that 'The arguments used by the proponents of war have veered from regime change to humanitarian necessity'. Glover also derided the inconsistency of those 'Leftish critics of this Anglo-American action [who] supported the attack on Kosovo in 1999', but was no more consistent himself. Having in 1999 rejected arguments for 'ethical' intervention in Kosovo, Glover now justified the invasion of Iraq on comparable 'ethical' grounds, arguing that it was necessary because 'Saddam is a totalitarian leader of exceptional evil', who ought to be removed from power.

According to those who wished to extend the logic of Kosovo to Iraq, left-wing opponents of the invasion had adopted the right's arguments about the importance of sovereignty. In an article explaining why he had resigned from the *New Statesman* magazine over just this issue, John Lloyd said that by 'defending sovereignty in the name of anti-imperialism, opponents of war undermine their claim to champion the oppressed'. Accusing the French and German governments of failing to act 'against murderous tyrannies or collapsed states throughout the 1990s – in Somalia, Rwanda, Bosnia, as well as Iraq', Lloyd emphasised that 'Where action to overthrow dictatorial regimes has been taken in Kosovo, Bosnia, Afghanistan and now Iraq, it has been taken either with US prompting, or with the US military in the lead' (*Guardian*, 11 April). In the same day's edition of the *Independent*, Hari accused anti-war critics of having 'become similar to the right-wingers who fetishise state sovereignty and say that protecting a bunch of foreigners is none of our business; they have abandoned the great internationalist tradition of the left'. In fact, as we shall see, left-leaning commentators did not defend the principle of sovereign equality in 2003 any more than conservatives had done in the 1990s. Despite the divergence between the sorts of explanation favoured by different papers, political dividing lines were too blurred for this debate to be understood in terms of a straightforward left/right distinction.

Imperial hegemony

The anti-war papers most often framed the war as an assertion of American power or imperial dominance. This theme usually cast the war in a critical light, as the ideologically driven project of neo-conservatives around Bush, and questioned US motives. In the *Guardian*, for example, Iraqi exile Sami Ramadani argued that:

> the US hawks, now prominent in the Bush administration, have been advocating a war on Iraq for the past 12 years – not to liberate the Iraqi people, or to protect the world from weapons of mass destruction, but to impose US hegemony on a strategically important country. (18 March)

Similarly, an article by Andrew Murray, the chairman of the Stop the War Coalition, described British troops as fighting 'for a reactionary and dangerous US administration' which demanded 'unconditional subordination to US imperial power' (*Guardian*, 21 March). These were obviously guest commentaries, but the *Guardian*'s comment page editor, Seamus Milne, took a similar view himself, describing the war as a 'piratical onslaught' and as 'a demonstration war, designed to cow and discipline both the enemies and allies of the US' (27 March). Furthermore, both the *Guardian* and the *Independent* adopted this explanation in their editorial columns. 'This is a political war, a war of power largely orchestrated by the ideologues and zealots who surround that most implausible of presidents, George Bush', said the *Guardian*'s 20 March leader, for example, while the *Independent* highlighted the 'tightly knit group of politically motivated men at the heart of this administration' who had long advocated war as 'a projection of American power, a punitive and exemplary war to deter America's enemies' (31 March).

Similar explanations also appeared, although less frequently, in the pages of the *Times* and the *Mail*. Matthew Parris, for example, explained the war as 'the beginning of a new and swelling American assertiveness worldwide' and suggested that for the neo-conservative 'authors of the invasion' it was part of a larger strategy to compel the 'forces of disorder and un-Americanism in the world … [to] bow, one by one, to Washington's will' (*Times*, 12 April). Similarly, describing the war as 'America's crusade', Hastings explained it as driven by Bush's 'extravagant dreams' and the ambitions of 'Washington hawks' to transform the Middle East (*Mail*, 16 April). Interestingly, although he did not oppose the war, Hastings expressed unease at the official emphasis on ethical justifications, saying that 'Blair's strong moral streak has always seemed disturbing'. Claiming to have hoped that Blair's support for Bush was merely 'pragmatic' and 'driven by the demands of the Atlantic alliance', Hastings recalled Blair's 2001 Labour conference speech about 'using Britain's Armed Forces to bring succour to the oppressed of the world' and said that such sentiments 'frightened the life out of some of us'. Yet in his 22 March commentary praising Blair's 'brave decision' (quoted above), Hastings had framed the war in ethical terms himself, emphasising 'the lives that will be saved by ending Saddam's tyranny' and reminding his readers that 'Through most of modern history, the British have taken up arms in just causes, against the forces of evil'.

As this suggests, in terms of how the causes of war were understood, there was less distance than might be expected between those who endorsed the invasion as an ethical war of liberation and those who denounced it as the ideological project of empire-building Washington hawks. *Mail* commentators Ann Leslie and Melanie Phillips, for example, tried to portray neo-conservatism as a decisive break from a former liberal/leftist consensus, but implicitly praised it as a tougher version of the same outlook. Arguing that during the 'touchy-feely' Clinton years 'rogue states, and the terrorists they support' had come to view the US as 'too soft, too decadent, too liberal, too "politically correct" to be willing to stand up for its own security interests', Leslie welcomed what she saw as a break from an 'effete liberalism [that] actually damages the cause of the oppressed people it supposedly champions' (12 April). Yet Leslie's implication was that, by taking on 'the world's most brutish dictators', neo-con toughness would properly defend the oppressed in a way that 'effete liberalism' had proved unable to do. With the same political axe to grind, Phillips hoped that victory in Iraq would overturn a left-wing consensus that had 'subverted everything from the defence of the realm to family, authority and the notion of self-restraint and replaced them by an illiberal political correctness' (17 March). Yet although she criticised Blair as a 'universalist' with 'fantasies of international brotherhood', the terms in which Phillips explained America's 'governing ambition to restructure the Middle East' sounded remarkably similar to the language of ethical foreign policy. 'Iraq is to be liberated', she declared, in a 'just war' of 'good versus evil' (24 March) and she hoped that this would usher in 'a new order that will uphold democratic values' (4 April).

Positive assessments of the 'Bush doctrine' also appeared in the liberal broadsheets. In the *Independent*, for example, Donald Macintyre expressed concern that the war was a 'hugely risky experiment', but was open to the possibility that 'the new and emerging transatlantic doctrine of systematic intervention in totalitarian-terrorist and failed states' might be 'proved right for our times' (18 March), while Stephen Pollard challenged the caricature of 'trigger-happy neo-conservatives centred around the Pentagon' and praised their outlook as embodying 'the idealism which is the only way the world can be changed for the better' (3 April). Tellingly, those on the anti-war side of the argument sometimes tried to rescue the principle of 'ethical' regime change even as they denounced Bush for putting it into practice. In the *Guardian*, for example, Jonathan Freedland said this was a 'thoroughly un-American war' because by 'get[ting] into the empire business' Bush had 'cast off the restraint which held back America's 42 previous presidents' (2 April). This was 'a break with everything America has long believed in', argued Freedland, including 'the model that shaped American foreign policy since 1945', because 'the sovereignty of the state of Iraq has been cheerfully violated by the US invasion'. Yet although Freedland objected to the aggressive assertion of US power – arguing that America was caught in a contradiction since it 'holds sovereignty sacred for itself … [but] ignores it for others' – he did not defend the principle of sovereign equality. Conscious, no doubt, that in the 1990s he had been equally cheerful about violating the sovereignty of weak states, Freedland immediately added: 'That can be defended', citing the argument that 'sovereignty is "forfeited" by regimes which choke their own peoples'. Similarly, recalling Blair's 'great Chicago speech, stirring Clinton to save the Kosovans in 1999' and his October 2001 speech on the 'moral power of the world acting as a community', Polly Toynbee lamented that such idealism no longer had any influence (16 April). If the neo-conservatives seemed to echo the 'Blair doctrine', she suggested, this was only because 'Bush sometimes borrows Blairish words as camouflage' for military action undertaken 'at the time and place of US choosing, for US reasons'. Like Freedland, she disliked American unilateralism but was not about to abandon the aspiration for an ethical approach in which 'the dictates of universal human rights would trump the sovereignty of national borders'. Hence, notwithstanding her sharp criticism of Bush, Toynbee conceded that the invasion might yet be justified if it led to peace in the Middle East or if 'a domino effect triggers demands for democracy across the Arab world'.

Understanding the war as an imperial project designed by neo-conservatives in order to demonstrate American power led commentators such as Freedland and Toynbee to oppose it, even though they supported the principle of extensive international interference in weak states on ethical grounds. Yet identical explanations of the war led other commentators to support it, for identical 'ethical' reasons. In the *Times*, for example, Anatole Kaletsky found he could 'fully agree with the peaceniks' about the motives of 'neo-conservative ideologues', identifying America's main objectives as being to boost Iraqi oil output and to 'demonstrate military power' (20 March). Nevertheless, Kaletsky supported the war on 'humanitarian' grounds. As he put it in a later article, despite the 'largely cynical and self-regarding' motivations of the Bush administration, 'good things often happen for bad reasons' (17 April). There was little difference between Kaletsky's position and that of an anti-war commentator such as the *Independent's* Deborah Orr, who said that 'all who abhor this war hope feverishly that it can somehow turn out to be relatively benign' and who criticised the US for being 'not terribly interested in the business of nation building' (21 March). Despite the apparently polarised debate about the war, there was considerable underlying agreement on the desirability of regime change, as reflected in the sorts of descriptions of Saddam and his regime set out in Box 7.1, all of which come from sources or writers who took an explicitly anti-war position.

Prescriptions

This blurring of the lines between pro- and anti-war commentators was also evident in the editorial positions taken by the papers in our sample. Analysts who identify a clear left/right division in press coverage are correct in the sense that papers did indeed divide along these lines in voicing support or opposition to the war. Yet in some respects there was little distance between them.

Division

In the run-up to the war, the most obvious disagreement was over the degree of danger presented by Iraqi WMD and whether war was necessary to deal with this threat. The *Times* said it was 'right to have taken the fateful step and initiated this campaign' because the threat from WMD made military action 'imperative and urgent' (20 March), while the *Mail* highlighted 'the new threat of disorder and chaos from brutal regimes such as Saddam's, with their weapons of mass destruction, and from extreme terrorist groups', arguing that 'to avoid future dangers … we have to fight it out now' (21 March). Both the *Guardian* and *Independent*, in contrast, called for the 'peaceful disarmament of Iraq, accomplished through diplomacy' (*Independent*, 18 March) and both characterised the war as 'unnecessary and avoidable' (*Guardian*, 20 March).

These different risk assessments were usually expressed through a broader political disagreement over the importance of working multilaterally and the

---

Box 7.1 Descriptions of Saddam and his regime by anti-war writers and sources

Saddam
- 'this amoral tyrant' (Iraqi exile)
- 'a brutal dictator' (British Foreign Secretary Robin Cook)
- 'a bloody dictator' (French socialist Jack Lang)
- 'the Iraqi dictator' (German Chancellor Gerhard Schroeder)
- a cruel dictator
- an abhorrent dictator
- militarised dictator
- the dictator
- Iraq's dictator
- 'a tin-pot dictator, and a rather vulgar one' (George Galloway, MP)
- tyrant
- a tyrant
- a hated tyrant
- Iraq's despotic President
- tormentor
- a megalomaniac
- 'a product of his country's violent and bloody past, not its cause' (former government advisor David Clark)
- a mad and bloodthirsty despot
- a loathsome killer
- a mass murderer
- wicked
- America's puppet and then ... America's monster

- a monster
- gravel-voiced Tikriti
- a cur of an underdog
- a master of playing victim when he is in the act of killing, a man who thinks nothing of smearing the innocent to propagate his own version of history
- twisted old leader
- clearly a bad man
- ghastly
- the most revolting dictator in the Arab world
- the monster of Baghdad
- Butcher
- the mightiest of Iraqi warriors ... the second Salahedin ... Fascist ... with a bit of Don Corleone thrown in
- the would-be Saladin
- 'evidently something of a Churchill scholar' (George Galloway)
- 'a friend to the Palestinians and to all the Arabs' (relative of dead Palestinian)
- 'a good Arab leader' (another Palestinian relative)
- vulpine and diabolical
- a bombastic bully who ruled through fear alone

Regime
- 'Saddam's tyranny ... his dictatorial state' (Iraqi exile)
- Saddam Hussein's tyranny
- hollow tyranny ... dictatorship
- 'dictatorship' (Charles Kennedy MP)
- odious
- 'an evil regime' (Andrew Lansley MP)
- evil regime
- dictatorship ... tyranny
- a police state
- a brutal government
- the towering tyranny of one man
- the bloodstained Ba'ath regime
- the Iraqi tyranny
- the whole world thinks the Baathists are monsters
- an evil regime
- Vile
- a megalomaniac ruling elite
- a rotten regime
- 'totalitarian' (George Galloway)
- the Iraqi torturers
- 'dictatorship' (French Prime Minister Jean-Pierre Raffarin)
- one of the cruellest and bloodiest tyrannies on earth

Descriptions are in quotation marks where they appeared that way in the original; attributions are given where the article attributed a phrase.

---

legitimacy of taking military action without explicit UN approval. The *Times* took the toughest stance, deciding by 15 March that there was 'little to be gained in spending another week moving commas and watering down language in the hope of achieving a UN consensus, only to have France exercise its ego and veto'. Describing the British Attorney General's legal justification for war as 'crisp and clear' (18 March), the *Times* saw no barrier to Anglo-American action and reminded critics that 'In Kosovo, the allies acted without the Security Council's blessing' (13 March). The *Mail* did not question the war's legality and although it acknowledged public 'doubts and concerns', it said these should be put aside until after the war. The paper was dismissive of the UN for being 'feebly impotent' and 'unwilling to enforce its own resolutions', although it also agreed with Blair on the danger of America losing 'all trust in international co-operation and [taking] an increasingly unilateralist stance' (17 March). For the *Guardian* and *Independent*, meanwhile, the lack of UN approval was of paramount importance. Although they also criticised France for the breakdown of diplomacy, both papers identified US belligerence as the main cause of what the *Guardian* called 'the mad, maddening rush to arms'

(20 March). According to the *Independent*, the Americans' determination to 'impose their vision of a new world order' amounted to 'a doctrine that might is always right', undermining the 'half-century-old system of international arbitration' (18 March), while the *Guardian* declared that 'The deliberate scuppering of the UN diplomatic process and the launching of war against Iraq in the next few days without explicit UN authorisation cannot be supported' (17 March). Of the two, the *Guardian* was the most forthright and consistent opponent of the war; it emphasised that the coalition had 'no legal mandate to attack, let alone a mandate for regime change and an indefinite occupation'.

Consensus

Despite these sharp disagreements, however, all four papers concurred on the desirability of 'liberating' the Iraqi people. While they echoed the official rationale for war on the grounds of WMD, the pro-war papers also implied that it should be judged as a war of liberation. The *Times* predicted that the war's perceived legitimacy would depend on 'whether the response of ordinary Iraqis suggests that they have been liberated, not conquered' (20 March), while the *Mail* looked forward to 'the moment Saddam's victims are liberated' (21 March). At least to begin with, this argument seemed to work in blunting the objections of anti-war critics. The *Independent* conceded the most ground to the pro-war camp, arguing that 'The liberation of the Iraqi people is, on its own terms, a desirable and laudable aim' and, notwithstanding its continuing suspicion of the US, said that 'For all the spin, for all Mr Bush's disastrous diplomacy and his dubious motives … the restoration of freedom and democracy to the Iraqi people is a noble aim' (21 March). Similarly, after the fall of Saddam's statue in Baghdad, the paper declared that 'the toppling of Iraq's Baath party regime in the very centre of its tyranny is a victory to savour' (10 April). The *Independent* adopted the method of cost–benefit analysis in deciding whether to support the war, arguing, for example, that 'The unprovoked invasion of a sovereign state sets an uncertain precedent; but it will be mitigated by the emphasis on Saddam Hussein's tyranny' (21 March). The fact that the paper took this pragmatic approach – not to mention its record of supporting Western military intervention throughout the 1990s – indicated that the principle of applying force to effect regime change was not at issue.

The *Independent*'s support increased when the war's potential benefits appeared to outweigh the costs and decreased when things went badly. In its 29 March editorial the paper explained that it had 'opposed the decision to go to war … because the potential benefits of removing a dictator … were outweighed by the horrendous costs of war' but acknowledged that 'had Saddam been assassinated in the first, opportunistic bombing raid … the costs and benefits would have been more balanced'. Since at this stage the 'human and financial costs' looked high, the *Independent* concluded that it was anti-war. By 10 April, however, after seeing the pictures of the falling statue, the paper felt that 'if the people of Iraq can use their new liberty to improve their lives and build a free and prosperous country, the cost – in lives, money and shattered diplomacy – may ultimately be vindicated' (10 April). There appeared to be no issue of principle involved. Indeed, in a different context, the *Independent*'s 2 May leader welcomed the fact that 'the world's superpower is throwing its weight around for the benefit of Africa', arguing that American pressure on Zimbabwean President Robert Mugabe to step down showed that the US could 'still be a power for good'.

The *Guardian* did attempt to construct a principled objection to the project of regime change. On the eve of war the paper argued that, 'In principle, it is far from ideal that the government of a sovereign nation, even that of Iraq, should be overthrown' by force, adding that the 'odious nature of Saddam's regime and the future threat it might pose' did not mitigate concerns over the war's legitimacy (19 March). This argument was the closest any newspaper came to defending the principles of non-interference and sovereign equality. Even when the fall of Saddam's statue seemed to many commentators to symbolise a vindication of the project of regime change, the *Guardian* still insisted that it 'does not mean future pre-emptive, unilateral, illegal war-making is now somehow OK' (10 April). Yet it seemed that the habits of thought developed over a decade of arguing for greater 'ethical' intervention, even when it entailed the violation both of international law and of the sovereignty of weak states, had not gone away. The paper's 19 March leader arguing that regime change was illegitimate largely undermined its own case. Urging that 'Iraq must surrender', the *Guardian* advised the Iraqi leadership to 'relinquish power and place the country under the protection of the UN', allowing Iraq to be 'peacefully occupied by military forces operating under UN auspices and with a fresh UN mandate'. Not unlike the fixation with obtaining a second Security Council resolution, this rather gave the game away: the *Guardian* was all in favour of multilateral, UN-approved intervention in Iraq. The next day the paper suggested that 'The prospect that Iraq's dictator will at last be deposed is perhaps the only clear-cut benefit of this entire adventure' (20 March); and the day after that, the *Guardian* said that 'If US forces had succeeded in killing Saddam Hussein' in the campaign's opening airstrikes, 'there would without doubt have been general rejoicing' (21 March). Conceding that 'Most people would be glad to see the back of Saddam and for the greater good ... killing him might be considered justified', the paper offered only the appearance of a principled objection in observing that 'State-ordered assassination sets an abominable precedent that encourages unwelcome emulation'. The *Guardian*'s alternative solution – that 'it would be far preferable to try him for his crimes' – took for granted the right of the West to stand in judgement over the leaders of rogue states.

As shown in Figure 7.1, across all coverage Iraqi civilians were much more likely to be described as 'liberated' (29.2 per cent of descriptions) than as 'occupied' or 'invaded' (11.7 per cent): a similar ratio to that found in television coverage by Lewis and Brookes (2004: 135–6). The pro-war papers very rarely characterised Iraqis as occupied or invaded (7.3 per cent of descriptions in the *Times* and 2.5 per cent in the *Mail*) but the anti-war papers did not tip the balance the other way. Descriptions in the *Independent* were more likely

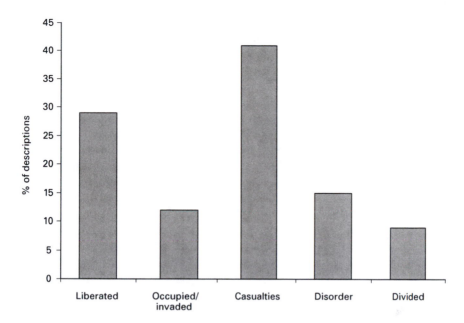

Figure 7.1 Descriptions of Iraqi civilians. Categories are not mutually exclusive, since 94 of the 572 articles with descriptions of Iraqi civilians featured more than one type, for instance describing Iraqis as liberated but also highlighting civilian casualties.

to describe Iraqis as liberated (16.8 per cent of descriptions) than as occupied or invaded (9.8 per cent). The *Guardian* was the most even-handed, characterising Iraqis as liberated (25.8 per cent) only slightly more often than as occupied/invaded (23.8 per cent). Against this, however, has to be set the fact that the biggest single descriptive category was 'casualties', which, at 41.3 per cent, is again very close to the proportion found in television news by Lewis and Brookes. Descriptions of Iraqi civilians as casualties were more likely to feature in the *Guardian* (45.0 per cent of description) and *Independent* (54.9 per cent) than in the *Times* and *Mail* (28.5 and 32.9 per cent, respectively), which suggests that this type of description reflected a more critical view of the war. Descriptions of Iraqis as either engaged in or affected by looting and disorder, or as divided along ethnic or religious lines, also tended to suggest a negative assessment of the effects of the war, although in this there was no significant difference between newspapers.

Re-division

Despite widespread agreement on the desirability of liberating the Iraqi people, it was a difficult justification to sustain in the longer term, as reports of cheering crowds and falling statues gave way to accounts of looting and demonstrations against the occupation. As the Iraqi regime crumbled, the main point of editorial agreement was that 'liberated' Iraq was chaotic and hostile, and earlier disagreements over the importance of UN authority continued in the debate over who should reconstruct the country.

As a weak opponent of war, the *Independent* was anxious to heal international divisions and re-establish the legitimacy of international intervention in Iraq, agreeing with what it understood to be Blair's position: that 'a post-Saddam Iraq should be placed under the auspices of the United Nations as soon as possible and transferred to civilian, Iraqi rule as soon as possible after that' (26 March). This editorial seemed to suggest that putting the UN in charge would not only herald 'a return to the spirit of multilateralism and international co-operation' but would turn the invasion into a war of liberation by demonstrating to 'Iraq and the world that in going to war, the United States and Britain did indeed have Iraq's best interests at heart'. Similarly, the paper identified the 'overriding imperative' as being to 'make it clear that the Allies are there for the sake of the Iraqi people' (12 April) and recommended that although the war 'should never have happened', the UN's role must be defined in 'a way that makes the post-war arrangements legitimate in the eyes of Iraqis and of the world' (18 April).

The *Guardian* also wished to mend fences, arguing from the outset that 'it is essential for global stability that Europe and the US should now work to reunite around a political agenda with the UN at its centre' (22 March) and that 'a Europe so divided internally by the Iraq crisis and so alienated from the US should now forge a common policy with Washington under UN auspices' (28 March). Disagreements over the UN's post-war role were more sharply posed by the *Guardian* than by the *Independent*, as it argued that what was needed was not merely a 'role' for the UN but 'UN rule' (3 April). Maintaining its suspicions of the US, the *Guardian* hinted at the danger of Iraq being turned into an American colony; it drew attention to the 'doling out of contracts to carpet-bagging private US companies linked to government figures' and insisted that 'Iraq's territory and its rich resources belong to all Iraqis and to Iraqis alone' (28 March). When it said, in this editorial, that 'The occupying powers have no business [in Iraq] once Saddam is gone', however, the *Guardian* did not mean that the coalition should withdraw. Responding to an article by Robin Cook which appeared to call for British troops to be pulled out, the *Guardian* said that an immediate withdrawal would be 'wrong and irresponsible', since it would 'again leave Iraqi citizens abandoned to Saddam Hussein's vengeance, as they were during the first Gulf war' (31 March). In the same spirit, once the regime had fallen the paper was adamant that 'there must be long-term follow-through' (10 April). Although much less sanguine than the *Independent*, the *Guardian* also hoped some positive, 'liberating' outcome would be retrieved from a war it had opposed, although quite how this would be achieved by placing the country under 'UN rule' remained unclear.

As the staunchest supporter of the war, the *Times* was also the most upbeat about victory and the only paper not to argue for the UN to be in charge of post-war arrangements. Yet even as it hailed the overthrow of Saddam's statue as 'an historic day of liberation', the *Times* warned of the danger of 'a catastrophic collapse of living standards, endemic violence and ethnic or tribal disputes' (10 April). Similarly, the paper's 26 April leader greeted the spectacle of Shia pilgrims 'chanting and flagellating themselves in a frenzy of religious fervour' as both 'heartening' and 'ominous'. On the one hand, such scenes could be interpreted as showing 'what freedom means to an oppressed people', enjoying their new liberty to 'worship without fear of arrest'; but on the other, they also seemed to signal the growth of an 'Islamic zeal, bordering on fanaticism', which had 'quickly taken on a radical, anti-Western tinge'. Although generally more optimistic than other papers, the *Times* was hardly confident about the future of the 'liberation'.

The *Mail* was even less convincing in its attempts to face down critics of post-war disorder. It argued that it was unfair to expect Western troops to have 'brought tranquillity to the streets overnight', but acknowledged in the same editorial that 'Mobs of looters rampage through Mosul.... Chaos engulfs Baghdad', and described Iraq as 'sliding into anarchy' (12 April). The *Mail* did not make an issue of who should lead post-war reconstruction except in its 9 April editorial, which welcomed Bush's repeated references to 'the "vital" role of the UN in rebuilding Iraq' and sharply criticised the 'triumphalist rhetoric from Washington' which suggested that 'Iraq could be run almost as an American fiefdom, while the Israel–Palestinian issue hardly registered'. Such sentiments would not have seemed out of place in the *Guardian*. Perhaps more typical of the *Mail* was its description of Iraq as 'a country with no democratic traditions and no free institutions, which is split on religious and ethnic lines and could easily fall apart' (9 April). Before the month was out, such concerns had led the paper to abandon any pretence that the invasion had had positive results, as it declared that 'A mere two weeks after the symbolic toppling of Saddam Hussein's statue in Baghdad, the size and complexity of the task of rebuilding Iraq are plain for even the most purblind triumphalists to see' (24 April). Pointing, like the *Times*, to 'the twin threats of fragmentation and fundamentalism', the *Mail* said that victory had 'opened a Pandora's Box'.

Criticism

Overall, 504 articles voiced criticisms of the war, 10.8 per cent of total coverage. As would be expected, the *Guardian* devoted the greatest proportion of its coverage to criticism (16.3 per cent) and the *Times* the least (6.4 per cent). In addition, 236 articles reported Iraqi civilian casualties, although on this topic it was the *Independent* which carried the most articles (95), while the *Mail* carried the least (26). As in other case studies, the main limitation of criticism was one of quality, rather than quantity.

The most common topic of criticism was that the war was illegal or illegitimate because it lacked UN authority, a point which featured in 192 articles, accounting for 38.1 per cent of all critical pieces. Not surprisingly, this objection was most common in the *Guardian* (79 articles) and the *Independent*

(58 articles), which developed the same sorts of arguments in their editorial columns, with similar limitations. In the *Guardian*, for example, Polly Toynbee spelt out the logic of those who opposed the war on the grounds that it lacked UN approval, acknowledging that she 'would reluctantly have supported war with UN acquiescence' (19 March), while the *Independent's* Deborah Orr wrote that it was 'still possible to hate the war, but to give thanks for regime change' (8 April), evidently missing the fact that by welcoming the war as 'liberation' critics fatally weakened their case.

As supporters of the war were quick to point out, many opponents of military action in 2003 had been among the keenest advocates of it in 1999, under similar legal circumstances. Indeed, in 1999 the *Independent* had used the example of Iraq as an argument in favour of intervention in Kosovo. According to the paper's 22 March 1999 editorial, critics of the bombing of Yugoslavia were 'similar to those who say that the sanction Saddam Hussein should face for trying to acquire weapons of mass destruction is a telling-off'. Back then, it seemed so self-evident to the *Independent* that Iraq ought to be bombed that this could be offered as a clinching argument in favour of bombing Yugoslavia. The same article approvingly quoted Blair's justification for the Desert Fox airstrikes against Iraq in 1998, saying he had 'set out with admirable clarity the principle that should govern the new world order', namely that 'when the international community agrees certain objectives and then fails to implement them, those that can act, must'. This was exactly the argument reiterated by coalition leaders in 2003. Similarly, the *Guardian* argued in a 26 March 1999 leader that, since the UN's 'constitution is a recipe for inaction', the authority of Security Council resolutions 'cannot be the sole trigger for international action to right an obvious wrong'. Given this background, it is difficult to take seriously the liberal broadsheets' arguments in 2003 about the importance of UN authority and legality. A clue to their real objection was the *Guardian's* comment in the 1999 editorial just quoted that, in deciding whether to take military action, 'the test must surely be whether such action is more than the pursuit of American self-interest cloaked in noble phraseology'.

As noted above, suspicion of American motives informed the most common explanation of the war, framing it as a demonstration of US imperial power, while the next most common explanation, that it was a war of liberation, acclaimed coalition motives. What appeared to be a debate about international law and the UN system, in other words, can better be understood as a disagreement over whether Bush's America could be trusted. This is why apparently sharp divisions over the war began to look more blurred on closer examination: both critics and supporters could see it as potentially 'liberating' the Iraqi people, since neither side truly questioned the assumption that international interference for the right, 'ethical' reasons was justified. The mistake of coalition leaders was to present the war in terms of pre-emptive self-defence against an imagined threat and only belatedly to prioritise the theme of liberation. At several points, when a different turn of events appeared to be possible – with a second UN resolution, with cheering crowds of Iraqis welcoming their liberators, with 'UN rule' in post-war Iraq – many critics seemed on the verge of being won over.

The *Independent's* 19 March editorial, for example, praised Blair as presenting 'the most persuasive case yet made by the man who has emerged as the most formidable persuader for war on either side of the Atlantic'. The Prime Minister was said to have 'made a coherent case ... that while disarmament and not regime change is the legal basis for the war, the prospect of the latter makes it possible to pursue the former with a "clear conscience and a strong heart"', and to have set out a 'chilling catalogue of repression by the Baghdad dictatorship'. With critics like the *Independent* saluting him as an 'increasingly impressive' leader, Blair hardly needed supporters. In this editorial, the *Independent* found that the 'most telling argument of all' was Blair's warning that inaction would strengthen tyrants and terrorists and would provoke 'a retreat into unilateralism by the United States'. However, Blair's opportunistic attempts to win round critics by talking up the threat and by acknowledging suspicions of the US while promising to influence it in a more positive direction were also a mistake.

The two next most common criticisms of the war, each featuring in 48 articles, or 9.5 per cent of total criticism, were, firstly, that military action would actually increase the risk of terrorism and, secondly, that joining the coalition entailed British subservience to American power. Where the coalition sought to justify war by inflating the risks from WMD and terrorism, its critics countered with their own nightmare scenarios. Anti-war MP Alan Simpson, for example, predicted that Western troops would be 'permanent targets for both liberation and fundamentalist movements' (*Independent*, 22 March); the *Guardian's* Seumas Milne said the war would inevitably give 'a powerful boost to nuclear proliferation and anti-western terror attacks' (10 April); and Egyptian President Hosni Mubarak's forecast that the invasion would produce 'a thousand Osama bin Ladens' was widely quoted.

Where the British government presented itself as the ethical conscience of America, pushing for greater humanitarian aid and progress on a Middle East peace settlement, critics had only to point to the fact of American dominance which Blair's argument implicitly acknowledged. The Stop the War Coalition's Andrew Murray said Blair had 'subordinated our country' to the US (*Guardian*, 21 March); anti-war MP George Galloway spoke darkly of 'the people who have betrayed this country ... [and] sold it to a foreign power' (*Guardian*, 1 April); and Polly Toynbee complained that 'Now we look like the 51st state, and a puny one at that' (*Guardian*, 21 March). This was a weak criticism in itself, since it tended to absolve Britain of blame for the war, finding the government guilty only of, as Galloway put it, 'playing Mini-Me to the Dr Evils of the Bush regime' (*Guardian*, 23 April). *Independent* columnist Yasmin Alibhai-Brown even went so far as to cast Britain as a hapless colony of American empire. Complaining of 'pervasive American domination over our land', she wrote: 'Trust me, I have lived under imperialism.... Another power controlling your destiny is hard to bear' (*Independent*, 24 March). While Alibhai-Brown described Blair as 'the Viceroy of the US', Labour Party stalwart Mark Seddon said the British had become 'America's sepoys' (*Guardian*, 4 April). For such critics, the domination of Iraq by Anglo-American power sometimes seemed a secondary concern compared with the supposed subordination of Britain.

Where coalition leaders offered opportunistic justifications for war, critics responded in kind.

As in Afghanistan, the promise of a quick and clean war with maximum humanitarian assistance and minimal 'collateral damage' may have backfired by encouraging attention to these issues. Initially, critics of the war saw its careful conduct as a saving grace, the *Guardian*'s 25 March editorial, for example, praising the coalition's 'unprecedented' care to avoid killing civilians, in contrast to the lack of care for civilian life shown by Saddam's forces. There was also much vigilance in early reports against the possibility that the Iraqis would use casualties as a propaganda ploy. This was most marked in the *Mail*, whose reporter in Baghdad, Ross Benson, frequently cast doubt on the veracity of casualty claims and pinned the blame for civilian deaths on Saddam (for example in his reports of 3, 4 and 5 April) but other correspondents also included warnings that displays of injured civilians were 'orchestrated by the authorities' (*Independent*, 28 March). As noted above, the pro-war papers gave less attention to casualties, particularly the *Times* (although in part this resulted from the paper's decision to withdraw its reporter, Janine di Giovanni, from Baghdad when the war began) and their columnists complained that coalition forces should drop what Simon Heffer called their 'softly-softly' approach (*Mail*, 29 March) and, in Michael Gove's phrase, 'stop pussyfooting' (*Times*, 26 March). Yet both the *Times* and *Mail* carried editorials criticising the killing of Iraqi civilians at coalition checkpoints (both 2 April) and in the longer term the mounting civilian death toll and continuing coalition losses, even after the moment of supposed 'liberation', could not be ignored, adding to critical assessments of the war's conduct and results.

During the war, the most hard-hitting criticism offered by the press was in articles challenging the idea of 'liberating' Iraq by invading it. Writing on the 200th anniversary of the death of the Haitian revolutionary leader Toussaint L'Ouverture, for example, Gary Younge said that 'Toussaint's life taught us that liberation cannot be imposed from above, let alone be imported from outside' (*Guardian*, 7 April). *Independent* columnist Mark Steel ridiculed the claim that Iraqis were being 'given back their country' (10 April) and Jonathan Glancey drew some telling parallels between the current occupation and Britain's brutal history of imperial rule in Iraq after the First World War (*Guardian*, 19 April). Such pieces were relatively rare, however: articles contesting the claim that the invasion could be seen as a war of liberation accounted for only 7.3 per cent of criticism (less than 1 per cent of total coverage).

The main issue which emerged as a focus for criticism after the war (and even more strongly after the period covered by this case study) was, of course, the absence of WMD. In our samples of press coverage, 70.6 per cent of articles mentioning WMD implied that Iraq possessed them, 24.3 per cent raised doubts about their existence and 5.1 per cent presented both views. This is, again, broadly similar to what Lewis and Brookes (2004: 135) found in television coverage, but with a somewhat higher proportion of articles raising doubts – probably because of the greater scope for journalists to express their own opinions in newspaper journalism. This is borne out by the fact that if we distinguish between those articles in which an opinion on WMD was offered by a journalist from those only reporting the views of sources, the proportion of 'doubting' articles is greater for the first type. Setting aside the small number of articles which presented both views even-handedly, where sources were quoted as expressing a view on WMD (in 254 articles), 85.8 per cent implied that Iraq possessed such weapons while 14.2 per cent doubted their existence: almost exactly the proportions found by Lewis and Brooks in television news. Where journalists were voicing an opinion (in 172 articles), a much higher proportion questioned the existence of WMD – 42.4 per cent – although still the majority presumed that Iraq had them.

It might be supposed that journalists followed the lead of sources in giving credence to official claims that Iraq possessed WMD, yet they clearly did not do so with regard to the claim that Saddam's regime was linked to international terrorism. Overall, 53.8 per cent of references assumed such connections existed, while 42.9 per cent questioned the claim and 3.3 per cent put both views. However, if we again distinguish between the opinions of journalists and sources, the proportions are quite different. While 83.8 per cent of references by sources assumed that Iraq was linked to terrorism, only 35.3 per cent of references by journalists did so. Where journalists themselves offered an opinion on the issue, 64.7 per cent of references threw doubt on official claims. Curiously, journalists expressed doubts about WMD claims less often, despite the fact that questions about the coalition's 'evidence' had been widely aired before the war and the government's official dossiers ridiculed as 'dodgy'. Possibly this is because, as noted earlier, British government sources had dismissed claims of a link between Iraq and 9/11, and also because the issue of terrorist connections was seen as much less important. While the existence or absence of WMD was a fairly significant theme, featuring in 449 articles, nearly 10 per cent of total coverage, the topic of Iraq's alleged terrorist links was much less prominent, occurring in less than 2 per cent of total coverage. However, it should be noted that, to the extent that doubts about the existence of WMD were voiced in the press, these did not diminish once the war started: in fact, most of the doubting articles appeared during our second sample period, when the proportion of references to Iraq's WMD which questioned their existence rose to 30.8 per cent, compared with only 9.4 per cent in our first sample period. The problem was not that sceptical journalists fell into line once the fighting started but that immediately before the war they did not air doubts which came to the fore later. Since, on the issue of Iraq's alleged terrorist links, journalists showed themselves to be perfectly capable of questioning official sources when they chose to do so, later complaints that they had been misled by similar claims about WMD are probably best understood as a way of signalling the growing unpopularity of the war and a rationalisation of the failure to challenge it more forcefully earlier.

Conclusions

In some respects, the coverage of Iraq stands out as different from other case studies, most obviously because of the sharp divisions over the wisdom of

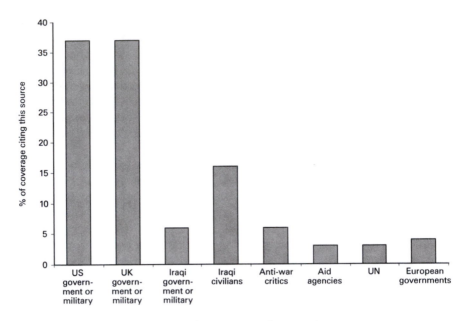

Figure 7.2 Prominence of the different types of source, Iraq coverage.

military intervention. Although, not surprisingly, the US and British governments and military were by far the most frequently cited sources, there were
several sources who voiced criticisms of the war's rationale and effects, including UN officials, aid agencies and Iraqi civilians, as indicated in Figure 7.2. The
category 'anti-war critics' includes prominent parliamentary opponents of the
war as well as representatives of the popular anti-war movement, which helps
to account for the relative prominence of this type of source. Theirs was still a
minority voice in terms of sources cited, but critical anti-war views gained more
of a hearing in 2003 than in other cases examined in this book. Further articles
also reported the activities of anti-war protestors and critics without citing
them as sources, so that nearly 9 per cent of total coverage registered the fact
that many people opposed the war. The significance of such coverage should
not be overstated, since a third of all articles which mentioned opponents of
the war were critical of them. Writers in the *Mail*, particularly, were inclined
to characterise anti-war critics negatively, as committing 'an act of treachery',
as 'harmless … loonies', or – in the case of young people on anti-war demonstrations – as errant children, for example (*Mail*, 20 and 24 March, 1 May).
However, the most prominent explanation of the war, which understood it as
an assertion of American hegemony, echoed the views of those who opposed
it rather than those of its official supporters.

Notable by its absence was the 'war on terror' frame, which had been so pervasive in Afghanistan. Official claims about links between Iraq and al-Qaeda
received little attention and were questioned by journalists, even though they
usually failed to question similarly false claims about WMD. As far as the

British press was concerned, it would seem that the supposedly powerful 'anti-terror' framework was not really seen as relevant in 2003 and the suspicions about US motives which appeared in some of the coverage of Afghanistan loomed larger in relation to Iraq. The main criticism of the war – its illegality and lack of UN authority – again marked a contrast between this and other case studies, particularly Kosovo. At the same time, however, the desirability of 'liberating' Iraq was very rarely questioned, suggesting an element of continuity with previous instances of 'ethical' intervention. This meant that, while there was much critical commentary, the substance of the critique offered in newspapers was rather weak and inconsistent.

CHAPTER 8

Conclusions: framing post-Cold War conflicts

The breakdown of the long-established Cold War ideological framework has been widely understood as presenting a problem for journalists seeking short-hand explanations of new crises and conflicts, but no clear understanding has so far emerged of how the media have responded to this situation. Greg McLaughlin, for example, observes that in the 1990s the first potential replacement for the Cold War frame – the idea of a New World Order – was only a short-lived success, which soon gave way to an inchoate idea of generalised disorder and a cacophony of individual reporters' own 'personalised perspectives' (McLaughlin 2002: 142, 152). As discussed in Chapter 1, many critics have suggested that a new model of 'ethnic' or 'tribal' conflict became dominant in the 1990s, a model which offered misleading explanations of why conflict had broken out in Yugoslavia and Rwanda, and which apparently justified inaction rather than intervention. At the same time, it is also claimed that greater attention to the suffering of victims of human rights abuses or humanitarian crises offered the possibility of a new role for journalists in pricking the conscience of the West and encouraging greater, more 'ethical', international activism. Since 9/11, the 'war on terror' has seemed to some commentators to supply a new comprehensive frame, offering a model of global 'bipolarity' comparable to the Cold War framework (McLaughlin 2002: 206). There is a grain of truth in all these views, each of which captures some particular aspect of media coverage, and of the wider public debate about how the West should understand and respond to post-Cold War conflicts. Returning to the questions posed at the beginning of this book (page 17), it is possible to discern some overall patterns in the way that conflicts and the international responses to them have been framed in press coverage.

Ethnic war and genocide

One of the most misunderstood elements of media coverage of recent conflicts is the theme of ethnicity. A surprise finding of this study is that in coverage of Bosnia, when 'ethnic hatred' is often said to have been a prominent, or even the dominant theme, in fact such ideas barely registered in comparison with the dominant view that the war resulted from the aggression of one side. On the evidence examined here, the supposed consensus that conflict was the product of mutual ethnic antagonisms did not exist: it was only ever a minor theme. Even in the case of Rwanda, when notions of 'tribal conflict' did initially predominate in news coverage, the importance of such explanations has been overstated by most analysts: this was the prevailing framework, but only for a brief period, and even then it had to compete with a variety of other explanations and did not go uncontested.

The significance claimed for 'ethnic' explanations tends to centre on the assertion that this way of framing conflict discourages effective international action, provides an alibi for non-intervention and distances news audiences from the suffering of victims portrayed as 'other'. Although the argument seems a logical one, it is not borne out by the evidence considered in this study. Firstly, the extent of 'ethnic' framing has been exaggerated in cases where it is held to have discouraged greater intervention, particularly Bosnia. Secondly, the presence of similar ideas about 'ethnic' or 'tribal' divisions in other cases – Somalia, Afghanistan and Kosovo – in no way challenged the consensus in favour of intervention. Indeed, it seems to have had the opposite effect in the case of Somalia, since the more chaotic and 'tribal' the country was thought to be, the greater the perceived need for long-term international involvement. In practice, there is no straightforward correspondence between 'ethnic' explanations and a non-interventionist policy orientation. Similarly, in Afghanistan the focus on the country's backward, tribal culture could serve the argument that greater 'nation-building' efforts were needed just as well as it could support the argument that British peacekeepers would be at risk in such hostile circumstances.

In terms of both its prominence and its implicit prescriptive significance, 'ethnic' framing appears to have been set up as a straw man by advocates of greater Western interventionism, eager to delineate who were the villains and who the victims in Bosnia and elsewhere. At the same time, the alternative explanations favoured by such advocates have sometimes reintroduced the faulty assumptions ostensibly rejected in the critique of 'ethnic' explanations of conflict. In the case of Rwanda, for instance, many commentators have rejected the idea that violence was the spontaneous product of innate tribal hatreds, yet the proposed alternative explanation, seeing the violence as premeditated and systematic genocide, did not produce any greater understanding when it was taken up in press coverage. Where reporting of 'tribal massacres' naturalised supposed differences between Hutu and Tutsi, later reporting of 'genocidal massacres' presented the whole country, and indeed the wider region, as defined by its difference, inherently prone to explosive violence, permanently on the edge of a further descent into evil. Simplistic and misleading ideas about tribalism were replaced with equally simplistic ideas about the peculiar and 'psychotic' culture of Rwandan society, which had turned tens of thousands of people into obedient killers. Similarly, where the 'ethnic' explanation of conflict in the former Yugoslavia tended to imply that all sides were equally prone to violent hatreds, the alternative view which sought to identify clear villains against whom the West could intervene simply transferred ideas about savagery and irrational 'bloodlust' into descriptions of the Serbs. By the time of the Kosovo conflict, the idea that conflict was 'medieval' could sit alongside the idea that it was Nazi-style genocide with little sense of incongruity.

It is striking that the term 'genocide' was used in relation to every conflict considered in this book except Afghanistan, including descriptions of Somalia's 'suigenocide' and Saddam's 'genocidal regime'. Usage was often very loose and in some cases little attempt was made by press commentators to develop any sort of explanation on the basis of this idea. Although, in other cases, explicit explanations were sometimes elaborated, in general, accusations of genocide are best understood mainly as a way to indicate that particular events or groups of people deserved the strongest possible moral opprobrium. This was particularly marked in the case of Kosovo, when the term genocide was used very freely but with almost no attempt to develop this into a proper explanation. Instead, it was hurled around in an effort to assert the most zealous possible 'moral' case for intervention. The outrage usually directed at anyone questioning this frame or adopting an alternative explanation suggests that it has been used more as a badge of moral attitudes than as a genuine attempt at explanation. From this perspective, to ask whether recent conflicts can properly be understood as genocide appears as a refusal to acknowledge the suffering of victims by putting violence into its proper moral framework. Yet we can agree that the consequences of conflict are terrible and sympathise with its victims without sacrificing understanding for spurious moral certainty.

Indeed, the genocide frame is highly selective in deciding which groups may be considered 'worthy victims', and it allows violence even against civilians associated with groups defined as evil to be ignored, minimised or justified. The disturbing feature of many accounts, including those in the media, which explain post-Cold War conflicts in terms of genocide is that the quest for moral simplicity involves distortion. In Bosnia, the adoption of this framework seriously impeded understanding of the nature of the conflict, apparently deliberately, as journalists went out of their way to portray it as a one-sided war of Serbian aggression. Even in Rwanda, where there is a stronger case for characterising the violence as genocide, the idea tended to be used in a highly simplistic fashion. Important questions about the impact of Western interference prior to April 1994 were closed off and the recent context of civil war was bracketed out, leaving only the suggestion that Hutu refugees were in thrall to a genocidal ideology and that violence against them was therefore justified. In Kosovo, the distortions again appear to have been largely deliberate, with signs that journalists were fully aware that talking up genocide was a calculated propaganda ploy by Nato governments but went along with it anyway.

Collusion and collaboration

Given what has been established by many previous studies of the news media, it is not surprising that in every case examined official Western sources were the most dominant. More significantly, in the majority of cases the editorial position taken by newspapers closely coincided with the line of the British and American governments. Even where criticism was expressed, the most common complaints tended to be either that Western governments were not intervening enough, or that they were intervening in the wrong way. The idea that they *should* somehow be intervening was, as discussed further below, almost never contested.

However, it would be misleading to suggest that journalists simply followed the lead of official sources. In some cases they certainly did, most clearly in the case of Kosovo. Yet in other cases considered here there was not the same sort of concerted and coordinated propaganda effort by Western governments as there was in 1999. At least as far as the 'ethical' interventions of the 1990s are concerned, journalists were active collaborators in writing the script rather than simply colluding with the presentation offered by official sources. The use of the term 'ethnic cleansing' in discussing Bosnia is a case in point. First put into circulation by Western officials wishing to promote greater intervention by their governments, it was eagerly taken up, elaborated and selectively applied by like-minded journalists, whose reports then contributed to the evidential basis for expert judgements about how the war should be understood. By the time of the Kosovo conflict, the sorts of justifications promoted by Nato leaders – framing the bombing as an epic struggle of good against evil, drawing comparisons with the Holocaust and justifying military action in terms of moral values based on human rights – drew on ideas and themes which had been developed by journalists advocating tougher action in Bosnia.

In at least some cases it is clear that media commentators knew that morally simplified justifications for intervention entailed misrepresentation and distortion, but pressed ahead regardless. As we saw in the case of Somalia, for example, there was a disconnection between, on the one hand, reports which pointed out that the extent of the crisis was being exaggerated in order to justify intervention, and which also sometimes drew attention to the deliberate creation of media-friendly events by the US, and, on the other, editorial commentaries which chorused approval of the tremendous moral mission supposedly being undertaken by the West. In general, the media were neither ignorant of the reality of the crises they covered nor entirely uncritical of the policy justifications offered by Western governments. Rather, journalists and political leaders were engaged in a common project of both struggling to understand the post-Cold War world and trying to find a new and meaningful role for Western powers within it.

Legitimacy and sovereign inequality

The legitimacy of Western military intervention was almost never questioned in the press. In this respect – whatever explanations were adopted in relation to particular conflicts – the key organising idea was that of sovereign inequality. The principles of sovereign equality and non-interference which underpinned the post-Second World War UN system were quickly abandoned as outdated and irrelevant after 1989. With the demise of the Soviet Union as, at least in principle, a counterweight and deterrent to Western power, there no longer seemed any reason to respect the sovereignty of weak states. States which abused their own citizens' human rights, which could not cope with humanitarian emergencies or which presented, through their internal instability and lawlessness, a threat to international order were seen to lack the legitimacy of 'full' sovereignty. This perspective has been institutionalised in various ways since the end of the Cold War, including through the apparatus of international criminal courts, as well as being expressed through armed intervention.

It is striking just how quickly this idea was established, appearing as a fully developed justification for international intervention in the 1992 'humanitarian mission' to Somalia. Indeed, in retrospect, it is clear that the idea was already implicit in the notion of a 'New World Order' in which the US and its allies would be able to adopt 'moral' policies, following an ethical imperative to intervene against illegitimate regimes rather than following the amoral dictates of *realpolitik*. Already at the end of the 1991 Gulf war, when Western leaders were roundly criticised in the media for not 'finishing the job' and overthrowing Saddam, the presumption was that Iraq had forfeited any right to be regarded as an equal sovereign state. Part of Iraq's territory could be taken out of its control, its airspace could be patrolled by the Western military and the country regularly bombed, and its economy could be regulated and controlled through a stringent sanctions regime. Regardless of the controversies surrounding the issue of WMD in 2003, the argument that the West had the right to intervene in Iraq had decisively been won long before.

In light of our case studies of Bosnia and Rwanda, it is also significant that the idea of the West's moral imperative to intervene in problem states arose both as an official justification for action and as a criticism of inaction by Western governments. President George Bush Snr presented a 'moral' case for intervention against Saddam in 1991 and was then criticised for not intervening enough. In Somalia, the US staged an elaborate and highly publicised 'humanitarian' military intervention, justified in terms of a moral obligation to act, and was criticised for not doing enough or for lacking stamina and commitment. In the case of both Bosnia and Rwanda, the criticisms were similar, with the West apparently lagging behind the demands of media commentators anxious to see ever-tougher intervention. The media's concern with declining Western prestige and credibility in Bosnia, or their condemnation of the West's moral failure in Rwanda, appears as a harsh and critical judgement on their own governments, but it was a criticism which presumed more common ground than disagreement. Again, it is best thought of as a collaborative effort on the part of both political leaders and journalists to find ways to bolster Western prestige and to delineate a new and positive role in a changing international landscape. Of course, there have been different ideas about how such a role should be defined, and there have been disagreements over particular policies and particular crises. Yet through this comparative study it has become apparent that the underlying similarities stand out more than the superficial differences.

Sovereign inequality can be conceived of in a variety of ways. It can be presented in terms of a 'clash of civilisations', or as a struggle of the civilised against the primitive and barbaric. It can be understood as a moral obligation to help people who are suffering and to end abuses, or as a defensive move against potential sources of instability and disorder. How arguments are made in specific circumstances matters very much at the time, but in the long run much of the debate about how to explain particular conflicts and how to rationalise specific policy choices is secondary to the fact that all these conceptions of the West's role are ways of thinking about its superiority. This superiority can be presented in particularist terms, as a defence of national or Western values, or dressed up in the pseudo-universalist garb of human rights. Either way, the results tend to be similar. Looking back, it has been humanitarian and human rights which have provided the more influential and effective formulations. This is a pseudo-universalism because it divides the world, according to 'moral' (as opposed to civilisational or cultural) criteria, into the law-givers and the criminals. In doing so, unequal status and unequal treatment are presumed to be justified on the basis of whether a state is deemed to possess 'full' sovereignty. The sovereignty of the weak state is 'conditional' on the verdict of the strong.

The suggestion, discussed in Chapter 7, that in the 1990s liberal advocates of ethical intervention came into conflict with conservative defenders of traditional ideas about national sovereignty (or indeed the idea that in 2003 left-leaning critics of the Iraq war belatedly became defenders of sovereign equality in order to oppose regime change) is largely untrue. While conservative thinkers in Britain in the 1990s sometimes mounted a defence of their own country's national sovereignty against the feared encroachments of the European Union, the principle of sovereign *equality* was almost never defended by anyone. The habitual differences of tone and stance which have been described in the newspapers analysed for this study cannot easily be understood in terms of straightforward left/right divisions. A traditional emphasis on national interests is often identified with a right-of-centre or conservative outlook, while the promotion of multilateral frameworks for 'humanitarian' or otherwise 'ethical' action tends to be associated with liberal or left-leaning writers. As we have seen, the divisions have rarely been as neat as this. It was left-wingers who lamented Britain's supposed subservience to imperial America in 2003 and protested that Britain must look to its own interests rather than serving those of the US, while the right-leaning *Times* was a consistently forceful advocate of 'ethical' military intervention in Somalia, Bosnia and Kosovo. Although it is true that objections to British involvement in 'other people's wars' were sometimes couched in terms of there being no British national interest, over the course of the 1990s such arguments were largely superseded by the development of rationales for action on the basis of both interests and values. This was most clearly formulated by Tony Blair in relation to Kosovo, when military action was justified in terms of both an altruistic wish to help the victims of oppression and a self-interested desire to bring stability to a nearby region and prevent refugee flows. In the effort to make intervention appear not only necessary but also meaningful in terms of the West's positive role in the post-Cold War world, the accent has usually been on the 'values' which military action is held to express. But in any case, in practice the arguments which were raised against intervention in particular crises virtually never contested the legitimacy of Western intervention as such.

After 9/11: no new Cold War

A key finding of this study is that the sorts of explanatory frames which developed in the 1990s have been adapted for the 'war on terrorism', with the most significant underlying continuity again being the presumption of sovereign inequality. At first glance it seems very odd to try to turn a response to a terrorist attack into a quasi-humanitarian mission involving aid drops and measures to end human rights abuses, or to switch from scaremongering about WMD to promises of liberation and democracy. Understandably, many critics have seen such 'add-on' justifications as mere window-dressing, as throwing some loftier-sounding rhetoric into the mix in order to win round sceptics and shore up both domestic and international support. Indeed, the proliferation of different sorts of explanations and rationales itself probably adds to the suspicions of anti-war critics that there must be some hidden conspiracy or interest involved. In fact, however, the combination of different reasons for waging war in the case of both Afghanistan and Iraq was premised on the idea that intervention is justified on the grounds of sovereign inequality, summed up in the idea that the former was a problem because it was a 'failed' state, or that the latter presented a threat because it was an 'outlaw' state. Either way, these were not 'proper' states and needed to be transformed for both security and moral reasons. These were attempts to restate the 'interests and values' formula offered by Blair as his 'doctrine of international community' in 1999 (see Chapter 5, page 136).

It was on the basis of the broader arguments about 'values' that the liberal broadsheets put aside their antipathy to Bush and, albeit conditionally and reluctantly, supported the war on terrorism in Afghanistan. So long as it could be understood as not merely a war of self-defence or of US national interest, but a war which would deliver humanitarian relief and improve human rights while diplomatic efforts concentrated on resolving the grievances of the Middle East – so long, in other words, as it entailed an ethical mission to transform the region as much as possible – the *Guardian* and *Independent* were in favour. Even more strikingly, as US policy began to be reassessed in a more critical light in December 2001, with the *Guardian* especially mistrustful of US motives, the objection was not that the future government of Afghanistan was decided in Bonn, not Kabul, by Western donors, not Afghans. Rather, the criticism was that the US was not sufficiently committed to long-term nation-building. The attempts of the new Afghan government to limit the number of foreign troops and to halt US airstrikes, which continued to cause civilian casualties, were brushed aside. Such was the consensus in favour of intervention that this high-handed treatment attracted no critical comment, even from those who had expressed misgivings about the war. As seen time and again in this study, from Somalia in 1992 to Iraq in 2003, the loudest complaint voiced in the press has been that the West does not do enough to reorganise other societies.

We might think that the combination of values and security interests had found a near perfect expression in the war on terrorism. The enemy, so far as one can be identified, professes open antipathy to Western values, while the shocking destruction of 9/11 surely made the threat real enough. Given the underlying agreement on the legitimacy of Western interference in weak states, it is perhaps difficult see why, at least in Britain, the war on terrorism has proved to be rather a flop. Whereas, to a greater or lesser extent, all newspapers supported British and/or American military action in almost every other case considered in this book, they divided sharply over the 2003 Iraq war, and despite the media's wide take-up of the anti-terror theme in 2001 there has been little sign of any enthusiasm for defending either the interests or the values which are supposed to be at stake.

The war on terrorism cannot plausibly be seen as a viable replacement for the Cold War framework. It is true, of course, that neo-conservative thinkers have sought to present it in these terms, but their efforts have not been very successful. The main limitation is the difficulty of articulating the distinctive values which are to be defended and propagated. Since these are supposed to be shared by some but hated by others, notably Islamist terrorists and their sympathisers, some critics have accused politicians and the media of adopting a 'clash of civilisations' framework or of conducting a crusade against Islam. Yet while a few right-wing ideologues might wish to frame contemporary conflict in these terms it is hardly a popular idea; nor is it likely to become so. Instead, the promotion of the idea of defending 'our' values is defensive and apologetic. As we saw in the coverage of Afghanistan, the supposedly confident and aggressive espousal of 'Western values' in the war on terror was transformed almost instantly into an admission of past failures, as the problem of failed states was widely understood in terms of 'blowback' from previous Western policy, and a feeling that terrorist attacks must be an expression of understandable grievances caused by earlier Western wrongdoing. Notwithstanding Bush's 'with us or against us' rhetoric, the war on terror has not galvanised popular enthusiasm for Western values but has instead, in the case of Iraq, produced divisions within and between Western nations.

A further limitation of the war on terrorism frame is that, in the formulation of interests and values, the 'interests' half of the equation is presented in terms of fear. The attempt to inspire action through fear is apt to backfire, of course, when threats turn out to have been exaggerated or made up. More importantly, fear is at least as likely to be interpreted as a reason for inaction as it is to inspire action. Debates about war in recent years have often been couched in terms of whether to act now to avert danger or whether acting in itself increases the risks. Neither side of the discussion questions the assumption that Western intervention in weaker states is legitimate in principle, and since the 2003 Iraq war the US and Britain have again been criticised for not intervening more, in

Sudan and elsewhere, just as they were in Rwanda and Bosnia a decade earlier. It appears that any contemporary formulation of America's 'manifest destiny' or Britain's global role is likely to be cut from essentially the same cloth as the ethical interventionism of the 1990s, whatever the political orientation of the next incumbents of the White House or Downing Street.

Notes

Notes to Chapter 1

1 SIPRI (2001: 64) defines 'major armed conflicts' as those involving at least 1,000 battle-related deaths in at least one one-year period since the onset of hostilities. In 1990–2001, the lowest number of major conflicts (19) occurred in 1997 and the highest (33) in 1991.

2 'Humanitarian Intervention: A Forum', *The Nation*, 14 July 2003, www.thenation.com/doc.mhtml?i=20030714&s=forum.

3 There have, however, been some studies of the propaganda role of the non-Western media, particularly in the former Yugoslavia (Thompson 1999; Skopljanac Brunner et al. 2000) and Rwanda (Article 19 1996; Kellow and Steeves 1998).

4 Remarks by the President to Employees at the Federal Bureau of Investigation, 25 September 2001, www.whitehouse.gov/news/releases/2001/09/20010925-5.html; Address to a Joint Session of Congress and the American People, 20 September 2001, www.whitehouse.gov/news/releases/2001/09/20010920-8.html; State of the Union Address, 29 January 2002, www.whitehouse.gov/news/releases/2002/01/20020129-11.html.

5 A more obvious choice for a fourth newspaper might be the *Telegraph*. However, at the time of writing the newspaper had withdrawn its archives prior to 2000 from all electronic databases. The *Mail* was chosen because of its right-of-centre political stance, and in order to allow some comparisons to be drawn between the broadsheet press and a mid-market tabloid.

6 Online news databases are not without their problems. Archives can be unreliable and incomplete, and discrepancies can arise when different newspapers' data are recorded differently. One particular problem which deserves mention is that whereas the broadsheets usually split 'in brief' columns into separate stories, the *Mail* often bundled more than one item into a single 'article'. In this study, no changes were made to the way in which newspapers separated their articles, except for editorials, which were always counted as single articles. Where data were evidently incomplete, the ProQuest database was used as an alternative source, although this did not always yield better results. Where the database included different versions of the same article, the longest was selected. For these reasons, figures for total coverage in the case studies should be treated as approximate. A more general problem with electronic versions of newspapers is that they do not include layout, photographs or other illustrations. It would be desirable to integrate the textual analysis attempted in this study with the type of

framing approach to news images offered by Griffin (2004), but on this occasion the limitations of a text-only analysis were felt to be outweighed by the advantages it affords in terms of handling larger quantities of coverage.

Notes to Chapter 2

1 Their 10 December 1992 *Los Angeles Times* article, 'Disaster Pornography from Somalia', is available at www.medialit.org/reading_room/article105.html. Their views were also reported in the *Independent* on the same day.

2 'The Comprehensive Report on Lessons Learned from United Nations Operation in Somalia (UNOSOM), April 1992–March 1995' (undated but c. 1996), paragraph 64, http://pbpu.unlb.org/PBPU/Download.aspx?docid=509.

3 George H. W. Bush, 'Address to the Nation on the Situation in Somalia', 4 December 1992, http://bushlibrary.tamu.edu/research/papers/1992/92120400.html.

4 Table 2.1 gives the numbers of relevant articles. A LexisNexis search was carried out using the term 'Somalia' for all the periods listed and all articles were checked for relevance. Readers' letters and articles mentioning Somalia only in passing were excluded. The date ranges of the five periods of coverage selected were determined as follows: Period 1 is the calendar month of August, since the airlift began mid-month, on 14 August 1992. Period 2 covers the week before President Bush issued the order for Operation Restore Hope, on Friday 4 December 1992, and the following three weeks. Period 3 is from three weeks before the end of Operation Restore Hope (on 4 May 1993) until one week after. Period 4 is the calendar month of October, since the clash with General Aidid's militia was at the beginning of the month (3–4 October 1993). Period 5 is the four weeks preceding the 1 April 1994 deadline for the withdrawal of US forces.

5 The *Guardian* carried 25 articles in which causes were addressed briefly, accounting for 22.5 per cent of the paper's total coverage of Somalia during the periods examined; the *Independent* carried 20 (15.2 per cent of its coverage); the *Times* 20 (17.5 per cent); and the *Mail* 6 (22.2 per cent).

6 The number of explanatory articles during the remaining two periods was three at the end of Operation Restore Hope, in April/May 1993 (27.3 per cent of the coverage for that period), and two as US forces withdrew in March 1994 (9.1 per cent).

7 This type of limited explanation was not found in any other articles.

8 Terms such as these, suggesting the violence was criminal, occurred in 6 of the 11 articles; in two instances the violence was presented in the context of civil war ('factional fighting' by 'guerrillas'); and in three instances both criminal and civil war frames were invoked.

9 Of the 71 articles offering brief explanations, 46 made this connection (64.7 per cent), although only 36 of these offered some explanation of the war itself.

10 This article evidently formed the basis for the *Times* editorial of 28 March 1994 discussed earlier. Kiley wrote that: 'Operation Restore Hope aimed to put an end to the looting of food aid and the protection rackets which were the main cause of famine costing relief agencies tens of millions of pounds a year. For, unlike the Ethiopian famine of 1984, the disaster in Somalia was entirely man-made' (5 May 1993).

11 Fifteen articles had more than one target of criticism: six focusing on both the military and the aid operation; five on both the media and the aid operation; and four on the media and the military. 'Criticism' includes both direct criticism by journalists and also the reported criticism of others, such as politicians, NGO spokespersons and Somalis.

12 In order to be as inclusive as possible, a LexisNexis search was conducted of all UK national newspapers, including Sundays, from 1 January 1992 to 31 December 1995 using the terms 'Somalia' AND 'African Rights' OR 'de Waal' OR 'Omaar'. The *Telegraph*'s archives were not available.

13 George H. W. Bush, 'Address to the Nation on the Situation in Somalia', 4 December 1992, http://bushlibrary.tamu.edu/research/papers/1992/92120400.html.

14 The search, using NUDIST, was not for whole words only, so that 'child' also includes 'children'; 'militia' also includes 'militiamen', and so on. Without checking the context of every mention of each term, this technique provides only a crude indication of the changing emphasis in the coverage: for example, while 60.6 per cent of articles in August 1992 mentioned the word 'child' or derivatives, only 23.4 per cent of articles were coded as drawing attention to children's suffering. With this caution, the overall pattern presented here may be taken as broadly accurate, since there is no reason to suppose a greater number of irrelevant mentions of a term in one period than in any other.

15 The *Guardian* and the *Times* also reminded readers of this story in later coverage, each running an article comparing the December 1992 landings with the shocking images of dead soldiers in October 1993, and each carrying a report contrasting the televised arrival of US troops with their departure in March 1994.

16 George H. W. Bush, 'Address to the Nation on the Situation in Somalia', 4 December 1992, http://bushlibrary.tamu.edu/research/papers/1992/92120400.html.

Notes to Chapter 3

1 'Bosnia War Marks Anniversary', *BBC Online*, 6 April 2002, http://news.bbc.co.uk/2/hi/europe/1914133.stm.

2 Formally signed in Paris on 14 December 1995.

3 'Muslim' was designated as a 'nationality', rather than simply a religion, in Yugoslavia in 1971. For a discussion of the reasons for, and effects of, this decision see Johnstone (2002: 157–8). The 1991 census data here are from Woodward (1995: 33).

4 The Bosnian Institute, 'Chronology 1985–1995', www.bosnia.org.uk/bosnia/viewitem.cfm?itemID=690&typeID=386.

5 Table 3.1 indicates the total numbers of relevant articles. A LexisNexis search was carried out using the term 'Bosnia' for all the periods listed and all articles were checked for relevance. Readers' letters and articles which mentioned Bosnia only in passing were excluded.

6 The quantity of articles for the other periods was as follows: focusing mainly on causes, three in the 1993 sample period, one in 1994 and one in 1995; mentioning causes briefly, 21 in 1993, four in 1994 and three in 1995.

7 Despite its 10 April 1993 report that the US had 'subtly changed tune', on 15 April the *Times* quoted a 'senior American diplomat' as explaining that 'In Europe, the feeling is that this is a civil war but in the US there is a greater sense that it is a war of aggression'.

8 The numbers of articles explaining the war as the result of Serbian aggression were as follows: focusing mainly on causes, four (out of a total of nine) during the 1992 sample period, one (out of three) in 1993, none (of one) in 1994 and one (of one) in 1995; mentioning causes briefly, 28 (out of a total of 37) in 1992, nine (out of 21) in 1993, three (of four) in 1994 and three (of three) in 1995.

9 The *Mail* (7 April) also said that the Serbs 'were being blamed' but cited no sources to this effect apart from Izetbegovic.

Notes

10 The coincidence of the 'crusade' or 'holy war' idea appearing in the *Guardian*, *Independent* and *Times* within three days of each other suggests that it may have come from a shared source, although none was cited. Such similarities are evidence of the 'pack mentality' that critics have identified in Bosnia coverage. The most striking examples of this in our samples were in articles by the *Independent*'s Emma Daly and Stacy Sullivan of the *Times*, who offered very similar 'first-hand' accounts based on interviews with victims of the war. The same anecdote from a Sarajevan woman appeared in Daly's 22 November 1995 report as in Sullivan's report the following day; and on 27 November both journalists based stories around an interview with the same man.

11 The other two articles advancing this explanation were in the *Guardian* (23 April 1992) and the *Mail* (7 April 1992).

12 The remaining two articles advancing this combination of 'Western interference' and 'Serb–Croat carve-up' explanations were in the *Times* (5 and 24 April 1993).

13 This issue deserves more extensive treatment than can be attempted here, although we return to it in Chapter 5.

14 United Nations Convention on the Prevention and Punishment of the Crime of Genocide, 9 December 1948.

15 The equivalent Russian term (*etnicheskoye chishcheniye*) was used by the Soviets to describe Azeri assaults on Armenians in Nagorno-Karabakh in the 1980s (see for example Banks and Wolfe Murray 1999: 152). Here there is a linguistic similarity, but no direct relationship with its use in the former Yugoslavia.

16 US Federal News Service, State Department Briefing, 14 May 1992.

17 Kenney resigned in protest over the US government's failure to take a tougher stance on Bosnia, but later changed his mind and became an opponent of military intervention in the Balkans. All quotations from Kenney here are from personal correspondence.

18 The figures on US media were kindly obtained for me by David Peterson via a Lexis-Nexis database search.

19 One report in our 1992 sample did mention a 'violent clean-out' of Zvornik by the Serbs (*Independent*, 14 April) and another described the Yugoslav army as 'mopping up' in Visegrad while Serbian gunmen 'moved around the town … to ensure it had been "cleansed"' (*Guardian*, 16 April). A search of all incidences of the term 'clean' (and variants, such as cleansed) for our four chosen newspapers revealed seven similar uses of the term in 1991. Six of these referred to 'clean up' or 'clean out' operations, in all cases but one describing the actions of Croatian forces. The only instance in which 'cleansing' was linked to ethnicity was in a 9 July 1991 article by Tim Judah in the *Times*, which reported the fears of a Serb in Croatia: 'Zarko Cubrilo, aged 48, said that he had lost his job after 20 years as a building supervisor. He said that all the Croats in his company had kept their jobs. "Many of us have been sacked because they want an ethnically clean Croatia." Mr Cubrilo said that Croatia's ruling party wanted "either to conquer us and make us loyal citizens who will only be allowed to sweep the streets, or kick us out."'

20 The Bosnian Muslim government successfully obtained a decision from the International Court of Justice (also in April 1993) ordering Serbia to prevent 'acts of genocide' in Bosnia, and later threatened to take the British government to the same court for complying with Serbian genocide.

21 See notes 758–825 to this section of the report. Aside from news articles, other sources used here included books by journalists (Misha Glenny and Roy Gutman) and specialist publications such as Radio Free Europe/Radio Liberty research reports, as well as Western NGOs and US Congressional committees.

22 The totals for other periods were: 18 articles in 1992 (16.2 per cent of coverage for that period); 77 in 1993 (19.4 per cent); and 36 in 1995 (19.4 per cent).

23 Counting only those articles which mentioned a British angle in their headlines, this type of coverage accounted for 8.2 per cent of the total. Comparing different periods, adoption of a British news angle was most prominent in 1994 (13.1 per cent of coverage for that period); comparing different newspapers, it was most marked in the *Mail* (21.8 per cent of the paper's total coverage).

Notes to Chapter 4

1 Common estimates of the number of victims range from 500,000 to 1,000,000, and occasionally more. The figure of 800,000 is given by the UN International Criminal Tribunal for Rwanda (see the Tribunal's *Handbook for Journalists*, http://69.94.11.53/ENGLISH/handbook/index.htm). The estimate of deaths among Hutu opposition party supporters is from Mamdani (2001: 5).
2 See George Washington University's National Security Archive site, www.gwu.edu/~nsarchiv/NSAEBB/NSAEBB53/index.html.
3 Seth Sendashonga, the Hutu Interior Minister in the new government established by the RPF, said the RPF's victory was followed by a 'killing spree', which was halted only temporarily by its need to secure international aid. Sendashonga was sacked from the government in August 1995 and later assassinated because of his criticism of the regime (Terry 2002: 209).
4 Terry (2002: 210) notes that UN personnel physically counted 4,000 dead and 650 wounded before they were stopped by the RPF; the higher estimate of 8,000 was given by aid agencies at the time.
5 Table 4.1 gives the total numbers of relevant articles. A LexisNexis search was carried out using the term 'Rwanda' for all the periods listed and all articles were checked for relevance. Readers' letters and articles mentioning Rwanda only in passing were excluded.
6 The numbers given for explanatory articles refer only to those attempting to explain the mass killings of April–June 1994. Explanations of other events, such as the flight of refugees, are treated separately below.
7 The quantity of explanatory material in the different sample periods examined was as follows: April 1994, 21 articles (25.3 per cent of total coverage for that period), comprising eight in which the causes of violence were the major focus and 13 in which it was a minor focus; July 1994, 13 articles (9.4 per cent of coverage), comprising five in which the causes of violence were the major focus and eight in which it was a minor focus; April 1995, one article which took the causes of violence as its main focus and three in which it was a minor focus (6.6 per cent of coverage); November 1996, three articles (1.8 per cent of coverage), all of which took the causes of violence as their main focus.
8 The quantity of explanatory material in different newspapers was as follows: the *Guardian* carried 16 articles (9.9 per cent of its total coverage), of which five took the causes of violence as their major focus; the *Independent* carried 14 articles (10.4 per cent of its total coverage), eight of which were focused mainly on the causes of violence; the *Mail* carried five articles (23.8 per cent of the coverage examined), two of which focused mainly on causes; and the *Times* carried six (4.7 per cent of its total coverage), again with two focusing mainly on causes.
9 Of the 21 articles offering explanations in this period, 11 adopted the 'tribal' framework (52.4 per cent): five of eight articles focusing mainly on causes and six of 13 mentioning causes briefly.
10 The editorial praised Overseas Development Minister Linda Chalker, whose claim that

'These camps are full of Hutu extremists with weaponry' was also reported in the same day's edition of the *Times*, but not reported in other papers.

11 It might be thought that calling Zaire the 'heart of darkness' suggested itself simply because it was the setting for Conrad's novel. Yet the idea apparently suggested itself most forcefully to *Times* journalists. Although this 14 November article used the heart of darkness metaphor, the *Independent* also carried a commentary by Andrew Marshall, entitled 'Heart of Prejudice', which offered a critique of 'the attitudes that still blind us to the realities of Rwanda and Zaire' (20 November 1996).

12 Of 101 articles dealing with the refugee camps in November 1996, 40 offered an explanation of why the refugees had not returned to Rwanda, and 30 of these said that the refugees were being forced to stay by their leaders.

Notes to Chapter 5

1 For a summary of these initiatives see Defence Select Committee (2000: Annex B, 'Chronology').

2 'Moral Combat: Nato at War', *Panorama* television broadcast, BBC2, 12 March 2000. Transcript at http://news.bbc.co.uk/hi/english/static/events/panorama/transcripts/transcript_12_03_00.txt.

3 This and other similar German government documents are posted at: http://emperors-clothes.com/articles/german/Germany.html. Since these reports were issued in response to requests for asylum by Kosovo Albanians, their objectivity may be questionable. But the picture they reveal is borne out by KVM monitor Jacques Prod'homme, who is reported to have said that 'in the month leading up to the war, during which he moved freely throughout the Pec region, neither he nor his colleagues observed anything that could be described as systematic persecution, either collective or individual murders, burning of houses or deportations' (Rouleau 1999). Post-war assessments issued by the US State Department, the ICTY and the OSCE all corroborate Prod'homme's statement (Chomsky 2000c).

4 'Moral Combat: Nato at War', *Panorama* television broadcast, BBC2, 12 March 2000. Transcript at http://news.bbc.co.uk/hi/english/static/events/panorama/transcripts/transcript_12_03_00.txt.

5 *Ibid.*

6 *Ibid.*

7 Tom Walker and Aidan Laverty, 'CIA Aided Kosovo Guerrilla Army', *Sunday Times*, 12 March 2000. In addition, two private US military training companies, Dyncorps and Military Professional Resources Inc., which had earlier operated in Croatia and Bosnia, sent their personnel to Kosovo; and Johnstone (2002: 235) notes that from 1996 the German intelligence services also provided training and equipment to the KLA.

8 Vickers (1998: 225–6) notes that in the 1980s cash obtained from narcotics was used in an organised fashion to enable the purchase of land from Serbian families in Kosovo. The combined Serbian and Montenegrin population in the province declined from 27.4 per cent in 1961 to 8.6 per cent in 1991 (Vickers 1998: 318, 320).

9 BBC News, 25 and 26 March 1999.

10 John Goetz and Tom Walker, 'Serbian Ethnic Cleansing Scare Was a Fake, Says General', *Sunday Times*, 2 April 2000. The Germans based their claims on a Bulgarian intelligence report (which actually concluded that 'the goal of the Serbian military was to destroy the Kosovo Liberation Army, and not to expel the entire Albanian population'),

invented a codename for the alleged 'plan' (inadvertently using the Croatian variant of Serbo-Croat) and drew up fake maps in order to provide supporting documentation.

11 As Binder (2000) notes, this means that a greater proportion of Serbs and Montenegrins than ethnic-Albanians fled Kosovo during the bombing.

12 In addition, as KLA soldier Lirak Qelaj admitted, 'it was KLA advice, rather than Serbian deportations, which led some of the hundreds of thousands of Albanians to leave Kosovo' (Jonathan Steele, 'KLA Player Longs to Retire from World Stage', *Guardian*, 30 June 1999).

13 Robert Fisk, 'Taken in by the Nato Line', *Independent*, 29 June 1999.

14 'The Kosovo Cover-Up', *Newsweek*, 15 May 2000. See also Andrew Gilligan, 'RAF Admits Failings in Kosovo Inquiry', *Sunday Telegraph*, 25 July 1999.

15 This estimate is based on information from the UN Mission in Kosovo's Office of Missing Persons and Forensics, press release, 3 February 2003, www.unmikonline. org/press/2003/pressr/pr917.htm. Requests for more up-to-date figures met with no response and no more recent information appears on its website.

16 A LexisNexis search was carried out using the term 'Kosovo' for both periods and all articles were checked for relevance. Readers' letters and articles which mentioned Kosovo only in passing were excluded. However, in the case of the *Guardian*'s coverage during 17 March–14 April 1999, the database was found to be faulty. This was evident from both the uncharacteristically small quantity of coverage returned from the Lexis-Nexis search and by references in some articles to others which were missing from our sample but clearly relevant. The *Guardian* articles for this period were therefore taken from the ProQuest database instead, using the same procedure as for other searches.

17 The *Guardian* carried 65 explanatory articles (11.0 per cent of its total coverage), the *Times* carried 53 (9.2 per cent), the *Independent* 42 (6.6 per cent) and the *Mail* 26 (8.8 per cent). Four explanatory articles addressed both the conflict in Kosovo and the Nato intervention: to avoid double counting, these were included in the latter category of 'explanation'.

18 Briefing by the Foreign Secretary, Mr Robin Cook, and the Chief of the Defence Staff, General Sir Charles Guthrie, Ministry of Defence, London, 29 March 1999, www. kosovo.mod.uk/brief290399.htm.

19 Press conference of the Nato spokesman, Jamie Shea, and Air Commodore David Wilby, Nato HQ, 31 March 1999, www.nato.int/kosovo/press/p990331a.htm.

20 Speech by the Prime Minister, Tony Blair, to the Economic Club of Chicago, Hilton Hotel, Chicago, USA, 22 April 1999, www.globalpolicy.org/globaliz/politics/blair.htm.

21 *Ibid.*

22 Overall, the *Times* carried 36 editorials, the *Guardian* and *Independent* 25 each and the *Mail* 23.

23 The only British national newspaper which opposed intervention was the *Independent on Sunday*, which took a different editorial stance from its weekday equivalent.

24 The *Guardian*'s 98 articles made up 16.5 per cent of its coverage; the *Times* carried 65 critical articles (11.2 per cent of its total) and the *Independent* 76 articles (11.9 per cent).

Notes to Chapter 6

1 Tony Blair was reportedly advised by the British Attorney General that the sole legal justification for the war was self-defence and that he 'would be in breach of international law if he was to portray the attack as a retaliation or punishment' (*Guardian*, 4 October).

2 President George W. Bush, 'Address to a Joint Session of Congress and the American People', 20 September 2001, www.whitehouse.gov/news/releases/2001/09/20010920-8.html.

3 'International Campaign Against Terror Grows', Remarks by President Bush and Prime Minister Koizumi of Japan, 25 September 2001, www.whitehouse.gov/news/releases/20 01/09/20010925-1.html.

4 President George W. Bush, 'Address to a Joint Session of Congress and the American People', 20 September 2001, www.whitehouse.gov/news/releases/2001/09/20010920-8.html.

5 Tony Blair, speech to the Labour Party conference, October 2001, available at http:// politics.guardian.co.uk/labourconference2001/story/0,1220,561985,00.html.

6 See Solomon's *Media Beat* columns of 12 October ('Killing Them Softly: Starvation and Dollar Bills For Afghan Kids', www.fair.org/media-beat/011012.html) and 25 October 2001 ('War Needs Good Public Relations', www.fair.org/media-beat/011025.html). For a critical assessment of the claimed 'humanitarian' dimension of the war, see Mahajan (2002: 33–43).

7 BBC, 'War in Afghanistan: Editorial Policy Guidelines', 25 September 2001, www.bbc. co.uk/guidelines/editorialguidelines/assets/meetings/war_guidelines_october02.doc.

8 A third possibility would have been to take both sample periods and examine how the story changed over a longer time-span. This option was considered, but the large quantity of coverage and the limited time-frame for completing the study made it impossible.

9 A LexisNexis search was carried out using the term 'Afghanistan' for both periods and all articles were checked for relevance. Readers' letters and articles which mentioned Afghanistan only in passing were excluded, although, as discussed below, an exception was made in the case of the *Guardian*, allowing more articles than usual to pass the test of relevance.

10 The *Times* also used the strap-line 'War on Terror', but this was not included in its electronic archives on LexisNexis or ProQuest and so could not be counted.

11 The paper's use of strap-lines was checked on microfilm copies at the British Library.

12 The only instance of the term 'revenge' being used in the context of support for the war was a report that a US government advisor had told members of Congress to 'remember that revenge is better eaten cold' (*Guardian*, 8 October).

13 This was from the introduction to a long feature debating the question 'Can Islam liberate women?', which took a sympathetic view of Islam, with articles based on interviews with Muslim women and a commentary by Egyptian novelist Ahdaf Soueif (*Guardian*, 8 December). In our samples, two articles highlighted human rights abuses in Afghanistan in the context of an explicitly anti-war argument: a *Guardian* interview with the Revolutionary Association of the Women of Afghanistan (8 October); and an anti-war commentary by *Independent* columnist Natasha Walter, who argued that: 'In this war, if we look dispassionately at the situation of women, we can clearly understand that military attacks are not going to eradicate the problems of the region' (10 October).

14 The *Independent* carried 109 critical articles (16.1 per cent of its total coverage), the *Times* carried 80 (11.1 per cent) and the *Mail* 41 (13.8 per cent). Most criticism appeared during October (288 articles, as against 84 in December), when, despite the greater quantity of total coverage, it also accounted for a higher proportion (14.8 per cent, compared with 12.6 per cent in December).

15 As compared with 15 such articles in the *Independent*, seven in the *Times* and three in the *Mail*.

16 The *Independent* carried 11 articles making this point, the *Mail* eight and the *Times* and *Guardian* seven each.

Notes to Chapter 7

1 Data presented by Lucas Robinson and Steven Livingston (2006: 28) indicate that US media interest in this story peaked during September 2002. President Bush and Vice-President Dick Cheney persisted in making such allegations even after the official report of the National Commission on Terrorist Attacks Upon the United States concluded that there was no evidence of such a link. See Walter Pincus and Dana Milbank, 'Al Qaeda-Hussein Link Is Dismissed', *Washington Post*, 17 June 2004, and Dana Milbank, 'Bush Defends Assertions of Iraq–Al Qaeda Relationship', *Washington Post*, 18 June 2004.

2 The two dossiers are available online: 'A Decade of Deception and Defiance', 12 September 2002, www.whitehouse.gov/news/releases/2002/09/20020912.html; 'Iraq's Weapons of Mass Destruction: The Assessment of the British Government', 24 September 2002, www.number10.gov.uk/output/Page271.asp.

3 Deputy Secretary Wolfowitz interview with Sam Tannenhaus, *Vanity Fair*, 9 May 2003, www.defenselink.mil/transcripts/2003/tr20030509-depsecdef0223.html.

4 'Iraq: Its Infrastructure of Concealment, Deception and Intimidation', 3 February 2003, www.number-10.gov.uk/output/page1470.asp; 'US Secretary of State Colin Powell Addresses the UN Security Council', 5 February 2003, www.whitehouse.gov/news/releases/2003/02/20030205-1.html.

5 Speech by The Rt. Hon. Charles Kennedy MP, Leader of the Liberal Democrats, Hyde Park, 15 February 2003, www.libdems.org.uk/news/story.html?id=4205&navPage=news.html.

6 The full text of Cook's resignation speech, 17 March 2003, is available at http://news.bbc.co.uk/go/pr/fr/-/2/hi/uk_news/politics/2859431.stm.

7 Rangwala first aired his analysis of the dossier in a post to the Campaign Against Sanctions on Iraq email discussion list (www.casi.org.uk/discuss/2003/msg00457.html). It was subsequently picked up by Channel 4 News and other media outlets.

8 See Rangwala's work at http://middleeastreference.org.uk/iraqncbfurther.html.

9 'President Discusses Future of Iraq', 26 February 2003, www.whitehouse.gov/news/releases/2003/02/20030226-11.html. The British government also issued a less controversial dossier in December 2002 entitled 'Saddam Hussein: Crimes and Human Rights Abuses', available at http://iraqfoundation.org/hr/2002/cdec/irdp.pdf.

10 A LexisNexis search was carried out using the term 'Iraq' for the dates selected and all articles were checked for relevance. Readers' letters and articles which mentioned Iraq only in passing were excluded.

11 There were 58 explanatory articles in our first sample, 190 in the second and five in the third. Explanatory articles made up 4.8 per cent of coverage during the invasion.

12 The *Mail* carried 49 explanatory articles, the *Times* 56, the *Guardian* 77 and the *Independent* 71.

References

Ackerman, Seth and Jim Naureckas (2000) 'Following Washington's Script: The United States Media and Kosovo', in Philip Hammond and Edward S. Herman (eds), *Degraded Capability: The Media and the Kosovo Crisis*. London: Pluto Press, pp. 97–110.

African Rights (1993a) *Operation Restore Hope: A Preliminary Assessment*. London: African Rights.

—— (1993b) *Human Rights Abuses by the United Nations Forces*. London: African Rights.

—— (1995) *Rwanda: Death, Despair and Defiance* (revised edition). London: African Rights.

Ahmed, Akbar S. (1995) '"Ethnic Cleansing": A Metaphor for our Time?', *Ethnic and Racial Studies*, 18(1), pp. 1–25.

Ali, Tariq (2002) *The Clash of Fundamentalisms*. London: Verso.

Allard, Kenneth (1995) *Somalia Operations: Lessons Learned*. Washington, DC: Institute for National Strategic Studies/National Defense University Press, www.au.af.mil/au/awc/awcgate/ndu/allard_somalia/allardcont.html.

Allen, Tim (1999) 'Perceiving Contemporary Wars', in Tim Allen and Jean Seaton (eds), *The Media of Conflict*. London: Zed Books, pp. 11–42.

Allen, Tim and Jean Seaton (1999) 'Introduction', in Tim Allen and Jean Seaton (eds), *The Media of Conflict*. London: Zed Books, pp. 1–7.

Amnesty International (2004) News Release: 'Annual Report 2004: War on Global Values', 26 May, http://news.amnesty.org/index/ENGPOL100162004.

Arnove, Anthony (2000) 'Introduction', in Anthony Arnove (ed.), *Iraq Under Siege*. London: Pluto Press, pp. 9–20.

Article 19 (1996) *Broadcasting Genocide*. London: Article 19.

Baker, James A., with Thomas M. DeFrank (1995) *The Politics of Diplomacy: Revolution, War and Peace, 1989–1992*. New York: G. P. Putnam's Sons.

Banks, Marcus and Monica Wolfe Murray (1999) 'Ethnicity and Reports of the 1992–95 Bosnian Conflict', in Tim Allen and Jean Seaton (eds), *The Media of Conflict*. London: Zed Books, pp. 147–61.

Bantimaroudis, Philemon and Hyun Ban (2001) 'Covering the Crisis in Somalia: Framing Choices by *The New York Times* and *The Manchester Guardian*', in Stephen D. Reese, Oscar H. Gandy and August E. Grant (eds), *Framing Public Life*. London: Lawrence Earlbaum, pp. 175–84.

Beattie, Liza, David Miller, Emma Miller and Greg Philo (1999) 'The Media and Africa: Images of Disaster and Rebellion', in Greg Philo (ed.), *Message Received*. Harlow: Longman, pp. 229–67.

Bell, Martin (1996) *In Harm's Way* (revised edition). Harmondsworth: Penguin.

—— (1998) 'The Journalism of Attachment', in Matthew Kieran (ed.), *Media Ethics*. London: Routledge, pp. 15–22.

Bell-Fialkoff, Andrew (1993) 'A Brief History of Ethnic Cleansing', *Foreign Affairs*, 72(3), pp. 110–21.

—— (1999) *Ethnic Cleansing*. New York: St Martin's Griffin.

Binder, David (1994–95) 'Anatomy of a Massacre', *Foreign Policy*, No. 97, Winter, pp. 70–8.

—— (2000) 'The Ironic Justice of Kosovo', *MSNBC News*, 17 March, available at www.agit-prop.org.au/stopnato/20000319balkamsnus.htm.

Bishop, Ronald (2006) 'The Whole World Is Watching, But So What? A Frame Analysis of Newspaper Coverage of Antiwar Protest', in Alexander G. Nikolaev and Ernest A. Hakanen (eds), *Leading to the 2003 Iraq War*. New York: Palgrave, pp. 39–63.

Bogdanich, George and Martin Lettmayer (2000) *Yugoslavia: The Avoidable War* (documentary film). New York: Frontier Theatre and Film.

Brock, Peter (1993–94) 'Dateline Yugoslavia: The Partisan Press', *Foreign Policy*, No. 93, pp. 152–72.

—— (1995) '"Greater Serbia" vs. the Greater Western Media', *Mediterranean Quarterly*, winter, pp. 49–68.

—— (2005) *Media Cleansing: Dirty Reporting*. Los Angeles, CA: GM Books.

Brown, Robin (2003a) 'Spinning the War: Political Communications, Information Operations and Public Diplomacy in the War on Terrorism', in Daya Kishan Thussu and Des Freedman (eds), *War and the Media*. London: Sage, pp. 87–100.

—— (2003b) 'Clausewitz in the Age of CNN: Rethinking the Military–Media Relationship', in Pippa Norris, Montague Kern and Marion Just (eds), *Framing Terrorism*. London: Routledge, pp. 43–58.

Callahan, David (1997) *Unwinnable Wars: American Power and Ethnic Conflict*. New York: Hill and Wang.

Callamard, Agnes (2000) 'French Policy in Rwanda', in Howard Adelman and Astri Suhrke (eds), *The Path of a Genocide*. New Brunswick, NJ: Transaction Publishers, pp. 157–83.

Campbell, Alastair (1999) 'Kosovo: Communications Lessons for NATO, the Military and the Media', speech at the Royal United Services Institute, London, 9 July.

Carruthers, Susan L. (2000) *The Media at War*. Basingstoke: Macmillan.

Chandler, David (2000a) 'Western Intervention and the Disintegration of Yugoslavia, 1989–1999', in Philip Hammond and Edward S. Herman (eds), *Degraded Capability: The Media and the Kosovo Crisis*. London: Pluto Press, pp. 19–30.

—— (2000b) *Bosnia: Faking Democracy After Dayton* (second edition). London: Pluto Press.

—— (2002) *From Kosovo to Kabul: Human Rights and International Intervention*. London: Pluto Press.

—— (2004) *Constructing Global Civil Society: Morality and Power in International Relations*. Basingstoke: Palgrave.

Chomsky, Noam (1990) 'The Real Cold War's Not Over', *Living Marxism*, No. 18, April, pp. 6–9.

—— (1999) *The New Military Humanism: Lessons from Kosovo*. Monroe, ME: Common Courage Press.

—— (2000a) *A New Generation Draws the Line: Kosovo, East Timor and the Standards of the West*. London: Verso.

—— (2000b) *Rogue States: The Rule of Force in World Affairs*. London: Pluto Press.

—— (2000c) 'In Retrospect', *Z Magazine*, April/May 2000, www.zmag.org/ZMag/articles/chomskyapril2000.htm.

References

Cigar, Norman (1995) *Genocide in Bosnia*. College Station, TX: Texas A&M University Press.

Clarke, Walter and Jeffrey Herbst (1996) 'Somalia and the Future of Humanitarian Intervention', *Foreign Affairs*, 75(2), www.mtholyoke.edu/~jwestern/ir317/clark.htm.

Cohen, Roger (1999) 'Ethnic Cleansing', in Roy Gutman and David Rieff (eds), *Crimes of War*. London: W. W. Norton and Company, pp. 136–8.

Coleman, Mary (1993) 'Human Sacrifice in Bosnia', *Journal of Psychohistory*, 21(2), pp. 157–69.

Collins, Barrie (1998) *Obedience in Rwanda: A Critical Question*. Sheffield: Sheffield Hallam University Press.

—— (2002) 'New Wars and Old Wars? The Lessons of Rwanda', in David Chandler (ed.), *Rethinking Human Rights*. Basingstoke: Palgrave Macmillan, pp. 157–75.

Cooley, John K. (2000) *Unholy Wars: Afghanistan, America and International Terrorism* (second edition). London: Pluto Press.

Cooper, Robert (2004) *The Breaking of Nations* (revised edition). London: Atlantic Books.

Couldry, Nick and John Downey (2004) 'War or Peace: Legitimation, Dissent and Rhetorical Closure in Press Coverage of the Iraq War Build-Up', in Stuart Allan and Barbie Zelizer (eds), *Reporting War*. London: Routledge, pp. 266–82.

Crocker, Chester A. (1995) 'The Lessons of Somalia – Not Everything Went Wrong', *Foreign Affairs*, 74(3), www.pbs.org/wgbh/pages/frontline/shows/ambush/readings/lessons.html.

Curtis, Mark (1998) *The Great Deception*. London: Pluto Press.

—— (2004) 'Psychological Warfare Against the Public: Iraq and Beyond', in David Miller (ed.), *Tell Me Lies*. London: Pluto Press, pp. 70–9.

Cushman, Thomas and Stjepan G. Mestrovic (eds) (1996) *This Time We Knew*. New York: New York University Press.

de Waal, Alex (1997) *Famine Crimes*. London: African Rights.

—— (1998) 'US War Crimes in Somalia', *New Left Review*, No. 230, pp. 131–44.

Defence Select Committee (2000) *Fourteenth Report*, www.parliament.the-stationery-office. co.uk/pa/cm199900/cmselect/cmdfence/347/34702.htm.

Destexhe, Alain (1995) *Rwanda and Genocide in the Twentieth Century*. London: Pluto Press.

Dorman, William A. and Steven Livingston (1994) 'News and Historical Content', in W. Lance Bennett and David L. Paletz (eds), *Taken by Storm*. Chicago: Chicago University Press, pp. 63–81.

Dowden, Richard (1995a) 'Covering Somalia – Recipe for Disaster', in Edward Giradet (ed.), *Somalia, Rwanda and Beyond*. Dublin: Crosslines Global Report, pp. 91–7.

—— (1995b) 'Media Coverage: How I Reported the Genocide', in Obi Igwara (ed.), *Ethnic Hatred*. London: ASEN Publications, pp. 85–92.

Edwards, David and David Cromwell (2004) 'Mass Deception: How the Media Helped the Government Deceive the People', in David Miller (ed.), *Tell Me Lies*. London: Pluto Press, pp. 210–14.

Entman, Robert M. (1993) 'Framing: Towards Clarification of a Fractured Paradigm', *Journal of Communication*, 43(4), pp. 51–8.

Foreign Affairs Select Committee (2000) *Fourth Report*, www.publications.parliament. uk/pa/cm199900/cmselect/cmfaff/28/2802.htm.

Fox, Fiona (2000) 'The Politicisation of Humanitarian Aid'. Unpublished discussion paper for Caritas Europa.

—— (2002) 'Conditioning the Right to Humanitarian Aid? Human Rights and the "New Humanitarianism"', in David Chandler (ed.), *Rethinking Human Rights*. Basingstoke: Palgrave, pp. 19–37.

Freedman, Des (2003) 'The *Daily Mirror* and the War on Iraq', *Mediactive*, No. 3, pp. 95–108.

Gil-White, Francisco (2002) 'How the Media and Scholars Write about Slobodan Milosevic', *Emperor's Clothes*, 9 February (accessed electronically).

Giradet, Edward (ed.) (1995) *Somalia, Rwanda and Beyond*. Dublin: Crosslines Global Report.

Glenny, Misha (1996) *The Fall of Yugoslavia* (third edition). London: Penguin.

Gordon, Michael, Carol Morello, Lois Raimondo, Tom Squitieri and Kevin Whitelaw (2003) 'Afghanistan', in Stephen Hess and Marvin Kalb (eds), *The Media and the War on Terrorism*. Washington, DC: Brookings Institution, pp. 163–82.

Gourevitch, Philip (2000) *We Wish To Inform You That Tomorrow We Will Be Killed With Our Families*. London: Picador.

Gowan, Peter (2000) 'The War and its Aftermath', in Philip Hammond and Edward S. Herman (eds), *Degraded Capability: The Media and the Kosovo Crisis*. London: Pluto Press, pp. 39–55.

Gowing, Nik (1994) 'Real-Time Television Coverage of Armed Conflicts and Diplomatic Crises: Does It Pressure or Distort Foreign Policy Decisions?' (Working Paper 94-1). Cambridge, MA: Shorenstein Barone Center, Harvard University.

——(1996) 'Real-Time TV Coverage from War', in James Gow, Richard Paterson and Alison Preston (eds), *Bosnia by Television*. London: British Film Institute, pp. 81–91.

—— (1997) 'Media Coverage: Help or Hindrance in Conflict Prevention?' (Report to the Carnegie Commission on Preventing Deadly Conflict). New York: Carnegie Corporation.

—— (1998) 'New Challenges and Problems for Information Management in Complex Emergencies', paper presented to the 'Dispatches from Disaster Zones' conference, London, 27–28 May, www.usip.org/events/pre2002/gowing.pdf.

—— (2003) 'Journalists and War: The Troubling New Tensions Post 9/11', in Daya Kishan Thussu and Des Freedman (eds), *War and the Media*. London: Sage, pp. 231–40.

Griffin, Michael (2004) 'Picturing America's "War on Terrorism" in Afghanistan and Iraq: Photographic Motifs as News Frames', *Journalism*, 5(4), pp. 381–402.

Halvorsen, Kate (2000) 'Protection and Humanitarian Assistance in the Refugee Camps in Zaire: The Problem of Security', in Howard Adelman and Astri Suhrke (eds), *The Path of a Genocide*. New Brunswick, NJ: Transaction Publishers, pp. 307–20.

Hammond, Philip (2004) '"Humanitaere Intervention" und "Krieg gegen den Terror": Das Verhalten der Medien vom Kosov vis zum Irak', in Martin Loeffelholz (ed.), *Krieg als Medienereignis II*. Wiesbaden: VS Verlag für Sozialwissenschaften, pp. 99–117.

Hansen, Lene (1998) 'Western Villains or Balkan Barbarism?' PhD dissertation, University of Copenhagen.

Hartmann, Florence (1999) 'Bosnia', in Roy Gutman and David Rieff (eds), *Crimes of War*. London: W. W. Norton and Company, pp. 50–6.

Heuer, Uwe-Jens and Gregor Schirmer (1998) 'Human Rights Imperialism', *Monthly Review*, 49(10), www.monthlyreview.org/398heuer.htm.

Hudson, Kate (2003) *Breaking the South Slav Dream*. London: Pluto Press.

Hudson, Miles and John Stanier (1997) *War and the Media*. Stroud: Sutton.

Human Rights Watch (1999) *Leave None to Tell the Story*. New York: Human Rights Watch, www.hrw.org/reports/1999/rwanda/.

Hume, Mick (1997) *Whose War is it Anyway?* London: Informinc.

—— (2000) 'Nazifying the Serbs, from Bosnia to Kosovo', in Philip Hammond and Edward S. Herman (eds), *Degraded Capability: The Media and the Kosovo Crisis*. London: Pluto Press, pp. 70–8.

References

Huntington, Samuel P. (1993) 'The Clash of Civilizations?', *Foreign Affairs*, 72(3), summer, pp. 22–48.

ICISS (International Commission on Intervention and State Sovereignty) (2001) *The Responsibility to Protect*. Ottawa: International Development Research Centre.

Ignatieff, Michael (1998) *The Warrior's Honor: Ethnic War and the Modern Conscience*. London: Chatto and Windus.

—— (2000) *Virtual War: Kosovo and Beyond*. New York: Metropolitan Books.

IICK (Independent International Commission on Kosovo) (2000) *The Kosovo Report*. Oxford: Oxford University Press.

IISS (International Institute for Strategic Studies) (1999) *The Military Balance, 1999/2000*. Oxford: Oxford University Press.

Iyengar, Shanto and Adam Simon (1994) 'News Coverage of the Gulf Crisis and Public Opinion', in W. Lance Bennett and David L. Paletz (eds), *Taken by Storm*. Chicago: Chicago University Press, pp. 167–85.

JEEAR (Joint Evaluation of Emergency Assistance to Rwanda) (1996) 'The International Response to Conflict and Genocide; Lessons from the Rwanda Experience', www.reliefweb.int/library/nordic/.

Johnstone, Diana (2000) 'Humanitarian War: Making the Crime Fit the Punishment', in Tariq Ali (ed.), *Masters of the Universe?* London: Verso, pp. 147–70.

—— (2002) *Fools' Crusade*. London: Pluto Press.

Judah, Tim (2000) *Kosovo: War and Revenge*. New Haven, CT: Yale University Press.

Kagan, Robert (2004) *Paradise and Power* (revised edition). London: Atlantic Books.

Kaldor, Mary (1999) *New and Old Wars*. Cambridge: Polity.

Kampfner, John (2003) *Blair's Wars*. London: Free Press.

Kaplan, Robert D. (1993) *Balkan Ghosts. A Journey Through History*. New York: St Martin's Press.

—— (1994) 'The Coming Anarchy', *Atlantic Monthly*, 273(2), www.theatlantic.com/politics/foreign/anarchy.htm.

Karim, Karim H. (2002) 'Making Sense of the "Islamic Peril"', in Barbie Zelizer and Stuart Allan (eds), *Journalism After September 11*. London: Routledge, pp. 101–16.

Keane, Fergal (1995) *Season of Blood*. Harmondsworth: Viking.

Keeble, Richard (1997) *Secret State, Silent Press*. Luton: John Libbey.

Keegan, John (1993) *A History of Warfare*. London: Pimlico.

Keen, David (1999) '"Who's It Between?" "Ethnic War" and Rational Violence', in Tim Allen and Jean Seaton (eds), *The Media of Conflict*. London: Zed Books, pp. 81–101.

Kellow, Christine L. and H. Leslie Steeves (1998) 'The Role of Radio in the Rwandan Genocide', *Journal of Communication*, 48(3), pp. 107–28.

Kenney, George (1999) 'Rolling Thunder: The Rerun', *The Nation*, 14 June, www.thenation.com/doc/19990614/kenney.

Kern, Montague, Marion Just and Pippa Norris (2003) 'The Lessons of Framing Terrorism', in Pippa Norris, Montague Kern and Marion Just (eds), *Framing Terrorism*. London: Routledge, pp. 281–302.

Klare, Michael (2005) *Blood and Oil*. London: Penguin.

Knaus, Gerald and Felix Martin (2003) 'Lessons from Bosnia and Herzegovina: Travails of the European Raj', *Journal of Democracy*, 14(3), www.journalofdemocracy.org/articles/gratis/KnausandMartin.pdf.

Knightley, Phillip (2001) 'Tell Them Nothing Till It's Over And Then Tell Them Who Won', Center for Public Integrity, 31 October, www.public-i.org/report.aspx?aid=285.

Lewis, Ioan and James Mayall (1996) 'Somalia', in James Mayall (ed.), *The New Interventionism, 1991–1994*. Cambridge: Cambridge University Press, pp. 94–124.

Lewis, Justin and Rod Brookes (2004) 'Reporting the War on British Television', in David Miller (ed.), *Tell Me Lies*. London: Pluto Press, pp. 132–43.

Little, Allan (2001) 'The West Did Not Do Enough', BBC Online, 29 June, http://news.bbc.co.uk/hi/english/world/from_our_own_correspondent/newsid_1413000/1413764.stm.

Littman, Mark (2000) *Neither Legal Nor Moral: How NATO's War Against Yugoslavia Breached International Law*. London: Committee for Peace in the Balkans.

Livingston, Steven (1997) 'Clarifying the CNN Effect' (Research Paper R-18). Cambridge, MA: Joan Shorenstein Center on the Press, Politics and Public Policy, Harvard University, http://ksgwww.harvard.edu/shorenstein/research_publications/papers/research_papers/R18.pdf.

Livingston, Steven and Todd Eachus (1995) 'Humanitarian Crises and US Foreign Policy: Somalia and the CNN Effect Reconsidered', *Political Communication*, 12(4), pp. 413–29.

—— and —— (2000) 'Rwanda: US Policy and Television Coverage', in Howard Adelman and Astri Suhrke (eds), *The Path of a Genocide*. New Brunswick, NJ: Transaction Publishers, pp. 209–28.

Madsen, Wayne (1999) *Genocide and Covert Operations in Africa, 1993–1999* (African Studies Vol. 50). Lewiston, NY: Edwin Mellen Press.

Mahajan, Rahul (2002) *The New Crusade: America's War on Terrorism*. New York: Monthly Review Press.

Malcolm, Noel (1996) *Bosnia: A Short History* (revised edition). London: Macmillan.

Mamdani, Mahmood (2001) *When Victims Become Killers*. Princeton, NJ: Princeton University Press.

Mann, Michael (2005) *The Dark Side of Democracy*. Cambridge: Cambridge University Press.

Maren, Michael (1997) *The Road to Hell*. New York: Free Press.

McChesney, Robert W. (2002) 'September 11 and the Structural Limitations of US Journalism', in Barbie Zelizer and Stuart Allan (eds), *Journalism After September 11*. London: Routledge, pp. 91–100.

McLaughlin, Greg (2002) *The War Correspondent*. London: Pluto Press.

McNulty, Mel (1999) 'Media Ethnicization and the International Response to War and Genocide in Rwanda', in Tim Allen and Jean Seaton (eds), *The Media of Conflict*. London: Zed Books, pp. 268–86.

Melvern, Linda (2000) *A People Betrayed: The Role of the West in Rwanda's Genocide*. London: Zed Books.

Mermin, Jonathan (1999) *Debating War and Peace*. Princeton, NJ: Princeton University Press.

Mestrovic, Stjepan G. (1995) 'Postemotional Politics in the Balkans', *Society*, 32(2), pp. 69–77.

Miller, David (ed.) (2004) *Tell Me Lies*. London: Pluto Press.

Minear, Larry, Colin Scott and Thomas G. Weiss (1996) *The News Media, Civil War and Humanitarian Action*. Boulder, CO: Lynne Rienner.

Moeller, Susan D. (2004) 'A Moral Imagination: The Media's Response to the War on Terrorism', in Stuart Allan and Barbie Zelizer (eds), *Reporting War*. Abingdon: Routledge, pp. 59–76.

Mugabe, Jean-Pierre (2000) 'Declaration on the Shooting Down of the Aircraft Carrying Rwandan President Juvenal Habyarimina and Burundi President Cyprien Ntaryamira on April 6, 1994', International Strategic Studies Association, 21 April, www.globalresearch.ca/articles/MUG109A.html.

Musabyimana, Tatien (1995) 'Massacres in Rwanda: Ethnic Crisis or Political Crisis?', in Obi Igwara (ed.), *Ethnic Hatred*. London: ASEN Publications, pp. 93–7.

References

Myers, Garth, Thomas Klak and Timothy Koehl (1996) 'The Inscription of Difference: News Coverage of the Conflicts in Rwanda and Bosnia', *Political Geography*, 15(1), pp. 21–46.

Nacos, Brigitte L. and Oscar Torres-Reyna (2003) 'Framing Muslim-Americans Before and After 9/11', in Pippa Norris, Montague Kern and Marion Just (eds), *Framing Terrorism*. London: Routledge, pp. 133–57.

Neuman, Johanna (1996) *Lights, Camera, War*. New York: St Martin's Press.

Norris, Pippa, Montague Kern and Marion Just (2003) 'Framing Terrorism', in Pippa Norris, Montague Kern and Marion Just (eds), *Framing Terrorism*. London: Routledge.

O'Neill, Brendan (2002) 'Blair's Dodgy Dossier', *Spiked*, 24 September, www.spiked-online. co.uk/Articles/00000006DA63.htm.

Ottosen, Rune (1999) '"Rambo" in Somalia? A Critical Look at Media Coverage of Operation Restore Hope', in Kaarle Nordenstreng and Michael Griffin (eds), *International Media Monitoring*. Cresskill, NJ: Hampton Press, pp. 163–96.

Parenti, Michael (2000) *To Kill a Nation*. London: Verso.

Pellett, Peter L. (2000) 'Sanctions, Food, Nutrition, and Health in Iraq', in Anthony Arnove (ed.), *Iraq Under Siege*. London: Pluto Press, pp. 151–68.

Peterson, Scott (2000) *Me Against My Brother*. London: Routledge.

Petrovic, Drazen (1994) 'Ethnic Cleansing – An Attempt at Methodology', *European Journal of International Law*, 5(3), pp. 342–59.

Philo, Greg, Lindsey Hilsum, Liza Beattie and Rick Holliman (1999) 'The Media and the Rwanda Crisis: Effects on Audiences and Public Policy', in Greg Philo (ed.), *Message Received*. Harlow: Longman, pp. 213–28.

Pilger, John (1993) 'The West Is Guilty in Bosnia', *New Statesman and Society*, 7 May, pp. 14–15.

—— (1999) *Hidden Agendas*. London: Vintage.

—— (2001) 'There Is No War on Terrorism', *New Statesman*, 29 October, www.zmag.org/pilgernowar.htm.

—— (2004) 'Crime Against Humanity', in David Miller (ed.), *Tell Me Lies*. London: Pluto Press, pp. 29–33.

Pottier, Johan (1995) 'Representations of Ethnicity in Post-genocide Writings on Rwanda', in Obi Igwara (ed.), *Ethnic Hatred*. London: ASEN Publications, pp. 35–57.

Power, Samantha (2001) 'Bystanders to Genocide', *Atlantic Monthly*, September, www.bard.edu/hrp/resource_pdfs/power.bystanders.pdf.

—— (2004) 'Reporting Atrocity: War, Neutrality, and the Danger of Taking Sides', *Press/Politics*, 9(3), pp. 3–11.

Preston, Alison (1996) 'Television News and the Bosnian Conflict: Distance, Proximity, Impact', in James Gow, Richard Paterson and Alison Preston (eds), *Bosnia by Television*. London: British Film Institute, pp. 112–16.

Prunier, Gerard (1995) *The Rwanda Crisis 1959–1994: History of a Genocide*. London: Hurst and Co.

—— (2000) 'Operation Turquoise: A Humanitarian Escape from a Political Dead End', in Howard Adelman and Astri Suhrke (eds), *The Path of a Genocide*. New Brunswick, NJ: Transaction Publishers, pp. 281–305.

Rampton, Sheldon and John Stauber (2003) *Weapons of Mass Deception*. London: Robinson.

Rashid, Ahmed (2001) *Taliban*. London: Pan Macmillan.

Reese, Stephen D. (2004) 'Militarised Journalism: Framing Dissent in the Persian Gulf Wars', in Stuart Allan and Barbie Zelizer (eds), *Reporting War*. London: Routledge, pp. 247–65.

Refugees International (1997) *The Lost Refugees: Herded and Hunted in Eastern Zaire*. Washington, DC: Refugees International.

Rendall, Steve and Tara Broughel (2003) 'Amplifying Officials, Squelching Dissent', *Extra!*, May/June, www.fair.org/index.php?page=1145.

Ricchiardi, Sherry (1996) 'Over the Line?', *American Journalism Review*, September (accessed electronically).

Rieff, David (1995) *Slaughterhouse: Bosnia and the Failure of the West*. London: Vintage.

—— (1999) 'A New Age of Liberal Imperialism?', *World Policy Journal*, 16(2), www.world-policy.org/journal/rieff2.html.

—— (2002) *A Bed for the Night*. London: Vintage.

Ritter, Scott and William Rivers Pitt (2002) *War on Iraq*. London: Profile Books.

Robertson, Geoffrey (1999) *Crimes Against Humanity*. London: Penguin.

Robertson, George (2000) 'Law, Morality and the Use of Force', 16 May, www.nato.int/docu/speech/2000/s000516a.htm.

Robinson, Piers (2002) *The CNN Effect*. London: Routledge.

Robinson, W. Lucas and Steven Livingston (2006) 'Strange Bedfellows: The Emergence of the Al Qaeda–Baathist News Frame Prior to the 2003 Invasion of Iraq', in Alexander G. Nikolaev and Ernest A. Hakanen (eds), *Leading to the 2003 Iraq War*. New York: Palgrave, pp. 23–37.

Rotberg, Robert I. and Thomas G. Weiss (eds) (1996) *From Massacres to Genocide*. Washington, DC: Brookings Institution.

Rouleau, Eric (1999) 'French Diplomacy Adrift in Kosovo', *Le Monde diplomatique*, December (accessed electronically).

Rowell, Andy (2004) 'No Blood for Oil?', in David Miller (ed.), *Tell Me Lies*. London: Pluto Press, pp. 115–25.

Sadkovich, James J. (1998) *The US Media and Yugoslavia, 1991–1995*. Westport, CT: Praeger.

Shaw, Martin (1996) *Civil Society and Media in Global Crises*. London: Pinter.

—— (2005) *The New Western Way of War*. Cambridge: Polity.

Shawcross, William (2000) *Deliver Us From Evil*. London: Bloomsbury.

Silber, Laura and Allan Little (1996) *The Death of Yugoslavia* (revised edition). London: Penguin/BBC Books.

Simpson, John (1998) *Strange Places, Questionable People*. London: Macmillan.

SIPRI (Stockholm International Peace Research Institute) (1992) *SIPRI Yearbook, 1992*. Oxford: Oxford University Press.

—— (2000) *SIPRI Yearbook, 2000*. Oxford: Oxford University Press.

—— (2001) *SIPRI Yearbook, 2001*. Oxford: Oxford University Press.

Sirota, David and Christy Harvey (2004) 'They Knew...', *In These Times*, 3 August, www.inthesetimes.com/site/main/article/899/.

Skoco, Mirjana and William Woodger (2000) 'War Crimes', in Philip Hammond and Edward S. Herman (eds), *Degraded Capability: The Media and the Kosovo Crisis*. London: Pluto Press, pp. 31–8.

Skopljanac Brunner, Nena, Stjepan Gredelj, Alija Hodzic and Branimir Kristofic (eds) (2000) *Media and War*. Zagreb and Belgrade: Centre for Transition and Civil Society Research/Agency Argument.

Solomon, Norman and Reese Erlich (2003) *Target Iraq*. New York: Context Books.

Strobel, Warren P. (1997) *Late-Breaking Foreign Policy*. Washington, DC: United States Institute of Peace Press.

Taylor, Philip (2003) *Munitions of the Mind* (third edition). Manchester: Manchester University Press.

References

Terry, Fiona (2002) *Condemned to Repeat? The Paradox of Humanitarian Action*. Ithaca, NY: Cornell University Press.

Thomas, Raju G. C. (2003a) 'Prologue: Making War, Peace and History', in Raju G. C. Thomas (ed.), *Yugoslavia Unraveled*. Lanham: Lexington Books, pp. vii–xx.

—— (2003b) 'Sovereignty, Self-determination, and Secession: Principles and Practice', in Raju G. C. Thomas (ed.), *Yugoslavia Unraveled*. Lanham, MD: Lexington Books, pp. 3–39.

Thompson, Mark (1999) *Forging War*. Luton: University of Luton Press.

Thussu, Daya Kishan and Des Freedman (2003) 'Introduction', in Daya Kishan Thussu and Des Freedman (eds), *War and the Media*. London: Sage, pp. 1–12.

Tumber, Howard and Jerry Palmer (2004) *Media at War: The Iraq Crisis*. London: Sage.

UN Commission of Experts (1994) 'Final Report of the United Nations Commission of Experts Established Pursuant to Security Council Resolution 780 (1992), Annex IV: The Policy Of Ethnic Cleansing' (S/1994/674/Annex IV), 28 December.

UNHCR (United Nations High Commissioner for Refugees) (1999a) 'UN Inter-Agency Update on Kosovo Humanitarian Situation Report 82', 4 March, wwww.reliefweb.int/w/rwb.nsf/0/29291b9f2df28d62c125672b004a07fa?OpenDocument.

—— (1999b) 'Kosovo Crisis Update', 30 March, www.unhcr.org/cgi-bin/texis/vtx/news/opendoc.htm?tbl=NEWS&page=home&id=3ae6b80dc.

US Committee for Refugees (1999) 'Fighting Heats Up Kosovo Winter; Fresh Displacement', March, p. 26, www.refugees.org/data/refugee_reports/archives/1999/1999Jan-June.pdf.

Vickers, Miranda (1998) *Between Serb and Albanian*. London: Hurst and Co.

Vulliamy, Ed (1994) *Seasons in Hell*. London: Simon and Schuster.

—— (1999) '"Neutrality" and the Absence of Reckoning: A Journalist's Account' (reproduced from the *Journal of International Affairs*, 52(2), 1999), in *Preventing Deadly Conflict: Publications of the Carnegie Commission on Preventing Deadly Conflict*, CD-Rom. Washington, DC: Carnegie Corporation.

Wall, Melissa A. (1997) 'A "Pernicious New Strain of the Old Nazi Virus" and an "Orgy of Tribal Slaughter": A Comparison of US News Magazine Coverage of the Crises in Bosnia and Rwanda', *Gazette*, 59(6), pp. 411–28.

Weiss, Thomas, Margaret Crahan and John Goering (eds) (2004) *Wars on Terrorism and Iraq*. London: Routledge.

Woodward, Susan L. (1995) *Balkan Tragedy: Chaos and Dissolution After the Cold War*. Washington, DC: Brookings Institution.

Index

Note: 'n.' after a page number indicates the number of a note on that page

Index

CPSIA information can be obtained at www.ICGtesting.com
Printed in the USA
BVOW042353160212

283134BV00002B/18/P